ELECTRONIC COMMERCE:

LAW AND PRACTICE

Second edition

AUSTRALIA
LBC Information Services Ltd
Sydney

CANADA and USA
Carswell
Toronto

NEW ZEALAND
Brooker's
Auckland

SINGAPORE and MALAYSIA
Sweet & Maxwell (Asia)
Singapore and Kuala Lumpur

ELECTRONIC COMMERCE:

LAW AND PRACTICE

Second edition

Michael Chissick

FIELD FISHER
WATERHOUSE

and

Alistair Kelman

LSE THE LSE COMPUTER
SECURITY RESEARCH
CENTRE ■

enformatica

London
Sweet & Maxwell
2000

Published by
Sweet & Maxwell Limited of
100 Avenue Road,
Swiss Cottage, London NW3 3PF
(http://www.sweetandmaxwell.co.uk)
Typeset by Dataword Services Limited of Chilcompton
Printed in Great Britain by
Bookcraft (Bath) Ltd

A C.I.P. catalogue record for this book
is available from the British Library

ISBN 0421 70800 X ✓

No natural forests were destroyed to make this product,
only farmed timber was used and replanted

To Diana

AK

To Don

MPC

FOREWORD

The "new economy" is about to carry us away. Like passengers in an airliner we have waited for our take-off slot. We seem to have moved down the runway with agonising slowness, but now the nose of the plane has gone up and we're about to leave the ground!

What sort of flight do we want? A smooth, steep climb to a high altitude, or a bumpy, lurching ride, skimming the treetops? For a smooth ride, we need the best information we can get about the weather ahead. In e-commerce terms, we need thorough, clear guidance to legal and regulatory air flows.

This new edition of *Electronic Commerce — Law and Practice* comes at a critical time, when the words "dot com" are to be seen everywhere, and when the Government is doing all it can to promote e-commerce take-up in the United Kingdom. More than ever it is vital that everyone has access to clear, accurate and comprehensive information about the legal underpinning of e-commerce — from domain names to distance selling; from digital signatures to direct taxation.

Electronic Commerce — Law and Practice provides this kind of access in easily understood language. Short examples show how things happen in real life, and all the current references to vital Acts and case law are there.

The legal and regulatory environment for e-commerce is changing all the time and affects everyone with an interest in the new economy. Guides like this are an essential way of navigating that environment.

Alex Allan
e-Envoy
Office of the e-Envoy
Room 111
Cabinet Office
70 Whitehall
London SW1A 2AS
http://www.e-envoy.gov.uk

PREFACE TO THE SECOND EDITION

Our thanks go to Edward Cheng for his valuable assistance with respect to Chapters 3 and 4 in the first edition and to Siman Aral for his contribution to updating the second edition. Our thanks also go to Charles Whiddington for the Competition Law section, to Kirstene Baillie of Field Fisher Waterhouse for contributing Chapter 9 on Financial Services, to Hayley Stallard of Field Fisher Waterhouse for contributing Chapter 10 on Webvertising and to Graeme Nuttall for contributing Chapter 11 on taxation of e-commerce.

We give particular thanks to John Hartle who has reviewed the entire text and to Dr James Backhouse and Mr Peter Sommer for their constructive criticism of the chapters in which they were involved. Our thanks go also to Amanda Ritchie for typing most of this text. Naturally all mistakes are our joint responsibility.

Since writing the first edition in 1998 this book has already changed both our lives. At the time in 1998 e-commerce was at its infancy and neither of us could have predicted the **.com** revolution which has followed.

Michael's practice at Field Fisher Waterhouse in the area of e-commerce has quadrupled in eighteen months and Field Fisher Waterhouse now represents over 180 e-commerce clients.

Alistair's life has changed even further — in December 1999 he ceased practising at the Bar to concentrate on developing his e-commerce patent applications (**www.fastclear.com** and **www.datafreeze.com**), to become e-commerce counsel of enformatica Limited (**www.enformatica.com**), a technology foundry, and to participate in an interdisciplinary team at the LSE in the production of a new professional distance learning course on Electronic Commerce for their Computer Security Research Centre.

The law of e-commerce is the most active branch of law with changes and new legal and technological developments occuring constantly. It is therefore important that the reader should be in possession of the latest information as as soon as possible and this book should be treated as a starting point rather than as a conclusive document. The book is no substitute for professional legal advice.

We have tried to restrict references to web pages either to home pages or to pages which appear unlikely to be moved in the near future. However, websites do get redesigned and altered and readers will find, over time, that the detailed web references at some future date may not always lead to the sought document. When this situation occurs we would recommend readers to put the text description of the web references into a web search engine to find the reference's new location. We have found the Northern Light search engine (**www.northernlight.com**) and the Google search engine (**www.google.com**) to be particularly useful to performing these tasks.

The law is given in this edition as it stood on January 1, 2000, although during the proofing stage in March 2000 certain sections have been updated to incorporate some of the developments as of March 31, 2000.

	Michael Chissick	Alistair Kelman
Address and e-mail	**ffw** **FIELD FISHER WATERHOUSE** **Field Fisher Waterhouse** 35 Vine Street London EC3N 2AA **mpc@ffwlaw.com**	**enformatica** "The JoinedUpInternet Company" **enformatica Limited** Chelford Court Robjohns Road Chelmsford CM1 3AG Essex, U.K. **alistair.kelman** **@enformatica.com**
Telephone	+44(0)20 7861 4000	+44(0) 1245 611300
Other Professional Address		**LSE THE LSE COMPUTER SECURITY RESEARCH CENTRE** **The LSE Computer Security Research Centre** St Clements Buildings The London School of Economics Houghton Street London WC2A 2AE
Auther's web Pages	http://www.ffwlaw.com/profiles/chissick__m.htm	http://csrc.lse.ac.uk/People/KelmanA/KelmanA.htm
Author's corporate websites	http://www.ffwlaw.com http://www.ecommerceincubator.co.uk	csrc.lse.ac.uk www.fastclear.com www.enformatica.com www.telepathic.com

CONTENTS

TABLE OF CASES

E.C. CASES

TABLE OF STATUTES

TABLE OF STATUTORY INSTRUMENTS

TABLE OF EUROPEAN LEGISLATION

TABLE OF INTERNATIONAL TREATIES AND CONVENTIONS

LIST OF ABBREVIATIONS AND GLOSSARY OF TERMS

As with most technology the Internet is full of buzz words and jargon. Listed below are the most common words along with their plain English explanations.

Access provider   A company that sells Internet connection. Known variously as Internet access or service providers (**IAPs** or **ISPs**), *e.g.* Demon, CompuServe or America Online.

Anonymous FTP server   A remote computer, with publicly accessible file archives, that accepts "anonymous" as the log-in name and an **e-mail address** as the password.

Archie   A program that searches Internet **FTP** archives by file name.

Applet   A small program which is embedded within another application — usually a web **Browser** — and which can run on any system that runs the other application.

ASCII   The American standard code for information interchange. A text format readable by all computers.

Asymmetric cryptography   An encryption/decryption system in which it is impossible to derive the decryption key from the encryption key or the other way around.

Authentication   Authentication is the process of validating the identity of someone or something.

Bandwidth   The term used to describe the amount of data which can be sent over a telecommunications link to the Net. The higher the bandwidth, the faster data can flow.

Baud rate   A measure of the bits per second (bps) that a device can communicates or the bps that can be carried on a given communications circuit. Commonly used to describe the speed of a **modem** when transmitting data.

BBS   **Bulletin Board** System. A computer system accessible by modem. Members can dial in and leave messages, send e-mail, play games, and trade files with other users.

Block Encryption

An encryption method that encrypts and decrypts data in blocks rather than one bit (or byte) at a time in a stream. Block encryption is typically associated with the use of a single **Symmetric cryptography** key for both encryption and decryption.

BlowFish

The 64-bit BlowFish block cipher developed by Bruce Schneier which uses a simplification of the principles used in **DES** to provide the same security with greater speed and efficiency than **DES** in software. BlowFish is the precursor to **TwoFish**.

Bookmarks

A Web **browser's** file used to store **URLs**.

Browser

A software program, such as Netscape Communicator or Microsoft's Internet Explorer, that allows you to read and **download** web documents.

Bulletin board

One computer running software allowing multiple people to access the same information and to post information. Virtually all **bulletin boards** are text and graphics only, although they could become capable of displaying audio visual works.

Chat room

A section of an online service where interactive textual communication occurs amongst a collection of people.

Click

People click on a mouse button to instruct the cursor on screen to activate something.

CGI

Computer graphical interface.

CPU

The central processing unit of control of a P.C. which executes programs.

Cryptography

Cryptography is the science of keeping communications private. A central element of cryptography is encryption, which is the transformation of data into an unintelligible form. Encryption and decryption (the reverse of encryption) using computers require the use of some information, usually called a key. Some encryption systems use the same key to encrypt and decrypt (**Symmetric cryptography**), while others rely upon the two parties having different, but mathematically related keys (**Asymmetric cryptography**).

Cryptographic algorithm

A cryptographic algorithm is a mathematical function that takes intelligible information (plain text) as input and changes it into unintelligible cipher text.

Cyberspace	A term coined by science fiction writer William Gibson, referring to the virtual world which exists within the marriage of computers, telecommunication networks, and digital media.
Database	A computerised filing system for storing, arranging and retrieving information.
DES	The Data Encryption Standard. A block algorithm that has been endorsed by both the U.S. National Institute for Standards and Technology (NIST) and the American National Standards Institute (ANSI) as providing adequate security for unclassified sensitive information.
Dial-up	A term used to describe use of telephone lines or **ISDN** communication networks to connect a computer to the WWW.
Digital certificates	A digital certificate indicates the ownership of a public key by an individual or other entity. It allows verification of the claim that a given public key does in fact belong to a given individual. Certificates help prevent someone from using a phoney key to impersonate someone else. In their simplest form digital certificates contain a public key and a name. More sophisticated versions also contain an expiration date, the name of the certifying authority that issues the certificate, a serial number, and the digital signature of the certificate issuer. The most widely accepted format for certificates is defined by the X.509 international standard. Therefore certificates can be read or written by any application complying with X.509.
Digital signature	A digital signature verifies the contents of a message and the identity of the signatory. It also provides a way of ensuring that a document was in fact sent by a particular sender. This feature is known as non-repudiation. So long as a secure cryptographic hash function is used to generate the digital signature, there is no way to extract someone's digital signature from one document and attach it to another, nor is it possible to alter a signed message in any way. The slightest change in a signed document will cause the digital signature verification process to fail.
Direct connection	A connection, such as SLIP or **PPP**, whereby your computer becomes a live part of the Internet. Also called full IP access.
Domain	A part of the Internet name that specifies certain details about the **host** such as its location and whether it is part of a commercial, governmental, or educational entity. The address is written as a series of names separated by full stops.

Download	The transfer of a file from one computer to another.
E-commerce	A broad term describing business activities with associated technical data that are conducted electronically.
Electronic Commerce	See **E-commerce**.
E-mail	E-mail is a way of sending messages electronically to other people from your P.C.
E-mail address	The unique private Internet address to which your e-mail is sent. Takes the form of user@host.
Encryption	The mathematical processing of securing text or data by making it unintelligible to all but the intended recipient. Encryption is based on two components — a **Cryptographic algorithm** and a key.
Firewall	A collection of hardware and/or software components or a system that sits between the Internet and a network through which all traffic from inside to outside, and vice-versa, must pass through and which ensures that only authorised traffic, as defined by the local security policy, is allowed to pass through it. The firewall itself has to be immune to penetration.
Flame-mail	An inflammatory, aggressive, abusive or deliberately anti-social e-mail.
FTP	File transfer **protocol**. The standard *de facto* method of sending and receiving files over the Internet.
Gopher	A menu-driven system for retrieving Internet archives, usually organised by subject. It is a text-only service which is being supplanted by the www.
GUI	Graphical user interface. A method of driving software through the use of windows, icons, menus, buttons and other graphical devices.
Hash function	A hash function is a one-way mathematical function that takes a variable-length input string (sometimes called a pre-image) and outputs a fixed-length string (called a hash, hash value, hash word or message digest). The iterative process that computes a hash from a pre-image is termed hashing. Hashing is used in proving that electronic commerce messages have not been modified, corrupted or altered.
Home page	Either the first page loaded by your **browser** at start-up, or the main Web document for a particular group, organisation, or person.

Host	Your host is the computer you contact to get on to the Net.
HTML	**Hypertext** mark-up language. The language used to create documents on the www.
HTTP	Hypertext transfer protocol is the standard method of transferring **HTML** documents between **browsers** and **web servers**.
Hypertext	Text where any word or phrase may be linked to another point in the same or another document. These links trigger other documents to be displayed.
Internet	A co-operatively run global collection of computer networks with a common addressing scheme: the **TCP/IP** protocols.
Intellectual property	The legal rights which result from intellectual activity in the literary, artistic, industrial and scientific fields.
Intranet	The deployment of Internet technology inside an organisation which uses the Internet protocols. An intranet needs no connection to the global public Internet.
IP	Internet protocol. The most important protocol on which the Internet is based. It defines how **packets** of data get from source to destination.
ISDN	Integrated services digital network. A digital telephone network, ISDN can dramatically speed up transfer of information over the Internet or over a remote LAN connection, especially rich media like graphics, audio or video or applications. Out-of-band signalling is used to communicate information simultaneously, over fewer channels than would otherwise be needed. Typically an domestic ISDN line runs 128kb per second although far higher speeds are possible with commercial links.
ISP	Internet service provider. A company that sells access to the Internet and other online services.
Java	A computer language developed by Sun Microsystems. Java was designed to meet the challenges of application development in the context of heterogeneous, network-wide distributed environments. Paramount among these challenges is secure delivery of applications that consume the minimum of system resources, can run on any hardware and software platform, and can be extended dynamically.

Java applet	A small program written in Java which is embedded within another application — usually a web **Browser** — and which can run on any system that runs the other application.
JPEG	A graphic file format that is preferred by Net users because its high compression reduces file size, and thus the time it takes to transfer.
Key	A mathematical value (usually a large number) used by all modern cryptographic algorithms that determines the outcome of the encryption and decryption functions.
Key Escrowing/ Key Archiving	A set of policies, procedures, and mechanisms that provides backup access to cryptographic keys necessary to decrypt data outside of a normal application. Key escrow in particular carries connotation of key storage with a third party, whereby law enforcement agencies might be able to acquire keys used to decrypt messages from suspected criminals. Key archiving more generally refers to the topic of key storage for the purpose of recovering encrypted data when the original decryption key is lost, stolen, or needed for some other purpose.
Key Generation	The creation of a key or a distinct pair of Public and Private keys.
Key length	Encryption strength is a function both of the algorithm and the key length used with the algorithm. As a rule, the longer the key length, the greater the security.
Key Management	The generation, storage, distribution, deletion, archiving, and application of keys in accordance with an established security policy.
Link	A connection between two items of **hypertext**.
Message Digest function	See **Hash function**.
MD5	MD5 is a Hashing algorithm (sometimes termed a Message Digest algorithm). It is used for digital signature applications where a large message has to be compressed in a secure manner before being signed with the private key. MD5 takes a message of arbitrary length and produces a 128-bit hash or message digest. A message digest or hash can be considered a digital fingerprint of the larger message.
Modem	Modulator/demodulator. A device that allows a computer to communicate with another over a telephone line, by converting the digital information into analogue signals and vice versa.

Netiquette	The etiquette of using the Internet.
Newsgroup	**Bulletin boards** on the Internet covering every conceivable subject (see **Usenet**).
Online	A network connection to another computer.
Packet	A unit of data. In data transfer, information is broken into packets, which then travel independently through the Net. An Internet packet contains the source and destination addresses, an identifier and the data segment.
PGP	See **Pretty Good Privacy**.
PIN	A Personal Identification Number. Used similarly to a password to access and manipulate information electronically.
PKI	Public Key Infrastructure. See **PKIX**.
PKIX	(Public Key Infrastructure X.509): This is a working group of the Internet Engineering Task Force (IETF) concerned with defining standards for interoperability of public key infrastructure components such as security administrators, certification authorities, users, and directories.
POP	Point of presence. An access provider's local dial-in points to reduce the cost of telephone charges for customers dialling in.
PPP	Point to point protocol. A protocol which allows your computer to join the Internet via a modem. Each time you log in, you are allocated a temporary **IP** address. It is a more efficient system than the old SLIP connections, and easier to configure.
Pretty Good Privacy (PGP):	PGP or Pretty Good Privacy is a high-security cryptographic software application that allows people to exchange messages in privacy.
Private Key	A key for encryption and decryption that is paired with a **Public Key** and is kept secret by its owner.
Protocol	An agreed way for two network devices to talk to each other.
Public Key	An encryption or decryption key that is paired with a **Private Key** and is publicly known.
Public-key cryptography	Another name for **Symmetric cryptography** which is sometimes shortened to PKC.

RC4

RC4 is a **Symmetric cryptography** cryptosystem designed by Ron Rivest of RSA Data Security. It is a variable key-size operation that runs very quickly in software. While the algorithm is confidential and proprietary to RSA Data Security, Inc, it has been scrutinised under non-disclosure conditions by independent analysts and it is considered secure.

Robot

A "crawler" program that trawls the web to update search **databases** such as InfoSeek and Lycos.

Router

A special-purpose computer (or software package) that handles the connection between two or more networks. Routers spend all their time looking at the destination addresses of the packets passing through them and deciding which route to send them on.

RSA

RSA is an **Asymmetric cryptography** cryptosystem for both encryption and authentication invented in 1977 by Ron Rivest, Adi Shamir and Leonard Adleman. RSA's system uses a matched pair of encryption and decryption keys, each performing a one-way transformation of data.

Search engine

A computer program that utilises key word identification to find websites and establish **hypertext** links to them.

Server

A central computer which provides multiple users simultaneous access to data and services.

SMTP

Simple mail transfer protocol. The Internet protocol for transporting mail.

Spam

An inappropriate attempt to use a mailing list, or USENET or other networked communications facility as if it was a broadcast medium (which it is not) by sending the same message to a large number of people who did not ask for it. The term comes from a Monty Python sketch which featured the word "spam" repeated over and over.

SET

The Secure Electronic Transactions (SET) protocol is being developed by a consortium including VISA, Mastercard, Microsoft, Netscape, IBM and others. It aims to establish a single technical standard for protecting credit card purchases made over the Internet.

SSL

Secure Sockets Layer: a protocol designed by Netscape Communications to enable encrypted, authenticated communications across the Internet. SSL is used mostly (but not exclusively) in communications between web browsers and web servers. **URLs** that begin with "https" (rather than "http") indicate that an SSL connection will be used.

Symmetric cryptography	An encryption/decryption system in which knowledge of the encryption key is equivalent to knowledge of the decryption key.
TCP/IP	Transmission control protocol/Internet protocol. The protocols that drive the Internet, regulating how information is transferred between computers.
Telnet	A remote Internet log in service. It allows users to access another Internet site as if they are directly connected.
Trojan Horse	A program used to capture unsuspecting people's log on and passwords.
TwoFish	The U.S. government has sought public submissions of an improved block cipher which would serve the specific purpose of protecting the unclassified communications of the U.S. government. The block cipher that is accepted will be called the AES, for Advanced Encryption Standard and will replace **DES**. TwoFish developed by Bruce Schneier as a successor to his 64-bit **BlowFish** block cipher is the leading candidate for the AES.
URL	Uniform resource locator. The standard addressing system for the World Wide Web.
Usenet	User's network. A collection of networks and computer systems that exchange messages, organised by subject into over 27,000 discussion areas, called **newsgroups**. About half the Usenet machines are on the **Internet**.
Web	The World Wide Web or WWW the generic terms for a network of graphic/hypermedia documents on the Internet that are interconnected through hypertext links.
Website	A collection of web pages about a particular subject or organisation.
Web server	A computer on the Internet that stores web pages and sends them to web **browsers**.
X.509	A standard which specifies the format of **Digital certificates**, to provide a way to securely tie a name to a **Public Key**.

— 1 —

ELECTRONIC COMMERCE UNLEASHED

> "Electronic commerce will be an engine of economic growth in the Twenty-first Century, with the potential to invigorate economies by enhancing productivity, streamlining distribution, facilitating trade and revamping corporate structures. The United Kingdom and the United States have already taken steps domestically to realize the full potential of electronic commerce."[1]

INTRODUCTION

Everybody agrees[2] that electronic commerce[3] has started to revolutionise spending habits and will change the way everyone does business. The reasons for this are many and varied; globalisation and the dismantling of trade barriers, the deployment of smart cards, the Internet, and the *de facto* emergence of English as the global language.[4] Yet the certainty is tinged with concern. Predicting how fundamental technological change will affect society is a doomed task since nobody's imagination can cover all the interactivities that follow on from a radical cost shift. In the nineteenth century the development of the railways affected commerce by reducing the cost of shipping a ton of goods tenfold when compared to transportation by wagon or canal barge. Victorian railways meant that local goods could be sold nationally instead of regionally and gave support to the creation of a national system of trade marks and trade reputation. But railways also led to the creation of national daily newspapers and weekend holiday trips and improved the nation's health by making perishable goods such as fish and fruit more widely available. It is these latter changes which dominate our modern perception of the power of railways rather than the economics of train travel. Yet it is the economics that rebuilt the nineteenth century world.

1.01

---

[1] Part of a Joint Statement made in Washington D.C. by Vice President Al Gore and Prime Minister Tony Blair (January 30, 1999). **http://www.usembassy.org.uk/it71.html**.
[2] Since putting forward this statement in the First Edition we have not found a single dissenting opinion. For consumer sales to date the major impacts have been in book and music sales.
[3] See the Glossary for definitions of all terms of art.
[4] This opinion is supported by the fact that many meetings on scientific subjects in European Commission funded projects now take place in English even if English is not the language of any of the participants.

Electronic Commerce repeats this process at the beginning of the twenty-first century by effectively eliminating the cost of transporting of information. By doing so it speeds up a fundamental economic change which has been underway for some time — the globalisation of the world economy based on free trade without tariff barriers. We can measure and predict the direct economic impact of these changes without too much trouble. But we cannot predict the secondary effects which, in the long term, are likely to be far more significant.

FRICTION FREE CAPITALISM

1.02   In early October 1996 the journalist Tim Jackson[5] devoted his weekly column, reviewing new e-commerce businesses in the *Financial Times*, to what he termed "one of the few genuinely useful shopping services on the World Wide Web". The service was Amazon, a company which since then has revolutionised the global book trade and is fast changing the whole world of commerce.

> "The key is that Amazon.com has live electronic links with a dozen wholesalers. Apart from 500 bestselling titles, the company keeps zero inventories. When a customer orders a book, Amazon.com orders it from the wholesaler — and when the book arrives in its Seattle warehouse, it is barcoded and sent by the company's computer to a bin where the customer's order is being assembled. When all the books in an order have arrived, usually the same day, a manifest is printed and the books are packed up for shipping by UPS."

Amazon's website that October was accessible from any PC with a browser and contained a catalogue of two thirds of the 1.5 million English books in print. It was already the world's biggest book store but only had 106 employees. Its financial projections had it doubling in size every 2.4 months and moving into profit on schedule in 1998.

1.03   Today Amazon remains a phenomenon, the "success story" of the web which has not yet moved into profit. In January 1999 Amazon said its sales revenues reached $250 million in its fourth quarter, translating into a $1 billion annualised sales level.[6] But the company warned those high figures would not translate to lower losses in the quarter. "Significant sales of video and music lowered gross margins, as did aggressive product pricing," said Joy Covey, Amazon.com chief financial officer (CFO). "In addition, the strong growth combined with an all-out push to service customers resulted in higher fulfilment expenses." In plain English the company was finding that its profit margins were being squeezed. It opened a seven-acre distribution centre in Nevada to meet its "rapid growth" but, within a couple of months, serious rivals such as online booksellers BarnesandNoble.com and Books On Line from Bertelsmann AG were making the book trade a far, far tougher market in which to operate. By the early summer of 1999 Amazon was engaged in a price war offering exceptionally big discounts on all the best selling American books. By the end of 1999 fourth-quarter sales for BarnesandNoble.com has seen a threefold increase, from $25.9 million in the earlier quarter to $81.5 million. During this same period Amazon.com had only doubled its sales and still was making

---

[5] Tim Jackson, an award winning journalist for his books on Richard Branson, Intel and the Japanese economy, later founded the European Web auction house QXL which was floated on NASDAQ in the autumn of 1999 making Tim a multimillionaire.
[6] Newsbytes, January 5, 1999.

terrible losses. In January 2000 a new front in the booksellers' war broke out as BarnesandNoble.com and Microsoft announced that they would form an online bookstore to sell electronic books that could be read on Microsoft's handheld computers.

One vision of the future of web trade is called "Friction Free Capitalism". The term, coined by Bill Gates in his 1995 book "The Road Ahead",[7] describes a marketplace in which buyers and sellers have almost perfect knowledge of the true supply and demand for a particular product. In a web-based business distance can be irrelevant. In our post GATT[8] world restrictive regulations are disappearing. With new comparative price search engines[9] imperfect consumer information is being eliminated. So profit margins are squeezed as the economic friction, everything that keeps markets from working according to the textbook model of perfect competition, disappears.

Companies faced with new web-based competitors are being schooled in strategies **1.04** such as Lanchester's Second Law of Warfare[10] and the Trafalgar Technique[11] in their struggle to retain market share and ruthlessly crush the "alien invaders from cyberspace". Yet according to the guru Dr Ted Lewis[12] in the friction-free economy, where, supposedly, the cost of manufacturing and distributing a product approaches zero , "the only thing that matters is market share." Market share leads to "lock-in" which means that the customers are committed to (or stuck with) the biggest supplier. It does not matter how market share is acquired; giving away your product,[13] paying exorbitant fees to attract customers[14] or discounting the product 50 per cent.[15].

Lawyers faced with Dr Lewis' proposals will quickly identify all his recommended strategies as being likely to fall foul of competition law in the United Kingdom and Europe and anti-trust law in the United States. For this reason we have expanded our coverage of competition law in the second edition of this work.

MICROSOFT AND THE DEPARTMENT OF JUSTICE

No discussion on e-commerce can sensibly avoid a consideration of Microsoft[16] and its **1.05** control over the personal computer desktop through the Windows operating system. Whether the desktop is an open competitive environment or a closed proprietary zone which unfairly benefits one particular company is a central issue for companies wishing to develop e-commerce applications.

---

[7] ISBN 0140260404.

[8] General Agreement on Tariffs and Trade — The Uruguay Round which is leading to the steady elimination of protective tariffs hindering the free movement of goods and services between countries.

[9] *e.g.* http://www.mysimon.com.

[10] Lanchester, an air warfare theoretician in the first half of this century, codified the strategy by arguing that you should only target opponents who are within your "shooting range" — that is, who have market-share positions similar to or weaker than your own. Thus David never goes after Goliath, but stays busy picking on dwarfs of his own size.

[11] The Trafalgar Technique is a combat strategy adopted from the famous naval Battle of Trafalgar in which Admiral Lord Nelson defeated superior French and Spanish forces by targeting a weak point and breaking though their lines. In web business terms this means: analyse your competitors businesses for critical weaknesses in their supply chain which can be targeted by you.

[12] *e.g.* Author of "The Friction-Free Economy: Marketing Strategies for a Wired World." ISBN 08873084730,1.

[13] The Netscape model (Netscape was taken over by America Online which subsequently took over Time Warner in January 2000).

[14] The America Online model — which ran into difficulties in the U.K. when faced with the Dixon's Freeserve business.

[15] The current Amazon model.

[16] For a never ending report of the Microsoft trial see **http://www.theregister.co.uk/981020–000020.html**.

In 1995 the U.S. Justice Department ended an investigation into Microsoft's business practices by a consent decree which prohibited Microsoft from tying sales of any other product to sales of its operating systems. The agreement, however, allowed the company to develop "integrated products."

In the autumn of 1998 the U.S. Justice Department sued Microsoft over its insistence that PC makers who licensed the Windows 95 operating system also licensed its Internet Explorer browser. The two are separate products. The Justice Department argued that the requirement of bundling Internet Explorer with Windows 95/98 was a violation of the consent decree. Microsoft argued that Internet Explorer was an integrated part of Windows and that the Government knew at the time of the consent decree that Microsoft planned to integrate the two.

In December 1998, U.S. District Judge Thomas Penfield Jackson issued a preliminary injunction ordering Microsoft to offer PC makers a version of Windows without the browser. The software firm complied with the court order, but its method of compliance led to a furious side battle about how Internet Explorer should be removed and what files could be considered part of the browser: the integrated product battle once again. It appealed against the judge's decision and won when an appeal court struck out the injunction and noted that it was inclined to see Internet Explorer and Windows as an integrated product.

1.06   But Microsoft's victory was short-lived when broader charges were filed by the Justice Department and 20 state Attorneys General regarding its market dominance and the manner in which Microsoft has maintained its position. Problems for Microsoft arose through the disclosure of internal e-mails which totally contradicted what its witnesses had said in evidence (or introduced in written testimony) at the trial, and which Microsoft's lawyers had written in court-filed pleadings. By the early summer of 1999 Microsoft's witnesses had little credibility.[17] The internal e-mails told the story of Microsoft's predatory actions, contradicting in every material respect the "legitimate business justifications" put forth by Microsoft.

There was thus little surprise within the industry when on November 5, 1999, Judge Thomas Penfield Jackson ruled, as a "finding of fact", that Microsoft had monopoly power in the market for personal-computer operating systems. But the court's finding that Microsoft was a monopolist that had harmed consumers by using its market muscle to block competition went far beyond what even the company's strongest critics had expected. In his 207 page judgment, the judge totally backed the allegations of the Justice Department and 19 states that Microsoft expanded its market share in order to hurt competitors. "Microsoft has demonstrated that it will use its prodigious market power and immense profits to harm any firm that insists on pursuing initiatives that could intensify competition against one of Microsoft's core products," the judge wrote. He added that some innovations "that would truly benefit consumers never occur for the sole reason that they do not coincide with Microsoft's self-interest" and that harm to consumers was "immediate and easily discernible."[18]

---

[17] Microsoft's evidential position parallels the antitrust dispute in *United States v. Corn Products Refining Company* [1916], where it was alleged that the starch producer had engaged in illegal monopolisation. Corn Products had preserved evidence on typewritten memoranda from company executives. Judge Learned Hand wrote: "The documents were never intended to meet the eyes of anyone but the officers themselves, and were, as it were, cinematographic photographs of their purposes at the time they were written." A witness's attempts to contradict the validity of these memos, "served only to affect the general credibility of his testimony".

[18] see: **http://interactive.wsj.com/articles/SB94183999660138969.htm**. For the full text of Judge Thomas Penfield Jackson's "findings of fact," see: **http://interactive.wsj.com/documents/microsoft—ruling19991105.html**.

At the date of completion of this book the matter remains unresolved. Microsoft's executives indicated that the focus of the case would shift to an appeal court hearing and that settlement with U.S. antitrust regulators was unlikely. Talk of a break-up of the company or continued regulatory oversight with "behavioural" conditions continued in Washington DC. In mid January 2000 Bill Gates announced that Steve Ballmer would take over as chief executive of Microsoft and that he would stay on as chairman of the company's board and dedicate himself to work on Microsoft's software development.[19]

But the Department of Justice anti-trust trial is not Microsoft's only battle. There are a **1.07** number of other civil actions from other computer software companies which are coming up for trial. One of them, Caldera, a small software maker, was due to commence its Federal trial against Microsoft in January 2000 claiming that Microsoft used anti-competitive measures in the late 1980s and early 1990s against its DR-DOS software, which competed with Microsoft's MS-DOS operating system. Microsoft, which marketed its Windows 3.1 graphical shell with MS-DOS, denies the Caldera claims. The case began in 1996 when Caldera acquired DR-DOS from Novell Inc. and filed suit. The company alleges Microsoft engaged in a broad pattern of anti-competitive behaviour, including the planting of "bugs" in Windows to create errors when used with DR-DOS. The evidence[20] in Caldera's favour included e-mails from Bill Gates which fully support Caldera's allegations. Caldera claimed $590 million in damages, which could have been tripled to $1.77 billion as punitive damages if the matter had gone to jury trial.

On January 7, 2000 there was a meeting, at Microsoft's request, in a mediator's office in Seattle, and a settlement was agreed. The terms are confidential, but Microsoft has admitted that it has made a substantial payment to Caldera. Microsoft was also able to control the text of the press release that announced the settlement. Microsoft said it would take a three cents charge in the present quarter, but it is not known whether this represents the whole of the settlement. Certainly the cost to Microsoft will be several hundreds of millions of dollars.

Within the software industry the sentiment from the Department of Justice and Caldera cases strongly suggest that Microsoft will find it difficult to dominate the e-commerce marketplace through its "ownership" of the desktop in this new century.

OPEN SOURCE SOFTWARE: THE NEW KID ON THE BLOCK

While Microsoft has had to face a firestorm of litigation regarding predatory tactics, the **1.08** software that actually runs the majority of Internet servers, deciding what destinations packets should go to, transferring e-mail, serving up World Wide Web pages, is free and open to all. Not only can people download these programs for nothing, they can also read the source code, make changes and even distribute a modified version for others to

---

[19] Days earlier in a clever media manipulating move at the CES show in Las Vegas Gates and Baller opened their presentation with sleek and self-effacing video based on the hit "Austin Powers" movie. In the video Ballmer was cast as Dr Evil, who single-handedly ruins the U.S. stock market by replacing the real Ballmer. The hero Gates, resplendent in full Austin Powers costume ("I put the 'sin' in syntax, baby") saves the day and Gates delighted the audience by dancing, mugging, and using a faux British accent as the would-be superhero. The U.S. political landscape is changing as reporters, laughing at Gates and Ballmer's self effacing humour, cease thinking of Microsoft as "the Great Satan" of the software industry.
[20] In the Caldera litigation where Microsoft has decided to file a document publicly, albeit redacted, it makes them into slide images so that each page (there are hundreds) has to be printed separately from very slowly-rendering pages. They cannot of course be searched since the text is an image. By this means Microsoft tries to limit the damage which would come from its documents being classified and indexed by search engines.

use. Microsoft, Netscape Communications and others have all tried to make inroads into the market for Internet server software, but the free Apache Web server, an Open Source product, still accounts for more installations than all other server packages combined,[21] and its market share is growing. Some advocates predict that Open-Source programs will eventually dominate the entire software market.

There is a increasing volume of evidence that Open Source Software is more reliable than conventional commercial closed source software.[22] However a full discussion on the merits of Open Source Software and its business model is outside of the scope of this book.[23]

Nevertheless although Microsoft's Windows operating system is still a *de facto* standard for the desktop, its fastest-growing competitor is the revolutionary[24] open-source operating system Linux, a Unix variant that has an estimated 10 million or more adherents. Anyone can download Linux from a huge number of different websites or purchase a CD-ROM with the code for as little at $2. A number of major companies, including IBM,[25] have released versions of their software that run under Linux.[26] Furthermore, internal Microsoft memos leaked to the web[27] indicate that it considers Linux a significant threat, especially since it has captured the hearts, minds and resources of countless computer science students and recent graduates.

Linux was originally designed by programmers for programmers. Only in the past eighteen months has the Linux movement begun to dream of "taking the desktop" from Microsoft. It is bewilderingly complex, requires a steep learning curve and often demands a willingness for the installer to get down and dirty with arcane text-based "configuration files." Yet it seems likely that within in the near future these limitations will disappear as

---

[21] According to Netcraft of the 1,269,800 sites they surveyed in 1996, 42% ran Apache.

[22] See Reliable Software and the Year 2000 at **http://www.law.warwick.ac.uk/jilt/99–1/kelman.html**

[23] The main reference site for Open Source information is **http://www.opensource.org**.

[24] On June 14, 1999, in an article entitled "Anti-Microsoft 'subculture,'" Beijing's China Youth Daily took a look at the growth of the Linux-based operating system. "The rise of Linux is legendary," reads the article, "a little like the peasant uprising of Chen Sheng and Wu Guang. In a world of hegemony long suppressed, many feel oppressed but the majority doesn't know where their suffering originates. Once someone stands up, he will have followers like clouds. We can slowly accumulate a whole room of books; as similar knowledge products, software should be affordable too. No matter what, for two CDs to sell for over ¥10,000 is not acceptable to ordinary users. Apple Computers recently publicised the core of their operating system when upgrading the OS X Server, and took the first step towards freeware [open source software]. True competition between freeware [open source software] and commercial software has begun. This is a conflict between software beliefs: Are CDs with almost zero cost more valuable, or is technical service and human labour more valuable? The software industry will give us a conclusion in the next 10 years." Chen Sheng and Wu Guang are famous figures from ancient Chinese history, labourers on the Great Wall who began a rebellion in 206 B.C. against the tyrant emperor Qin Shi HuangDi. The Chen Sheng-Wu Guang rebellion is often employed by Chinese writers as a kind of code phrase to talk about the era when Chairman Mao Zedong (the latter-day Qin Shi HuangDi) ruled China, but it is also generally useful for describing any situation in which the righteous masses take action to overthrow a corrupt and overweening ruler. This appears to be the first time that the analogy has been applied to the world of software. http://www.sinopolis.com.cn/Archives/TOPSTORY/ts—990615.htm.

[25] In August 1999 IBM announced the general availability of both the DB2 database and WebSphere application server for Linux. Both products were to be "ServerProven" for Linux which is an IBM term meaning that the software will been optimised to run on IBM servers. In January 2000 IBM announced it was going to make the computer operating system Linux the centre of its hardware plans and that it would "essentially Linux-enable all our platforms," (Sam Palmisano, head of the IBM Server Group) "We believe we are now on the brink of another important shift in the technology world. The next generation of e-business will see customers increasingly demand open standards for inter-operability across disparate platforms". IBM also announced it was to donate key programming code developed for its mainstay computer systems to Linux, in order to boost its reliability.

[26] Caldera — once champion of Dr–DOS — now bets on the future of Linux.

[27] See **http://www.opensource.org/halloween.html**. Vinod Valloppillil warned that Linux and open source "poses a direct, short-term revenue threat to Microsoft." In the long run, he worried, the open-source model's "free exchange of ideas" could hurt the Microsoft even more.

new computer companies start moving the home computer market away from the hardware box with user installed software towards the set-top box sold as a commodity like a hi-fi system. In the late summer of 1999 this new type of personal computer was promised for the U.S. market. Costing around $199 these "white box" computers will come with Linux pre-installed[28] as well as the mainstream applications desired by ordinary users.[29]. Within days of the units being announced various bundled deals were being offered from U.S. Internet Service Providers offering these new Linux computers with unlimited Internet access for $20 per month inclusive. U.K. and European equivalents were promised. Then, in early January 2000, Intel announced that some of its forthcoming web appliances would run Linux instead of Windows.

STANDARDS FOR SECURE BROWSERS

It must also not be forgotten that e-commerce is also linked to a standards battle in **1.09** authentication technologies. Like the VHS/Betamax confrontation in early video recorders (which was finally won by VHS) the e-commerce marketplace is littered with implementations of competing technologies all of which want to become accepted as the single global standard for e-commerce. Many countries have their national champions and government support for particular e-commerce technologies is often rooted in partisan national interests rather than technical superiority or genuine risk.

The most well knows standards battle involves SET, the Secure Electronic Transaction, a technical standard for safeguarding payment card (debit and credit card) purchases made over open networks. The SET protocol was developed jointly by VISA and MasterCard and requires the use of public key certificates to authenticate the parties to each other at every step along the way.

In the first edition of this book we suggested that SET might not be the eventual winner in e-commerce. We cited the view that SET was an overcomplicated solution to a problem which appeared to be adequately addressed for consumer purposes by the Secure Hypertext Transfer Protocol (S-HTTP) and Secure Socket Layer (SSL) technology. We said: "If e-commerce takes off on non-SET systems then there will be no reason for companies to incur the additional overheads imposed by SET. Unless governments decide to interfere."[30]

Over the past eighteen months our prediction appears to have come true. Consumer e-commerce has flourished without SET. Additionally, at a management level, concerns have arisen regarding the anti-competitive implications of a single public key certificate supplier as against the security vulnerabilities of allowing cross-certification of public key certificates by a variety of suppliers. These anti-competitive and security concerns have further delayed the deployment of SET. Only if fraud undermines consumer confidence in personal e-commerce will SET stand any chance of success.

---

[28] The equivalent Microsoft Windows personal computer would cost an extra $80 as the operating system licence fee paid by the manufacturer to Microsoft.

[29] *e.g.* word processing, spreadsheet, graphics, database.

[30] A explanation of these emerging technologies is set out in Chapter 5: Payment mechanisms: Encryption and Digital Signatures.

THE CHANGING REGULATORY LANDSCAPE

1.10   Over the next few pages we outline some of the immediate potential problems which face governments all over the world. None of these problems pose barriers to the technology being deployed. Rather, they indicate that governments will act in concert to protect their revenue bases and may need to establish sensible security standards to protect national economies from being riddled with commercial racketeering and criminality. The transition between well understood conventional commercial systems and their jargon (Letters of Credit, Bills of Exchange, INCOM terms, etc.) to secure e-commerce and its jargon (digital certificates, Trusted Third Parties, DES, TwoFish, etc.) will require the world economy to pass through a short period of vulnerability to fraud until the risks are well understood and controlled.

We make no apology for including this speculative analysis of the future regulation of e-commerce environment in a textbook which is mainly intended for use by commercial lawyers. Moneylaundering legislation impinges upon everyone (including solicitors and accountants acting for clients)[31] and it is essential that practitioners are aware of the dubious and doubtful uses of e-commerce so that they can protect themselves from personal and professional catastrophe. Lawyers also need to know not simply what the law currently is but how the law is likely to evolve. English lawyers are slowly coming to terms with the purposive approach to the interpretation of U.K. legislation to give effect to the United Kingdom's obligations under European Union Directives, even if this involves a departure from the strict and literal application of the words used in the U.K. legislation.[32] With highly technical subjects such as control over encryption and digital signatures it is essential for the lawyer to understand the law of e-commerce in context. Governments will undoubtedly bring in new laws to regulate the use of e-commerce in moneylaundering and to maintain national tax revenues.

Even though long term prediction is a doomed activity, short term prediction can be a pleasurable vanity. At the end of this chapter, after trying to put some figures on the size of the market, we look a few years into the future at how e-commerce might impact upon the ordinary daily life of an imaginary lawyer — Samantha Wesley.

GLOBALISATION AND THE DEMATERIALISATION OF TRADE

1.11   If we think of pop stars and politicians as commodities, then the way that they are marketed and sold has undergone a revolution in the closing decades of this century. Complex commercial synergies arise in blockbuster films with "product placements" reinforced by tie-in merchandise associated with music albums and videos. Media campaigns by politicians at election times enjoy similar choreography and staging and can lead to unholy alliances between politicians and media magnates.

---

[31] On July 14, 1999 the European Commission put forward a proposal (IP/99/498) to amend Council Directive 91/308 to extend its coverage to organised crime and fraud and corruption affecting E.U. financial interests and to impose record keeping and reporting requirements on, *inter alia*, estate agents, accountants, notaries and lawyers involved in financial transactions. See **http://europa.eu.int/rapid** for further details.
[32] The House of Lords recognised this approach to construction in *Pickstone v. Freemans* [1989] 1 A.C. 66 and *Lister v. Forth Dry Dock and Engineering Co. Ltd (In Receivership)* [1990] 1 A.C. 546.

But what of the future? Today every pop star and every politician has several websites promoting them. Some of these already sell tie-in merchandise. How soon will it be before we have the commodified global political party selling books, speeches, videos, CD–ROMs from websites to fund political campaigns and voter registration programmes in selected nations?[33]

These visible changes reflect the rise in importance of intellectual property rights, particularly trade marks. In a global market place pop stars and political parties all need to protect their "brand" and associated merchandise. We are in the post GATT-TRIPs world when every country has undertaken to strengthen and unify their protection of intellectual property rights. By the early years of the next century all nations should have fulfilled their treaty obligations with improved reciprocal enforcement of rights.

The trend towards better enforcement of intellectual property rights will have a positive effect on global trade in commodities containing intellectual property (videos, CDROMs, microprocessors, books, etc.)[34] But problems are already arising in dematerialised commodities, such as software and music, which is sold over the Internet. Should sales tax or VAT be paid on these sales or should everything sold in cyberspace be tax free? Is it unfair to European Internet Service Providers for non-European Internet Service Providers to offer web space to European customers and not levy VAT on their invoices?[35]

At the moment these concerns are not of major importance to governments. But as world trade moves into cyberspace and there is a general loss of government revenue, the entire basis of commercial taxation may have to be reviewed with new directives and legislation.[36]

WHERE THE SMART MONEY IS HEADING

We are all already familiar with the concept of a credit-card sized piece of plastic which **1.12** will contain digital cash; several systems are just about to be launched onto the European, American and Asian markets having undergone extensive trials in towns and communities. At the moment these remain interesting local experiments — with no one system taking a lead.[37] But once a significant amount of commercial activity is being done

---

[33] We are already getting cross-over between political speeches and commercial advertising. The South African restaurant chain "Nando's" has had a very successful radio campaign in Australia based around the right-wing politician Ms Pauline Hanson whose extreme racial views have made her subject to death threats. The campaign featured a soon-to-be grilled chicken parodying a recording made by Ms Hanson to be played in the event of her assassination.

[34] But *pace* the problems with trade marks, copyright and exhaustion of rights — See Judgment C–355/96 *Silhouette International Schmied GmbH & Co. KG v. Hartlauer Handelsgesellschaft mbH*, July 16, 1998 **http://europa.eu.int/cj/en/cp/cp9849en.htm**.

[35] This matter is now partly addressed by revised VAT legislation in the U.K. which took effect from July 1, 1997 relating to telecommunications services. These measures are only temporary and will be replaced by definitive changes to the Sixth Directive (77/388) before the end of 1999. For further information see Chapter 13 of *Internet Law and Regulation* (2nd ed., Sweet & Maxwell, London, 1997).

[36] But maybe not — see **http://www.easyClear.com**.

[37] The digital cash market place over the past eighteen months has turned into a two-horse race with the smart card behemoth alliances, Mondex and VisaCash , well ahead of the field and with the resources to stay the distance. First Virtual dropped out of the running in July 1998. CyberCash's CyberCoin never caught on. Digital Equipment, now part of Compaq Computer, is not proceeding with its Millicent electronic cash, and IBM is doing little with its product called Minipay. The promising outsider DigiCash, which had a very elegant software solution, filed for bankruptcy in November 1998 (**http://www.news.com/News/Item/0,4,28360,00.html**). Its sad story in the original Dutch from an anonymous insider "How DigiCash Blew Everything" can be found at **http://www.nextmagazine.nl/ecash.htm**.

using digital cash a number of economic effects are likely to be felt, all of which will have to be addressed by legislation or bank regulation. Digital cash will ultimately replace a significant part of the legal tender issued by the central banks, which will have implications for their own revenues and activities. It must not be forgotten that central banks actually sell their cash to the banks.

In economic terms the "float" is the amount of cash in circulation in the United Kingdom. Traditional cash is a major source of float for central banks, as it is a non-interest bearing liability. When real cash is withdrawn from a bank, that money is no longer owned by the bank: it becomes a debt of the central bank to the bearer of the cash. But when money in bank current accounts is withdrawn from a bank by converting it into digital cash on a smart card, it is not really leaving the bank, and the bank can continue to use it. The main economical effect of digital money will be to transfer the "float" from the central banks to the commercial banks who issue digital cash.[38]

In July 1999 the float in the United Kingdom, was approximately £28.7 billion.[39] If half the cash in circulation in the United Kingdom were to be digital cash the Government's interest earning float would be reduced to around £14 billion, leading to a very significant loss of interest and an increase in the Government's borrowing requirements to maintain public services

1.13   In anticipation of the deployment of digital cash by the banks, both the Bank of England and the Bank of Canada have had very serious discussions with the banks who want to enter the digital cash arena in order to reach an agreement on a fair apportionment of this float. No agreement has as yet been reached.

Then there is the "escheatment" issue. Currently, banks have to return to the central banks any monetary value that has been unclaimed for a long period of time (unused bank accounts, traveller's cheques, etc). All the major organisations who are proposing to issue digital cash have announced that their digital cash is exactly like cash: they will not refund the value left on lost cards. Moreover, there are already talks that some banks will offer an insurance for lost cards, an additional source of revenues.

Currently, when traditional cash is lost, it is to the benefit of the central banks since cash is a liability for them. Overall, we can say that it is to the benefit of the whole society. When digital cash is lost, this is no longer true because this float is not owned by the central banks, but rather by the commercial banks

It therefore seems that commercial banks will, at least initially, benefit from escheatment. If governments decided to address this through the use of specific legislation to force them to give these sums back to the State, there could be serious problems with some systems. The Mondex system, for example, is designed in a manner to ensure that the digital cash is not traceable — consequently, the issuing bank would not have any information regarding how much Mondex value had been lost on a missing card.

---

[38] This issue does not just concern digital cash — it can also relate to propriatory tokens. In the early 1990s the Japanese Government forced NTT (Nippon Telephone and Telegraph) to deposit at the Japanese central bank half of the $700 million float that was "locked" on their phone cards.
[39] Source: Bank of England — web site: **http://www.bankofengland.co.uk**.

CYBERLAUNDERING AND NET-SMURFING

Doug Drug Dealer is the CEO of an ongoing narcotics corporation who wishes to convert hard currency, the profits of his enterprise, into legitimate money. Doug employs Linda Launderer to hire couriers to deposit funds under different names in amounts between $7500 and $8500 at branches of every bank in certain cities [below the $10,000 cash transaction reporting limit]. This is repeated twice a week for as long as required. Linda has in the meantime been withdrawing these same funds and depositing the money with Internet banks that accept e-cash. To be safe she limits these transfers to $8200. Now that the currency has been converted into digital e-cash, the illegally earned money has become virtually untraceable and Doug Drug Dealer has access to legitimate electronic cash.[40]

1.14

In moneylaundering[41] jargon the couriers who deposit small amounts of illegal money are called "smurfs" and those that are engaged in this kind of activity in cyberspace are called "net-smurfs" or "cybersmurfs". The problem which regulatory authorities face in combating cyberlaundering is multifaceted:

- Present day legislation to combat moneylaundering is based on what is termed "suspicious transaction reporting". The banker is under a duty to file a suspect transaction report if he/she suspects that a transaction is laundering illegally obtained money. But the suspicion-based system breaks down when there is no banker involved in the transaction who is capable of becoming suspicious. Most cross-border transactions are conducted purely electronically, without anyone physically seeing them.[42]

- Many digital money cards issued by banks come in two forms: attributable and non-attributable. Attributable cards are used to debit sums against a specified account. These are loaded onto a rechargeable card. Non-attributable cards cannot debit or credit bank accounts, but can accept transfers from other cards. Transfers are made with a computer (with Internet access) and telephone, as well as by putting cards into a special wallet which moves sums from one card to the other. Where transactions involve a non-attributable card, the "record" shows "private". Peer to peer transfers are possible without requiring the parties to contact a third party. Hence, just like an actual cash transfer, the transaction is entirely anonymous. No data is held by banks on transfers. Money can be held on cards or PCs and transferred as long as both parties have non-attributable cards. One central concern with this type of card is that cards with very high capacities could be used to move large sums across borders to provide a parallel banking system in such a way as to by-pass international wire transfer reporting requirements.

---

[40] Mark Bortner "Cyberlaundering: Anonymous Digital Cash and Money Laundering. Internet (**http://www.law.miami.edu/froomkin/seminar/papers/bortner.htm** February 19, 1997.

[41] The issue of moneylaundering and the technical discussion of its prevention is outside of the scope of this book. The authors would direct readers to the literature on this topic and would recommend as a definitive starting point: U.S. Congress, Office of Technology Assessment, Information Technologies for Control of Money Laundering, OTA-ITC–630 (U.S. Government Printing Office, Washington, DC, September 1995).

[42] See further Bercu, "Towards Universal Surveillance in an Information Age Economy" (1994) 34 Jurimetrics J 383; Gold M. and Levi M., *Money Laundering in the U.K.: An Appraisal of Suspicion-Based Reporting* (Police Foundation, London, 1994).

Disintermediation, where money flows through non-traditional banking channels, is a growing problem for governments wishing to have control over their national economies and e-commerce is likely to increase the extent of the problem.[43]

1.15   Not surprisingly, the problems with suspect transaction reporting are being technologically addressed through pattern matching other computer-based detection regimes. But developing effective technologies for reporting or searching for relevant intelligence concerning e-commerce transactions is likely to impose significant capital and recurrent costs on those who have to install and operate the systems necessary for the reporting and/or searching. U.K. financial institutions, like their U.S. counterparts, have generally accepted money laundering reporting requirements as one of their general expenses of doing business. But in the "Brave New World" of falling margins and greater competition for financial services, it is going to be considerably harder to persuade bankers that they should bear the cost of what is, in effect, the investigation arm of a government anti-moneylaundering enforcement agency. There maybe a good case for tax credits or bounty sharing with bankers to offset the expenses incurred in policing the digital money marketplace.

In the embryonic e-commerce market there are currently no special controls regulating cyberlaundering. Yet it is easy to see envisage how e-commerce could be used to disguise such activities:

> Charlie Crack is a member of a drug gang which markets crack cocaine to schoolchildren. His boss wants the money Charlie's gang gets for its sales to appear to be the profits from a legitimate business rather than drug dealing. So the boss sets up a soft porn website selling "tasteful" shots of naked teen idols. Charlie is instructed not to accept money but to give bags of crack cocaine to children who show, using the records from their digital purses, that they have paid to download a proprietary image from the boss' website within the past 12 hours. The boss gets untraceable digital cash from a business which appears to be making clean money.

HOW MUCH IS HYPE?

1.16 | If Europeans are looking to their governments and the European Union to make e-commerce as cosy as doing business in their own back yards, they will wait in vain. If they look to governments to create regulations that might hold back the competitive challenges that e-commerce could create, they might just as well seek highway speed limits to suit the horse and buggy.[44]

---

[43] For further discussion on this point see para. 4.2.3 of "SECURITY OF ELECTRONIC MONEY" Report by the Committee on Payment and Settlement Systems and the Group of Computer Experts of the central banks of the Group of Ten countries (Basle, August 1996). The authors consider this Report to be a very useful primer on the underlying technical security issues affecting the use of Smart Cards.

[44] Louise Kehoe, *Financial Times* — September 9, 1998. Louise's statement, is turning into an accurate prediction. In February 1999 the European Parliament voted in favour of imposing stringent copyright protection across the Internet. Pundits immediately called the policy unworkable. The move, which was acclaimed by artists' and musicians' unions as a success, would make it illegal to view unauthorised copyright material online, as web servers need to make temporary copies of the material in order to transmit it efficiently. One early reaction was that if material were posted online with the author's consent, anyone downloading it would have to pay the author. Even viewing it online could become an infringement, if a surfer uses web caching to avoid paying for

In 1998 there was a general consensus that continental Europe was in the slow lane regarding growth in e-commerce mainly due to its telecommunications costs which were approximately five times higher than in the United States.[45] This negative factor was considered to be compounded by fewer wired customers, higher hardware and software costs plus concerns about security, taxes and language problems.[46] During 1999 the United Kingdom narrowed the gap with the United States partly thorough the extraordinary growth of free Internet Service Provider (ISP) services such as www.freeserve.net from Dixons.

In our first edition we quoted a 1998 report which stated that business-to-business e-commerce in Europe was expected to reach $11.8 billion by 2001[47] with big companies encouraging their business partners to follow them online, thereby accentuating the demand for additional connections and bandwidth. $11.8 billion now looks like a very conservative estimate in the light of a June 1999 report from another trusted organisation[48] which said that after the United States, Germany has the second-highest level of e-commerce revenues in the world, at $1.5 billion in 1998 and $4.4 billion projected for 1999; the United Kingdom follows, with $1.49 billion in 1998 and $3.7 billion in 1999.[49]

In the business to consumer sphere Christmas 1999 confirmed the amazing growth in online transactions. Online spending over the Christmas period approached £200 million in the United Kingdom, a bit more in Germany and around £65 million in France.[50] For the United Kingdom this is more than the entire 1998 online sales volume in a period of roughly four weeks. And the deflationary effect of e-commerce was very marked — a number of goods sold in Christmas 1999 were significantly cheaper than the identical goods sold in 1998.

But before businesses can engage in e-commerce they have to be actively connected to **1.17** the Internet. To estimate this preliminary activity the 1999 U.K. Government's international benchmarking study, "Moving into the Information Age" introduced a "Connectivity Indicator" which assessed information Society preparedness by reporting the proportion of companies meeting at least one of three criteria:

- had a website

- frequent use of e-mail

- frequent use of EDI

---

the content. Author of the proposal, MEP Roberto Barzanti, conceded that enforcement would be a problem. "That is not the issue at this point, but it will probably be the responsibility of ISPs in the future." Despite insisting that partnership between governments and the technology industry is vital, he said: "If member states say that it is up to ISPs to enforce the E.U. directive, then they will have to comply." Barzanti admitted he has no direct experience with technology. A literature lecturer from Siena University, his political experience lies in regulating television content. "This is a very complex and novel area for me," For the full story see Silicon.com "MEPs vote to ban Web caching": Thursday, February 11, 1999.
[45] Source: Forrester Forum Europe, July 1998.
[46] Source: Interactive Media in Retail Group, July 1998.
[47] Source: Forrester Research Inc "European New Media Strategies service", July 1998.
[48] Source: eMarketer **http://www.emarketer.com./estats/062999—eglobalrpt.html**.
[49] In September 1999, in the Performance and Innovation Unit Report from the U.K. Cabinet Office the authors quoted broadly similar statistical projections but added that U.K. e-commerce transactions "have the potential to grow tenfold in the next three years . . . E-commerce tends to put downward pressure on inflation and increases economic growth " see e–commerce@its.best.uk. A copy of this report in HTML format will shortly be appearing on the Office of the E-Envoy's website.
[50] Estimate by Alan Taylor, Chief Executive of the e-commerce consultancy, E-Insight.

While United States and Canada were clear leaders against this metric, United the Kingdom, Japan and Germany all scored quite high, with only France and Italy trailing significantly in this preliminary activity:

Country	Percentage
USA	65 per cent
Canada	65 per cent
U.K.	63 per cent
Japan	60 per cent
Germany	59 per cent
France	39 per cent
Italy	34 per cent

The Connectivity Indicator
(data collected November 1998-January 1999)

1.18 During 1999 some politicians who call for an economic realignment of Britain away from continental Europe and back toward the British Commonwealth and America were given a statistical weapon in "An Analysis of the New Networked Economy".[51] This report measures distance in terms of relative cost of a telephone call. If a map were drawn on this basis the Netherlands would have Canada and the Virgin Islands as near neighbours, closer in fact than its neighbours in the old geography, such as Germany and Belgium. Thanks to early and progressive liberalisation of telecommunications, resulting in hot competition for customers' business and subsequent decline in the cost of international calls, the United Kingdom and Sweden have placed themselves next to the USA and Canada at the centre of the networked world. Taking the cost of calls between USA and United Kingdom as a distance of one unit, countries get further from world centre as their international calling costs increase. This means that some European Union countries are close to the centre, some much further from the centre. Greece and Portugal are twice as far from world centre as Hong Kong, four times as far as Sweden and further "out" in networked economy terms than Malaysia.

Country	Distance from the United States
United Kingdom	1.0
Sweden	1.3
Canada	1.4
Virgin Islands	1.5
Australia	1.6
Netherlands, Belgium, France, Germany	1.8
Denmark	1.9
Austria, New Zealand	2.0
Finland	2.1
Ireland	2.3
Hong Kong, Italy	2.4
Luxembourg	2.5
Mexico	2.6
Japan, South Korea, Spain	3.0

[51] Source: European Telework Online resources database **http://www.eto.org.uk/resource**.

Singapore	3.5
Malaysia	3.6
Taiwan	3.9
Portugal	4.3
Poland	4.5
Greece	4.8

Worldwide e-commerce was estimated in 1998 to be at about $10 billion. It was then expected to soar to $500 billion by 2002.[52] In the summer of 1999 a different consultancy stated that worldwide e-commerce revenues would grow from $98.4 billion in 1999 to over $1.2 trillion by 2003, with the U.S. continuing to enjoy a majority share of global e-commerce dollars in that year.[53] But, they said, European consumer Internet access spending will move at a much slower pace to America, climbing to an expected $4.6 billion in 2001. The causes of this appear to be more rooted in the structure and nature of European society and European business practices rather than any technological limitation.

In September 1998 Andersen Consulting pointed to huge differences between U.S. and   **1.19**
European attitudes towards e-commerce.[54] The consultants reported that although 82 per cent of the 300 European executives interviewed recognise the strategic importance of e-commerce only 39 per cent are doing anything about it. Furthermore, only 19 per cent of European executives regard e-commerce as a serious competitive threat to their business today. By September 1999 the U.K. Performance and Innovation Unit in the Cabinet Office was being rather more blunt about this problem:

"Many small companies for whom day-to-day survival is a challenge enough, have little time or inclination to address issues that seem complex, technical and irrelevant. Many larger companies appear 'frozen in the headlights' — aware of the likely impact, yet paralysed by the potential for reduced margins and unwilling to address a major transformation of business practice. There are serious skill shortages, both in technical areas and in the management of change in both private and public sectors. Government is not fulfilling its potential vital role as both purchaser and exemplar. Many individuals do not yet appreciate the scope for cost savings and improvements in quality of life possible with e-commerce."[55]

In our first edition we concluded this section by saying:

"Europe does appear to have grounds to worry. While there is legitimate concern regarding the need to establish a global scheme to deal with liability and regulatory issues involving digital signatures, cryptography and digital cash there can be no doubt that world business is moving into cyberspace at an amazing pace regardless of the lack of legal certainty. Continental Europe has very little time to influence the regulation of e-commerce and remains preoccupied with the Euro. The UK, which (unlike Germany and Italy) has loyally waited on European Union developments in this sphere,[56] may need now to take unilateral action to protect its national interests and create a framework where U.K. business and the City can safely participate in the American dominated e-commerce arena."

A little over a year later the lack of real progress in creating a Europe-wide legal infrastructure for e-commerce[57] continued the paralysis amongst continental businesses

---

[52] Source: Andersen Consulting **http://www.ac.com.**
[53] Source: eMarketer **http://www.emarketer.com./estats/062999_eglobalrpt.html.**
[54] Source: Andersen Consulting **http://www.ac.com.**
[55] Para. 1.13 of e–commerce@its.best.uk.
[56] To useful effect — See Chapter 5 Payment Systems where we show why the German digital signature legislation and its regulatory regime may be an unsuitable model for Electronic Commerce.
[57] Coupled with the legacy of the 1999 infighting and fraud allegations within the European Commission which had led to the mass dismissal of the European Commissioners.

which take their lead from political lobbying rather than the competitive marketplace. There are continuing worries about protectionism, free trade[58] and legal barriers.[59] Yet there are signs that the impotence of Fortress Europe in fighting off "alien invaders from cyberspace" is causing a few far-sighted European businesses to ignore their political arena and instead to concentrate upon replicating successful American e-business strategies in their local environment.[60]

In our first edition where we posed the question "how much is hype?" the clear answer now appears to be "very little is hype — the growth of e-commerce is exponential".

SAM'S STORY

1.20   To close this introductory chapter we introduce Samantha Wesley, an assistant solicitor in a City firm in the year 2004. Sam is an ordinary person, not especially computer literate but able to use computers in her ordinary daily life.

As usual Sam Wesley was already awake and washed as her radio alarm went off. It was raining and the radio confirmed that yesterday's rain sealed June 2004 as being the wettest English June on record. "Some things never change", muttered Sam as she bumped around the bedroom in the darkness trying not to disturb Tom. There was little chance of that — he could sleep through a thunderstorm. But the creaking floorboards moved the computer mouse on the work table which mistook them for start up requests and lit the screen up with the list of the day's reminders. Some were work related but most were pleasure. An urgent note flashed "Walking on Water", a reference to the new political musical which was opening at the Prince Alfred Theatre. Sam liked musicals but wanted to see the reviews of this one before committing herself. The temptation was too great. She sat down and clicked on the Electronic Telegraph icon, following the links to the review page.

"Is he waving or drowning? — John Diamond[61] reviews "Walking on Water" [Short review follows]

Sam read the piece to the end and decided to book tickets. She clicked on the booking link, the screen dissolved and she was at the Prince Alfred Bookings site. Two tickets at €90 in the Front Stalls were available but the order form stated that the view was obstructed. Sam clicked on the "show me" icon and saw a picture of the stage as it would appear from her seat. It was clear that a huge pillar would block the view which in any event was strongly angled. "Not right for such a spectacular". But there were Dress

---

[58] In the summer of 1999 Sir Leon Brittan, the European Commission Trade Commissioner, was replaced by Pascal Lamy, a Frenchman known as "Delors's Exocet" when he was chief of staff to the former commission president Jacques Delors. With France's reputation for protectionism and market intervention, the decision caused "astonishment" in Brussels and raised questions about the future direction of the EU's free trade agenda — Daily Telegraph (July 7, 1999).

[59] On September 9, 1999 an emergency European Union meeting took place to hammer out a directive to radically amend the Brussels and Rome conventions which had been identified as being serious impediments to the growth of Electronic Commerce in the European Union. For more information see Chapter 4 — International Contracts.

[60] *e.g.* Bertelsmann AG with "Books on Line" **http://www.bol.com**.

[61] John Diamond, the television and radio journalist and author of "C — because cowards get cancer too . . ." (ISBN 0–009–181665–3) gave permission to Alistair Kelman for his name to be used in this piece of fiction. For John Diamond see **http://www.the–times.co.uk/JohnDiamond/index2.html**.

Circle seats available at €105[62] each and their views were unobstructed. She clicked to make a booking. The computer interrupted "Real or Pseudo Identity?" Was Sam prepared to give the theatre her real name? "Real" clicked Sam — she did not normally mind being known as a theatregoer and getting special offers from the Theatre Bookings Web site. But sometimes, when on a view for a client, Sam used a Pseudo Identity. She had done so last week when checking out "Maestro" the play about the new Lord Mayor of London which was alleged to libel one of the firm's clients in a scene in a railway station.

The computer interrupted again "Collect Tickets or E-Tickets?" With a real identity the **1.21** theatregoer could collect the ticket from the theatre by showing his credit card or could ask for e-tickets which were fully transferable electronic vouchers which were downloaded onto a smart card like digital money and could be transferred from card to card. Only at the theatre when the anonymous smart card was waved before the sensor would the paper tickets be printed and the electronic vouchers voided on the card. The ticket agencies loved them and E-tickets to rock concerts were always high sellers on the web auction sites. "E-tickets" clicked Sam. A moment later the workstation told her that there were two paid tickets for "Walking on Water" on the hard drive ready for transfer to her Smart Card.

Sam was turning to leave the workstation when a flashing icon caught her eye. It was the stock monitor flashing yellow with no sound, not critical but requiring attention. Sam clicked on the icon to open up her ESI stockwatch. Overnight in Tokyo, Kuji Chemical had announced research collaboration with Lanchester Molecular. Sam had a few shares in Lanchester Molecular in her portfolio and the computer was telling her that the company had been mentioned in news story within the last 12 hours. "I'll hold" she muttered to himself. But this caused her to look at her portfolio. Like most independent professionals Sam liked managing her own affairs. For three years she had been a Sponsored Member of CREST the United Kingdom's registration and settlement system, developed by the Bank of England. This allowed her to benefit from all the advantages of electronic settlement of U.K. stocks and shares whilst continuing to keep her name on the company's registry thereby enabling her to receive all the shareholder rights direct from the company. But in recent months Sam had become interested in the revitalised Asian stock markets and had become a private customer of E*TRADE U.K. which allowed her to trade on the Singapore stock market. She reviewed the overnight trading — the U.S. trade figures had had little effect on trading in that part of the world although NASDAQ stocks were down. Looking at the figures changing from one market to the next Sam could almost see the tides of money ebbing and flowing around the world as night followed day.

There was no good reason to sell or buy and Sam, a student of Warren Buffett, always **1.22** played the long game with her stock portfolio. It was time to get down to work.

And work meant problems. This morning was the second meeting with the receivers of Melvilles — it was hard to believe that the company had gone under despite the popularity of their goods. The *Financial Times* had called it "The First Roadkill on the Information Superhighway" and the litigation was predicted to go on for years.

Melvilles were an American department store with a good mail order division. They had gone onto the web in a big way in the late 1990s mainly selling smart casual clothing under the slogan "The Passport to Pleasure". But it had all gone wrong in a spectacular manner.

---

[62] We have retained the fiction from the first edition that by 2004 people in the U.K. will be using the Euro rather than the pound. This does however seem rather unlikely.

Melvilles' mail order telephone sales operations had been in the Deep South of America taking advantage of low wages and cheap 1–800 services. It had seemed logical to build their web sales operations on the same system. But this was their first mistake. The local computer staff did not know of a world outside of Georgia. This mirrored the company: Harvey Melville Senior who had founded Melvilles in the 1940s never had gone outside of America and like most Americans did not have a passport. Melvilles assumed that doing business over the web was going to be just like their telephone order business in the USA. It was not.

Melvilles problems had started in the Christmas of 1999 when it received a flood of orders from Germany all paid for by credit cards over the web. It debited the cards and shipped the goods. But a large proportion of the goods were rejected because the customer claimed either that he had not ordered the goods or that no agreement to purchase had been made under German law — because of a lack of paper signatures. The German credit card companies refunded all their customers and redebited Melvilles.

Why had the Germans rejected the goods? The answer lay in a message in a Usenet Group. Melvilles had been the target of a "hate campaign" aimed at the owner Senator Harvey Melville Junior. Senator Melville had been behind a strident campaign in the U.S. Congress which attacked unilateral German restrictions on the import of genetically modified soya beans from the United States. Bavarian farmers, steeped in thousand year old pure barley and water legislation on the quality of beer, believed that American was poisoning Europe for profit. The Usenet message, posted anonymously using a remailer, had outlined a no-risk plan to hit Melvilles using pages of genuine Credit Card numbers and Addresses. The highly computer literate German enviromentalists and patriots reacted almost instantly placing thousands of orders for American shirts, pants and linen, each order carefully designed to be over $250 and therefore subject to the Credit Card companies guarantees against misuse.

1.23   The timing was perfect. Melvilles serviced thousands of orders, 97 per cent of which were rejected. As the reports started coming back in the Year 2000 bug bit[63] and there was massive data loss of Internet records. Then the German Postal Authorities demanded extra storage payments from Melvilles, which was unable to meet them. So it dumped the parcels on international charities and, as a result, Latvia ended up with the best dressed refugees in the world. *Newsweek* called the saga "The Revenge of the Soya" and many hackers claimed to have been the authors of the original anonymous Usenet message.

Melvilles struggled on for a few months more — a patriotic call to U.S. consumers to buy their goods fell on deaf ears — and then sought Chapter 11 protection. They had tried to sue the local law firm who had advised them on their contracts but the action collapsed when it turned out that they had never commissioned any new legal work when they created their website out of their mail order operation. The web designers who created their site were "code fodder", kids newly out of college who worked on short contracts for peanuts. Melvilles' bankers, all local firms, were protected from the debacle by their agreements — it turned out that Melvilles had never sought explicit permission to take payments from credit cards over the Internet although the local bank managers knew that this was happening.

A final complication arose when Melvilles sent threatening letters to the thousands of credit card customers who had rejected the parcels. Several complaints were laid before

---

[63] This is fiction — we know that the Year 2000 bug had very few effects on business. However when this little drama was written in 1998 it looked as though there were going to be a large number of traumatic outcomes arising from its impact.

the Berlin Data Protection Commissioner who had then instigated an enquiry into the security and auditability of Melvilles' data protection compliance.

But before she could turn to the Melville papers Sam spotted a new item in her business folder from "Starline DNA Testing". Curious she clicked on the message icon:

"Do you really know who your relatives are? Are you really related to someone wealthy who died without knowing of your existence. Every year the IRS benefits from thousands of wealthy people dying without any known next of kin. Instead of the IRS getting rich you might be getting rich.

All it takes is a cotton bud wiped around your mouth and five dollars. Send us the cotton bud, a photograph, your personal details and the money and we will register your DNA on our database. Starline take similar swabs from all dead or dying citizens in all of the United States — our representatives are in every funeral parlour. Once we find a match we will notify you of your lost relative. For 45 per cent of your inheritance Starline provide you with the proof you require to enable you to regain what is yours."

"Junk mail" thought Sam, "nothing can get rid of it — only the messages get weirder." But as she deleted it she pondered was Starline really a front for an illegal human DNA classification project? "Anything is still possible in America".[64]

The doorbell chimed and Sam went down to collect the mail. There was a recorded **1.24** delivery item — a new smart card. This one was the "CentralServices" smart card, able to hold biometric data. "Hold the package up with the bar code facing the camera", said the Delivery man, taking his time stamped delivery photo. Sam posed, the camera flashed and she signed the touchpad with the stylus. "You will be e-mailed the receipt within ten minutes. Reply to the message and sign it with your digital signature".

Back inside, after drinking a cup of coffee, Sam unwrapped the package. The CentralServices smart card was a multifunction product. It was a credit card, a bank debit card, an electronic purse and a National Identity Card and Driving Licence.[65] It was also useless.

Or at least it was until it was authenticated. Sam read the instructions. "Plug your card into the PC Card slot in your computer. Older machines may refer to this as the PCMCIA slot. Follow the instructions on screen as we connect you to the Internet for authentication".

The card inserted Sam waited. The CentralServices logo appeared on the screen, a rotating image of the Euro coin which each time it spun displayed a different national version of its face. "Trying to connect you" said the prompt at the bottom of the screen.

In less than a minute the card got the computer to connect it to the issuer's switching centre. A picture stated to appear on screen — it was Sam at her front door holding up the package containing the card. "If you can confirm that this is you please reply to this message using your digital signature. Sam digitally signed the photograph and returned it. Up came the message "VoicePrint — Read the following sentence in your normal speaking voice"[66]

---

[64] In 2004 Starline was actually a sting operation set up by the FBI to gain U.S. citizens DNA samples for profiling against DNA taken from unsolved scene of crime investigations.

[65] Under an E.U. directive agreed to by the British Government some years ago all U.K. Driving Licenses from the year 2000 onwards contain a photograph of the driver and act as *de facto* identity cards. In January 2000 the Passport Office released a mock-up of a new miniature passport which civil rights groups objected to as being a *de facto* identity card. We are anticipating that by 2004 there will be legislation allowing for a U.K. Driving Licence to be included within an approved Smart Card which will also serve the purpose of being an identity card for the citizen.

[66] In October 1999 part of this fiction became reality as an Irish company "Buytel" demonstrated their "Voicevault" voice verification system authenticating customers by their voice at a major biometrics in financial institutions conference in Barcelona. See **http://www.buytel.com**.

1.25   Sam read "It was the best of times, It was the worst of times".[67] The computer prompted "Please confirm that you are not suffering from any temporary medical condition which is altering your voice". Sam confirmed that she was not. Another couple of phrases appeared to be read "Click your heels together three times",[68] "The secret of success is honesty and fair dealing. If you can fake those, you've got it made".[69]

The voiceprint verification ended with a tiny beep: "Your card with be validated for use in 10 seconds. If it is lost or stolen telephone the call centre immediately you discover the loss. Thank you for using CentralServices". Moments later the computer beeped again. Sam removed her activated smart card then changed her mind and plugged it back in. A few keystrokes later she had transferred her e-tickets to "Walking on Water" onto the new card ready for the show.

Having put the smart card into her purse Sam turned back to the computer to check her e-mail. There was an urgent message from her Cluster Manager, Fabrio Lopez. She clicked on the icon:

> Sam, I need you to take over the Alsace copyright dispute today instead of continuing with the Melville matter. Jimmy tells me that you have got him up to speed on it and thinks he can cope. Alsace is a different matter. Disclosure was a disaster — the client "forgot" about the automatic electronic journal on his network which the other side demanded. The Chancery Master has ordered it to be handed over by 4.30 pm tomorrow. Tonight I reviewed it and it appear to contradict almost everything we have been told in the witness statements. Thank God we didn't serve them early as I had been minded to do just before the Without Prejudice meeting!
> I need you, as a matter of urgency, to make an annotated version of the Witness Statements cross referenced to the Electronic Journal with queries on every entry where the one does not corroborate the other. Remember that Exchange of Witness Statements is due in eight days and we go for trial in the middle of next month.
> Here are the files. They are too big for you to work on at home. Toni has pencilled in a video conference with the client to discuss the statements on Friday starting at 6 am (sorry about the hour but the client is in Islamabad)
> Regards, Fabrio

1.26   Sam glanced at the size of the attachments. They were massive: far too big to print out. Yet that was not the problem. Electronic disclosure meant that she should do the comparison work on screen. But to do so lawfully she needed at least a twenty-one inch display[70] rather than the fifteen inch one she had at home; electronic disclosure always required a lot of screen comparisons and could easily lead to excessive eye strain. A 2002 Health and Safety Executive case[71] had ruled that an employer whose employees teleworked had to supply its staff with a safe system of working and this meant that the employee's home workstation had to comply with the minimum EU requirements. Failure to require an employee to use a large high definition monitor for electronic disclosure applications was a clear breach of the employer's duty under Health and Safety requirements.

Fabrio knew this which was why he said that they were too big for Sam to work on at home. The computer systems with twenty-one inch screens were all at Cluster Support HQ in town.

So Sam started putting on her business clothes ready for the commute. And as she sprayed on her perfume she noticed that she was running low in "Reality".

---

[67] Source: Charles Dickens — opening words of "A Tale of Two Cities".
[68] ". . . and you will be back in Kansas" Source: Frank Baum "The Wizard of Oz".
[69] Source: Groucho Marx.
[70] This being a flat screen display rather than a monitor.
[71] Please note — there is no such case, this was fiction written in late 1998 [and reviewed in late 1999].

"Reality" by Jean Paul Gaites was the "passionate expression of the next generation". It was the first totally synthetic perfume made not from traditional flower and animal extracts but in a biotechnology plant at a secret location.[72] The perfume was not available in supermarkets or chain stores but was only stocked in Europe in Business Class boutiques at selected airports and in one store on Faubroug St Honoré in Paris.

But Europe was not the world as the manufacturer has discovered. "Reality" could be bought for one tenth its normal European retail price on the Internet. And there was nothing that Jean Paul Gaites could do to stop it save for restricting his sales only to Europe. He had sold a very large shipment of "Reality" to a distributor in India in the belief that India was like the European Union which allowed manufacturers to use European trade mark owners to stop the importation of identical goods sold outside of the European Union.[73] Indian law however was different and had a policy of "exhaustion of rights" whereby a local trade mark owners rights were said to be "exhaused" if they were used against goods or services which had been lawfully put on the market by the manufacturer anywhere else in the world. The Indian dealer sold the shipment to SuperNorvge the Norwegian supermarket chain who promptly put it on sale on their website as well as in their stores. Like India, Norway also had international exhaustion of rights as part of their law. Outside of "Fortress Europe" it was able to cut the best trade deals for its population. But as it was also a member of European Free Trade Association (EFTA) there was no lawful way that that the European Union could stop or hinder exports from Norway. And if a person bought goods from a Norwegian website it was like them travelling to Norway and buying the goods there.

1.27

Sam connected to the SuperNorvge site — an easy task since she had "bookmarked" the page in her browser. "Smart Shopping?" it asked. Sam clicked "Yes" and inserted her new CentralServices card. The list of SuperNorvge goods at discount prices screened endlessly across her display — designer jeans, trainers, exclusive makes of accessories and stockings. "May we update your personal record?" Sam had no worries regarding giving SuperNorvge access to the size-related personal information on her smart card — her body size and personal characteristics — since Norway had one of the toughest data protection regimes in the world. But today it was just "Reality" that concerned her and she ignored the prompt and clicked on "perfume". The site checked her smart card and prompted "Reality". She pulled the perfume bottle icon into the virtual shopping basket and clicked OK. "Your purchase including express courier shipping will cost you €97 (including delivery, U.K. import duty and U.K. VAT). Delivery within 4 hours — Confirm?"

It was an easy decision to make.

---

[72] The advertising suggested that "Reality" was created by the Gods out of pure atoms of spring water and electricity. It was in fact made in part of a disused chemical plant on Merseyside.
[73] See Judgment C–355/96, *Silhouette International Schmied GmbH & Co. KG v Hartlauer Handelsgesellschaft mbH*, July 16, 1998, **http://europa.eu.int/cj/en/cp/cp9849en.htm**.

— 2 —

THE ESTABLISHMENT OF A BUSINESS: WORKING ELECTRONIC COMMERCE

"There will be no such thing as internet companies in the future because all companies whatever their business, will be internet companies"[1]

INTRODUCTION

There are a number of requirements which need to be considered when establishing an electronic commerce business (e-business). One novel requirement concerns domain names. These are a new species of intellectual property with their own complex regulatory framework and are considered in Chapter 3. Another emerging area of legislation is spamming.[2] There are also other more conventional topics: the European Distance Selling Directive regulates the content of websites and gives consumers buying goods and services various rights. There are also many goods and services whose sales are specifically regulated. Some cannot be sold at all, others can only be sold on specific terms. We explore the need for websites to have disclaimers brought to visitors' attention. Web auctions are a particularly interesting phenomenon which have the potential for creating a global free market in standard products and services. But there currently are a number of problems which have to be resolved before they can grow out of their niche markets. Finally, as the importance of e-commerce grows, so do the competition law issues which arise. All of these topics we address below. **2.01**

DOMAIN NAMES

A domain name is a human comprehensible alternative to the string of numbers, *e.g.* 234.532.80.69 called an I.P. (Internet protocol) address, which web servers use to identify each other on the Internet. The creation of memorable domain names as an alternative to numerical I.P. addresses has spawned a new industry and a trade in valuable domain names. **2.02**

---

[1] Rick Lockridge of CNN "Even experts still puzzling out how-to's of Net business" (March 27, 1998).
[2] Technical terms such as this are defined in the Glossary.

When a company decides it wants to establish a website, the first issue it needs to address is the choice of its domain name. Ideally, the company would like to have many highly memorable domain names which would all "map" onto the same string of numbers. But domain names are a scarce resource and disputes arise when more than one company tries to get the same name. Each domain name must be unique. This obviously causes an immediate conflict with the trade mark system.[3]

Registration of domain names is meant to be a simple procedure of applying to the appropriate national registry with a registration fee. Traditionally, domain names have been allotted on a "first come, first served" basis. In practice, and especially for commercial companies, it is sensible to use a domain registration agent who will have established facilities to register domains in national registries all over the world. Domain registration agents all have websites where a potential customer can instantly check, free of charge, to see if a particular domain name is available. The best domain registration agents give detailed advice regarding national registration requirements and administrative problems. For example, the French national registry will not allow anyone to have a **.fr** registration unless the applicant has offices in France and is registered for VAT in France. Other countries such as Ireland and Australia have imposed strict guidelines for registration in an effort to minimise the conflict between domain names and trade mark registrations.

In the United Kingdom the body in charge of domain names is Nominet; in the United States it is InterNIC under a contract from the National Standards Institute (NSI). Each national registry has different policies of domain name allocation, and most have adopted a dispute policy and rules specifying what can and cannot be registered. You can carry out searches on domain name availability for U.S. and U.K. domain names at **http://www.networksolutions.com** and **http://nominet.org.uk** respectively.

Types of Domain Names

2.03   There are two main kinds of domains — generic domains and country domains. Generic domains are the most prized and are meant to indicate a global presence. The U.S. National Standards Institute (NSI) regulates their use under a fairly relaxed regime which is slightly biased towards U.S. interests. Although, in theory, all U.S. bodies should use their country domain rather than a global domain the NSI established a system whereby U.S. organisations treated the generic domains as though they were really the U.S. country domain. Thus American colleges[4] use the global stem **.edu**; the U.S. navy[5] uses the global stem **.mil** without any country indication and the U.S. Democratic Party[6] uses the stem **.org** again without any country indication. But the relaxed NSI registration rules have meant that the **.com** domain is open to anyone. Any company with global ambitions can apply for a generic registration — there are many U.K. and European companies whose domain names have the stem **.com**.[7] For example, the web address of Field Fisher Waterhouse, the law firm of one of the authors, is: **www.ffwlaw.com**.

---

[3] Simply put the same trade mark can be used for a number of different types of goods. A U.K. trade mark (*e.g.* "Polo") can be registered to different companies for confectionery, clothing and motor cars. But only one company could have the domain **http://www.polo.co.uk/**.

[4] *e.g.* Harvard University is **http://www.harvard.edu/** (and not **http://www.harvard.ac.us/**).

[5] **http://www.navy.mil/**.

[6] **http://www.democrats.org/**.

[7] *e.g.* the BBC, which one might think of as being totally British, (with key domains of **http://www.bbc.co.uk/ http://news.bbc.co.uk/** and **http://www.bbcresources.co.uk/**) today indicates its global ambitions with **http://www.beeb.com/** and **http://www.bbcworldwide.com/**.

Country domains are based upon the international two letter code (the ISO-3166 list). Within each country domain are sub-domains for different types of activity. For example, http://www.country bookshop.co.uk is an Internet bookstore in England. The **.co** is a sub-domain indicator showing that it is a commercial site within a country domain. The **.uk** stem indicates that the domain is located in the U.K. and is regulated by Nominet.

The shortage of global domain names has led to a number of proposed new domains **2.04** (**.shop .web .arts .info .rec .firm .nom .eu**) to allow businesses and individuals to have unique but meaningful web addresses. Originally, these new domain names were scheduled to become active in February 1998, but plans were upset by the release on January 30, 1998 of the U.S. Government's "Green Paper" — a proposal describing its views on how the Internet's Domain Name System should be run. In February 1998 the European Union and many other international groups publicised their response which castigated the U.S. Government for assuming authority over the Internet and dismissed many of the ideas set out in a Memorandum of Understanding about the introduction of the new names. As a result in June 1998 the U.S. Government issued a "White Paper" suggesting that the entire process be re-examined by a group of 15 representative organisations. At present there is still some discussion on how the implementation of new top level domain names will be managed. As we will see below, an important part of implementing a consistent approach to domain name registration is the process by which conflicts between individuals' domain names and trade marks are resolved.

The Internet Corporation for Assigned Names and Numbers (ICANN), a non profit organisation established in early 1999 to administer the allocation of the new top level domain names, has recently been involved in an ongoing dispute with its predecessor Network Solutions Inc (NSI) as to who will have the right and the ability to profit from the registration of new top level domain names. NSI refused ICANN access to its database of registrants thereby making it impossible for ICANN to manage the registration of new domain names. As at October 1999 NSI and ICANN have agreed a compromise under which ICANN would be given access to the database while NSI would become one of several ICANN-accredited domain name registrars.[8]

Trade Marks and Passing Off

A trade mark is any sign capable of distinguishing goods or services of one origin from **2.05** those of others. A trade mark can be protected by registration. In the U.K. there are two routes to protection. A national registration can be obtained through the U.K. Patent Office under the Trade Marks Act 1994 or a mark can be registered as a Community trade mark under European Community Law.[9] If someone has registered a domain name incorporating a trade mark then the domain name holder could be in breach of the Trade Marks Act 1994. Section 10 of the Trade Marks Act 1994 states that:

> "A person infringes a registered trade mark if he uses in the course of a trade a sign which identical or similar to the registered trade mark in relation to identical or similar goods or services."

The tort of passing off is committed if a defendant wrongly represents in the course of trade that there is a connection between the defendant and the claimant. This is

---

[8] There is an information site at **http://www.gtld.com/** which contains the latest news and comment about the proposed new names.
[9] Council Regulation 40/94 on Community Trade Mark which is administered by the Office for Harmonisation in the Internal Market.

considered further in the next section in the important case of *Marks & Spencer's v. One in a Million* in the context of "cybersquatting". Trade Marks are considered in detail at section 5.30 below.[10]

Domain Name Disputes

2.06   The case of *Prince plc v. Prince Sportswear Group Inc.* is a good example of the type of domain name dispute which arises between companies.[11] The source of the dispute is a fundamental mismatch between trade mark rights and the domain name system.

In January 1997, Prince Sports Group, a manufacturer of tennis racquets, sent a "cease and desist" letter to Prince PLC, a U.K.-based information technology (I.T.) company. The letter complained about the I.T. company's registration and use of the domain name **prince.com**. The letter claimed that the sports group had a number of PRINCE trade mark registrations (including in the United Kingdom) and alleged that the I.T. company's use of the domain name amounted to trade mark infringement and unfair competition under the Lanham Act. Prince Sports Group also complained to the NSI requesting that the domain name be put on hold, pending the resolution of the dispute.

Since 1995 Prince PLC had operated a website under the domain name **prince.com** which it had been assigned under the then "first come first served" policy of the NSI. However, in September 1996, the NSI issued its Domain Name Resolution Policy (Revision 2)[12] which has indirectly enabled any U.S. federal trade mark holder or holder of a foreign trade mark to pre-empt the rights of pre-registered genuine domain name holders.

2.07   Under this revised policy, if a second company can show that it is the owner of a U.S. federal registered trade mark or a foreign registered trade mark pertaining to that name, the first party which has registered the domain name loses that registration. Such a loss of registration can be put on hold if the first party can also either prove that it has a U.S. federal trade mark registration or a foreign trade mark registration, or has commenced proceedings in a "court of competent jurisdiction" to protect that domain name.

When NSI wrote to Prince plc intimating that it was about to re-allocate the domain name, Prince plc could neither show it owned a trade mark, nor confirm that it had commenced proceedings in a U.S. court (which some might say was the right "court of competent jurisdiction"), and so were in danger of losing the domain name in favour of Prince Sportswear Group Inc. However, the NSI advised Prince plc that it could commence proceedings against Prince Sports Group in any court of competent jurisdiction and further said that if Prince plc brought such a suit, NSI would not put the name on hold pending resolution of the action and would abide by any resulting court order.

Accordingly, Prince PLC filed suit in the High Court in London alleging that the statements made by Prince Sportswear Group Inc. (that Prince plc was "infringing and diluting its trade mark rights") constituted groundless threats under section 21 of the U.K. Trade Marks Act 1994. Neuberger J. granted Prince plc a declaration and injunction pursuant to section 21(2) of the Act. NSI accepted that the threats were groundless and Prince plc continues to have use of the **prince.com** domain name.[13]

---

[10] Court of Appeal, July 23, 1998.
[11] CH—1997—P No. 2355, July 18, 1997.
[12] For details of this policy see **http://www.rs.internic.net/domain+info/internic+domain+6.html**.
[13] CH—1997—P No. 2355, July 18, 1997.

The NSI's revised policy is a flawed attempt at dealing with the rights of trade mark **2.08** owners. It ignores the fact that the trade mark registrations may not cover the specific services and goods in relation to which the domain name is being used. Trade mark registrations should, in these cases, be irrelevant in resolving domain name disputes. Further, it takes no account of common law rights which a domain name registrant may have acquired — the unregistered trade mark or passing off rights.

However, the NSI revised policy is of some use in protecting legitimate traders from others passing off their websites as being associated with them. For example, it appears that a U.K. trade mark owner could invoke the NSI revised policy against a U.S. company which had acquired a **.com** registration and was passing off goods or services as being those of the U.K. company.[14]

Cybersquatting

The issue of cybersquatting was clarified and the practice of domain name piracy was **2.09** effectively buried in the United Kingdom in the *One in a Million* decision.[15]

The case concerned the business of One in a Million Ltd, which had registered the plaintiffs' names and trade marks as Internet domain names, without their consent, and then sought to sell them. The plaintiffs (Marks & Spencer Plc, J. Sainsbury Plc, Virgin Enterprises Ltd, British Telecommunications Plc, Telecom Securicor Cellular Radio Ltd and Ladbrokes Plc) claimed that the defendant was passing off and infringing their registered trade marks. They also claimed that the defendant's activities constituted threats of passing off and that they were entitled to injunctive relief. The defendant accepted that the trade names Marks & Spencer, Sainsbury, Virgin, BT, Cellnet and Ladbroke are well known brand names with substantial goodwill attaching to them. It had registered **ladbrokes.com, sainsbury.com, sainsburys.com, marksandspencer.com, marksandspencer.co.uk, cellnet.net, bt.org, virgin.org, britishtelecom.co.uk, britishtelecom.net** and **britishtelecom.com**. The defendant claimed that it registered domain names with a view to making a profit either by selling them to the owners of the goodwill, using the blocking effect of the registration to obtain a good price, or, in some cases, selling them to collectors or to other persons who could have a legitimate reason for using them. It argued that this could not amount to passing off or a threat to pass off.

The Court of Appeal, dismissing the appeal of *One in a Million* and granting a **2.10** permanent injunction, held that the registration of a distinctive name such as "marksandspencer" made a false representation to persons who consulted the register that the registrant was connected or associated with the name registered. This constituted passing off. The Court further held that the registration was an erosion of the exclusive goodwill in the name which damaged or was likely to damage Marks & Spencer Plc. Aldous L.J. felt that domain names comprising the names Marks & Spencer were instruments of fraud because any realistic use of the name would result in passing off.

---

[14] There have been several cases in the United States on domain names most of which have settled. In *MTV Networks v. Curry*, a former employee of the rock music cable television service obtained the site name **mtv.com** and offered reports on the rock music industry at the Internet site. The case settled on undisclosed terms. (*MTV Networks v. Curry*, 867 F.Supp. 202 (SDNY 1994)). In *Kaplan Education Center Ltd v. Princeton Review Management Corp.* 94 CV 1604 (S.D.N.Y. 1994) a test preparation service obtained a domain name that resembled that of a rival service and then placed disparaging material about its rival at the site. Despite Kaplan's demand for injunctive relief and damages (as well as attorneys' fees), the monetary claims were not established and the arbitration panel simply required PRI to release the name).

[15] *Marks and Spencer plc v. One in a Million Ltd*, July 23, 1998, CA.

This justified injunctive relief. The other trade names were all household names denoting the respondents. The Court decided that the defendant's motive was to use the respondents' goodwill, and to threaten to sell the domain name to another who might use it for passing off in order to obtain money from the respondents. The value of the domain name lay in the threat that they would be used in a fraudulent way. The registrations were made with the purpose of appropriating the respondents' good will. They were instruments of fraud and injunctive relief was appropriate. Aldous L.J. stated that:

"there was clear evidence of systematic registration by the appellants of well-known trade names as blocking registrations and a threat to sell them to others."

He went on:

"the purpose of the so-called blocking registration was to extract money from the owners of the goodwill in the name chosen. Its ability to do so was in the main dependent upon the threat, expressed or implied, that the [defendants] would exploit the goodwill by either trading under the name or equipping another with the name so he could do so."

2.11   The decision of the Court seems to have been influenced in no small measure by the attitude of the defendant. In August 1997, it had threatened to involve the media if British Telecommunications took legal action against it over the domain name bt.org. It later offered to sell the name for £4,700 plus VAT. The name **burgerking.co.uk** was offered for sale to Burger King for £25,000 plus VAT in September 1996, the defendant pointing out that if Burger King did not buy it, it "would be available for sale to any other interested party". A similar threat was made implicitly to Intertan U.K. Ltd (Tandy) at about the same time. After the case BT issued a statement containing the following:

"This judgment in proceedings in which BT has taken a leading role, represents a significant victory on behalf of businesses with valuable trade marks which have been the target of abusive activities by unprincipled domain name pirates and cybersquatters who seek to take speculative advantage of the goodwill established in well-known marks. It reinforces the view that the domain names clearly perform a trade mark function and that trade mark owners can legitimately expect to have their rights protected on the Internet. The message to those who want to register domain names and avoid conflict with trade marks is "don't imitate, differentiate!"

The defendant sought leave to appeal to the House of Lords but was refused.

This case, at the time of writing, is the highest considered U.K. case on domain names. Together with *Prince*, it indicates that it is important:

- when registering a domain name to undertake trade mark searches to avoid conflict with trade mark owners;

- when a potential conflict is discovered to seek agreement with the trade mark owners to avoid potential passing off problems. If it can be established that there is no likelihood of passing off or trade mark infringement the domain name should be safe to use;

- do not attempt to blackmail the trade mark owners (or, conversely, give in to intimidation by the trade mark owners when there is no likelihood of passing off or trade mark infringement — see *Prince*).

"First Come, First Served"

The 1997 decision of the Vice Chancellor, Sir Richard Scott, in *Pitman Training Limited et al*   **2.12**
v. Nominet U.K.[16] illustrates the support of the law to the "first come, first served" policy
of domain name registration and the importance of early registration.

The case concerned the domain name **www.pitman.co.uk** and arose because both of
the plaintiffs, Pitman Training Limited and PTC Oxford Limited (a franchisee of the first
plaintiff), and the second defendant, Pearson Professional Limited, were entitled to use
the name or style "Pitman" for their respective trading purposes. All these three parties
could trace back their rights in the name to Sir Isaac Pitman in the nineteenth century
who founded not only a publishing business, but also a training business and an
examination business.

In February 1996 Pearson Professional Limited sent a request to Nominet for
registration of the domain name **pitman.co.uk** for use in its publishing business. The
application was noted as received and confirmed on February 21, 1996. Thereafter,
Pearson Professional Limited did not have a nominal I.P. address assigned to the domain
name but left it as a registration in limbo while the company made plans for the
development of the site. However, in April 1996, the first plaintiff, Pitman Training
Limited, enquired as to whether the domain name **pitman.co.uk** was still available for
allocation. Owing to an error, Pitman Training was told that the name was indeed still
available, and it was duly registered to the company's business.

The first plaintiff started to use the domain name in July 1996. It was not until   **2.13**
December that year that Pitman Publishing, a training division of Pearson Professional,
which was then ready to go "live" with its e-mail service and website, found that its
domain name had been re-allocated to Pitman Training without its knowledge or
consent. The Vice Chancellor refused Pitman Training's claims to be allowed to continue
using the name and ordered the immediate reassignment of **pitman.co.uk** to Pearson
Professional.

It should, however, be pointed out that the litigation would not have arisen had
Pearson Publishing taken the prudent step of registering a temporary I.P. address with
the domain name **pitman.co.uk**. A single page announcing that the domain name had
already been assigned would have stopped Pitman Training from making an investment
based on the error.

There is a fully automatic system for changing the I.P. addresses associated with
particular domain names, and a switchover from a temporary I.P. to a new permanent
I.P. where a site has been constructed normally takes between 12 to 48 hours.
Consequently, although not legally necessary, it is sensible for any registration to be
immediately supported by connecting the domain name to a temporary page publicising
the domain name ownership.

Recent Developments

On April 30, 1999 the World Intellectual Property Organisation (WIPO) submitted its   **2.14**
report concerning intellectual property issues associated with domain name registration
to the Internet Corporation of Assigned Names and Numbers (ICANN). On the
September 29, 1999 ICANN responded by publishing its new policy in relation to domain

---

[16] *The Pitman Training Ltd v. Nominet U.K.* [1998] Tr.L.R. 173.

name disputes. The policy statement draws heavily on WIPO's recommendations and seeks to establish an efficient and cost effective procedure for resolving cybersquatting disputes. The procedure will, at this stage, only apply to registrations of **.com**, **.net** and **.org** domain names which are made in "bad faith".

The new procedure is estimated to take approximately 45 days, will be arbitrated over by "neutral person" and will cost approximately $1000. The arbitrator will decide whether the registration of the domain name will be confirmed, cancelled or transferred with both parties retaining a right to appeal the decision. The owners of a domain name will be forced to submit themselves to the procedure only in cases where the complainant alleges that the domain name has been registered in "bad faith" meaning that it is confusingly similar or even identical to complainants trade mark and that the owner of the domain name does not have a legitimate interest in the domain name. It is hoped that this procedure will eliminate registrations of domain names designed to disrupt a competitor's business or intended to extract a payment for the transfer of the domain name. The procedure is also intended to apply where a domain name is used to pass off the products or services on a site as those of a well known brand or where the domain name itself implies a connection with those products or services.

Where a dispute arises concerning a domain name that has not been registered in bad faith, the trade mark owners will have to look to the courts for a remedy as WIPO's recommendations on a further procedure allowing owners of well know trade marks to place a "block" on the registration of similar domain names were not adopted.

ICANN stated that it believed the granting of such rights to trade mark owners would severely obstruct the cheap and speedy registration of domain names which it considers a key feature of the Internet.

It is now anticipated that other administrators of domain names such as Nominet which administers the **.co.uk** domain names, will likewise adopt similar procedures.

How effective the implementation of these proposed dispute resolution procedures will be is yet to be seen, though it appears that there will be significant scope for argument on what may constitute a legitimate use of a domain name. ICANN's policy refers to the "legitimate non-commercial and fair use" of a domain name. How far that definition will stretch will no doubt be the focus of heated debate.

Strategies for registering Domain Names

2.15   So what is the most sensible strategy to adopt when seeking to register a domain name? Using the services of a domain name registration agent that can advise you on the requirements of registering a particular domain name can help you avoid difficulties after registration. As a general guide, and until the domain name registration process is expanded to deal with the substantive trade mark issues, a preventative strategy is preferable. In cases where a domain name registration is likely to cause objection or a conflict with domain names it is wise to undertake trade mark and domain name searches before registration. As more and more registries require warranties and indemnities on trade mark infringements (Australia, Singapore, United Kingdom) this procedure is vital in assessing the potential conflict and liability to trade mark owners.

Given the new procedures to be introduced by ICANN, conflicts with owners of similar domain names should also be examined. In cases of **.com**, **.org** and **.net** domain names consisting of or incorporating your trade marks, the owner of the conflicting domain name should be contacted to determine their right to the domain name and, if necessary, the ICANN dispute resolution procedure initiated in cases where you believe the current domain name owner has registered in bad faith. A conflict concerning the registration of a country specific domain name will have to be managed in accordance with the responsible administrative body (for example, Nominet's guidelines in the United Kingdom). A domain name registration agent will be able to provide you with more details on the dispute resolution procedures for a particular domain name should a conflict arise.

In cases where there appear to be no conflicts, you should register immediately. As you will appreciate from the above case law "first in time" registration of your domain name can be vital. If you intend to use your domain name internationally it is wise for you to seek registration of generic top level domain names such as **.com** as well as country-specific domains.

Registration in the jurisdictions in which you seek customers for the services featured **2.16** on your site is advisable, especially as the inconsistencies in the protection afforded trade mark owners in such jurisdictions allow unscrupulous operators to exploit/ dilute your trade mark or use it to unfairly compete with you. Seeking a registration of obvious variants of your domain name at the commencement of your "online presence" is also an effective method of deterring opportunist.

Issues that will generally be considered in a domain name dispute include whether the domain name is a trade mark or part of a trade mark that is afforded protection in the jurisdiction where the dispute arose, and whether the trade mark is actively used by the trade mark owner in that jurisdiction. Individuals seeking to register a trade mark as a domain name should also consider that the domain name including the domain designation such as **.com** or **.co.uk** may themselves be registered as trade marks if they are sufficiently distinctive. The value of such a registration is questionable, however, if the trade mark that forms the distinctive part of the domain name has already been registered.

In short, the most preferable strategy to protect your domain name consists of "first in time" registration of the domain name together with registration of the appropriate and corresponding trade mark in the jurisdictions in which the domain name is registered.

THE DISTANCE SELLING DIRECTIVE

The Distance Selling Directive[17] was adopted by the European Parliament and Council in **2.17** May 1997 and is due to be implemented by June 4, 2000.[18] The Directive is designed to protect consumers against some of the risks involved in distance selling. It will make significant changes in the practice of those who use the Internet to sell goods and services to European consumers. By protecting consumers against some of the risks involved in buying goods at a distance, it is intended to encourage and increase confidence in such methods of selling and also harmonise laws in all Member States so that all European consumers have equal access to goods and services in other Member States. Essentially, the Directive covers five main areas: the provision of information about the contract and its terms (Articles 4 and 5); the right of withdrawal (Article 6); the obligations as to performance by the supplier (Article 7); payment by card (Article 8) and inertia selling (Article 9).

---

[17] Directive 97/7.
[18] At the time of going to print the government had published a draft Statutory Instrument entitled The Consumer Protection (Contracts Concluded by Means of Distance Communication) Regulations 2000.

What is a Distance Contract?

2.18   A *distance contract* is any contract concerning goods and services concluded between a supplier and a consumer under an organised distance sales or service provision scheme run by the supplier, who, for the purposes of the contract, makes exclusive use of one or more means of distance communication up to and including the moment at which the contract is concluded.[19] The key to the applicability of the Directive is a contract where the supplier and the consumer do not come face to face prior to the conclusion of the contract (telephone sales, mail order or e-commerce). Therefore, a transaction where the seller makes initial contact by using a distance communication but concludes the contract face to face is not covered by the Directive. The ambit of the Directive is therefore very wide. Annexure 1 of the Directive contains an indicative list of the means of communication for distance selling. It includes unaddressed printed matter, press advertising, telephone sales with or without human intervention, videotex (microcomputer and television screen) with keyboard or attached screen and electronic mail.

Who is a Consumer and who is a Supplier?

2.19   A *consumer* is any natural person who, in contracts covered by the Directive, is acting for purposes which are outside his/her trade, business or profession. This is a rather strange definition since it appears to exclude protection for sole traders. This means that a computer programmer who buys software over the Internet for incorporation into his/her products would not be a consumer. However, the implications from early documentation and debate behind the legislation is that a consumer is a non specialist dealing with an undertaking in a superior bargaining position. It is thought likely that this purposive construction of the definition would be adopted in any contested case, thereby protecting sole traders.

A *supplier* is defined as any natural or legal person who, in contracts covered by the Directive acts in his/her commercial or professional capacity.

Excluded Contracts

2.20   Certain types of contract are excluded from the ambit of the Directive; other types of contract are exempted from some of the provisions of the Directive. The excluded contracts are:

- contracts relating to financial services — these are regarded as different from other contracts because they have specific legislation which is applicable and do not ordinarily gain protection of consumer protection legislation[20];

- contracts concluded by means of automatic vending machines or automated commercial premises. These are excluded because they are unlikely to create the same sort of issues as purchasing goods using distant methods;

- contracts concluded with telecommunication operators through the use of payphones. Again, this does not create the same sort of issues requiring consumer protection as other contracts;

---

[19] Art. 2(1).
[20] See Chapter 9.

- contracts for the construction of sale of land are excluded as a special category;

- contracts concluded at auction — the common practice whereby people bid by means of telephone or on-line such as www.qxl.com — are considered separate from other types of contract.

The obligations relating to prior information, written confirmation, the right to withdraw and performance within 30 days do not apply to contracts for the supply of food beverages and other such consumable items and to contracts for the provision of accommodation, transport, catering or leisure services where a supplier agrees to provide the services on a specified date.[21] This is only logical as it would make no sense if a consumer could book an air ticket, take the flight and then exercise the right of refusal.

Successive Operations

Many consumers buy books and CDs from so-called book and music clubs. The Directive **2.21** at recital 10 refers to these type of contract as comprising "successive operations" or "a series of separate operations over a period of time". Such transactions may be treated differently by Member States laws. The Directive is stated to require compliance at the time of the first of the series of successive operations, even though there may be a number of separate contracts. This has been criticised by some commentators[22] as concentrating on the fact that consumers only need to be notified of contractual terms on initially joining the club but they still need the protection of the Directive for matters such as the right of refusal and the provisions of inertia selling after the initial period.

Prior Information Requirements

Article 4 of the Directive specifies that prior to the conclusion of any distance contract, **2.22** (*i.e.* before the contract is entered into, not before performance is concluded) the consumer shall be provided with the following information:

- the identity of the supplier and, in the case of contracts requiring payment in advance, his/her address;

- a description of the main characteristics of the goods or services;

- the price of the goods or services including all taxes;

- delivery costs, where appropriate;

- the arrangements for payment, delivery or performance;

- the existence of a right of cancellation, except in certain cases specified in the Article where this right does not exist;

- the cost of using the means of distance communication, where it is calculated other than at the basic rate (such as premium phone lines);

- the period for which the offer or the price remains valid; and

- where appropriate, the minimum duration of the contract in the case of contracts for the supply of products or services to be performed permanently or recurrently.

---

[21] There is an exception in the case of outdoor leisure events where the supplier can reserve the right not to apply Art. 7(2) in specific circumstances.
[22] See the Art. by Robert Bradgate at 1997.4 Web JCI.

None of these requirements should cause a company selling via a website any difficulties. A failure to provide this information will lead to a supplier not being able to enforce the contract.

Provision of Information in a Comprehensible Manner

2.23   The Directive requires the consumer to be provided with the Article 4 information in a clear and comprehensible manner and in good time before the conclusion of any distance contract (meaning before the contract is made, not before performance of the contracts is concluded). In addition, the information must be provided in a way appropriate to the means of distance communication used with due regard to the principles of good faith in commercial contracts and the rules of protection of vulnerable people such as minors. The concept of providing information in good faith will be difficult to implement into U.K. law which does not recognise such general requirements. The requirement of good faith essentially means that people supplying goods using electronic commerce should deal openly with their consumers supplying the required information in a comprehensive and legible form.

One contentious issue was the language in which the requisite information should be supplied. The European Commission took the view that if the consumer replied to an advertisement in an English-language newspaper, it was reasonable that the information be supplied in English. In discussions certain Member States took the position of requiring the use of the consumer's language. Since the language to be used for distance contracts is a matter left to Member States, one can envisage situations where the language used is not that of the host country of the recipient. It is likely that any such deliberate use of a language which is different from that the host country supplier would be in breach of good faith requirements.

Written confirmation of Information

2.24   The Directive requires[23] that in distance contracts for the sale of goods, the consumer must receive written confirmation of most of the Article 4 information in a durable medium available and accessible by him/her. This recognises that using the World Wide Web and e-mail is ephemeral[24] due to the lack of permanence in the medium. In the case of services, the requirement is to provide confirmation in good time during the performance of the contract. There is a partial exemption for goods delivered by the supplier to a third party (such as gifts). No confirmation is required for either goods or services where the information has already been provided in writing with another durable medium. The consultation paper of the Department of Trade and Industry[25] indicates that the DTI considers e-mail meets the definition of confirmation in a durable medium.

Right of Cancellation

2.25   The most significant impact of the Directive is contained in Article 6 of the Directive which creates a general right to cancel. This is a right which many consumers already

---

[23] Art. 5.
[24] Recital 13.
[25] June 1998 Consultation Paper: "Distance Selling — implementation of E.U. Directive 97/7 on the Protection of Consumers in respect of Distance Contracts". A Further Consultation Paper was issued in November 1999.

have in other transactions such as when buying goods from magazines where the Mail Order Protection Scheme applies and in certain credit agreements regulated by the Consumer Credit Act 1974.[26] Every consumer who is party to a distance contract has at least seven working days (*i.e.* an actual period of between 10 and 12 ordinary days most of the year and two weeks at Christmas) to cancel the contract at will without having to give any reason. No penalty can be levied and a full refund is due to the consumer. Such refunds must take place within 30 days. Only the direct costs of the goods are payable. However, there are some significant exemptions to these rules. The "cooling-off" period will not apply to gaming/lottery services and travel services. Nor will it apply to unsealed audio or video recordings, records or computer software and CD-ROMs. Furthermore, it will not apply for newspapers, periodicals and magazines and certain other situations referred to in Article 6(3).

From the wording it would therefore appear that it will apply in the case of books that are not periodicals or magazines. Book shops that offer books over the Internet appear to be caught — it would be open to a consumer to order a few novels for Christmas, receive them, read them, decide that he/she did not like them and successfully demand his/her money back early in the New Year.

Performance

Unless the parties have agreed otherwise, the supplier must execute a customer's order **2.26** within 30 days from the day following that on which the consumer forwarded his/her order to the supplier.[27] Accordingly, it is open for a supplier to agree a longer than 30 day period with a consumer but this could lead to challenges under the Unfair Contract Terms Act 1977 and, in particular, the Unfair Terms and Consumer Contracts Regulations 1994.[28]

Where a supplier is unable to perform the contract because the goods or services are not available, the supplier must inform the consumer of this situation and refund any sums received within 30 days.

The draft U.K. Regulations provide that the supplier may provide the consumer with goods or services of equivalent quality or price provided that the consumer is informed of this possibility prior to the conclusion of the contract. It is further provided that the consumer must be informed of this possibility in a clear and comprehensible manner. The cost of returning the goods following the exercise of the right of withdrawal are to be borne by the supplier and the consumer must be informed of this. In any event, any contractual clauses which purport to permit a supplier to provide goods or services of the same quality and price but of a different description to those ordered will potentially be challengable by a consumer under the Unfair Contract Terms Act 1977 and the Unfair Terms in Consumer Contract Regulations 1994.

Payment by Card

It is estimated that 47 per cent of all disputes dealt with by Visa in the European Union **2.27** are directly related to Internet fraud. Due to the high rate of Internet related fraud on credit card transactions, Visa supports the swift adoption of the Secure Electronic

---

[26] See the Consumer Protection (Cancellation of Contracts Concluded Away from Business Premises) Regulations 1987.
[27] Art. 7(1).
[28] See para. 3.88.

Transaction protocol (SET). Developed by a consortium led by MasterCard and Visa and implemented since 1997, SET is a standard protocol that supports secure digital credit card transactions online. Visa also advocates parallel measures to enhance the security of transactions on the Net such as the adoption and standardisation of digital signatures.[29]

In response to rising fears of credit card fraud in electronic commerce transactions, the Law Commission of England and Wales issued draft proposals addressing the issue on April 27, 1999. If approved, they would fundamentally change fraud legislation in the area. Some of the proposed changes include:

- widening the range of actions included in the offence of "obtaining property by deception";

- "changing the criminal definition of fraud to include temporary, as well as permanent deprivation";

- altering the notion of "deception" in order to make it easier to apply;

- closing loopholes in the offence of obtaining services be deception.[30]

The success of e-commerce depends on consumers having the confidence that when they make payment prior to delivery or performance of goods or services they will be protected. There is also concern regarding fraudulent use of credit and debit cards. Article 8 provides that a consumer may request cancellation of a payment where fraudulent use is made of his/her payment card and that in the event of such fraudulent use the consumer is to be re-credited with the sums paid.

2.28   But there remain problems with goods purchased from abroad using credit or debit cards. In respect of credit cards section 75 of the Consumer Credit Act 1974 provides that, for transactions in excess of £100, if a credit card holder (a *debtor*) has "any claim against the supplier in respect of a misrepresentation or breach of contract, he shall have a like claim against the creditor". On the face of it, a U.K. consumer should be able to bring a claim against his/her U.K. card issuer if goods supplied by an overseas supplier are not of satisfactory quality. Although there are a few tenuous arguments which suggest that a U.K. card issuer could avoid liability[31] the better view is that section 75 covers overseas credit card transactions.[32]

The same cannot, however, be said to apply to debit cards where the consumer uses a debit card and receives unsatisfactory goods. In these circumstances the consumer will have no claim against his/her card issuer. Within the European Union he/she currently has to pursue an action against the supplier in the country where the contract was made — effectively litigating abroad. But, after the Directive has been brought into force the customer will be able to sue the foreign supplier locally in respect of contracts made in the European Union. Thus an English consumer will be able to bring a complaint against a German supplier in an English court with English law being applicable. The judgment of the court will be fully enforceable against the German supplier. And national consumer protection organisations will work together to ensure compliance with the highest consumer standards.

---

[29] EBL, June 1999, vol.1, no. 5 at p.1. — also covered in Chapter 6.

[30] *ibid.*

[31] See the discussion in Guest, A.G. & Lloyd, M.G. *Encyclopedia of Consumer Credit Law*, para. 2–076.

[32] See the Director General of Fair Trading's review of s.75 in *Connected Lender Liability* (March 1994) at pp. 26–28 and Report No. OFT 132 "Connected lender liability — a second report by the Director General of Fair Trading on section 75 of the Consumer Credit Act 1974" May 1995, where the Director General stated that his view was (and remains) that overseas transactions are covered by the law as it stands.

Inertia Selling

The Directive requires Member States to take measures necessary to prohibit the supply **2.29** of goods and services to a consumer without them being ordered by the consumer beforehand and where such supplier involves a demand for payment. In the United Kingdom the Unsolicited Goods and Services Act 1971 has effectually outlawed some inertia selling. The Act makes it an offence to demand payment for unsolicited goods. Since the Directive applies to both goods and services, U.K. law will need to be amended to extend the protection of this Act to services.

Binding Nature

Article 12(1) of the Distance Selling Directive expressly states that the consumer may not **2.30** contract out of or waive rights conferred by the Directive. The second leg of Article 12, which is addressed to Member States, requires them to implement legislation which will invalidate any attempts to deprive consumers of their rights under the Directive through a non-E.U. Member State choice of law.

Burden of Proof

In the case of a dispute the burden of proof concerning information, confirmation, time **2.31** limits and consumer consent will be on the supplier rather than the consumer.

Conclusion of the Distance Selling Directive

The Directive is the first consumer-oriented legislation which is primarily focused on **2.32** e-commerce. Distance selling is subject to little specific statutory regulation in the United Kingdom although there is an element of self regulation by codes of practice and trade associations. However, the Directive fails to address certain crucial legal issues such as:

- which legal system should be applied to transactions?
- how should transactions be authenticated?
- how can electronic privacy and data protection be ensured?

On the first issue, this appears to fall within the Rome Convention of the Applicable Law and the Brussels Convention on Jurisdiction and Enforcement of Judgments.[33] The law of the consumer's home State would normally be applicable (Rome Convention, Article 5.3.4) and the courts of his/her place of residence would normally have jurisdiction. In practice, because of the dispute resolution provisions, this is not likely to be a real problem. The Directive (Article 11(2)) provides for mutual recognition of consumer bodies who could bring legal actions or administrative complaints if such actions or complains were allowed under the Member State's law. Taking the explicit role of Member States and consumer bodies in protecting consumers' rights arising out of distance selling agreements, a company will be faced with a losing battle if it attempts to engage in sharp practice with choice of law clauses and purported waiver of consumer rights.

---

[33] See Chapter 4.

The question of how a transaction should be authenticated is best answered by a practical approach. It is wise to use the best mature technology and always be able to "unwind" transactions.[34] Business is creating professional standards which are likely to be acceptable paradigms of authentication.[35] But these are still being developed. Until there is consensus it is prudent only to use secure servers for all direct selling activities over the web, with proper firewalls and well documented procedures that are fully auditable. Suppliers should also ensure that individual transactions with particular customers can be unwound within the necessary time frame, as customers who pay by credit card will have to have their accounts recredited within a reasonable time. Although the Directive makes no mention of any time to recredit, it is likely that a period of 30 days or less will be imposed as a benchmark by reference to Article (6)(2).

MANAGING THE SITE

Commenting on the site

2.33 A fact which seems obvious but which is often forgotten, is that companies inviting people to send e-mail must ensure that they read it and respond to it in a timely manner. They must also handle the personal information supplied by the potential customer in a lawful way.

The customer may be asking a question, commenting on some part of the site, warning you of a danger or complaining about your product. A good way of responding is to design the website so that every e-mail receives a standard automatic response. An example of this is shown below.

> This is an automatic response — thank you for your message. All e-mails to us are reviewed. However, this process takes time and, owing to the volume of e-mail received, we do not undertake to respond personally to your message.

Having made the statement that all e-mails are reviewed, it is important to follow through. This should be one of the responsibilities of the Webmaster — the company official in charge of the site.[36] He/she will be able to sift and sort out the messages, forwarding those which are important to the appropriate people in the company and responding in a suitable manner to those which deserve a personal reply.

The customer will often supply the company with personal information — his/her name, age, interests, etc. Companies need to have a policy regarding dealing with this data, the safest policy being to discard it after review. Personal data should not be gathered from this source without a suitable warning being given — only when the customer has registered his/her interest through filling in an electronic form with appropriate warnings should the data become a company asset.

---

[34] On technical reasons concerning the use of SET for authentication see the section in Chapter 5 on "Secure Electronic Transactions and the Microsoft Patent".

[35] See the section in Chapter 6 on "Principles of Good Practice — the BSI and DISC codes".

[36] Additionally a new type of software termed an automated Message Centre is a key feature of many major commercial systems. The Message Centre downloads the incoming mail from customers, stores it in a database, and then sends back an acknowledgement with a tracking number. Mail is sorted into "pools", depending on its subject or other criteria. Individual employees of the company then retrieve mail and respond to it. Their answer goes back to the Message Centre, which then tracks the response for future reference (*e.g.* ISO 9002) before forwarding it to the customer with the appropriate tracking number intact.

Registering for automatic notification

One very useful modern feature of a number of sites is automatic notification of changes. **2.34** Customers give their names and e-mail addresses; whenever the specified section of the site changes, an e-mail is sent directly to them, telling them that the site has changed.

This service is often free for both the company and the customer — it is paid for by advertising. The notification message contains an advertisement for some product or service selected by the notifier. The notification message also always contains a message telling the customer how to stop receiving further notifications of changes.

Use of notifiers with unsolicited advertisements is not considered to be improper — the Legal Advisory Board of the European Commission uses one of these services on its pages. However, problems could arise if the notifier accepted advertisements for goods and services which were not of a kind considered suitable for the target market. For example, strict controls exist in Sweden regarding advertising and children; a toy company could therefore encounter problems regarding unsolicited advertising to children if it used a notifier service that targeted them.

With notifiers, the personal data, the link between the name and the e-mail, is not normally supplied to the company but is retained by the notifier. Care should therefore be taken in selection of the notifier to ensure that the organisation is handling personal data in a legal and decent manner. Dangers arise if, through inadequate computer security, the mailing list used by the supplier is passed to a spammer.

Registering interest by filling in an online form

Under data protection laws, every time a customer completes an online form, important **2.35** issues and duties arise regarding the acquisition of data.[37] The first issue concerns the manner in which the information may be acquired and the nature of the information being sought. Other issues include important duties regarding the management and the re-use and storage of data. This section looks only at the initial issues of acquisition of data and its nature.

Acquisition of data

Principle 1 of the Data Protection Act 1998 says: "The information to be contained in **2.36** personal data shall be obtained, and personal data shall be processed, fairly and lawfully". The term "lawfully" is easy to determine; stealing a customer list is clearly wrong. But the term "fairly" raises subjective issues. In determining whether information has been obtained or acquired fairly, Schedule 1, Part 2 of the Act provides that regard shall be had to the method by which it was obtained, including in particular whether any person from whom it was obtained was deceived or misled as to the purpose or purposes for which it is to be held, used or disclosed.

It would therefore be unfair to encourage customers to complete a form under the representation that they are entering a competition to win a prize if the personal data so obtained were to be used for a mailing list, unless this fact was made known to the customers at the time and they had the opportunity to tick a box saying that they did not want to be included on the mailing list.

---

[37] See Chapter 7.

Codes of Practice

2–37   There are now a number of code of practice to which e-businesses can sign up which give consumers assurances that certain minimum standards are met. The Appendix to this book contains *Which Web Traders Code of Practice.*

SPAMMING

Spam is the term given to unsolicited e-mail on the Internet which is often sent by e-businesses trying to sell goods and services. Spam is a characterised by users sending extremely large (often 50 million plus) numbers of e-mails which can block Internet Service Providers (ISP) services,[38] making it impossible to carry normal traffic to and from their customers. ISPs have found that the bogus use of addresses on their systems has caused them to be blacklisted so that their honest customers are unable to exchange mail with parts of the outside world.

The problem of "spamming" led Washington State to enact the world's first legislation designed to prevent it.[39] The Washington law makes it illegal to use a dummy or forged return address and to put false or misleading information in the subject line. Lawbreakers may be subject to pay the recipient $500 and the Internet Service Provider $1,000 for each offence. It has been reported that a Seattle man has collected $200 from a company who sent him spam mail under this law.[40]

Trespass

2.38   In the first Internet case of its kind in the United Kingdom, Virgin Net Ltd launched a suit against Adrian Parris of ProPhoto U.K. in April 1999, alleging that Parris sent up to a quarter of a million junk e-mails, through his e-mail account. Claiming that Parris was in breach of the terms of his subscriber contract and that bulk e-mail constitutes trespass, Virgin Net hopes to send a strong message to spammers that such actions will not be tolerated in future.[41] Virgin officials indicated that customer complaints, loss of goodwill and disruption of services resulting from being "blackholed" by the RealTime Blackhole List (RLB), a system which blocks messages from ISPs known to tolerate spam, were reason enough to pursue legal action.[42] Legal actions of this type may become more prevalent as companies attempt to deter spammers and rebuild their reputations with customers after spamming incidents.

In the United States there has been over 20 reported cases.[43] These have involved some of the largest U.S.-based ISPs (AOL, CompuServe and Prodigy) instituting proceedings against spammers such as Cyber Promotions.[44] It was held that the transmission of electronic messages to CompuServe's server without CompuServe's permission was a trespass to CompuServe's property as the volume of spam was burdensome enough to

---

[38] A report by Novell in April 1998 found that spam cost U.K. businesses up to £5 billion in lost time.

[39] The U.S. State of Nevada also now has such laws and California is considering their introduction.

[40] See in http://www.sjmercurty.com (San Jose Mercury News) for September 1998.

[41] *E-Commerce Law and Policy*, vol.1, Iss. 4, May 1999, at p.1.

[42] BBC News, "Virgin sues spam man", April 20, 1999, Published at 14.54 GMT 15.54 U.K. **http://news.bbc.co.uk/hi/english/sci/tech/newsid_323000/323817.stm.**

[43] These are listed and some transcripts are available at **http://www.fmls.edu/cyber/cases/spam.html.**

[44] Case No. C2–96–1070, United States District Court for the Southern District of Ohio. Final consent order and other judgments are available at **http://tigerden.com/junkmail/cases/index.html.**

CompuServe's server to be sufficient to constitute a trespass, even though no actual physical damage was suffered.

Yahoo! has also begun to combat spam through legal channels. In a suit naming World **2.39** Wide Network Marketing and the Information Technologies Corp, Yahoo! has charged the organisations with trade mark infringement and forgoing thousands of spam messages with Yahoo! related headers and e-mail addresses made to look as if they originated from **Yahoo.com** addresses. Stressing loss of reputation and customer complaints as driving forces behind Yahoo!'s decision to sue, Jon Sobel, associate general counsel for Yahoo, indicated that "Spamming obviously costs companies like us money, but we filed the law suit because we want to protect Yahoo's name and our users' experience."[45]

In the U.K. it is also likely that a court would find spamming to be trespass. The Torts (Interference with Goods) Act 1977 created a tort of wrongful interference with goods. Section 1 of the 1977 Act provides that wrongful interference means:

> "(a) conversion of goods (also called trover);
> (b) trespass to goods;
> (c) negligence so far as it results in damage to goods or to an interest in goods;
> (d) any other tort so far as it results in damage to goods or to an interests in goods".

"Goods" are defined in section 14 of the 1977 Act as "all chattels personal other than things in action or money". This provided stated meanings to the common law of torts.[46]

Therefore, the U.K. Government noted in "Building Confidence in electronic **2.40** commerce" that in the case of spamming "if industry approaches prove ineffective, further legislation may become necessary". Furthermore, the Department of Trade and Industry announced that under the Telecommunications (Data Protection and Privacy) (Direct Marketing) Regulations 1998, from May 1, 1999, it has been illegal to send unsolicited, direct marketing faxes to individuals.[47] All of these efforts indicate a concern that lost profit and goodwill due to spamming and a willingness to take legal action to deter future spamming and redress harms to companies and customers alike.

The question which the U.K. courts may one day have to determine is whether the act of spamming causes a sufficient impact with someone's property for there to be a tort. So long as the spamming is of sufficient significance to cause some damage to the ISPs server then an action for trespass could be made out. Dumping very large quantities of mail on a relay server can (and usually does) saturate the server's capabilities and/or connectivity. If — as usually happens with spam — a large proportion of the addresses are undeliverable, and the alleged originator's address is also undeliverable (for obvious reasons) the server keeps trying to return the undeliverable mail.[48]

However, it may be that the courts in the United Kingdom will not get to consider this issue as MSN and other ISPs have announced that they have introduced anti-spamming e-mail software in their services and introduced I.P. filtering. These technologies (termed "spamicide") appear to be reasonably effective.

---

[45] *E-Commerce Law and Policy*, Vol. 1, Issue 4, May 1999 at p. 2.
[46] See para. 3.05 of Chapter 3 for further discussion on meaning of goods.
[47] *E-Commerce Law and Policy*, Vol. 1, Iss. 4, May 1999, at p.1.
[48] A number of network administrators have told one of the authors that they have had to take their mail servers down for several days after being used as an (unauthorised) spam relay point.

The Computer Misuse Act 1990

2.41   The Computer Misuse 1990 Act was enacted to deal with hackers and those who sent and planted computer viruses. Since spamming was not known about when the 1990 Act was implemented, it was certainly not the intention of Parliament for the Act to cover such activities. Under section 3 of the Act:

> "A person is guilty of an offence if . . . he does any act which causes an unauthorised modification of the contents of any computer; and at the time when he does the act he had the requisite intent and the requisite knowledge".

Section 3(2) sets out the requisite intent required under section 3(1). This states that the intent is:

> "An intent to cause a modification of the contents of any computer and by so doing:
>
>   (a) to impair the operation of any computer;
>   (b) to prevent or hinder access to any program or data held in any computer; or
>   (c) to impair the operation of any such program or the reliability of any such data."

A prosecution under this Act will only be viable if the specific type of intent in section 3(2) can be shown. However, since the originator of the spam will have had to disguise his/her originating address, the legitimacy of his/her activities will already be questionable and it would not be too difficult for a jury to conclude that the person had sufficient intent for the criminal offence under section 3(2) to be made out.[49]

Trade Mark Issues of Spamming

2.42   Spamming may also raise trade mark concerns when unsuspecting users receive spam mail which is sent using e-mail addresses consisting of domain names and trade marks owned by other entities. This misleads the recipients into believing that the owner of the trade mark sent or endorses the e-mail, thereby causing confusion and potentially damaging the trade mark owner's reputation. In the U.S. case of *Hotmail Corp v. Van Money Pie Inc.*, Hotmail (the Microsoft owned e-mail provider and owner of the Hotmail trade mark and domain name) was granted an injunction against the defendants who sent spam e-mail messages advertising pornographic material with return Hotmail electronic mail addresses.[50]

DISCLAIMERS

2.43   A website, whether it is for information purposes only or as part of an e-business to buy and sell goods, can create legal liability for the e-business in each country from which someone accesses the site. Disclaimers (or health warnings) should be included in all websites to try to limit the legal liability of the e-business or publisher.

---

[49] The s.3 offence does not cover "reckless" damage or modification and this limitation was said to be a safeguard to ensure that people would not be prosecuted for merely inadvertent acts. However use of a false address could be said to indicate that the spammer knew that his activities would or were likely to cause damage. See *Akdeniz Y.* [1996] 3 Web JCLI, "s.3 of the Computer Misuse Act 1990: an Antidote for Computer Viruses!" **http://webjcli.ncl.ac.uk/1996/issue3/akdeniz3.html** and Battcock, R. (1995) "The Computer Misuse Act 1990: 5 years on" (includes a complete list of cases prosecuted under Computer Misuse Act 1990 up to July 1995) at **http://www.strath.ac.uk/Departments/Law/student/PERSONAL/R—BATTCOCK/**.
[50] [1998] W.L. 388389, 47 U.S.P.Q. 2d 1020 (N.A. Cal., April 16, 1998) (No. C–98 JW PVT ENE, C98—20064 JW).

The extent to which liability can be excluded or restricted can vary from country to country. It is not possible to draft a disclaimer which will work in every country from which a website can be accessed. Apart from the obvious language problems, different countries permit different exclusions. Under U.K. law, it is not possible, for example, to exclude liability for death or personal injury caused by negligence[51] or for defamation.[52] Accordingly, a disclaimer may minimise the risk of legal liability but whether a court would uphold an attempt to exclude liability will depend on the circumstances.

The governing law of a disclaimer is normally the one in which the page is accessed by a viewer. It may not work, but it is prudent to provide that the viewer accepts the law which governs the disclaimer is English law if the website owner is a U.K. business.

It is important that a disclaimer is brought to the attention of a viewer. They should **2.44** not be included on a separate legal page which a viewer can optionally visit. Possibilities for locating a disclaimer include:

- on the web page which contains the product or services information;

- on the entry page which requires a visitor to acknowledge before gaining entry to the rest of the website;

- a prominent link entitled "Product Disclaimer" which should be placed at various places on the site.

The following is an example of a disclaimer of liability:

> With respect to the information available on this site [ABC Limited] expressly excludes any representation or warranty (express or implied) to the fullest extent possible. [ABC Limited] makes no representations about the materials in this site or any sites linked to this site. You agree to accept the application of English law to govern matters between [ABC Limited] and yourself.

Web Site Mandatory Content Requirements

In addition to the information required to be given to all consumers pursuant to the **2.45** Distance Selling Directive (see para. 2.22 in this chapter), there may be other website content requirements with which an e-business must comply. Most U.K. e-businesses are run through companies registered with the U.K. Register of Companies. Section 349 of the Companies Act 1985, requires a company to state on all invoices and notices (which by extension will include a website) its name, place of business registration, registered number and address of registered office. The Business Names Act 1985 which applies to all businesses requires that invoices and written orders for goods must state a corporate name and U.K. address in case a document has to be served on the business. A website form will also need to comply with the Business Names Act. There may also be specific requirements based on the regulation of the industry or sector in which the e-business operates. For example, a travel company may be obliged to show its ABTA and ATOL details on the website. There may also be codes of practice and accreditations (such as the

---

[51] Unfair Contract Terms Act 1977.
[52] But note that wider s.1 of the Defamation Act 1996, there is a codification and expansion of the defence of innocent dissemination making it available to printers, and broadcasters in respect of unrecorded statements by persons for whose acts the broadcaster is not responsible. s.1 should inform U.K. Internet Service providers about defamation liability.

Which Code of Practice (see the Appendix)) which carries with it a *Which* watermark/
accreditation seal which may be appropriate.

AUCTIONS

2.46   There has been a dramatic growth in online auctions aimed both at consumers and
businesses. Not surprisingly, there is no specific legislation dealing with online auctions
but this trend does raise interesting legal questions. An auction is merely a particular
manner of contracting and rules relating to when an offer is accepted and when it is
revoked, considered in Chapter 3, apply equally to auctions.

What makes online auctions interesting is the question of the method of acceptance by
the auctioneer. Section 57(2) of the Sale of Goods Act 1979 states that "a sale by auction is
completed on the fall of the auctioneer's hammer or in any other customary manner."
With online auctions there is the practical problem that there is no auctioneer's hammer.
In practice, this problem seems to be resolved by setting a closing time on the website by
which all bids must be placed. The highest bidder at the time the auction closes is bound
to contract unless the reserved price has not been reached.

Section 12(2) of the Unfair Contracts Terms Act 1977 states "in the sale by auction the
buyer is not in any circumstances to be regarded as dealing as a consumer". Therefore,
people engaging in online auctions may not receive the wider protection of consumer
legislation and any exclusions of liability may not be subject to the reasonableness test.
However, this does not place a consumer in any different position to ordinary auctions.
The Distance Selling Directive specifically excludes auctions from the ambit of the
Directive.

2.47   It is particularly important with online auctions that the terms and conditions for sale
are brought to any potential bidder's attention. In addition, there are some statutory
formalities which apply to auction sales and which, by analogy, will apply to online
auctions. Thus, section 57(3) of the Sale of Goods Act 1979 requires the auctioneer to
display their full name and residence and copies of the Auctions (Bidding Agreements)
Act 1927 and 1969 in a conspicuous part of the auction room and to keep them there
during the time the auction is being held. Online auctioneers entering into contracts
governed by English law will need to ensure that the website has appropriate links to
copies of these Acts.

Although no auction licence is required to conduct an auction, some London boroughs
have introduced codes of practice and licence conditions relating to auctions conducted
in their locality. Conducting an online auction may therefore be a way of bypassing such
controls.

However, Internet auctions remain prone to what is delicately termed "accidental
fraud". Participants often fail to pay for goods or fail to deliver goods on time, not
because they have a fraudulent intent but because they forget, go on holiday or are not
really expecting to make a purchase and then find themselves obligated. To deal with
these problems a new type of intermediary is appearing. These companies, for a fee,
provide assurance that goods are delivered and paid for with a money back guarantee. If
something goes wrong, the company takes the loss.

In a very traditional auction such as Sotheby's and Christies the contractual
relationship between the parties is clear. The seller enters into a contract with the auction
house, appointing the auction house as his/her agent with authority to make a sale on
behalf of the seller. The successful purchaser then enters into a contract directly with the

auctioneer who acts as the seller's agent. The auctioneer delivers the purchased item to the purchaser who then pays the auction house. The auction house then deducts its commission from the sale proceeds. However, it is the seller who gives warranties as to good title via the auction house who passes them on to the purchaser. However, with an online auction the legal structure is different. Online auctions are normally structured as contracts between the auction house and the seller and between the auction house and each bidder. The auction house does not become a party to any contract of sale it is merely the conduit who introduces the seller to the purchaser. Normally the auction house is involved in collecting payment. The auction house accordingly has no liability in the event that there is a failure with respect or title or quality. It has been pointed out[53] that in many online auctions there is a purported contract of sale between a seller and a purchaser when the seller and purchaser do not know each other's identity. All dealings are made with the auction house who sets out the terms of sale in lengthy terms on conditions. This may mean that there could be difficulties with this chain of events in establishing a contract of sale between the purchaser and seller.

REGULATED ACTIVITIES

Many goods and services which may be sold or traded online have specific laws, rules **2.48** and regulations which either restrict or regulate those goods and services. Any person proposing to sell particular goods or services online should check the relevant rules which regulate that particular class of goods or service. It is outside the ambit of this book to give a detailed consideration to specific rules which apply in particular industries. The following sections provide only summaries of the relevant legal environment for just a few of the main products which are commonly sold online.

Gambling

Gambling is predicted to be one of the real growth areas of e-commerce. It has been **2.49** estimated that £6 billion will be gambled online by 2002 as bookmakers take advantage of the Internet's huge audience reach and cost savings.[54]

In the U.S. in particular, there are concerns about the legality of gambling online, with only some U.S. states permitting gambling, and there are further concerns about the proliferation of illegal online gambling. In 1997 Senator Kyl introduced a Bill, to be called the Internet Gambling Prohibition Act of 1997, to amend the Federal criminal code to prohibit and set penalties for gambling via the Internet and for engaging in the business of gambling on the Internet. The Bill, known as the "the Kyl Bill" passed the Senate amid controversy but not the House vote required for adoption of the legislation. After this impasse, a second version of the Bill was introduced which eliminated unpopular criminal penalties for those placing bets, indicated its intention not to criminalise "Fantasy Leagues" already legal in some states, and stated that under the act, ISPs may be required to block access to gambling sites. If empowered, this legislation would extend the force of the Wire Act 1961 to include cable and satellite operations in order to combat the establishment of cybercasions.[55]

In addition, the U.S. National Gambling Impact Study Commission, created by Congress in 1996 to investigate the social effects of gambling, also intends to recommend

---

[53] Robin Bynoe at **http://www.zdnet.co.uk/news/1999/48/ns-11934.html**.
[54] Datamonitor.
[55] *E-Commerce Law and Policy*, Vol. 1, Iss. 4, May 1999 at p. 13; **www.senate.gov/~kyl/p3-23-99.htm**.

a nationwide ban on gambling via the Internet, citing the potential negative social effects of legalised or under regulated gambling through difficult to regulate media such as the Internet.[56]

In March 1998, the authorities in Manhattan charged 14 American owners and managers of six offshore companies with illegally using interstate telephone lines in relation to online betting, even though the defendants claimed to have been granted licences in the places where their offshore companies were based, namely the Caribbean and Central America.

In contrast to the U.S.'s prohibitive stance, some states are taking a more enlightened approach. For example, InterLotto is licensed in Lichtenstein to run an Internet lotto. In New Zealand and Australia, Internet gambling licences are available to individuals who satisfy stringent requirements, the theory being that disreputable organisations will not get involved.

2.50   In November 1997, the First International Symposium on Internet Gambling Law and Management met in Washington D.C. The legal issues considered included: different cultures' attitudes to gambling, the fact that some jurisdictions, particularly in the Pacific and Caribbean, are actively promoting online gambling in their territories because of the taxation revenue, and whether an international treaty was necessary.

In Great Britain, there have so far not been any legislative attempts specifically to regulate or prohibit Internet gambling, In fact, the E.U. Directive on E-Commerce, published in December 1998, "explicitly excludes gambling from its rules and application"[57] so it is necessary to look at legislation drafted before the invention of the Internet. Gambling is governed by a complex regulatory regime, with different regulations applying depending on whether the gambling involves betting, gaming or lotteries. The relevant Acts are the Betting, Gaming and Lotteries Act 1963, the Gaming Act 1968, the Lotteries and Amusement Act 1976 and the Betting and Gaming Duties Act 1981.

The gambling related offences under these Acts include the following:

- to promote or be concerned in a foreign lottery.[58]

- to promote or be concerned in a lottery in Great Britain unless it is part of the National Lottery or falls into one of the other limited exceptions.[59]

- to sell lottery tickets using a machine, which may preclude the sale of lottery tickets via the Internet. However, if a person is involved in the sale, then it may not be prohibited.

- to use premises (other than an approved racecourse or licensed track) for the purposes of betting with persons resorting to them unless the premises are duly licensed.[60]

2.51   In relation to Internet betting, the following question arises: does a website constitute "premises" and therefore need to be licensed? The courts have defined premises to include any place or vessel. It is not necessary to prove that people have "resorted to" the premises unless the only evidence of the betting is that a transaction took place, in

---

[56] EBL, June 1999, vol. 1, no. 5 at p.1.
[57] *E-Commerce Law and Policy*, Vol. 1, iss. 4, May 1999.
[58] Lotteries and Amusements Act 1976, s.2(1).
[59] Lotteries and Amusements Act 1976, s.1.
[60] Betting Gaming and Lotteries Act 1963, ss.1(1) and 9(1).

which case physical resorting must be proved. The courts have also held that there is no need to prove physical entrance to the premises, it is enough to show a "close physical connection" between the person and the premises.[61] It is arguable that a connection to a website hosting an Internet casino, for example, would fall within the definition, in which case the website should be licensed.

- under the Gaming Act 1968, it would not be permissible to set up an online casino or bingo club because the club would require a licence, the licence can only be granted to a members' club, and the members must be present when the gaming takes place.

- betting may not take place in the streets or other public places.[62] Public places are not defined in the relevant Act, but it is certainly arguable that the Internet constitutes a public place.

- to advertise a gaming establishment in public.[63]

In addition, there are various regulations which apply to anyone carrying on general betting businesses in Great Britain. These include obligations to keep such books, records and accounts as the Commissioners of Customs & Excise may direct. Electronic records may not be sufficient for these purposes.

Pornography

The United States Supreme Court recently upheld a ban on the transmission of lewd or   **2.52** obscene e-mail. The Court affirmed the 1996 Communications Decency Act, which prohibits obscenities in communications including e-mail and held that such prohibitions were not unconstitutional. The Act had been challenged as overly broad by ApolloMedia Corp., the creators of **annoy.com** which allowed senders to send indecent material anonymously to public officials and others by e-mail.[64] Much of the sophisticated technology which has made the Internet so powerful has been pioneered by the world of adult entertainment. Sales of pornographic magazines are falling because cyberporn is such a big market. It is ironic, then, that these developments have led to so much debate over the dangers of the Internet. It has led to worldwide discussion on how to regulate the online porn industry. This in turn has led to extra concerns for Internet Service Providers (ISP) worried about their liability for obscene or indecent material transmitted via their services, whether hosting Usenet newsgroups or simply providing Internet access.

In the United Kingdom, a lot of the law relating to pornography is contained in the Obscene Publications Act 1959 (as amended by the Criminal Justice and Public Order Act 1994). Under this Act, it is a criminal offence for any person either (1) whether for gain or not, to *publish* an obscene article; or (2) *to have* an obscene article for publication or gain.[65]

Material is obscene if its effect, or the effect of part of it, is such as to tend to deprave and corrupt persons likely to read, see or hear it.[66] A pornographic article or photograph

---

[61] *R. v. Brown*, 1995.
[62] Betting Gaming and Lotteries Act 1963, s.8.
[63] Gaming Act 1968, s.5(1).
[64] EBL, June 1999, vol. 1, no. 5 at p. 4.
[65] Obscene Publications Act 1959, s.2(4).
[66] *ibid.*

displayed on the Internet would be accessible to such a large number of people, including children that it is more likely to be categorised as obscene than a pornographic photograph in a magazine with limited circulation and access because it is kept on a top shelf in a newsagent.

2.53   Publication of obscene material includes the display, showing or circulation of the material. Since the Criminal Justice and Public Order Act 1994, this includes the transmission of electronically stored data. An Internet Service Provider is at risk of being liable for the offence of publication if it, for example, hosts a Website displaying obscene material.

ISPs are also concerned about unknowingly committing an offence of possession. The possession offence involves ownership, possession or control of an obscene article, for publication or gain. It is possible that an ISP acting as a host, charging a subscription fee giving access to the material is committing the offence. Simply providing access may not constitute the possession offence.

Other criminal offences include the following:

- under the Telecommunications Act 1984 it is an offence to send, by means of a public telecommunications system, a message (or other matter) which is grossly offensive or of an indecent, obscene or menacing character.[67] This includes the transmission of data via a telecommunications system such as the Internet.

- the Broadcasting Act 1990 contains offences of publication and possession in relation to programme services, which could cover live or recorded material available online.

- the Protection of Children Act 1978, as amended by the Criminal Justice and Public Order Act 1994 makes it an offence to take, make, permit to be taken, distribute, show, possess intending to distribute or show, or publish any indecent photograph or "pseudo photograph" of a child. Photograph includes data stored on a computer disk or by other electronic means which is capable of being converted into a photograph/image.

- under the Criminal Justice Act 1988 it is an offence to possess an indecent photograph of a child.

- the Indecent Displays (Control) Act 1981 makes it an offence publicly to display indecent matter. This is particularly relevant to cybercafes and libraries providing Internet access. However, it is not an offence if the place charges a fee for access to the material and is barred to people under 18 years of age. The Act could apply to Internet Service Providers.

- it is an offence to incite or conspire to commit certain sexual offences abroad.[68] This legislation is directed at sex tourism and applies to Internet e-mails sent or received in England and Wales.

2.54   There are some defences available to Internet Service Providers. If the ISP has not examined the obscene article and has had no reasonable cause to suspect that it was obscene material, it will not be guilty of the offence.[69]

---

[67] Telecommunications Act 1984, s.43(1).
[68] Sexual Offences (Conspiracy and Incitement) Act 1996.
[69] Obscene Publications Act 1959, s.2(5).

Of particular interest to ISPs, is the defence set out in the Broadcasting Act 1990: a person or company would not be liable for the offence of publishing or possessing obscene material if it did not know and had no reason to suspect that the programme or material would include material making it liable to be convicted of an offence. A service provider hosting a Usenet newsgroup involving suspicious sounding names would probably not be able to take advantage of this defence as it would probably know, or should have suspected, that the material was obscene.

Online service providers were also concerned about the implications of the 1998 conviction of the director of CompuServe in Germany who was sentenced to two years in prison and a fine (suspended) for the distribution of child pornography through newsgroups. The Internet community was shocked by this result, partly because the director and the company had taken steps to block the newsgroups it was told about and then discovered as a result of its own investigations. In addition, German legislation provided defences broadly similar to the defences described above (no knowledge or reason to suspect material was obscene), which many thought would protect the director. The conviction was overturned on appeal but considerable concern was raised by the first instance court's decision.

The online community is taking steps to self-regulate. Organisations such as the Internet Watch Foundation and the Internet Service Providers Association have been set up to self-regulate areas including cyber porn.

Travel

Airlines and businesses in the travel sector have proved to be amongst the earliest **2.55** success stories of e-commerce. Airlines have regarded Internet sales and e-tickets as means of reducing distribution costs and saving money in terms of ticketing paperwork and staffing. However, the travel industry is heavily regulated. The Package Travel, Package Holidays and Package Tour Regulations 1992 (the "Package Travel Regulations") apply to those who organise and sell "packages" (as defined) or those to whom packages are sold, in other words tour operators and travel agents. The Package Tour Regulations will apply to material placed on the World Wide Web. The extent of application depends upon whether, before booking, a customer obtains additional information from other sources or if a customer can book directly from the Internet without obtaining any other information. In addition, the Civil Aviation (Air Travel Organiser's Licensing) Regulations 1995 may also apply. In most respects material on the World Wide Web for sale of travel and holidays is regulated in the same way to brochure material.

The Package Travel Regulations only apply to "packages" sold or offered for sale in the **2.56** United Kingdom. A package is defined as a pre-arranged combination of at least two of three components, namely transport, accommodation, and other tourist services not ancillary to transport or accommodation and accounting for a significant proportion of the package. Regulation 4 provides that a tour operator or travel agent is liable to compensate a consumer for any loss suffered as a result of misleading information contained in any descriptive matter concerning a package, the price of a package or other conditions applying to the contract. Hence, any inaccuracy in any descriptive material on the Internet which concerns a package does create the risk of a civil claim for damages, whether for a tour operator or travel agent

"Consumer" is defined in the Package Travel Regulations as the person who "takes or agrees to take the package . . .". Hence, before Regulation 4 has any application a booking will have to have been made. The consumer will need to demonstrate not only loss but that that loss arose as a result of misleading information in the Internet material.

Regulation 5 is concerned with brochures and imposes various requirements about the contents of brochures. While, at first blush, this might seem wholly inapplicable, ABTA and various Trading Standards Officers have publicly stated that they regard any material from which a package can be booked as constituting a brochure for the purposes of Regulation 5.

Regulation 7 provides that, before a contract is made, a customer must be given information about passport and visa requirements applicable to British citizens, about health formalities required for the journey and the stay and the financial protection arrangements entered into by the tour operator providing the package. Hence, material on the World Wide Web will need to contain this information, unless it can be guaranteed that, before a contract is made, customers will be given this information from another source.

2.57   Where material on the Internet does not contain the information required by Regulation 5 and/or Regulation 7 but that information is contained in a brochure, tour operators are advised to refer specifically to such a brochure, and to include a statement that the details which are contained on the Internet are not full details but merely introductory ones.

Regulation 9 provides that, before the contract is made, the consumer must be given the terms of the contract "in writing or such other form as is comprehensible and accessible". The effect of Regulation 9 is that the information detailed above would either have to be contained in the material on the Internet or, if not, given to the customer before the issue of a confirmation invoice. If the terms are not given to consumers before the contract is made, they will not be incorporated in the contract. Particularly where there are terms limiting liability and taking advantage of compensation limits in International Conventions, it would be somewhat unfortunate, to say the least, to lose that protection.

COMPETITION LAW

Introduction

2.58   In *Washington Post v. Total News Inc.*, the *Washington Post*, with others, claimed that *Total News* had designed a parasitic website which re-published news from other websites without using any of its own material. *Total News* linked to sites such as the *Washington Post* and framed material from those third party sites along side banner advertisements which belonged to *Total News*. Claiming copyright and trade mark infringement, false advertising and unfair competition, the *Washington Post* alleged that *Total News* generated revenue from others material and threatened the goodwill of the *Washington Post* and others through its actions. The parties eventually settled out of court. By the terms of the settlement, *Total News* was allowed to continue linking to material but forced to abandon its embedded frames and properly cite sources of the material.[70]

As discussed elsewhere, general principles of law have and will prove themselves well able to adapt to the new environment of e-commerce. The same can be said for

---

[70] EBL, May 1999, vol. 1 no. 4 at p. 12; Chissick Michael, *Internet Law: A practical guide for business* (*Financial Times* Marketing Brief, Media and Telecoms, 1997).

competition law whose application to e-commerce and new electronic media is already being seen in antitrust scrutiny of mergers and joint ventures between companies in the converging telecoms and media industries; the review and replacement of the U.S. Government's contract with NSI; the major E.U. push for de-regulation in the telecommunication field; and challenges brought by competition authorities in the United States and the E.U. against alleged abuses by Microsoft.

What is clear is that even though the new environment presents new challenges, the same general principles of competition law will apply to conduct affecting e-commerce as to any other type of commercial activity.

E.C. Competition law

The main pillars of E.C. competition law are found in Articles 81 and 82 (formerly Articles **2.59** 85 and 86)[71] of the Treaty of Rome, in the E.C. Merger Regulation[72] and in the Regulations made under the Treaty of Rome.

Article 81

Article 81 provides as follows: **2.60**

"1. The following shall be prohibited as incompatible with the common market: all agreements between undertakings, decisions by associations of undertakings and concerted practices which may affect trade between Member States and which have as their object or effect the prevention, restriction or distortion of competition within the common market, and in particular those which:

(a) directly or indirectly fix purchase or selling prices or any other trading conditions;
(b) limit or control production, markets, technical development, or investment;
(c) share markets or sources of supply;
(d) apply dissimilar conditions to equivalent transactions with other trading parties, thereby placing them at a competitive disadvantage;
(e) make the conclusion of contracts subject to acceptance by the other parties of supplementary obligations which, by their nature or according to commercial usage, have no connection with the subject of such contracts.

2. Any agreements or decisions prohibited pursuant to this Article shall be automatically void.
3. The provisions of paragraph 1 may, however, be declared inapplicable in the case of:

— any agreement or category of agreements between undertakings;
— any decision or category of decisions by associations of undertakings;
— any concerted practice or category of concerted practices;

which contributes to improving the production or distribution of goods or to promoting technical or economic progress, while allowing consumers a fair share of the resulting benefit, and which does not;

(a) impose on the undertakings concerned restrictions which are not indispensable to the attainment of these objectives;
(b) afford such undertakings the possibility of eliminating competition in respect of a substantial part of the products in question."

In brief, the main elements are as follows: **2.61**

- *"agreements . . . decisions . . . concerted practices"*

There is no requirement for a formal written agreement for Article 81 to apply. An agreement may be oral, informal or a "gentleman's agreement". An agreement may also

---

[71] The Amsterdam Treaty re-numbered the Treaty of Rome and came into force on May 1, 1999.
[72] Council Regulations 4064/89 and 1310/97.

be inferred from the conduct of the parties and this would include e-mails or agreements made electronically. "Concerted practices" denotes co-ordinated conduct which may fall short of a concluded agreement; practical co-operation replaces the risks of competition.[73]

- *"undertakings"*

To fall within Article 81, an agreement must be between undertakings. This term is defined very broadly and includes all natural and legal persons carrying on a commercial or economic activity. Whether or not a profit is realised, is irrelevant.[74] Although, in the absence of dominance, Article 81 would not catch unilateral conduct by one undertaking, the Commission may readily infer agreements (such as a network of smaller agreements) in order to capture an anti-competitive activity.

2.62   - *"restriction of competition"*

Article 81 prohibits agreements whose object or effect is to prevent, restrict or distort competition. It does not matter whether it is the object of the agreement to restrict competition or is merely the effect.

Article 81(1) sets out a non-exclusive list of examples of the types of restrictions which might be caught. A practical example which can be given is in relation to comparison-shopping on the Internet. Junglee and Netbot are both Internet comparison-shopping companies. Consumers visiting their websites are offered a service to find the best price for a product. Junglee has recently been acquired by Amazon.com, which sells books and CDs. If it chooses not to permit Junglee to provide price comparisons with other booksellers then, whilst this might be restrictive of competition in a broad sense, it would not be caught by Article 81(1) because agreements between parents and subsidiaries are not caught.

Netbot has also been acquired, by Excite. Netbot may now not comparison-shop for books and CDs: consumers being allowed to search only one bookseller — Amazon. If this was a result of a market-sharing agreement or other restrictive agreement between Excite and Amazon, then this could be caught by Article 81(1) if the other criteria of Article 81 were satisfied (in terms of market foreclosure and effect on trade between Member States, which are considered below).

- *"Effect on trade between Member States"*

In order for an agreement to be caught by Article 81 there must be an effect on trade between Member States. The pattern of trade must be influenced, directly or indirectly, actually or potentially. Where an agreement encompasses the whole territory of a Member State then it will be considered to have an intra-community effect. In the case of e-commerce its universal scope means that this requirement should easily be satisfied.

Appreciability

2.63   In determining whether an agreement is caught by Article 81, the effect on trade between Member States must be appreciable. Agreements of minor importance are ignored. The Commission has issued a statement of its policy, the Notice on Agreements

---

[73] See *ICI v. Commission* [1972] E.C.R. 619.
[74] See *Van Landewyck v. Commission* [1980] E.C.R. 3125.

of Minor Importance. Under the Notice, the Commission states that as a matter of policy (*i.e.* it may change and is not binding on national courts) it does not consider that an agreement will have an appreciable effect on competition if the parties combined market share is less than 5 per cent (for horizontal agreements) or 10 per cent (for vertical agreements).[75]

The Commission has approved Microsoft's licensing agreements with ISPs by means of an administrative letter (so called "comfort letter"), following amendments to the agreements designed to prevent the market from being foreclosed in Microsoft's favour. An ISP maintains a permanent connection to the Internet and enables its subscribers to connect to the Internet via a telephone link to the ISP. In addition, the ISP may also provide its subscribers with World Wide Web pages.

In March 1997, the Commission launched an inquiry into various agreements between **2.64** Microsoft and some European ISPs for the licensing and distribution of Microsoft's Internet Explorer products. In February 1998, Microsoft formally notified to the Commission the amended versions of these agreements, after being advised to review the agreements to ensure that they did not contain restrictions that might have the effect of illegally foreclosing the market for Internet browser software from Microsoft's competitors, of illegally promoting the use of Microsoft's competitors and of illegally promoting the use of Microsoft's proprietary technology on the Internet. The main amendments are, first, that the ISP's failure to attain minimum distribution volumes or per centages of Internet Explorer browser traffic will no longer result in termination of their agreement; and secondly, that ISPs are not allowed to promote and advertise competing browser software. The notified agreements therefore no longer infringe E.U. competition rules.

However, the Commission stressed that it has not given any ruling on the global behaviour of Microsoft concerning the possible abuse of a dominant position and that the investigations into the Microsoft's ISP agreements could be reopened if there is any change in the legal or factual situation.

New Approach to Vertical Restraints

Following extensive consultation by the Commission on proposals to reform the **2.65** current vertical restraints policy, the Commission has confirmed that it will adopt a single "very wide block exemption" to replace the existing categories of block exemptions. The framework of the proposed new block exemption will exempt from the scope of Article 81 all restraints which are not "black listed", unless the undertakings concerned exceed certain market share thresholds. Key features of the new block exemption regulation will be the following:

- unlike previous block exemptions, it will now include both intermediate and final products, and also includes both goods and services. There will therefore no longer be any doubt as to its application to the software industry.

- the benefit of the block exemption will be limited by market share thresholds. It is not yet decided whether there will be a single or dual market share thresholds. If there is to be a single-threshold system, the benefit of the umbrella block exemption would be withdrawn completely when the market shares exceed 25–35 per cent. In the event of a dual-threshold system being adopted, the main market

---

[75] Commission Notice of January 30, 1997 (97/C29/03).

share threshold would be 20 per cent, above which there would be scope for exempting certain vertical restraints up to a higher level of about 40 per cent. The dual-threshold system thus provides for a graduated series of exemptions.

- agreements falling within the safe harbour would be presumed to be legal. Those falling outside the safe harbour would not be presumed to be illegal but might require individual examination. The Commission would have the burden of proof to establish that the agreement was in breach of Article 81(1).

2.66
- national courts and national competition authorities will be given the power to determine when to withdraw the application of the block exemption, and also to determine whether or not the agreement benefited from the block exemption in the first place.

- the following will be considered to be hardcore restrictions that always fall outside the scope of the block exemption:
  - fixed resale prices or minimum resale prices;
    restrictions on active or passive resales (other than the case of exclusive distribution);
  - restrictions on members of a selective distribution system from selling to unauthorised distributors;
  - restriction of cross-supplies between distributors at the same or different levels of distribution in an exclusive or selective distribution system;
  - a prohibition on the supplier of an intermediate good not to sell the same good as a repair or a replacement good to the independent aftermarket;
  - the combination, at the same level of distribution, of selective distribution and exclusive customer allocation.

The Commission Notice specifically states that agreements where the buyer of software sells on this software to the final consumer without obtaining any copyright over the software are considered to be agreements for the supply of goods for resale for the purposes of the block exemption.

Article 82

2.67 Unlike Article 81, which is concerned with anti-competitive agreements, Article 82 prohibits the abuse of a dominant position in a particular market. Article 82 provides:

"Any abuse by one or more undertakings of a dominant position within the common market or in a substantial part of it shall be prohibited as incompatible with the common market in so far as it may affect trade between Member States.
Such abuse may, in particular, consist in:

(a) directly or indirectly imposing unfair purchase or selling prices or other unfair trading conditions;
(b) limiting production, markets or technical development to the prejudice of consumers;
(c) applying dissimilar conditions to equivalent transactions with other trading parties, thereby placing them at a competitive disadvantage;
(d) making the conclusion of contracts subject to acceptance by the other parties of supplementary obligations which, by their nature or according to commercial usage, have no connection with the subject of such contracts."

In determining a party's position on a market it is necessary to define the relevant product and geographic market within which a party operates. In addition, the whole concept of e-commerce raises questions as to the jurisdictional application of the competition rules (at national as well as E.C. level).

Geographic Market

The very nature of the Internet is its global reach. A restrictive agreement between **2.68** e-commerce businesses can have universal effects. The Commission will have jurisdiction to investigate and enforce competition rules where effects are felt within the E.C., even though the parties may not have any physical connection with the E.C.[76]

Traditional constraints on the scope of a particular geographic market, such as transportation costs, are irrelevant in the context of e-commerce. As a result, other factors may come into play in narrowing the scope of the market, such as language or even territorial restrictions on the face of the webpage soliciting interest. For example, an e-commerce site offered only in Greek or Danish may lead to a market being defined by reference to Greece or Denmark. Similarly, the Commission will consider the extent to which consumers have access to computers and electronic commerce sites.

Product market

Jurisprudence from the European Court of Justice requires a product market to be **2.69** defined by reference to the products' characteristics which mean they are "particularly apt to satisfy an inelastic need and are only to a limited extent interchangeable with other products."[77] To the extent e-commerce is only another vehicle by which merchants sell their products, products sold over the Internet may not be defined as a separate product market. On the other hand, the Commission has been known to define product markets very narrowly, such as for spare parts.[78]

Dominance

In order to be caught by Article 82, a party must be in a position of dominance. **2.70** Dominance has been defined as the ability to an appreciable extent to act independently of customers, suppliers and competitors. Many factors will be taken into account, including:

- market share (including relative to other competitors);
- access to sources of supply and capital;
- technical knowledge of the undertaking and its competitors;
- barriers to entry; and
- the exclusionary effect of any distribution network.

The most important initial indicator is market share. A market share of 40 per cent has been held to constitute dominance and 85 per cent is conclusive evidence of dominance.[79]

Abuse

Article 82 gives a number of examples of abuse. Abuse may consist of exploitation of **2.71** customers, exclusion of potential competitors, discrimination without objective justification and may occur on a market on which the dominant undertaking is not

---

[76] See *the Wood Pulp case* [1985] E.C.R. 5193.
[77] See *Europemballage & Continental Can v. Commission* [1973] E.C.R. 215.
[78] See *Hugin v. Commission* [1979] E.C.R. 1869.
[79] See *United Brands* [1978] E.C.R. 207; *Hoffman La Roche* [1979] E.C.R. 461.

dominant. The most significant case in relation to such abuse is the current battle between Microsoft and the U.S. antitrust authorities alleged concerning Netscape, and the bundling by Microsoft of its Internet browser with its operating system (currently Microsoft Windows 98). Whether this is simply the addition of a new application or illegal tying by a dominant supplier remains to be determined by the courts.

In a case concerning *Digital Equipment Corporation*,[80] the E.C. found that Digital held a dominant position in relation to the maintenance of its own equipment. It was found to have abused its dominant position by tying the supply of hardware services and software services by, *inter alia*, ensuring that the prices of software services were considerably more attractive when included in a hardware and software package than when sold on a stand-alone basis. Digital undertook to offer hardware maintenance services for the systems on a stand-alone basis and to implement a pricing policy for its software support services based on the single flat fee per central processing unit.

U.K. Competition Act 1998

2.72   The Competition Act, which received Royal Assent on November 9, 1998, substantially redraws the landscape in the United Kingdom for competition regulation. The new law came into force on March 1, 2000 and has the following key features:

- The new law is a prohibition-based system modelled on Articles 81 and 82 of the E.C. Treaty and prohibits anti-competitive agreements and the abuse of a dominant position.

- Current domestic competition legislation — the Restrictive Trade Practices Act, the Resale Prices Act and most of the Competition Act — is repealed.

- Individual, block and parallel exemptions may be granted.

- Fines of up to 10 per cent of three years' U.K. turnover may be imposed for breaches.

- Sanctions may be imposed on corporate officers personally.

- Protection is given to agreements already exempted under E.U. law.

- The Director General of Fair Trading has extensive powers of investigation and enforcement.

- The Office of Fair Trading is primarily responsible for enforcing competition law.

- Sector regulators, including in particular Oftel, have concurrent powers of enforcement with the OFT.

The Chapter I Prohibition

2.73   Section 2(1) of the Act prohibits agreements which may affect trade within the United Kingdom and which may prevent, restrict or distort competition. The wording of the prohibition is substantively the same as the wording in Article 81(1) (which is set out above).

The Chapter I Prohibition sets out a non-exhaustive list of prohibitive practices, similar to Article 81:

---

[80] See E.C. Commission *Annual Report on Competition Policy* 1997, para. 69.

- fixing, purchasing or selling prices or other trading conditions;

- limiting or controlling production, markets, technical development or investment;

- sharing markets or sources of supply;

- applying dissimilar provisions to equivalent transactions with other trading parties;

- making the conclusion of contracts subject to acceptance of supplementary obligations which have no connection with the subject matter of such contracts.

Offending provisions are automatically void and unenforceable. The effect of this could be to render an agreement unenforceable, any amounts due irrecoverable and any intellectual property rights licensed unenforceable.

Section 60 of the Act requires that, as far as possible, the U.K. authorities and courts **2.74** interpret the prohibition of anti-competitive agreements in a manner which is not inconsistent with the principles laid down by the Treaty of Rome and the European Court in respect of E.C. competition law, with decisions of the ECJ and of the Commission, and also to have regard to any statements made by the Commission.

The Government's intention is that the Chapter I prohibition apply to horizontal agreements (*i.e.* between undertakings operating in the same level of production and distribution) and that, in general, the majority of vertical agreements (*i.e.* between undertakings operating in different levels of the production distribution chain) should be excluded on the basis that such agreements do not raise competition concerns. It is intended that specific provisions be introduced to exclude vertical agreements from the scope of the Chapter I Prohibition (other than in the cases of price-fixing agreements and reciprocal agreements between competitors).

Exemptions

The Director General of Fair Trading has the power to grant individual exemptions. An **2.75** individual exemption may be granted retroactively and subject to conditions and obligations. Any exemption granted must be for a fixed term, although this may be extended. In order to gain an individual exemption, the agreement must satisfy certain criteria which are the same as those set out in Article 81 (3) of the Treaty of Rome (as set out above).

The Director General is empowered under section 6 to recommend to the Secretary of State that certain classes of agreement which satisfy the exemption criteria should be exempted by way of a block exemption. An agreement which satisfies the criteria of any block exemption (either one specifically made under the U.K. Competition Act or under regulations of the European Commission) will be automatically exempt from the Chapter I Prohibition and there would then be no need to notify the agreement to the Director General for an individual exemption. As noted above in the discussion concerning Article 81, the environment for block exemptions under E.C. competition law is being revised through the introduction of an overarching block exemption.

The Chapter II Prohibition

The prohibition on the abuse of a dominant position (introduced by section 18(2) as the **2.76** "Chapter II Prohibition") is the most radical change to U.K. competition law. The prohibition is based very closely on Article 81 of the E.C. Treaty (which is set out above). Although certain types of conduct will be excluded by the legislation, no exemption can be granted from the prohibition. In addition, there will be a procedure under which clearance can be obtained from the Director General. Breach of the prohibition may result in the imposition of fines. The Director General will also be able to impose "cease and desist" orders.

The key elements of the Chapter II Prohibition are:

- any conduct amounting to an abuse;

- of a dominant position in a market;

- within any part of the U.K.;

- by one or more undertakings;

- which may effect trade within the U.K. or any part of it.

De minimis

2.77   Guidance Notes will be issued by the OFT and from the draft of the Guidance Notes the following points can be made:

- the Chapter I Prohibition applies to agreements which have an "appreciable" or significant effect on competition. The OFT takes the view that agreements will have no appreciable effect on competition if the parties' market share does not exceed 10 per cent.

- regardless of the market share held by the parties an agreement will be considered to be caught by the Chapter I Prohibition if it is made between competitors and directly or indirectly fixes prices or shares markets.

- other factors will also be relevant such as entry conditions or the characteristics of buyers and the structure of the buyers' side of the market.

- there is intended to be an annual turnover threshold below which the Director General will not impose penalties for breaches of the Chapter I Prohibition.

- in relation to the Chapter II Prohibition a firm with a market share below 20–25 per cent will generally not be regarded as dominant.

- conduct of minor significance is excluded from the scope of the Chapter II Prohibition and it is intended that an annual turnover threshold be set for determining what amounts to conduct of minor significance.

Investigation and Enforcement

2.78   The Director General will have primary responsibility for investigation and enforcement of the competition laws. His/her powers are intended to be comparable to those of the European Commission and he/she will have the following powers:

- to enter and search premises — unannounced where necessary;

- to examine and copy documents;

- to require "on the spot" explanations of documents found;

- to impose interim measures pending completion of the investigation.

Failing to co-operate with the Director General is a criminal offence. If the Director General finds that there has been an infringement of either the Chapter I or Chapter II Prohibitions, he/she may give directions to bring the infringement to an end and this include the termination or modification of an agreement or conduct.

Conclusion on Competition Law

The introduction into domestic U.K. law of competition rules substantively the same as **2.79** Articles 81 and 82 of the E.C. Treaty means that, given the global nature of e-commerce, conduct which might not meet the appreciability test for purposes of E.C. law might well meet the test within the domestic U.K. market. Since the Competition Act imports E.C. jurisprudence to assist in interpreting the Chapter I and Chapter II Prohibitions, Commission decisions and notices regarding some of the cases discussed earlier in this section will be relevant in determining, for example, whether particular conduct might be abusive or constitute restrictions of competition.

EXPANDING THE ELECTRONIC COMMERCE BUSINESS

It is beyond the scope of this book to examine all the means by which an e-commerce **2.80** business might seek to fund its expansion. Many of the more traditional sources of finance, such as the high street banks, are likely to take a sceptical view of early stage e-businesses with little in the way of tangible assets over which to take the security they invariably seek.

The approach of investors with some appetite for risk has been very different, however.

The Equity Markets

It is remarkable to see the speed with which the equity markets have caught e-commerce **2.81** fever. At the date of publication, the share prices of Internet-based stocks are continuing to rise rapidly as investors rush to stake a claim on the vast profits promised by e-commerce. Start up e-commerce companies have attained turnovers worth millions within weeks. In the first half of 1999, 565 Internet start-ups in the United States raised $6.3 billion, more than the $5.7 billion raised in the whole of 1998, and more than 1997 and 1996 combined.[81] Stock exchanges worldwide have admitted young e-commerce companies with short trading histories. The London Stock Exchange's Alternative Investment Market, Nasdaq's small capital market and Easdaq all designed or amended their admission rules to attract young e-commerce companies.

In January 1999 the London Stock Exchange made some significant relaxations to its Listing Rules to permit the admission of high tech companies without the usual track record. While the basic requirement for new applicant companies to have had an independent, revenue earning business for at least three years remains, the Listing Rules now permit the admission of non-compliant companies (specifically including high tech

---

[81] Report by Venture One, quoted in the *Industry Standard,* August 3, 1999.

companies), subject to special conditions and additional disclosure requirements.[82] Further, the requirement for a new board of directors or senior management of a new applicant company to have had responsibility for the group's major businesses for at least the immediately preceding three years has been removed. Instead, the Exchange must be satisfied that the directors and senior management have the appropriate experience and expertise to manage the group's business — a much more flexible test.[83]

2.82   Freeserve, an ISP, was launched in the United Kingdom on September 22, 1998. After just over 10 months of trading, on July 26, 1999, Freeserve plc floated on the London Stock Exchange with a market capitalisation of £1.4 billion, as the largest ISP in the United Kingdom.[84] Fuelled by e-commerce fever, Freeserve's share price rose almost 40 per cent on the first day of trading. It is perhaps an indication of the Exchange's enthusiasm to see this listing proceed that Freeserve was allowed to offer a considerably lower percentage of its shares to the public than would normally be required.

Freeserve published its prospectus over the Internet. E-commerce companies seeking to float increasingly making their prospectuses available over the Internet and in electronic format. This reduces costs and makes the prospectus easily accessible to a large number of potential investors. In the United States, investment bankers accompany prospectuses with "virtual roadshows", presentations which explain and sell the company to investors.[85]

In August 1999, the London Stock Exchange announced plans to launch Techmark, a new index for technology-based companies, enabling analysts more easily to compare high tech companies and encouraging the growth and quality of sector specialists.

Venture Capital

2.83   While a number of e-commerce start-ups have been able to move swiftly to flotation, the majority will need to go through some preliminary stages of funding. Many venture capital companies now have dedicated e-commerce groups and, with the prospect of swift growth, are willing to invest in appropriate e-commerce ventures at an earlier stage than would be normal in other industry sectors. The major problem at the time of writing is the sheer volume of applications from e-businesses with this venture capital companies are having to deal. Naturally enough, e-commerce itself is seeking the solution and a number of products are now on offer to groom e-commerce start-ups for, and guide them through, the fund raising process.[86]

---

[82] See rule 3.6A.
[83] See rule 3.8. The London Stock Exchange expects to issue a guidance note on the admission of high-tech companies as practice develops. The Exchange had not issued a note by the date of publication.
[84] At June 26, 99, Freeserve had the U.K.'s largest registered internet user base, with approximately 1.32 million active registered accounts. (Source: Freeserve mini prospectus.)
[85] Naturally, this kind of activity is highly regulated — see earlier in this chapter.
[86] See **ecommerceincubater.net**.

— 3 —

ONLINE CONTRACTS

"In some areas, government agreements may prove necessary to facilitate e-commerce and protect consumers. In these cases, governments should establish a predictable and simple legal environment based on a decentralised, contractual model of law rather than one based on top-down regulation."[1]

Prior to the Internet, most online or electronic contracts were conducted in the context of Electronic Data Interchange (EDI). EDI systems linked suppliers with retailers and assembly plants with parts manufacturers in order to reduce inventory, automate reordering procedures and eliminate paperwork. These systems were imposed on continuing relationships and thus pre-agreed "interchange agreements" or "trading partner agreements" could be made. The agreements, many of which were available in "model" form, were overriding contracts that specified everything pertaining to the future relationship: online contract formation, attribution of risk, operation procedures, security, even technical aspects such as the standard format of the data fields. Since interchange agreements were extremely detailed and explicit, very little litigation occurred in the area, making the structure they imposed a legal success. **3.01**

In sharp contrast, e-commerce and the new online contracts of cyberspace do not necessarily involve parties in a continuing relationship. Rather, e-commerce typically deals with real time, one-off transactions between parties who have never met. Thus, online contracts no longer have the luxury of a pre-agreed umbrella agreement that settles disputes; instead, parties must rely on their standard terms and conditions and the courts' interpretation of the law.

E-businesses and consumers alike have clamoured for legislation to deal with the lack of Internet specific laws. Many wonder whether English law can cope with transactions in the fast developing and virtual world of cyberspace. As this chapter shows, in most cases the English legal system does indeed possess the flexibility and laws to deal with this new commercial medium. E-commerce is not lawless and online contracts fit very nicely into the English law framework. **3.02**

This chapter deals with online contracts, from their inception to their completion. It is divided up into five sections. Paragraph 3.03 gives an introductory view of contracts and discusses the various subjects with which online contracts will likely deal. Paragraph 3.10.

---

[1] U.S. President William J. Clinton and Vice President Albert Gore, Jr., "A Framework for Global Electronic Commerce," March 18, 1998, Washington, D.C. **http://www.iitf.nist.gov/elecomm/ecomm.htm**.

examines pre-contractual considerations, such as advertisements and "knowing the customer." Paragraph 3.29. deals with online contract formation and applies to the online environment the four contractual requirements: offer, acceptance, consideration and intent to create legal relations. Paragraph 3.59. addresses writing and signatures, conventions left over from the paper world, and how they will figure in the realm of e-commerce. Paragraph 3.69. analyses standard terms and conditions, what they should include and how online vendors should display them.

CONTRACTS AND TYPES OF CONTRACT

3.03   A contract is an agreement which will be enforced by the law. In general, English law allows contracts to be formed in any available manner — orally, by telephone, by written document or by fax. It even allows a contract to be formed on the basis of the conduct of the parties. Accordingly, people are not debarred from forming legally binding contracts by e-mail and the World Wide Web. The virtual or "digital" nature of the agreement theoretically presents no impediment to its recognition under English law.

Some jurisdictions and model laws, concerned about the legal recognition of electronic contracts, have offered specific legislation affirming their validity. For example, the Model Law on e-commerce of the United Nations Commission on International Trade Law (UNCITRAL) states:

> "In the context of contract formation, unless otherwise agreed by the parties, an offer and the acceptance of an offer may be expressed by means of data messages. Where a data message is used in the formation of a contract, that contract shall not be denied validity or enforceability on the sole ground that a data message was used for that purpose or stored by electronic, optical or similar means, including electronic mail."[2]

3.04   A "data message" is defined as "information generated, sent, received." Singapore enacted a similar clause in its Electronic Transactions Act in July 1998. So far, the United Kingdom has not passed such specific legislation,[3] but there is no reason to believe that contracts made online will be treated any differently by the courts than those made by conventional methods simply because the contract has been made online.

On-line contracts and sales typically fall under three categories: goods, services, and digitised services. These three distinctions are important to online businesses when considering laws on consumer protection, implied terms and liability because many statutes define their scope based on whether a purchase is a good or a service.

Goods

3.05   Under the Sale of Goods Act 1979 (as amended by the Sale and Supply of Goods Act 1994), goods are defined as "all personal chattels other than things in action or money."[4] This includes consumer products such as toys, clothing, and books. Electronic sales of goods will usually involve ordering over the Internet (either through e-mail or a website) and a shipment of the goods by post or courier to the purchaser. Traditionally, a transfer of tangible property is required for a sale of goods but, as paragraph 3.07 below considers, this convention may change to accommodate the sale of digital information.

---

[2] UNCITRAL Model Law on Electronic Commerce (1996), Art. 11(1).
[3] The U.K.'s Electronic Communications Bill does not directly address contractual issues.
[4] Sale of Goods Act 1979 (as amended 1994), s.61(1) and Supply of Goods and Services Act 1982, s.18. The same definition is used in s.14 of the Torts (Interference with Goods) Act 1977.

Thus a sale of goods over the Internet is governed by the Sale of Goods Act 1979. Among other things (pre-contractual representations, etc.), the Act requires that:

> "Where the seller sells goods in the course of a business, there is an implied term that the goods supplied under the contract are of satisfactory quality."[5]

To determine satisfactory quality, a court considers whether the particular item was reasonably fit for its intended purpose, its price, defects, and other relevant attributes.

Services

Over the years, the courts have sought to distinguish between goods and services. It is **3.06** not always immediately apparent. The general overriding conclusion is that a service is where "the substance of the contract . . . is that skill and labour have to be exercised,"[6] or where the contract between supplier and consumer is unique in each case.[7] For example, purchasing a copy of standard software at a store is a sale of goods; a contract with a firm to write bespoke software is a sale of services.

Services, which include online banking, financial services, and gambling, are governed under the Supply of Goods and Services Act 1982, which imposes significantly less stringent standards on the merchant. Instead of requiring satisfactory quality, the contractor need only perform the service with reasonable care and skill to the degree "expected of a professional man of ordinary competence and experience."[8] In other words, the law focuses more on the ability of the performer, not necessarily the end result of his/her actions.

Digitised services

The Internet offers the opportunity to do what Negroponte calls "being digital."[9] Certain **3.07** products, such as software, video, books,[9a] music, and even newspapers and magazines, no longer have to be physically delivered in hard copy format to the purchaser. Suppliers can instead send the products in digital form over the Internet providing both time and cost savings.

However, a new question arises concerning digitised services: are they goods or services? As previously mentioned, e-businesses will find this distinction important because it determines the terms implied into the contract (see paragraph 3.79) and therefore the standard of quality that their products will have to satisfy.

United Kingdom courts have been far from definitive on whether digitised services and digital information constitute "goods". For example, in the Scottish case of *Beta Computers (Europe) Ltd v. Adobe Systems (Europe) Ltd,*[10] the court essentially regarded a contract for standard, non-customised software as *sui generis* (*i.e.* the only one of its kind):

---

[5] Sale of Goods Act 1979 (as amended), s.14.
[6] As in the case of an artist painting a person's portrait. *Robinson v. Graves* [1935] 1 K.B. 579 at 587.
[7] As (in the United States) the case of contact lenses. *Barbee v. Rogers* 425 SW2d 342 (1968).
[8] *Chitty on Contracts* at para. 13–024.
[9] Nicholas Negroponte, *Being Digital,* (A.A. Knopf, New York, 1995).
[9a] See Chapter 5, para. 5.24 for MP 3.
[10] *Beta Computers (Europe) Ltd v. Adobe Systems (Europe) Ltd* [1996] S.L.T. 604.

"It was not an order for the supply of disks as such. On the other hand, it was not an order for the supply of information as such. The subject of the contract was a complex product comprising the medium and the manifestation within it or on it of the intellectual property of the author."[11]

3.08   In contrast, the leading Court of Appeal case of *St Albans City and District Council v. International Computers Ltd,*[12] the highest judicial consideration so far in the United Kingdom of whether software is goods adhered to a traditional good/service distinction, Sir Iain Glidewell decided that while a computer program on a disk clearly falls within the definition of a "good", a computer program *per se* did not:

"In both the Sale of Goods Act 1979, s.61, and the Supply of Goods and Services Act 1982, s 18, the definition of goods includes 'all personal chattels other than things in action and money.' Clearly, a disk is within this definition. Equally clearly, a program, of itself, is not."[13]

The judgment in *St Albans*, however, runs into difficulty when applied to digitised services. If *St Albans* were not confined to its particular facts, it could lead to an illogical situation where identical digital products fell under different regimes merely because they were sold using a different medium. Computer programs sold to the licensee on a floppy disk would be goods, whereas programs transmitted directly via the Internet or over the telecommunications system would constitute a service. Similarly, a video bought at the store on a VHS tape would be a good but video-on-demand would not.

3.09   These illogical distinctions are likely to mean that the English courts will view digitised services as a dematerialised form of goods. In *Advent Systems Limited v. Unisys Corporation,*[14] the U.S. Court of Appeal for the third Circuit felt that there were strong policy arguments for classifying mass-market software as goods:

"Computer programs are the product of an intellectual process, but once implanted in a medium are widely distributed to computer owners. An analogy can be drawn to a compact disc recording of an orchestral rendition. The music is produced by the artistry of musicians and in itself is not a 'good', but when transferred to a laser-readable disc becomes a readily merchantable commodity. Similarly, when a professor delivers a lecture, it is not a good, but, when transcribed as a book, it becomes a good."[15]

Although the court in *Advent* refers specifically to intellectual property placed in a tangible form (book, disk, etc.), there is no reason why intellectual properties available in digitally-packaged form cannot be considered as merchantable commodities. Placing the software, music, or information into digital form is conceptually equivalent to placing it into a book, compact disc, or other tangible medium. Further emphasising the point, digital data have attributes which most closely resemble tangible goods; they are "moved", "distributed", "stored", etc. An alternative view is that they are certainly not services because they do not create a unique contractual relationship, nor do they depend on the exercise of skill or labour, and therefore should be considered as goods.

Back in the nineteenth century, a court once symbolically viewed the telegraph as a virtual pen of "copper wire a thousand miles long."[16] Using a similar mental leap, courts in the future are likely to view digitised services as a virtual version of "goods" in order to maintain a consistent legal framework.

---

[11] *ibid.* at 608 (cited in Lloyd at p. 415).
[12] *St Albans City and District Council v. International Computers Ltd* [1996] 4 All E.R. 481. First instance at [1995] F.S.R. 686.
[13] *St Albans v. ICL* [1996] 4 All E.R. 481 at 493. However, though a computer program is not a good (and therefore is not subject to the statutory implied term as to satisfactory quality), Glidewell L.J. ruled *obiter dicta* that the quality term is still implied under common law.
[14] *Advent Systems Limited v. Unisys Corporation* (1991) 925 F.2d 670, U.S. CA, Third Circuit, LEXIS 2396.
[15] *ibid.* at 675.
[16] *Howley v. Whipple (U.S.)* (1869) 48 N.H. 487.

PRE-CONTRACTUAL CONSIDERATIONS

Before transacting a sale and forming a contract with a customer, e-businesses have to **3.10** create a presence on the Internet through a website, newsgroup advertisement, e-mail list, etc. The culture of cyberspace encourages an attitude of "anything goes", with the principal maxim being *caveat emptor* (let the buyer beware). However, e-commerce is just like any other form of commercial activity and is bound by the same regulations and legal principles regarding pre-contractual behaviour. In addition, e-businesses may need to verify the identity of their customers, since they may not wish (or may not be legally allowed) to transact with all people from all jurisdictions. Failure to observe these considerations can have a major impact on the performance and enforceability of the subsequent contract.

Advertisement

Advertising and other means of promoting goods and services are subject to many **3.11** regulations which vary significantly among different jurisdictions. For example, Germany has strict rules against comparative advertising in contrast to both the United Kingdom and the United States.[17] Some advertising is further regulated by industry-specific rules (*e.g.* tobacco, bookmaking and gambling) and where it is aimed at a particular audience (such as children). A detailed examination of global advertising laws is beyond the scope of this book, although a more detailed analysis of U.K. advertising law can be found in Chapter 10. Nevertheless, the pre-contractual claims and representations made in advertising can have a significant impact on the resulting contract. This section addresses those concerns.

Unilateral v. Bilateral contracts

Generally, contracts are bilateral, meaning that both parties are bound; there is "the **3.12** exchange of a promise for a promise."[18] For example, when a person orders merchandise from a website, a bilateral contract is formed because the merchant promises to send the goods in exchange and the customer promises to pay.

However, online advertisements can create unilateral contracts, where only one party (*i.e.* the advertiser) is bound.[19] In a unilateral contract, an announcement offers money or some other reward for the performance of an action, and this announcement is considered to be a standing offer. The accepting party does not need to notify the advertiser; he/she only needs to do the required act. The well-known case of *Carlill v. Carbolic Smoke Ball Co. Ltd* concerned unilateral contracts. The defendant offered £100 to any person who contracted influenza after using its smoke balls as directed. The plaintiff did exactly as suggested, caught influenza, and sued for the £100; the court enforced the contract. Unilateral contracts are not only dangerous because a careless advertisement can create legal obligations, but also because they can be enforced by multiple parties. As Bowens L.J. suggested in *Carlill*, "It is an offer made to all the world."[20] If five people had

---

[17] Unfair Competition Act (Germany), s.1. cited in Dennis Campbell, ed., *Law of International On-Line Business*, (Sweet and Maxwell, London, 1998).
[18] *Chitty on Contracts* (ed., Sweet & Maxwell, London, 1999), para. 1–002.
[19] *Restatement of Contracts* (1932) s.12. *Restatement of Contracts* (2d, 1981) s.45 renames unilateral contracts as "option contracts." *Chitty on Contracts*, (ed., Sweet & Maxwell, London, 1999), para. 1–022.
[20] *Carlill v. Carbolic Smoke Ball Co. Ltd.* [1892] 2 Q.B. 484; affd [1893] 1 Q.B. 256.

used the smoke balls and contracted influenza, Carbolic would have been liable for £500; if ten, £1000.

Online advertisements therefore need to be carefully drafted to ensure that customers (and the courts) interpret them as advertisements, not unilateral contracts; otherwise a company with a website offering £500 to anyone finding a bug in its program may find itself liable for more money than originally anticipated. Merchants can use disclaimers to emphasise that the "webvertisement" is only an advertisement or an invitation to treat, not an offer or unilateral contract.

Express Terms

3.13   Historically, one principal problem faced by the courts in this area was whether a representation (often verbal) made prior to contract creation constituted an express term, even though it was not detailed in the written contract. At first, this possibility appears unlikely since, according to the parol evidence rule,

> "if there is a contract which has been reduced to writing, verbal evidence is not allowed to be given so as to add to or subtract from, or in any manner to vary or qualify the written contract."[21]

This restriction is not limited to oral evidence; it also includes drafts, preliminary agreements, and other prior representations. As a result, the weight and finality given to written contracts seems exceptionally high. If one assumes that computer documents constitute writing (paragraph 3.61), online contracts should theoretically be subject to only the specified terms.

However, the ambit of the parol evidence rule is extremely restricted; it applies only in instances where the court finds that the contract lies solely in the document. Thus, a court may find that part of the contract was verbal or in a previous statement, or, in the case of online contracts, in another e-mail or on a different web page. As the court ruled in *J. Evans & Son (Portsmouth) Ltd v. Andrea Merzario Ltd*, "the court is entitled to look at and should look at all the evidence from start to finish in order to see what the bargain was that was struck between the parties."[22] As a result, online statements made by e-mail or on web pages prior to contract formation may be interpreted as express contractual terms, despite their absence from the 'actual' contract written or otherwise. In addition, in the interests of fairness or justice, the courts might also use the Misrepresentation Act 1967 (paragraph 3.14) or the concept of collateral contract (paragraph 3.15) to hold an online merchant liable or contractually bound to a prior representation.

The lesson to be learned is that, if an online customer enters into a contract due to some representation made by the e-business, the courts have many ways of holding the e-business responsible. The representation can possibly be an express contractual term even (though not explicitly stated in the same location) part of a collateral contract, or a misrepresentation under the Misrepresentation Act 1967.

Misrepresentations

3.14   Pre-contractual statements or conduct, though they may not form actual contractual terms, do nonetheless affect a contractee's decision-making process. Hence, both common law and the Misrepresentation Act 1967 hold suppliers accountable for any untrue statements of fact which induce the customer to enter into a contract. A victim of

---

[21] *Goss v. Lord Nugent* (1833) 5 B. & Ad. 58 at 64, cited in *Chitty*, para. 12–081.
[22] *J. Evans & Son (Portsmouth) Ltd v. Andrea Merzario Ltd* [1976] 1 W.L.R. 1078 at 1083.

misrepresentation may affirm the contract or seek a remedy in the courts and obtain damages and/or rescission of the contract depending on whether the misrepresentation was made fraudulently, negligently, or innocently.[23]

E-commerce does not raise any new issues in this area. The Misrepresentation Act and the common law apply to online contracts just as to conventional ones and will impose liability for untrue statements of fact made on websites, by e-mail or elsewhere in cyberspace.

Collateral Contracts

> A millionaire goes to a website and reads the technical specification of a satellite navigation system. She commissions the construction of a yacht and in her contract with the boat builder specifies that the yacht should use the particular satellite navigation system. The system is faulty and in consequence the yacht hits a submerged rock and sinks.

A collateral contract is one which is independent of, but subordinate to, an agreement **3.15** affecting the same subject matter. If a representation induces a person to form a contract with a third party, the court may hold that there was a collateral contract with the representation. For example, in *Shanklin Pier Ltd v. Detel Products Ltd*,[24] the plaintiff relied on representations made by the defendant, a paint manufacturer, regarding the suitability of its paint, to form a contract with a third party, a painting contractor. (The contract stipulated the use of the defendant's paint.) When the plaintiff discovered that the paint was inappropriate, it successfully sued the defendant for damages under a collateral contract.

Product statements on a website can constitute the grounds for a collateral contract (possibly formed unbeknownst to the site owner). In the above scenario the millionaire may have a claim against the manufacturers of the satellite navigation system under a collateral contract. Thus, even if a business uses a website for purely promotional purposes and does not anticipate creating contracts online, it still must take care not to make misrepresentations.

Verifying Identity: Knowing the customer

Online merchants do not want to sell goods or services to everyone on the Internet. For **3.16** example, trade embargoes may block sales to particular countries, (*e.g.* Iraq, Cuba); local laws may prohibit the sale of certain goods or content (*e.g.* tobacco, pornography, etc.) to minors. Further, how does an e-commerce organisation know that the online person has the authority to buy or transact? Children purchasing goods without permission or the means to pay and hackers manipulating financial accounts are major concerns for the e-commerce business.

The faceless, impersonal nature of cyberspace makes it difficult for businesses to "know their customers." Although technical developments (*e.g.* digital signatures, smart cards, etc.) may provide effective solutions in the future, for now online businesses will have to resort to indirect methods for verifying identity and blocking web access from unwanted jurisdictions.

---

[23] For specifics on misrepresentation law, the reader is referred to a standard text on contracts, such as *Chitty*.
[24] *Shanklin Pier Ltd v. Detel Products Ltd* [1951] 2 K.B. 854.

Countries or States

3.17   There are a number of reasons why businesses will often want to limit the countries or jurisdictions with which they want to transact.

Export/import restrictions

Many products, such as encryption software and other dual-use technology, are subject to export restrictions (often for national security reasons) under laws such as the Dual Use and Related Goods (Export Control) Regulations 1995.[25] Failure to monitor the location of the transacting party, particularly for digitised services such as downloadable encryption software, could result in an online supplier being in breach of these statutes. On the flip side, many jurisdictions have import restrictions. For example, the United States Department of Agriculture rigorously regulates the importation of fruits and vegetables. Suppliers may wish to exclude these products as well.

Commercial embarrassment

In the media spotlight, the public quickly discovers the people and the countries with which a merchant does business. Even if not subject to government regulations, some businesses may choose to avoid dealing with particular countries, for public relations reasons.

Consumer Protection Legislation

As paragraph 3.82 details, many jurisdictions have consumer protection laws that imply mandatory terms into consumer contracts. Some of these terms may be surprisingly unfavourable to foreign merchants. On-line businesses wishing to avoid draconian legislation or foreign lawsuits may wish to refuse purchasers from some jurisdictions.

Illegal or regulated activity

Some online content or activities, such as financial services, gambling, or pornography, may be legal in some areas and illegal (or subject to heavy regulation) in others. To the relief of online businesses, many jurisdictions will not enforce their regulations and laws on Internet sites unless there is evidence of directed activity. The policy of the Financial Services Authority in the United Kingdom regarding financial services advertisements reflects this position.

3.18   However, even without purposely directed activity toward a particular jurisdiction, some long-arm statutes (often found in the United States) may seek to bring a website owner into the foreign court anyway. For example, in *Minnesota v. Granite Gate Resorts*,[26] a number of Minnesota residents accessed a Nevada website advertising a forthcoming international Internet gambling site. Consequently, a Minnesota court claimed personal jurisdiction, stating that the defendants had "purposefully availed themselves of the privilege of conducting commercial activities in [Minnesota]."[27] It should be noted that *Granite Gate* involved merely advertising, not even actual gambling activities.

A similar scenario regarding pornography occurred in *U.S. v. Thomas*.[28] A Federal court in Tennessee claimed jurisdiction, applied local obscenity standards, and convicted a

---

[25] Dual Use and Related Goods (Export Control) Regulations 1995 (S.I. 1995 No. 1191).
[26] *Minnesota v. Granite Gate Resorts* 568 N.W.2d 715.
[27] *ibid.*
[28] *United States v. Thomas* (1996) Nos. 94–6648/6649 FED App. 0032P (6th Cir.).

website owner based in California. The "passive" nature of a website provides no defence. As was held in *Playboy Enterprises Inc. v. Chuckleberry Publishing*[29]:

> "[An Internet site can be viewed as] an 'advertisement' by which [the foreign site] distributes its pictorial images throughout the United States. That the local user 'pulls' these images from [the foreign] computer . . . as opposed to [the site] 'sending' them to this country, is irrelevant. By inviting United States users to download these images, [the foreign site] is causing and contributing to their distribution within the United States."

Thus, there are a host of reasons why online merchants should regulate access to their sites and exclude users from unwanted jurisdictions. The consequences of carelessness in this area are not only potential embarrassment or difficult-to-enforce contracts, but possible civil liability and/or criminal sanctions (*e.g. U.S. v. Thomas*). Merchants of physical goods have less concern, since they can check the delivery address and act accordingly. However, merchants of digitised services face a tougher challenge, since the location and identity of the customer is not as apparent. Although near-perfect technical solutions (such as digital signatures, etc.) are not yet readily available, there are still a number of methods available to prevent unwanted site visitors and to minimise legal liability.

Web server checks

Every computer online has an Internet (I.P.) address (either permanently or tem-porarily assigned). Although this address does not necessarily indicate the customer's country of origin and can be masked,[30] a web server can perform this simple check as a preliminary verification. **3.19**

Alternatively, servers can utilise "cookies"[31] to get a general geographical location by detecting the time zone offset used by the customer. If the server only wants to do business within the United Kingdom, it could reject customers with time zone offsets other than zero (Greenwich Meridian) and +1 (British Summer Time).

These server checks are not foolproof but can provide a fair degree of protection against the risk and, furthermore, the fact that server checks were used would be taken into account by any court when determining whether the server was intending to sell its digitised services in the relevant jurisdiction.

Site disclaimers

Site disclaimers can exclude "unfriendly" jurisdictions through statements such as "This website is intended only for people inside the United Kingdom." These disclaimers discourage unwanted customers and can reduce the risk of legal liability by explicitly defining the intended audience. However, disclaimers must be consistent with the site owner's actions. In *Granite Gate*, despite the use of site disclaimers urging users to "consult with local authorities regarding restrictions," the court held that the defendants' subsequent actions were a "clear effort to reach and seek potential profit from Minnesota consumers."[32] **3.20**

Online contract construction

Online advertisements need to be carefully constructed so that they are only invitations to treat, not offers. This gives the online business the option to accept or

---

[29] *Playboy Enterprises Inc. v. Chuckleberry Publishing Inc.*, 939 F.Supp. 1044 (S.D.N.Y. 1996). See Chapter 4.
[30] IP addresses can be masked through a technique called "weaving," where a user connects to the web site via a number of other computers, creating layers which hide his original location.
[31] Cookies are pieces of information sent from the customers computer (web browser) to the web server for convenience. For example, cookies may contain the user's name, e-mail address, etc. See Chapter 8.
[32] *Minnesota v. Granite Gate Resorts* 568 N.W.2d 715.

refuse dealings with particular customers after obtaining their specific details (location, age, etc.) without raising the spectre of a breach of contract.

Impostors

3.21   To prevent fraud, some online services, particularly banks and financial services, need to verify the identity of a person before allowing him/her to make withdrawals or move funds. Authenticating a specific person presents a different problem from checking location, however, because the customer will often have already had a prior relationship with the online service provider. Therefore, the customer will likely possess a password, PIN (personal identification number), digital signature key, or some other form of identification.

Most of these on-going service contracts will specifically outline security procedures and attribute responsibility based on predetermined principles. Even without explicit terms, the courts are likely to find that if a password or PIN is used, the recipient (in this case, the online service provider) is entitled to rely on it unless notified of a problem. Responsibility for securing the authentication information lies completely with the owner of the key. The court in *Standard Bank London Ltd v. The Bank of Tokyo Ltd*[33] reached this conclusion regarding 'tested telexes' (telexes authenticated by a secret code):

> "The recipient would be able to rely on a tested telex unless it was on notice that the telex was not what it purported to be. Where a clear representation was made in the ordinary course of business, normally the recipient would be fixed with notice of dishonesty, or of facts that should put it on inquiry as to dishonesty, or if it had been wilfully blind."[34]

3.22   The problem authentication poses to the creation of a continuing online relationship (*e.g.* before a person establishes an online bank account) is quite similar to one already faced in the physical world. Traditionally, businesses such as banks rely on applications, letters of reference and other similar documents to vouch for a new customer's identity. On-line merchants will have to resort to analogous methods. Digital signatures and a framework of "trusted third parties" may make this process easier in the future, and are discussed in Chapter 6.

Authentication of a person is usually based upon:

(1) Something they know (*e.g.* password or PIN);

(2) Something they have (*e.g.* magnetic card or smart card);

(3) Something they are (*e.g.* voiceprint, fingerprint, etc.)

Current mass domestic market authentication technology is based upon passwords and PINs. Retailers and bank automatic teller machines use cards with magnetic stripes for authentication. Voice and fingerprint identification remain confined to specialist high security areas.

Difficulties arise when a supplier reduces authentication security to enable it to address a wider market. Catastrophic consequences can follow if the supplier reduces security by too great an amount as its contracts will require corroboration for their validity to be accepted in court. The determination of appropriate authentication security requires specialist professional risk assessment to take account of specific facts and circumstances.

---

[33] *Standard Bank London Ltd v. The Bank of Tokyo Ltd* [1996] 1 C.T.L.R. T–17.
[34] *ibid.*

Minors

In cyberspace, companies will have great difficulty discerning whether the customer **3.23**
is 48 years old or merely eight. Minors (anyone under the age of 18) thus present
two interesting problems to online merchants. First, the sale of certain goods and content
to minors, such as tobacco, alcohol, and pornography is unlawful. Without adequate
measures to ensure that customers are adults, website owners may again find themselves
liable to civil or criminal sanctions. Second, under English law, contracts made by minors
for things other than necessities (food, clothing, shelter, etc.) are voidable.[35] In addition,
although these contracts are unenforceable against the minor, they are enforceable
against the merchant.[36] The situation leaves online companies in a precarious position
which they have good reason to avoid. They must fulfil their contractual obligation, but
have little recourse if the child defaults on payment.[37]

Sale of illegal goods to minors
3.24

One remedy available to companies wishing to avoid dealing with minors online is the
Content Advisor found on most web browsers. The software is based on ratings created
by the Recreational Software Advisory Council (RSAC) to limit the degree of sex,
violence, and language accessible to children. To avoid legal action for distributing to
minors, providers of digitised services can acquire a rating that will restrict access
accordingly. On-line sellers of goods could use a similar tactic to ensure that only adult
customers made purchases. Unfortunately, the RSAC software only currently has four
categories: language, nudity, sex, and violence. RSAC would need to amend this list to
make it relevant to e-commerce activities such as gambling, the purchase of tobacco, etc.
On the basis that a parent who wanted his/her children protected from language, nudity,
sex, and violence would also wish to protect them from gambling and tobacco products,
it might be reasonable for a supplier to wrongly classify its site as containing nudity and
sex just to get the RSAC system to impose its current restrictions. Nevertheless, online
providers must still rely on parents to take preventative actions regarding their children.
The RSAC content advisor only works if parents enable it and change the relevant
settings.

Purchases by minors and their capacity for entering into binding contracts.

"The law on this topic is based on two principles. The first, and more important, is that the law must
protect the minor against his inexperience which may enable an adult to take unfair advantage of him or
induce him to enter into a contract which, though in itself fair, is simply improvident (*e.g.* if the minor
for a fair price buys something he cannot afford). This principle is the basis of the general rule that a
minor is not bound by his contracts. The second principle is that the law should not cause unnecessary
hardship to adults who deal fairly with minors. Under this principle certain contracts with minors are
valid; others are voidable in the sense that they bind the minor unless he repudiates; and a minor may
be under some liability in tort and in restitution."[38]

Over the past few years various U.K. companies have found themselves with unenforce- **3.25**
able contracts made with children. Telephone companies have installed telephone lines

---

[35] *Merchantile Union Guarantee Co. v. Ball* [1937] 3 All E.R. 1.
[36] Minors' Contract Act 1987, s.2. Originally, all aspects of contracts made by minors' were governed under the
Infants Relief Act 1874, but the Minors' Contract 1987 repealed it, reverting most of the relevant rules back to
common law.
[37] Under a breach, merchants can only recover the actual goods delivered to the minor, if the minor is still in
possession of them. Minors' Contract Act 1987, s.3.
[38] *Treitel: Law of Contract* (9th ed.) at p. 494.

for children without their parents' knowledge and have then been faced with unenforce-able telephone bills.

Minors in the United Kingdom are frequently issued with debit cards by banks and building societies. These are not credit cards but permit a minor to buy goods and services provided there are sufficient funds in the account. It is possible for a minor to go to a website and use his/her own debit card to make a purchase. The goods shall have been paid for before they are received. In practical terms this is of great significance since any dispute between the minor and the vendor will be an attempt by the minor for repayment of money and not an attempt by the vendor to get money out of a minor. To recover a wrongful payment the minor, as plaintiff, would have all the practical problems associated with litigating and, in particular, proving that the goods were not necessities. Consequently, in practical terms, it is fairly safe to sell goods and services to minors using their own debit cards.

It is difficult to contemplate circumstances where the e-business might be at genuine risk through accepting debit cards from minors for goods which it delivered to the minor on its normal terms of business. There might be an outside risk that a merchant whose business was selling goods which were not necessities (*e.g.* music CDs) could find itself at the receiving end of an action brought for repayment to a minor of monies paid for the goods. Furthermore, if a minor purchased goods from a merchant based in another jurisdiction the risk of litigation becomes almost insignificant.

3.26   The position is slightly different if the minor, having paid for the goods, changes his/her mind before the goods have been delivered. If the minor makes the vendor aware that he/she is a minor and wishes to withdraw from the transaction, the vendor would not be entitled to rely upon its normal terms of business regarding cancellations. The minor would be entitled to a full refund. Good business practice would require that the bank or building society who issued the minor with the debit card would find some means to charge back the transaction upon notice by the minor of the circumstances.

The position, however, is different when the contract is made by a child using a parent's credit or debit card without permission. In these circumstances the transaction should be treated as if the card had been stolen. Once the parent is made aware of the transactions having taken place, he/she has an opportunity either to ratify the trans-actions (in which case the contract will be with the parent), or deny the validity of the transaction. If the parent denies the validity of the transaction, the credit card company may have an action against the parent in negligence for failure to keep the credit card details confidential. On the basis of modern practice, though, this is unlikely to be pursued. All the information being sought to validate a "cardholder not present" transaction is present on the face of the card. It is unlikely that a court would deem this information to be confidential.

A more practical barrier to denying the validity of the transaction would be the associated problem of reporting the minor's crime to the authorities. Most parents would balk at having their children prosecuted for theft and the socially acceptable solution is to accept the validity of the minor's transactions and thereby save the minor from the implications arising from a prosecution for theft. But sometimes this is not possible.

Mistake

3.27   Related to the issue of whether a purchaser has the legal capacity to enter into a contract is the potential problem of mistaken identities in distant, impersonal transactions such as those under the rubric of e-commerce. As the parties to online contracts rarely meet, the firm establishment and acceptance of the identities of all involved is an issue at the heart of e-commerce. While technical means of reducing identification errors are discussed in paragraphs 3.16 to 3.22 above, the impact of mistaken identity on the validity of contracts is a separate, but equally important issue. In the summer of 1999 the click and brick retailer Argos was threatened with legal action unless it honoured orders for Sony Nicam television sets which it advertised at £3.00 each rather than the intended £299.99.

Issues of mistaken identity can easily arise in computer mediated environments. In fact, the mistake can be made on the part of the purchaser or the vendor of products or services. For example, imagine a customer who wishes to buy fishing equipment from Waterfish, the most reputable (fictional) dealer of fishing and fly fishing equipment in Europe. After much research and upon review of many suppliers, the customer chooses Waterfish specifically because of its reputation in the industry and its impeccable relationships with parts suppliers. Happy to have found the company, the eager customer hurriedly connects to **www.waterfish.com**, the homepage of a new start-up fly fishing establishment in Brighton. Not noticing the difference between the two companies online, the customer purchases a fly fishing rod and reel from the vendor and leaves a name and address for delivery. After delivery of the product, the customer realises that it was shipped from Brighton and that the warranties on parts are not as strong as those offered by the well known Waterfish. Having mistakenly bought goods from the wrong company, does the customer have a right to force a refund or are they stuck with the unwanted goods?

Under English law, a contract may be void in the case of a mistake such as this if (1) the mistake is "fundamental," (2) the mistake itself induced the contract, and (3) the mistake was "operative" in terms of the contract. If the mistake is fundamental, then it may negate one party's consent to the agreement of contract. In the example above, the mistaking of one company for another is considered fundamental in this capacity.[39] In the Argos situation one way they are likely to avoid responsibility is by claiming a mistake of fact. Furthermore, the mistake must have induced the entering into of the contract. In this case, the customer specifically wanted to purchase the product from a well known dealer because of its reputation and efficient supply of parts for its products. Therefore, the reputation and name of the company itself, in this case mistaken for another, induced the customer to enter into a contract with what they thought was the traditional, reputable Waterfish. However, satisfying these conditions, the contract remains valid until the mistake made is proven to be "operative." To be considered operative, the mistake must satisfy three criteria: where a reasonable person could not infer the intention of the parties involved in the transaction; where one party knew of the other's mistake; or where one party negligently, directly or indirectly induced the other's mistake.[40] While the law of misrepresentation remains unchanged in relation to e-commerce, the potential for non-negligent mistakes in computer mediated environments such as with e-commerce remains high. For this reason, it should be considered sound practice to state clearly who the vendor is during the transaction process (preferably in the terms of trading) in order to avoid unenforceable contracts, fraud by customers and general mistakes of identity in transactions. On the vendor side, a contract may be voided if the customer's identity was mistaken. For example, a company extending credit to someone on the basis of mistaken identity may retrieve goods or demand payment from a customer based on the above criteria.[41]

---

[39] *Cundy v. Lindsay* [1875] 3 App.Cas. 459.
[40] Haftke in Rowe & Haftke, *A Practitioner's Guide to the regulation of the Internet* (City & Financial Publishing, 1999/2000).
[41] *Cundy v. Lindsay* [1875] 3 App.Cas. 459.

Employees

3.28   Companies have devised elaborate procedures to ensure that there are checks and balances on the actions of employees.[42] For example, in order to make large purchases, an employee might require the "signing-off" of a superior. These paper-based methods are often slow and bureaucratic. One of the promises of e-commerce is to remove much of this inefficiency.[43] However, e-mail and web purchasing also allow greater opportunities to circumvent conventional procedures and controls if the business has not been re-engineered to reflect the new risks. Should employers be concerned about employees making unauthorised contracts? Are these online contracts enforceable?

English law provides that if an employee has the apparent authority to conclude a contract, the employer will normally be bound, regardless of whether the employee had the actual authority to do so or not.[44] Other jurisdictions, such as the United States, have similar doctrines.[45] Thus, as long as an online business is reasonable in assessing the authority of the purchaser/contractor, it will form fully enforceable contracts.

To prevent problems of unauthorised action by employees, employers need to establish clear policies delineating what employees can do with their e-mail accounts and Internet connections. Staff should also be educated and trained regarding the risks. In addition, since apparent authority is established through symbols of authority, such as business cards and letterhead, corporate policies should regulate representations such as the "signature tags" at the bottom of e-mails. It may also be wise for senior management to publish and circulate to all likely vendors a document setting out the true extent of the contractual authority granted to employees.

CONTRACT CREATION

3.29   Under English law, the formation of a contract requires four elements: offer; acceptance; consideration; and an intention to create legal relations. For example, online contract formation could proceed in the following manner:

> The consumer offers three euros (the offer price) to a music website to listen to a new track to be included on a forthcoming Elton John CD. The website accepts the offer and begins to download a high quality digital recording. In this situation, the parties exchange something of value (consideration), namely the three euros from the consumer to the website owner and the supply to the consumer of the digital recording of the music, and they intend on forming a binding agreement. Thus all the requirements for a binding contract are present.

An understanding of the contract formation process is critical to online businesses; a contract that fails to satisfy any of the requirements may be unenforceable. On the other hand, the courts might construe certain actions by consumers or e-businesses as

---

[42] This practice is also reflected in auditing where a company can find the reliability of its business records being questioned if there is an inadequate separation of responsibilities. See Chapter 5 "Evidence, Security, Watermarking and ECMS".

[43] Within companies, "groupware" technologies such as Lotus Notes allow the construction of an electronic equivalent of these paper-based procedures with electronic "chits" being signed off for approval or payment.

[44] *Chitty on Contracts,* para. 31–038.

[45] 3 Am. Jur. 2d Agency s.71 (1986); Restatement (Second) of Agency, s.8A (1958).

constituting the required elements, even though there was no desire to make an offer or acceptance at the time.

The exposition on the elements of contract below will enable businesses to be more mindful of their actions online. It will also indicate the methods for constructing websites to safeguard the commercial and legal interests of e-businesses.

Offer

When a person makes an offer, he/she is expressing a desire to enter into a contract **3.30** (based on specified terms and conditions) on the understanding that if the other party accepts it, the agreement will be legally binding. Offers can be made using virtually any form of communication — by post, fax, telex, telephone, and now by e-mail and the World Wide Web.

English law states that if a reasonable person would interpret a particular action or communication as an offer (a readiness to bind oneself), it is an offer whether the party intended it or not.[46] Thus, the appearance of an offer is more important than actual intent. This doctrine represents a significant danger to e-businesses. Careless online statements or poorly constructed websites can constitute making unintentional offers to the world that result in unwanted binding legal contracts once consumers accept.

Invitation to treat

To protect themselves from making unintentional offers, online merchants need to **3.31** observe the fine distinction between an offer and an invitation to treat. Invitations to treat are advertisements that promote the sale of products, but are not offers in themselves (nor unilateral contracts). For example, English law holds that shop displays and price-lists are invitations to treat. For example, in *Pharmaceutical Society of Great Britain v. Boots Cash Chemists (Southern) Ltd*,[47] the court held that:

> "It is a well-established principle that the mere exposure of goods for sale by a shopkeeper indicates to the public that he is willing to treat but does not amount to an offer to sell. . . . The customer is informed that he may himself pick up an article and bring it to the shopkeeper with a view to buying it, and if, but only if, the shopkeeper then expresses his willingness to sell, the contract for sale is completed."[48]

Similarly in *Fisher v. Bell*, the court said:

> "It is clear that, according to the ordinary law of contract, the display of an article with a price on it in a shop window is merely an invitation to treat. It is in no sense an offer for sale the acceptance of which constitutes a contract."[49]

When a customer approaches the store counter with a product it is only an offer to buy, not acceptance of an offer made by the store. The store then has the option of accepting the offer and complete the contract, or refusing it.

A similar principle is likely to apply to e-mail price lists and websites. Websites are the electronic analogue of shop windows and catalogues, advertising the descriptions of products and their prices. E-mail price lists similarly are analogous to circulars in conventional commerce. These analogies, however, are still conjecture, since no case law

---

[46] *Chitty on Contracts*, para. 2–002.
[47] *Pharmaceutical Society of Great Britain v. Boots Cash Chemists (Southern) Ltd* [1951] 2 Q.B. 795.
[48] *ibid.* at 801.
[49] *Fisher v. Bell* [1961] 1 Q.B. 394 at 399.

has yet verified websites as invitations to treat. Furthermore, pre-written order forms with the online merchants' standard terms and conditions could be construed (albeit unlikely) as offers, since they are designed and written by the supplier. In order to minimise the risk of an unfavourable court decision, websites and e-mail solicitations should have disclaimers explicitly defining them to be invitations to treat, and not offers. These disclaimers will ensure that e-businesses have the ability to select their customers and manage their supply of goods.

3.32 *Selection of customers*

As mentioned in paragraph 3.16, for many reasons, e-businesses merchants may not wish to deal with all customers from all jurisdictions. By retaining the power to accept or refuse, businesses can refuse undesirable customers and jurisdictions without fearing breach of contract. Additionally, if the vendor intends to accept orders from only U.K.-based customers, a notice on the website stating that "The contents of this website are for U.K. customers only" is advisable.[50]

Management of supply

One of the primary reasons why the courts introduced the invitation to treat principle was to protect traditional businesses from supply shortages or limited supplies. As the court decided in *Grainger & Son v. Gough:*

> "The transmission of a price-list does not amount to an offer to supply an unlimited quantity of the wine described at the price named, so that as soon as an order is given there is a binding contract to supply that quantity. If it were so, the merchant might find himself involved in any number of contractual obligations to supply wine of a particular description which he would be quite unable to carry out, his stock of wine of that description being necessarily limited."[51]

The same argument applies to e-commerce. On-line merchants cannot necessarily accurately assess the number of replies they will receive in response to a solicitation. If the website or e-mail price list were considered as an offer, the merchant would potentially have innumerable contracts with people throughout the world, all of whom could sue for breach if it did not deliver the advertised product.

3.33 *Errors or garbled offers*

E-mail can frequently become garbled due to transmission problems such as incompatible formats, changes in languages or keyboard sets, or even firewalls[52] removing attachments.[53] The offeror will probably not be held liable for the error if the recipient had reason to suspect a transmission problem. However, in certain circumstances (*e.g.* if the error is undetectable), the offeror could be held liable for inaccuracies if the offeree subsequently accepts the offer and forms a contract. Ensuring that e-mail solicitations are invitations to treat and requiring the customer to make the offer reduces this risk.

---

[50] See Chapter 2.
[51] *Grainger & Son v. Gough* [1896] A.C. 325 at 334.
[52] Firewalls are dedicated computers which guard the entrance to a network (usually belonging on a particular company or organisation). Their job is often to block any potentially malicious files (such as e-mails and their attachments) and to prevent intrusions by hackers.
[53] "Attachments" are formatted documents that are appended to e-mail messages. A good example of a formatted document is a word processing file that contains information regarding the text layout (font, font size, justification, bold text, etc). Informal studies have estimated that approximately 50 per cent of attachments to e-mail messages between organisations are lost or corrupted in their transmission. This loss or destruction arises owing to incompatibilities between different e-mail systems.

Acceptance

After the offer has been made, the offeree accepts it and thus creates a contract. In   **3.34**
cyberspace, acceptance is a contentious issue because the offeror and the offeree are
distanced in time and space. Where is the contract actually formed? How is it formed? In
what ways can acceptance be communicated? This section addresses these questions and
others related to the creation of an online contract.

As explained in the previous section, depending on how the courts interpret a website
or other online advertisement (as either an invitation to treat or an offer), the customer
response could be viewed as either an acceptance or an offer (respectively). This section
assumes that the website is an invitation to treat, that the customer response is an offer
and thus it is the vendor who accepts and forms the contract.

Attribution of computer acts to a person

One of the advantages of e-commerce is the automation of tasks which previously   **3.35**
required human involvement. Computers can receive orders online and, in some
electronic data interchange systems (EDI), even keep track of inventory and automatically place orders when supplies run low. This raises an important issue: can a
computer accept an offer and create a contract? For example, if a person wishes to buy a
book and makes an offer to an online bookseller, can the merchant's web server accept
the offer and create the contract?

English law and most other legal systems, have a tradition of attributing the actions of
a machine to the person who instruct it to execute a particular routine.[54] In *Thornton v.
Shoe Lane Parking,*[55] the court ruled that a customer contracted with a car park machine
(representing the owner) when he fed in his money and received a claim ticket. As
Denning L.J. suggested:

> "[The customer] was committed at the very moment when he put his money into the machine. The
> contract was concluded at that time. It can be translated into offer and acceptance in this way: the offer
> is made when the proprietor of the machine holds it out as being ready to receive the money. The
> acceptance takes place when the customer puts his money into the slot."[56]

In the United States case of *State Farm Mutual Auto. Ins. Co. v. Brockhurst,*[57] the court ruled   **3.36**
that since the computer only operated as programmed by the insurance company, it was
bound by the contract formed (in this case, an insurance renewal). Based on these two
precedents, the English courts would probably decide that a web server, as an agent of
the online business, can both make offers and accept offers in order to create contracts.
Web-automated contracts therefore need to be carefully constructed to prevent the
creation of unwanted contracts. Otherwise, as long as the customer reasonably believes
that the computer accepted the offer, the contract will be fully binding, regardless of
what bugs the server might have or what the online terms might state (*e.g.* price,
quantity, product, etc.). In addition, not only must merchants ensure that the prices,
terms and conditions are accurate, they must also be wary of "free-text" boxes that
would enable the customer to change the terms of the agreement. For example, if the sale

---

[54] For an early fictional account of how the law deals with computers acting on their own see *Haddock v. The
Generous Bank Limited, Computer* 1578/32/W1, The Magical Electronic Contrivances Limited and the Central
Electricity Board; one of Sir A. P. Herbert's "Misleading Cases" (Penguin 1963).
[55] *Thornton v. Shoe Land Parking Ltd* [1971] 1 All E.R. 686.
[56] *ibid.* at p. 689.
[57] *State Farm Mutual Auto. Ins. Co. v. Brockhurst* 453 F.2d 533, 10th Cir. (1972).

is for £500 and the customer can type into the free-text box, "I agree to the price of £50," the supplier might be held to the lower price.

Although the standard terms could state that the contract is a contract of adhesion (in which the conditions of the contract are fixed) those terms prohibiting amendments may not be enforced by the courts.[58] Thus, to minimise risk, a properly constructed website should not allow the customer to change or input additional terms into the contract. The customer is only presented with fixed prices and conditions, and can only click a button to send the offer.

Similar arguments apply for e-mail if an online business wants to provide a prewritten contract for the customer to send as an offer. Without some technical means of ensuring message integrity, the customer could easily change the standard terms and conditions to benefit himself/herself instead of the merchant. Use of technical solutions such as hash functions or digital signatures can prevent this problem.

Valid methods of acceptance

3.37   Acceptance is the unconditional agreement to the presented offer. It cannot be a message merely notifying the offeror that the offer has been received; nor can it involve a change of terms, as this amounts to a counteroffer (paragraph 3.50). Unless explicitly specified in the offer, acceptances can generally be made via any communication method that is "reasonable" in the circumstances. Speed and reliability of the method are taken into consideration in determining whether it is reasonable. For example, using the post to accept a time-sensitive offer originally made by e-mail may be unreasonable. Generally, accepting an offer by the same means by which it was originally communicated (or by a faster and more reliable method) should be sufficient,[59] unless the terms of the offer explicitly insist on a single method.

Contracts can even be accepted by a "click-wrap". A click-wrap is where the contract is presented in a window online, and the customer is asked to click an "Offer" or "I accept" button. Although English courts have not yet dealt with click-wrap agreements, a United States District Court held them to be enforceable in America.[60] An English court would probably similarly recognise click-wrap contracts.

3.38   The online merchant can implicitly accept a customer's offer through some form of action. For example, in *Brogden v. Metropolitan Railway*,[61] where the parties had acted in accordance with an unsigned draft agreement for the delivery of consignments of coal, it was held that there was a contract on the basis of the draft. That interference was drawn from the performance in accordance with the terms of the draft agreement.[62] Similarly, in *Weatherby v. Banham*,[63] the court ruled that the unsolicited sending of goods was an offer made by the supplier that was accepted if the recipient used them.[64] In cyberspace, the supplier can accept by sending the ordered goods, by transmitting the data.

---

[58] N.B.: In the normal context, however, a contract of adhesion is usually a take it or leave it *offer* by the supplier to be accepted by the customer. In this on-line scenario, the supplier is trying to impose terms on the customer's offer, further complicating matters.
[59] *Tinn v. Hoffman & Co* (1873) 29 L.T. 271 cited in Cheshire 51.
[60] *Hotmail Corporation v. Van Money Pie Inc.,* C98–20064 (N.D. Cal., April 20, 1998).
[61] Brogden (1877), 2 A.C. 666.
[62] *G. Percy Trentham Ltd v. Archital Luxfer Ltd and Others* [1993] 1 Lloyd's Rep. 25.
[63] *Weatherby v. Banham* (1832) 5 C. & P. 228.
[64] Under the Unsolicited Goods and Services Act 1971, such "inertia selling" is now prohibited in the U.K. In other words, the law views the merchant as having offered a gift to the consumer, and thus the consumer does not have to pay for the goods if he/she uses them.

Generally, acceptance cannot be assumed from silence.[65] However, for online contracts, since a prudent supplier will rigidly specify all the terms in the offer, silence may be construed as acceptance because one might reasonably assume that the supplier will accept its own terms. As always, the best method of removing this risk is for a supplier to specify in the contract how it will communicate an acceptance.

Contract creation

The instant of acceptance is the instant of contract creation. When and where a **3.39** contract is created can be critical if a dispute ever arises. The exact time of acceptance is important if there are competing acceptances (*e.g.* a unique object is sold to the first person to agree to the terms) or if the offer is revoked at some point. The location of acceptance plays a role in the law, jurisdiction and implied terms which will apply to the contract.

Historically, the instant of contract creation was less important because parties tended to be in the same country, and most contracts were formed in person. As businesses began to utilise post, phone, fax, and telex for transactions, the courts developed new rules. Even so, contracts were still generally confined within one country. However, global e-commerce makes choice of law (paragraph 4.22) and jurisdiction (paragraph 4.02) significant concerns. Thus, the moment of online contract creation takes on a new, greater level of importance.

The English courts developed two rules, the postal rule and the receipt rule, to determine the moment of acceptance for contracts formed by post and telex. An examination of these two rules, which attempt to most fairly distribute risk, might suggest how the courts will deal with e-mail and web contracts.

Postal Rule. According to Lindley J. in *Byrne v. Van Tienhoven*: **3.40**

> "It may be taken as now settled that, where an offer is made and accepted by letters sent through the post, the contract is completed the moment the letter accepting the offer is posted, even though it never reaches its destination."[66]

The postal rule, first established in *Adams v. Lindsell*,[67] seemingly places an unfair burden on the offeror, because the offeror is contractually bound to a contract before being notified. The reason for the principle is the attempt to distribute risk to those most able to control it. The offeror alone selects the method for communicating an acceptance. If the offeror wishes to use the post then the risks should fall to it. Also, once the acceptance is posted, the offeree loses control over the risks of miscommunication or non-delivery. Thus, the law minimises the risk for the offeree by default, but the offeror is well positioned to change it.

Receipt Rule **3.41**

The courts have used the receipt rule for instances in which the two parties have continuous communications. For example, if the two parties are communicating over the phone or in-person, the offeror must hear the acceptance, and only then is the contract created.

---

[65] *Felthouse v. Bindley* (1862) 11 C.B.N.S. 869.
[66] *Byrne v. Van Tienhoven* (1880) 5 C.P.D. 344 at 348, cited in *Cheshire* at p. 54.
[67] *Adams v. Lindsell* (1818) 1 B. & Ald. 681.

The receipt rule further applies to modern methods like telex. As Parker L.J. stated in *Entores Ltd v. Miles Far East Corp.*[68] concerning acceptance using telex:

"Where, however, the parties are in each other's presence or, though separated in space, communication between them is in effect instantaneous, there is no need for any such rule of convenience [postal rule]. To hold otherwise would leave no room for the operation of the general rule that notification of the acceptance must be received. An acceptor could say: 'I spoke the words of acceptance in your presence, albeit softly, and it matters not that you did not hear me'; or 'I telephoned to you and accepted, and it matters not that the telephone went dead and you did not get my message.'"[69]

3.42   The House of Lords later confirmed this ruling in *Brinkibon v. Stahag Stahl und Stahlwarenhandelsgesellschaft mbH*[70] which involved a telex acceptance. Essentially, the principle is that if both parties are in continuous communication during the acceptance, the burden of notification falls on the accepting party (offeree), who has immediate feedback. Even in the case of telex or fax, where both parties are not necessarily personally involved, the devices communicate with each other and there is feedback. The offeree is thus in the best position to discover a transmission fault and can re-send the message as needed.

One should note, however, that with respect to the time of contract formation, the time at which the telex, fax, or e-mail (see below) is expected to be read may be more important than the actual time of receipt. According to *Schelde Delta Shipping BV v. Astarte Shipping Ltd (The Pamela)*,[71] if an acceptance is sent outside of normal business hours, receipt is not effective until the opening of business the next day (or, in the case of *Schelde*, on the Monday morning after the weekend).

3.43 *Rules for online acceptances.*

In light of the postal rule and the receipt rule, where will e-mail and web contracts be formed? As previously mentioned, this question is important, because the place of creation affects many factors critical to dispute resolution such as implied terms, choice of law, and jurisdiction. No case law has decided this question yet, but looking at the attributes of both forms of communications may reveal what the courts might decide if such a dispute should arise as it inevitably will.

(1) Electronic Mail

As the electronic analogy of post, e-mail seems most suited for the postal rule. E-mail is not instantaneous and the sender does not normally receive any immediate or continuous feedback concerning the delivery of the message. Once the offeree clicks the "send" button, control of the messages is lost. The e-mail is sent off into the Internet and routed around by various computers until it reaches its destination. The same issues of uncertainty for sending messages through the post apply to e-mail as well. Whether e-mail acceptances are effective at the time of sending or at the time of receipt, one party will be uncertain as to whether contract creation has occurred. Thus, the courts might as well choose the rule that gives the earliest time of acceptance.

---

[68] *Entores Ltd v. Miles Far East Corp.* [1955] 2 Q.B. 327.
[69] *ibid.* at 336.
[70] *Brinkibon v. Stahag Stahl und Stahlwarenhandelsgesellschaft mbH* [1983] 2 A.C. 34.
[71] *Schelde Delta Shipping B.V. v. Astarte Shipping Ltd (The Pamela)* [1995] 2 Lloyd's Rep. 249.

If e-mail acceptances fall under the postal rule, online contracts would form at the instant the offeree sent the message. Consequently, unless there was a contractual term to the contrary, the residence or place of business of contract formation would be the location of the offeree, not at the offeree's mail server and certainly not at location of the offeror. If a merchant structures the contract negotiation process so that the solicitation is an invitation to treat and the customer makes the offer (as previously assumed), then the sequence works perfectly. When the merchant sends the e-mail acceptance, the contract is formed within the merchant's jurisdiction (indeed, exactly where the merchant is located).

Nonetheless, reasons also exist for arguing that e-mail acceptances be subject to the **3.44** receipt rule. The courts originally formed the postal rule on the basis that the post was reasonably fast and very reliable.[72] E-mail, however, is not as reliable as the post. In cyberspace, e-mails can get lost,[73] become garbled, and are often rejected by corporate firewalls.[74] In addition, unlike the postal service but similar to the telex in *Entores*, the sender (offeree) of an e-mail message is likely to know if a message does not arrive at its destination. If there is a transmission fault or a non-existent address the e-mail will often be "bounced back" to the sender with an error message indicating that it was not received by the intended person. Unlike the post, e-mail is usually fast enough (returned within a few hours) for the sender to take remedial action if an error should occur.

Nevertheless, just because an e-mail message arrives at its destination does not necessarily mean that the e-mail is coherent or complete. Normally, there should be enough information in an incoherent e-mail to enable the receiver (offeror) to ask the sender to re-send the message. However, severe incompatibilities or problems can result in both parties never understanding each other. (Here is a genuine difference between e-mail and postal mail; letters in the post do not get accidentally rewritten by the postal authorities at each end.) Given these reasons, particularly the reduced reliability and increased risk of non-delivery, does a postal rule for e-mail place an undue burden on the offeror? Perhaps the receipt rule is in order.[75]

If e-mail does fall under the receipt rule, then, the contract would form at the offeror's **3.45** location. However, a receipt rule for e-mail raises a number of other thorny issues. For example, where does receipt actually occur? Is receipt when the acceptance arrives at the offeror's mail server, when it is downloaded it onto the computer, or when the offeror reads it? The location of the mail server often differs from the offeror's computer and, depending on the frequency that a person checks and reads e-mail, the respective times can also significantly vary. Whether a person has a continuous Internet connection or a "dial-up" connection may also affect the time and location of receipt.

In determing the precise time of receipt, the courts will most likely use the aforementioned doctrine in *Schelde Delta Shipping B.V. v. Astarte Shipping Ltd (The Pamela)*,[76] based on the expected time of receipt. Accordingly, receipt will usually occur when the offeror downloads the message, since one would expect a user to read the message after

---

[72] After all, back in the nineteenth century, the Royal Mail delivered letters several times a day in London.

[73] Under the postal rule, if the e-mail acceptance is lost in the post, the contract is still binding. *Household Fire Insurance Co. Ltd v. Grant* (1879) 4 Ex.D. 216.

[74] Firewalls are dedicated computers which guard the entrance to a network (usually belonging on a particular company or organisation). Their job is often to block any potentially malicious files (such as e-mails and their attachments) and to prevent intrusions by hackers. N.B.: e-mails without attachments, that is to say simple ASCII messages are far less likely to get lost or corrupted than e-mail messages containing attachments.

[75] The receipt here must logically mean that the offeror has been able to read the message, not simply that the offeror's computer has received the message. The receipt should be intelligible to the offeror.

[76] *Schelde Delta Shipping B.V. v. Astarte Shipping Ltd (The Pamela)* [1995] 2 Lloyd's Rep. 249.

downloading it from the server. Whether or not the offeror actually reads the acceptance will probably be immaterial. If the offeror refuses to read the e-mail acceptance, the offeror will probably still be held liable. Additionally, the offeror is expected to download his messages with reasonable frequency. If the offeror seldom checks e-mail (or is, about to go on holiday) there is probably a duty of care to inform the offeree, otherwise the acceptance will probably be effective after a reasonable time.

3.46   An alternative perspective[77] on acceptance might hold that receipt occurs when it arrives at a computer under the offeror's control. To hold the sender (offeree) responsible for the e-mail after that point would be unfair since the offeror would then be in the better position to manage risks. Thus, if the offeror uses an Internet service provider (ISP), acceptance will be effective only after the e-mail is downloaded off the server onto the computer. In accordance with recent court decisions, this interpretation views ISPs as public telecommunication operators.[78] While the e-mail is on the ISP mail server, it is still technically "in transit" and the responsibility of the sender. However, if the offeror operates his/her own mail server then acceptance would be effected when the e-mail arrives there, transit being complete.

Irrespective of exactly where and when receipt is actually effective, the receipt rule for e-mail contract formation unfortunately does not work with the contract negotiation structure previously advocated for online merchants. If the supplier wishes to retain the option of acceptance/refusal (the price lists being merely invitations to treat), the customer must necessarily be the offeror. However, under the receipt rule, this arrangement necessitates that the contract forms in the customer's jurisdiction, where the customer receives the merchant's acceptance. E-businesses thus face the unwelcome prospect of forming and enforcing contracts in scattered jurisdictions throughout the world.

Selecting and applying one of the existing acceptance rules to e-mail acceptances will continue to pose problems because e-mail has attributes found both in posting messages and in more instantaneous forms of communication. If and when disputes arise on this subject, the courts will certainly have to make a difficult choice. In the meanwhile, there is a possible solution for e-businesses, discussed in paragraph 3.47 below, to reduce the risks and uncertantities.

3.47 *(2) Website contracts*

Unlike e-mail contracts, which fall somewhere in between the postal rule and the receipt rule and thus cause confusion, determining an acceptance rule for contracts made over the World Wide Web is more straightforward. The World Wide Web exhibits the features of a method of instantaneous communication (interactive and in real-time), the sender has almost immediate feedback, and errors or faults are readily apparent. As a result the receipt rule will probably apply to web contracts.

However, just as in the case of e-mail, use of the receipt rule hinders the creation of contracts within the e-businesses own jurisdiction. Again, if the e-commerce business retains the right to accept, the acceptance is not effective until it reaches the customer, thus creating the contract in the customer's jurisdiction. Paragraph 3.48 suggests a possible solution to this problem.

---

[77] Trystan C.G. Tether, Bird & Bird, "Contracting on the Internet," IBC Conference, January 28, 1998.
[78] *Zeran v. America Online* [1997] No. 97–1523 FED App. 1523P (4th Cir.). *Electronic Citation.*

Specifying the means of acceptance

The receipt rule gives e-businesses a choice between two means of acceptance. Due to **3.48** the sequence of exchanges necessary to form a contract, merchants can only use one or the other of the two following scenarios:

Scenario A: Merchants make it clear that their e-mail solicitations and website catalogues or displays are only invitations to treat. The customer makes the offer (under standard terms and conditions written by the merchant) so that the merchant can accept or refuse the contract at its discretion, protecting its interests (as discussed in paragraph 3.30). However, under the receipt rule, the merchant's acceptance is not effective until the offeror (customer) receives it. Thus, the contract is created in the customer's (possibly foreign) jurisdiction. If a dispute later arises, the merchant may need to sue the customer in a foreign court. (See paragraph 4.01 on choice of law and jurisdiction issues).

Scenario B: Although they may still disclaim their preliminary e-mails and websites as invitations to treat, at some point, the merchants have to make the offers. The customer accepts the offer, and under the receipt rule, the contract forms when the merchant receives the acceptance. This scenario thus ensures that the contract is formed in the merchant's jurisdiction. However, once accepted by the customer, the merchant can no longer refuse the contract because it would be a breach. If supply of the particular product becomes scarce, the online merchant would be still liable, unless it can escape through some other means such as frustration using the legal doctrines of or impossibility.

Fortunately, online merchants may not have to make this difficult choice. Under **3.49** English law, the receipt or postal rules only apply if the offer does not specify an explicit method of acceptance. Therefore, in most cases, the offeror can override the default rule and prescribe the method of acceptance.[79] Consequently, merchants might be able to act in accordance with Scenario A, but would additionally specify in the standard terms and conditions that acceptance is effective once sent (postal rule). This arrangement would succeed in retaining the online merchant's right to accept or refuse while ensuring that the contract is formed in the merchant's jurisdiction. Additionally, the standard contract should also have choice of law and jurisdiction clauses which are favourable to the supplier.

Whether or not the courts will decide that such favourable terms for the e-business are unfair (and thus invalid) is unknown. In addition, many jurisdictions have mandatory consumer protection laws that will invalidate this construction in the case of consumer contracts. However, since e-businesses essentially have nothing to lose, amending the standard terms and conditions to include these clauses may be worth considering.

Revocation and Counteroffer

Naturally, not all offers are eventually accepted. The offeree might reject the offer, or **3.50** propose a counteroffer. The offer may lapse after a specified time or event, or it may be revoked by the offeror. For the most part, under the prescribed method of contracting, online businesses will be in the position of the offeree (with the right to accept) and will not need to worry about revocation or counter offering. However, in some cases, businesses may find themselves making the offer and thus should keep the relevant legal rules in mind.

---

[79] *Chitty on Contracts*, para. 2–042.

Lapse and Revocation

Terms usually included in an offer determine the time during which the offer is effective. As a result, an offer may lapse after a period of time or after some specified event. If the period of validity is not specified, the courts will imply that the offer lapses after a reasonable period. Determination of this reasonable period depends on factors such as the contract's subject matter and the method of communication used by the parties.[80]

3.51 In addition to the automatic lapsing of an offer, the offeror may revoke it at any time up until the moment of acceptance, irrespective of any terms that specify the period in which the offer is valid.[81] However, a revocation must be received (*i.e.* the receipt rule) before it is effective, as was expressed in *Byrne v. Van Tienhoven*.[82] This rule was traditionally used to resolve disputes where a revocation was posted before, but not received before, an acceptance was sent. Nonetheless, such a situation is unlikely to arise in e-commerce, even if e-mails fell under the postal rule.

On the Internet, the offeror can revoke an offer using e-mail, but whether it can be revoked by placing a notice on a website is doubtful. Since the revocation notice needs to be actually received by the offeree, a web display will probably not suffice. This implication represents another reason why online merchants should be wary of creating unilateral contracts (paragraph 3.12).

Counteroffer and the Battle of the Forms

3.52 According to *Hyde v. Wrench*,[83] making a counteroffer necessarily means the rejection of the original offer.[84] If an offeree's counteroffer is subsequently rejected, it cannot then unilaterally resurrect and accept the original offer. The original offer is dead, and the original offeror is at liberty to restate the offer or not. Additionally, since an acceptance must be an unequivocal assent to all terms, if the "acceptance" contains additional or modified terms, it is technically a counteroffer and no contract is formed.

In the course of normal contract negotiations, e-businesses will, of course, seek to impose their own standard terms and conditions to protect their interests.[85] Although this situation will seldom occur in standardised web contracts, where the offeree has no opportunity to amend or change, it can certainly occur during e-mail negotiations. For example, Party A sends its offer on its e-mail template containing its standard terms and conditions. Party B, wishing to contract with A, sends the acceptance on its own standard e-mail template with different (and probably conflicting) terms and conditions. Essentially, the two parties agree on all major points, such as product, quantity, price, etc., but the standard terms differ on ancillary issues, such warranties jurisdiction or choice of law. This situation is known as the "battle of the forms".

3.53 As explained above, strictly speaking, no contract is formed. Neither party has unequivocally accepted the other's offer, but rather a series of counteroffers have been e-mailed back and forth. In *Butler Machine Tool Co. v. Ex-Cell-O Co.*,[86] Lawton L.J. favoured this "no-contract" viewpoint. However, since a "battle of the forms" occurs

---

[80] *Ramsgate Victoria Hotel Co. v. Montefiore* (1866) L.R. 1 Exch. 109.
[81] *Routledge v. Grant* (1828) 4 Bing. 653; *Dickinson v. Dodds* (1874) 2 Ch.D. 463, and *Chitty on Contracts* para. 2–059.
[82] *Byrne v. VanTienhoven* (1880) 5 C.P.D. 44.
[83] *Hyde v. Wrench* (1840) 3 Beav. 334. See also *Chitty on Contracts,* para. 2–063.
[84] *Trollope & Colls Ltd v. Atomic Power Constructions Ltd* [1962] 3 All E.R. 1035.
[85] Indeed, the reader will notice that construction of these standard terms and conditions is a substantial focus in this chapter.
[86] *Butler Machine Tool Co. v. Ex-Cell-O Co.* [1979] 1 All E.R. 965.

often in the commercial world, this view would invalidate many contracts. Lord Denning M.R. offered a slightly different perspective in *Butler:*

> "In many of these cases our traditional analysis of offer, counter-offer, rejection, acceptance and so forth is out-of date . . . The better way is to look at all the documents passing between the parties and glean from them, or from the conduct of the parties, whether they have reached agreement on all material points, even though there may be differences between the forms and conditions printed on the back of them . . . The terms and conditions of both parties are to be construed together. If they can be reconciled so as to give a harmonious result, all well and good. If differences are reconcilable, so that they are mutually contradictory, then the conflicting terms may have to be scrapped and replaced by a reasonable implication."[87]

Under Lord Denning M.R.'s interpretation, a contract is created, but neither party should benefit from the discrepancy in standard terms. The court must find mutual ground or else create some mutual benefit.[88]

Another perspective on the "battle of the forms", is found in the Uniform Laws on International Sales Act 1967, which is applicable only to international sale of goods and is only found in limited form in English law. However, it does offer an plausible alternative view. Article 7 of Schedule 2 states:

3.54

> "A reply to an offer which purports to be an acceptance but which contains additional or different terms which do no materially alter the terms of the offer shall constitute an acceptance unless the offeror promptly objects to the discrepancy; if he does not so object, the terms of the contract shall be the terms of the offer with the modifications contained in the acceptance."[89]

Under this interpretation, online merchants face a possible danger. If the offeree sends back an acceptance with new terms and conditions, and the offeror is silent, the offeror may become bound by the new terms unless a response is sent.

A similar danger derives from the actual facts in *Butler Machine Tool v. Ex-Cell-O Co.,* where the original offeror (the seller, Butler) received an "acceptance" with new terms and conditions and then proceeded to send back the acknowledgement slip. As the court ruled:

3.55

> ". . . an acceptance of that counter-offer [the 'acceptance' with new terms and conditions] . . . is shown by the acknowledgement which the sellers signed and returned to the buyers."[90]

By sending the acknowledgement, the seller implicitly accepted the buyer's conditions. In this case, the implied assent is arguably stronger than in the case of silence (above).

Disputes involving "battle of the forms" are complex. Consequently, online businesses should protect themselves by prudently refraining from any action that might implicitly indicate acceptance of the other party's terms and conditions. They should not return any forms provided by the other party, and should probably not even send e-mails acknowledging receipt of an "acceptance". Failing to observe this caution may result in being inadvertently bound to unfavourable terms.

Consideration

Consideration is the element which typically transforms a mere promise into a legally binding contract. Consideration is often defined as the exchange of something of value,

3.56

---

[87] *ibid.* at 968d.
[88] According to Cheshire 168fn, "Lord Denning's views here are reminiscent of his views in *Gibson v. Manchester City Council* [1978] 2 All E.R. 583, [1978] 1 W.L.R. 520, which were emphatically disapproved of by the House of Lords [1979] 1 All E.R. 972, [1979] 1 W.L.R. 294. . . . Of course, the *Gibson* case did not involve a battle of the forms.".
[89] Uniform Laws on International Sales Act 1967, Sched. 2, art. 7.
[90] *Butler Machine Tool Co. v. Ex-Cell-O Co.* [1979] 1 All E.R. 965 at 968a.

but can include a detriment to the promisee or a benefit to the promisor. In requiring consideration, common law represents contract as a sort of bargain where the promisee must pay or give something to the promisor in return for the goods, services, or other benefit it receives.

English courts interpret the consideration requirement, and often will even "invent consideration", regarding something as consideration even broadly though the promisor did not necessarily want it.[91] Consequently, the requirement of consideration is usually easy to satisfy. For normal commercial transactions, consideration poses no threat to online contracts and e-commerce. The goods, services, or digitised services provided by the online merchant and the payment given by the customer fully satisfy the requirement for consideration.

The only possibly novel situation is with so-called "web-wrap" or "click-wrap" agreements, where a website requires a customer to agree to certain terms and conditions before delivering a digitised service. Many of these click-wrap agreements protect free websites, shareware or freeware (software that is distributed on a trial or free basis respectively). Usually, the website requires a customer to agree to certain terms and conditions, which exclude liability or prohibit commercial use, before allowing the customer to download the digitised service. One concern is whether a click-wrap agreement has any consideration. Whether free software or access to a website represents a benefit and thereby consideration is probably likely, but unknown.

Intention to Create Legal Relations

3.57 The final element of contract formation, the intent to create legal relations, is also easily satisfied under most circumstances. Indeed, in a commercial transaction with an explicit contract, intention is automatically presumed. The onus of proving otherwise "is on the party who asserts that no legal effect is intended, and the onus is a heavy one".[92] Disputes regarding this requirement typically only arise when some part of a letter or offer specifically mentions that no legal consequences will arise from it.[93]

One should note that the intention to create legal relations discussed here does not relate to errors in judgment or belief. The former asks only whether the parties were interested in involving the courts in their agreement, as opposed to making an informal, friendly promise.[94] The latter, on the other hand, is dealt with by the doctrine of mistake which is applicable when one or both parties makes an error in judgment.

3.58 In the context of e-commerce, which typically involves commercial contracts, intent will normally automatically exist. However, there is one possible exception, where an unclear or perhaps deceptive website dupes a consumer into making an unwanted contract. For example, an online merchant offering a digitised service may construct a makeshift website which gives no purchasing information and merely displays the product and a "Save" or "Download Now" button. An unsuspecting customer will probably assume that the service is free and has no intention of creating a contract when he/she clicks the button. In the event of a dispute, the courts would most likely not allow the online merchant to demand payment for the digitised services delivered on the basis of an absence of intention to create legal relations.

---

[91] *Chitty on Contracts*, para. 3–008.
[92] *Edwards v. Skyways Ltd* [1964] 1 W.L.R. 349 at 355. Cited in *Chitty on Contracts*, para. 2–106.
[93] *Rose and Frank v. Crompton* [1923] 2 K.B. 261; reversed [1925] A.C. 445.
[94] As Cheshire and Fifoot suggests, "Agreements are made every day, in domestic and in social life, where the parties do not intend to invoke the assistance of the courts should the engagement not be honoured. To offer a friend a meal is not to invite litigation."

To avoid this possibility, e-businesses should ensure that websites explicitly state the prices and terms of their digitised services. The customer should go through a sequence of web pages detailing the transaction terms and conditions, culminating in a "last chance" screen where the customer either submits the offer or cancels it without legal ramifications. Establishing this purchasing framework will prevent misunderstandings and will lead to online contracts with greater enforceability.

WRITING AND SIGNATURE REQUIREMENTS

> The general rule of English law is that contracts can be made quite informally: no writing or other form is necessary.[95]

Probably the most common legal myth held by the general public is that contracts under English law must be in writing and have a signature. Indeed, most contracts, such as purchasing goods from a retailer, involve no written documentation at all. In most cases, English law does not require writing or signatures[96]; these requirements only manifest themselves in specific statutes. Today, only a few types of contracts are specifically required by statute to be signed and in writing. For example, under section 2 of the Law of Property (Miscellaneous Provisions) Act 1989, **3.59**

"A contract for the sale or other disposition of an interest in land can only be made in writing and only by incorporating all the terms which the parties have expressly agreed in one document or, where contracts are exchanged, in each."[97]

Additionally,

"The document incorporating the terms or, where contracts are exchanged, one of the documents incorporating them (but not necessarily the same one) must be signed by or on behalf of each party to the contract."[98]

Other instances which require writing and signatures include leases for over three years,[99] consumer credit,[1] certain forms of insurance, deeds, wills, and the transfer of shares. Failure to abide by the requirements may render the contract inadmissible as evidence, unenforceable, or completely void. **3.60**

As these examples make clear, there are only a few instances of when a signed, written contract is required in writing. Most e-commerce contracts will not be affected. Nevertheless, having signed and explicitly written contracts is generally helpful, since it increases certainty, provides evidence, and prevents the creation of hasty or careless contracts.

However, other jurisdictions may have far more stringent contract requirements. In the context of global e-commerce, online businesses may need to comply with foreign requirements to ensure enforceability of their contracts.

---

[95] *Chitty on Contracts*, para. 4–001.
[96] The only exception is that prior to 1960, corporations were required to contract under seal. However, even this requirement was abolished under the Corporate Bodies' Contract Act 1960.
[97] Law of Property (Miscellaneous Provisions) Act 1989, s.2(1).
[98] *ibid.*, s.2(3).
[99] Law of Property Act 1925, s.52.
[1] Consumer Credit Act 1974.

Article 9 of the Electronic Commerce Directive[2] requires Member States to adjust their national regime to remove restrictions on the use of electronic media to enter into contracts. The U.K. E-Commerce Bill will give power to remove restrictions which prevent e-commerce in place of paper.

The Requirement of Writing

3.61   Under the Interpretation Act 1978, writing is defined as "typing, printing, lithography, photography and other modes of representing or reproducing words in a visible form."[3] Unfortunately, this definition does not answer the question of whether a digital contract satisfies the requirement of writing. For example, if a contract is displayed on a computer screen, it is indeed in visible form, but it is neither tangible nor permanent. Without any relevant case law for guidance it is difficult to predict how the courts will decide this issue.

However, in recent times, Parliament and the courts have generally appeared amenable towards expanding the definition of writing to include digital documents. The Civil Evidence Act 1995 removed previous requirements that documents had to be "original" (in written form) in order to be admissible.[4] The Copyright, Designs and Patents Act 1988 defines writing as including:

> "any form of notation or code, whether by hand or otherwise and regardless of the method by which, or medium in or on which, it is recorded."[5]

Finally, the court in *Derby & Co. Ltd v. Weldon* held that computer databases (files) are valid documents for discovery:

> "The database, so far as it contains information capable of being retrieved and converted into readable form, is a document within the meaning of R.S.C. Ord. 24 of which discovery must be given . . ."[6]

3.62   These trends suggest that courts will probably deem online and other digital contracts as "writing". Other common law jurisdictions such as the United States have similarly attempted to extend writing to include digital forms. The Uniform Commercial Code defines writing as "printing, typewriting, or any other intentional reduction to tangible form."[7] This tradition goes back to the nineteenth century when a U.S. court in reference to the telegraph suggested that:

> "[i]t makes no difference whether that operator writes the offer or the acceptance . . . with a steel pen an inch long attached to an ordinary penholder, or whether his pen be a copper wire a thousand miles long."[8]

Similarly, other technologies such as telexes and faxes[9] were held to be writing in the U.S., culminating in this instructive opinion given in *Clyburn v. Allstate*:

> "In today's 'paperless' society of computer generated information, the court is not prepared, in the absence of some legislative provision or otherwise, to find that a computer floppy diskette would not constitute a 'writing' within the meaning of [the Statute]."[10]

---

[2] Proposal for a European Parliament and Council Directive 98/0325 on certain legal aspects of electronic commerce in the internal market dated November 18, 1998.

[3] Interpretation Act 1978, Sched. 1.

[4] Civil Evidence Act 1995, s.8. Evidentiary requirements are discussed in Chapter 6.

[5] Copyright, Designs, and Patents Act 1988, s.178.

[6] *Derby & Co. Ltd v. Weldon (No. 9)* [1991] 1 W.L.R. 652 at 654.

[7] Uniform Commercial Code s.1–201(46).

[8] *Howley v. Whipple* 48 N.H. 487 (1869).

[9] *Bazak International Co. v. Mast Industries, Inc.* 73 N.Y.2d 111, 7 UCC Rep. Serv. 2d 1380 (1989).

[10] *Clyburn v. Allstate* 826 F.Supp. 955 (D.S.C. 1993).

Signature Requirement

A signature is normally assumed to involve the writing of some name or identifying   **3.63**
mark on a document. However, just as the courts have extended the definition of writing
beyond and including on paper, so too have they broadened the concept of signature.
The English law definition of signature is best summed up by the decision in *Goodman v.
J. Eban Ltd*,[11] where the court validated the use of a rubber stamp as a signature:

> "Where an Act of Parliament requires that any particular document be 'signed' by a person, then, *prima
> facie*, the requirement of the Act is satisfied if the person himself places on the document an engraved
> representation of his signature by means of a rubber stamp . . . The essential requirement of signing is
> the affixing in some way, whether by writing with a pen or pencil or by otherwise impressing upon the
> document, one's name or 'signature' so as personally to authenticate the document."[12]

Consistent with this interpretation, the more recent case of *Re a Debtor (No. 2021 of
1995)* held that a faxed copy of a signature satisfied a relevant statutory signature
requirement. In the court's opinion, it was hard to see why some methods of "impressing
the mark on paper" would be more valid than others.[13] Indeed, Laddie J. even suggested
that if the signature was digitised and later appended to the fax (thus making the fax the
first tangible copy of the document), the document (or contract) should be regarded as
signed.

As these cases demonstrate, the key concept of signature is the authentication it
symbolises rather than its physical manifestation. A signature represents an endorsement
of the given document, and whether it is written, typed, or stamped makes no
difference.[14] All that matters legally is the person's intention to agree and to authenticate.

E-mail signatures

How will contracting parties "sign" online contracts? Under the broad interpretations   **3.64**
of signature given above, merely typing one's name at the end of an e-mail will probably
suffice, as long as there was an intention to authenticate. Additionally, the "signature-
file" often automatically or manually appended to e-mails could be considered as a form
of letterhead and thus a signature as well.

However, as in the case of evidence, admissibility does not equal weight. Just because
a court recognises a particular form of signature does not mean that it will give any
significant weight to it, and understandably so. The basic electronic signatures mentioned
above are can be easily forged: a fraudster need only type another person's name or "cut
and paste" over another signature-file. The forger does not even need to go through the
pains of stealing or recreating letterhead and the loops and lines of a "traditional"
signature.

To ensure that the courts give greater legal weight to signatures created online, more
sophisticated methods are required. Thus, in the future, particularly for larger transactions, merchants may use digital signatures (further discussed in Chapter 6) or other

---

[11] *Goodman v. J Eban Ltd* [1954] 1 Q.B. 550.

[12] *ibid.* at 557.

[13] *Re a Debtor* (No. 2021 of 1995) [1996] 2 All E.R. 345 at 351.

[14] Cases in the United States have subscribed to a similar position, holding the validity of signatures that are
typed (*Watson v. Tom Growney Equip. Inc.* 721 P.2d 1302 (N.M. 1986)), represented by company letterhead
(*Kohlmeyer & Co. v. Bowen* 126 Ga. App. 700 192 S.E.2d 400 (1972)), and faxed (*Beatty v. First Exploration Fund
1987 and Co. Limited Partnership*, 25 B.C.L.R.2d 377 (1988)), though this last case did not involve the U.S. Statute
of Frauds.

forms of authentication codes. Since these methods utilise secret information known only to the parties involved or only to the signer alone (in the case of digital signatures), they offer a far greater level of non-repudiation.

For example, in *Standard Bank London Ltd v. The Bank of Tokyo Ltd*,[15] the banks involved authenticated money transfers by using telexes with a secret code, or "validated telexes". In the case, a fraudster forged three telexes from the Bank of Tokyo, each a letter of credit for several million dollars. The court, however, ruled that a "validated telex" recipient was entirely entitled to rely on it unless otherwise notified or unless there was reason to believe that dishonesty was involved. This decision places significant responsibility on the sending party to secure the codes or keys since, after all, the sending party is in the best position to protect them.

Web signatures

3.65   Web-based click-wrap contracts, which may ultimately become the mainstay of e-commerce, may have difficulties fulfilling signature requirements, though they will seldom arise. Unlike e-mails, where acceptance is usually accompanied by the signing of a name, with web contracts the customer accepts by clicking a button. While actions like clicking a button can signify acceptance, they clearly do not satisfy a signature's definition of being a name or identifying mark.

One possibility for avoiding this problem is to find the signature elsewhere in the contract. The order form for most online contracts has input boxes in which the customer types his/her name, address, e-mail address, etc. A typed or written name, though not at the bottom of the contract, can be construed as a signature. For example, in *Durrell v. Evans*, the court said:

> "If the name of the party to be charged is printed or written on a document intended to be a memorandum of the contract, either by himself or his authorised agent, it is his signature, whether it is at the beginning or middle or foot of the document."[16]

3.66   However, this extremely broad interpretation of signature may not adequately protect consumers, especially in the case of click-wrap contracts. Thus, as a matter of public policy, the courts may rule that click-wrap contracts are not signed. One of the reasons for requiring a signature is its ceremonial implications. When people sign a document they understand that it represents a more serious legal step and consequently may proceed with greater caution. After all, even though signed contracts are generally not required by law, they are often used for their greater legal weight. For example, according to the court in *L'Estrange v. Graucob*,[17] although in unsigned contracts the plaintiff must prove that the defendant was aware of the contractual terms and conditions, no such requirement exists in signed contracts. As Scrutton L.J. suggests:

> "In cases in which the contract is contained in a railway ticket or other unsigned document, it is necessary to prove that an alleged party was aware, or ought to have been aware, of its terms and conditions. These cases have no application when the document has been signed. When a document containing contractual terms is signed, then, in the absence of fraud, or, I will add, misrepresentation, the party signing it is bound, and it is wholly immaterial whether he has read the document or not."[18]

---

[15] *Standard Bank London Ltd v. The Bank of Tokyo Ltd* [1996] 1 C.T.L.R. T–17.

[16] *Durrell v. Evans* (1862) 1 H. & C. 174 at 191.

[17] *L'Estrange v. Graucob* [1934] 2 K.B. 394.

[18] *ibid.* at 403 cited in Cheshire at p. 168.

Based on how the general public currently views online "clicks", click-wrap contracts offer few of the ceremonial elements found in signed documents. Consequently, click-wraps are far less effective in communicating the danger or legal implications of the situation. Furthermore, unlike in a traditional contract where all terms are immediately visible (albeit in small print), online documents often hide the contractual terms by providing a hyperlink reference. Thus, recognising click-wrap contracts as signed contracts may create a system whereby people are unknowingly bound to serious contracts, a situation that the signature requirement was originally intended to prevent.

Model Laws

A number of efforts, most notably the United Nations Commission on International Trade Law (UNCITRAL)'s Model Law on e-commerce 1996,[19] have attempted to remove writing and signature requirements to provide greater certainty to online contracts and to promote e-commerce. The Model Law focuses primarily on broadly redrafting statutes to encompass the electronic equivalents of writing and signatures. It first develops the concept of a "data message", the electronic equivalent of a written document, which includes e-mail, EDI, telex, etc.[20] Thereafter, in Articles 6 and 7, it redefines the concepts of writing and signature to fit into the digital world. **3.67**

The Model Law reduces writing to its most essential legal property, permanence. Article 6 ensures that data messages qualify as writing so long as they can be retrieved:

> "Where the law requires information to be in writing, that requirement is met by a data message if the information contained therein is accessible so as to be usable for subsequent reference."[21]

Similarly, it reduces signature to its endorsement or authentication property.

> "Where the law requires a signature of a person, that requirement is met in relation to a data message if:
>
> (a) a method is used to identify that person and to indicate that person's approval of the information contained in the data message; and
> (b) that method is as reliable as was appropriate for the purpose for which the data message was generated or communicated, in the light of all the circumstance, including any relevant agreement."[22]

The Model Law also verifies the enforceability of online contracts, providing that both offer and acceptance may be in the form of a data message, and that contracts "shall not be denied validity or enforceability on the sole ground that a data message was used for that purpose."[23] **3.68**

From the preceding discussion on online contracts, English law appears to agree wholeheartedly with the Model Law on issues such as writing, signatures and the enforceability of the online contract. However, one should note that most of the English precedents applicable to writing and signatures are from the period before computers and the Internet. Whether the courts will extend these principles into the digital age remains to be seen. Nonetheless, UNICTRAL's Model Law represents a good baseline and may hold some influence with the court should a dispute over online contracts arise.

---

[19] UNCITRAL's Model Law has met with some success, including its pivotal role in Singapore's Electronic Transactions Bill 1998.
[20] United Nations Commission on International Trade Law, Model Law on Electronic Commerce, Art. 2(a).
[21] UNCITRAL Model Law on Electronic Commerce, Art. 6(1).
[22] *ibid.*, Art. 7(1).
[23] *ibid.*, Art. 11(1).

ONLINE CONTRACT TERMS AND CONDITIONS

3.69 Most online contracts will not be formed after lengthy discussions and negotiations over specific terms and clauses. Rather, they will generally be standard form contracts, also called contracts of adhesion. Besides key issues, such as price and type/quantity of goods or services, the terms in these contracts are not negotiated but are offered on a "take-it-or-leave-it" basis. The standard terms and conditions are predrafted by the merchant to protect its interests, and the customer receives them only at the time of purchase, usually with neither the time nor the desire to scrutinise them.

The terms and conditions in these standard contracts often deal with more supplemental matters, such as payment method, exclusion or limitation of liability, warranties, choice of law, and jurisdiction. While e-businesses will understandably try to draft these terms to their advantage as much as possible, they must remain mindful of the restrictions imposed by legislation such as the Unfair Contract Terms Act 1977. English law recognises that customers generally bargain from an inferior position and have these standard terms imposed upon them. It requires that many exclusion clauses be reasonable in order to be enforceable.

Although a complete review of these topics is beyond the scope of the book they warrant detailed analysis because of the growing importance of standard form contracts in e-commerce. The global and virtual nature of the Internet creates new concerns often not considered in the past, such as how to adequately display terms and conditions.[24] On-line merchants will also need to place emphasis on new or different clauses, such as specifying a method of contract formation, limitation of liability, warranties, choice of law, and jurisdiction. This section addresses these issues.

Displaying contract terms online

3.70 The terms and conditions in a standard form contract will have no effect unless the customer is given "notice" of them before the contract is formed.[25] For example, in *Olley v. Marlborough Court Ltd*, a contract for a hotel room, having been signed at the hotel's reception desk, was not subject to terms found on a notice in the bedroom.[26] In general, this "timing issue" should not pose a significant problem for online contracts, because online merchants can easily display the standard terms before a customer submits the order.

However, the requirements of "notice" could pose a greater obstacle to online standard form contracts. Unless the customer signs the contract, in which case all specified terms should be effective,[27] merely displaying the terms somewhere may not be sufficient. In *Parker v. South Eastern Railway Co.*,[28] referring to standard terms printed on a railway ticket, the court (as interpreted by the court in *McCutcheon v. David MacBrayne Ltd*) divided the concept of notice into three questions of fact:

(1) did the passenger know that there was printing on the railway ticket?

(2) did he know that the ticket contained or referred to conditions?

---

[24] See the Data Protection Registrar's concerns about electronic forms not providing warnings to the customers until the end of the form which is acceptable on hard copy forms but less so with on-line forms.

[25] *Chitty on Contracts*, para. 12–009.

[26] *Olley v. Marlborough Court Ltd* [1949] 1 K.B. 532.

[27] *L'Estrange v. Graucob* [1934] 2 K.B. 394. See para. 3.63 Signature Requirement above.

[28] *Parker v. South Eastern Railway Co.* (1877) 2 C.P.D. 416.

(3) did the railway company do what was reasonable in the way of notifying prospective passengers of the existence of conditions and where their terms might be considered?[29]

Simply put by Lord Denning M.R. in *Thornton v. Shoe Lane Parking,* "the customer is **3.71** bound by the . . . condition if he knows that the ticket is issued subject to it; or if the company did what was reasonably sufficient to give him notice of it."[30] An online merchant must make some reasonable effort, not just to make the terms available but also to inform the customer about the existence and meaning of those terms and conditions.

For more onerous conditions, such as ones that deprive the customer of legal rights and remedies, English law demands an even greater effort by the merchant to give notice. In *Thornton,* which dealt with an exemption of liability for personal or bodily injury, Lord Denning M.R. suggested that:

> "It [the exemption] is so wide and so destructive of rights that the court should not hold any man bound by it unless it is drawn to his attention in the most explicit way. It is an instance of what I had in mind in *J. Spurling Ltd v. Bradshaw* [1956] 1 W.L.R. 461–466. In order to give sufficient notice, it would need to be printed in red ink with a red hand pointing to it — or something equally startling."[31]

World Wide Web

The World Wide Web complicates compliance with these notification requirements. **3.72** On-line merchants have various means by which they can inform the customer of their standard terms and conditions. The following list describes a number of them in increasing order of substantiality (*i.e.* greater notice to the customer). However, e-commerce businesses will need to balance legal weight and certainty with the resulting attractiveness of their websites. After all, the web pages are there to promote and sell goods, not as a legal exercise. Dense blocks of "legalese" could be off-putting.

- *Reference Statement without hyperlink* — Merchants could include a statement such as "This contract is subject to Company's standard terms and conditions" at the bottom of the order form. While this small statement may be commercially attractive, it may fail the reasonable notice requirement. The customer may not see the notice and, even if he/she does, there is no access to further information. Making the terms effective in this case would clearly be binding the customer to terms and conditions to which he/she did not assent.

- *Reference Statement with hyperlink* — The reference statement could be linked to a page containing the standard terms and conditions. This technique is popular with many web merchants because it achieves some legal credibility without substantial disruption to the promotional and commercial aspects of the order form or web page. Indeed, it may satisfy the reasonable notice requirement for "usual" terms. In *Parker v. South Eastern Railway,* a notice of "See back" on the front of a railway ticket with the terms and conditions on the back was held to be sufficient notice. This "See back" notice is strikingly similar to the hyperlink at the bottom of a web page.[32]

---

[29] *McCutcheon v. David MacBrayne Ltd* [1964] 1 W.L.R. 125 at 129, referencing *Parker v. South Eastern Railway Co.* (1877) 2 C.P.D. 416, cited in *Thornton v. Shoe Lane Parking* [1971] 2 Q.B. 163 at 171.
[30] *Thornton v. Shoe Lane Parking,* [1971] 2 Q.B. 163 at 170.
[31] *ibid.*
[32] *Parker v. South Eastern Railway* (1877) 2 C.P.D. 416.

3.73   An alternative view, however, is that the hyperlink seemingly hides the terms and conditions from the customer. Just because the terms are somehow accessible does not mean that the user is induced to examine them. For example, in the U.S. case of *Microstar v. Formgen*,[33] the court admonished the merchant for putting the restrictive terms in a separate, non-cross-referenced file that the customer did not necessarily have to view.[34]

For more onerous terms, such as long term financial commitments, the hyperlink method is likely to be inadequate, if one applies Lord Denning's example of using "red ink with a red hand pointing at it." In *Interfoto Picture Library Ltd v. Stiletto Visual Programmes Ltd*,[35] the court ruled that the vendor had a duty to drawn attention to particularly surprising or onerous terms using boldface type or a separately attached note. In that case, the surprising term was a particularly harsh penalty clause for the late return of photographs. Thus, e-businesses using the hyperlink method of displaying terms might best transfer the surprising terms and exclusion/limitation clauses off the 'legal page' and onto the actual order form.

- *Display Terms at Bottom of Page* — Instead of hyperlinking the standard terms and conditions, the merchant could stream the whole text at the bottom of the order form or web page. Since the terms are conspicuously displayed, this method has greater legal weight in terms of notice. However, it can easily make the web page visually unattractive. Also, the user is still a passive participant, since the web page has not required him/her to actively demonstrate that he/she had the opportunity to read the terms and conditions.

- *Dialogue Box* — One of the most elaborate display mechanisms is to create a dialogue box that forces the user to scroll through the terms and conditions before clicking "I agree" or "I have reviewed these terms". Notwithstanding the possibility of this 'click wrap' being held as a signature,[36] this rather draconian approach is legally powerful. The customer is not just given the opportunity to review the terms; indeed, he/she is forced to review them and to agree through a positive action (the "click"). The customer clearly realises that the contract is subject to certain terms and conditions.

3.74   Naturally, the most effective method legally is probably the most undesirable and unattractive method commercially. Not only is the customer's dialogue box filled with lines of legalese, but he/she must also waste time scrolling through and clicking the assent button. The process could be off putting to the customer, especially when purchasing only low value goods in services. However, this method is more visually attractive than simply appending the terms to the bottom of the web page or order form. At least here, the legalese is confined to the smaller dialogue box.

3.75   As previously mentioned, web merchants will have to balance the legal protection and the commercial desirability offered by the above methods. This last option, the dialogue box, however, appears promising. If it can be incorporated into the ordering process, its unattractiveness may be significantly diminished. For example, in the final stage of the order process, after review of the order itself, the web page could require the customer to scroll through the conditions before clicking on the final "Submit order and agree to above terms."

---

[33] *Microstar v. Formgen*, 942 F. Supp. 1312 (S.D. Cal. 1996).
[34] The court in *Microstar*, however, did not rule on the validity on the license in that case.
[35] *Interfoto Picture Library Ltd v. Stiletto Visual Programmes Ltd* [1989] Q.B. 433, [1988] 1 All E.R. 348.
[36] See para. 3.62 argues against the clickwrap signature, but it remains a possibility for the courts.

An alternative method could be only to have first-time customers perform the annoying 'scroll and click process,' assuming that on subsequent occasions the customer is already aware of the standard terms and conditions. As decided in *Spurling v. Bradshaw*,[37] previous dealings can bind a party to standard terms and conditions, even if the party is not presented with the terms on subsequent occasions. Nevertheless, the safest procedure is to present the terms and conditions in every instance.

Electronic mail

Complying with notice requirements in e-mail contracts probably offers the e-business **3.76** very little choice. Standard terms and conditions will probably have to be included at the bottom of the e-mail offer (or invitation to treat) in order to constitute proper notice. E-mails with "phantom" referencing statements such as "this contract is subject to the Company's standard terms and conditions" will not suffice.

Further, placing the terms and conditions in attachments or hyperlinks embedded in the e-mail will meet similar, if not more substantial, objections to the ones explained above for web contracts. For example, e-mail attachments often get removed by firewalls, and thus the terms may not even accompany the e-mail. Additionally, the hyperlinks assume that the e-mail program will support them and that the user has access to the World Wide Web (which will not be the case if a text-only connection is being used).

Express, Implied, and Mandatory Terms

Properly drafted and displayed to the customer, expressly stated standard terms and **3.77** conditions are useful devices for protecting the e-businesses best interests. However, just as in the case of "traditional" contracts, online contracts are subject to implied and mandatory terms. These either "fill in the gaps" between or go beyond the terms expressly stated. This section focuses on these three types of contractual term: express, implied and mandatory. A proper understanding of their distinctions and the issues they raise is essential to any online merchant who wishes to construct enforceable online contracts to their advantage.

Express Terms

In a standard form contract, express terms are found in the standard terms and **3.78** conditions. They directly and explicitly specify on what terms the merchant wishes to conduct business. Express terms can also specifically override any undesirable implied terms, protecting the merchant from unwanted liability or responsibility.[38] Under English law, once the parties have expressed some view on a particular matter in the contract, "they have expressed all the conditions by which they intend to be bound under that agreement."[39]

As the party in the position to draft standard terms and conditions, online merchants appear to have an inherent legal advantage. However, if they fail to exercise care in drafting their standard terms, this advantage can be easily squandered. When the courts interpret written contractual terms, they will focus almost exclusively on the outward appearances and meanings conveyed, not the actual underlying intention of the parties.[40]

---

[37] *Spurling v. Bradshaw* [1956] 2 All E.R. 121.
[38] See para. for a discussion of implied terms.
[39] *Aspdin v. Austin* (1844) 5 Q.B. 671 at 684 cited in *Chitty*, para. 12–078.
[40] *Smith v. Lucas* (1881) 18 Ch.D. 531–542.

The House of Lords confirmed this doctrine in *Deutsche Genossenschaftsbank v. Burnhope*, stating:

> "It is true the objective of the construction [of contract] is to give effect to the intention of the parties. But our law of construction is based on an objective theory. The methodology is not to probe the real intentions of the parties but to ascertain the contextual meaning of the relevant contractual language. Intention is determined by reference to expressed rather than actual intention."[41]

As a result, poorly drafted and ambiguous terms and conditions could result in judicial interpretations unfavourable to the online merchant. Indeed, the interpretations will almost certainly be unfavourable; in the case of vague or ambiguous terms, English law requires the courts to interpret the terms against the party who drafted them.[42] The customer will receive the benefit of the doubt.

Express terms are also subject to legal restrictions such as the Unfair Contract Terms Act 1977. To retain their legal advantage as "drafter", vendors will have to carefully craft their standard terms and conditions to avoid these pitfalls.

Implied terms

3.79 On-line contracts, like traditional written contracts, cannot possibly explicitly account for every single possibility. As a result, the law interprets contracts using the customs of society or the relevant commercial sector. These customs and the context they provide necessarily insert implicit contractual terms into areas where the explicit contract is silent. As the court suggested in *Hutton v. Warren*:

> "It has long been settled that, in commercial transactions, extrinsic evidence of custom and usage is admissible to annex incidents to written contracts, in matters with respect to which they are silent. The same rule has also been applied to contracts in other transactions of life, in which known usages have been established and prevailed; and this has been done upon the principle of presumption that, in such transactions, the parties did not mean to express in writing the whole of the contract by which they intended to be bound, but a contract with reference to those known usages."[43]

For example, when a customer purchases books online it is obviously expected that they will be of "satisfactory quality" "not warped".[44] No contractual term explicitly states this, but the term is implied by the context of the transaction.

The simple example above demonstrates an obvious case of an implied term. However, like many implied terms arising from commercial customs and practices, the notion of "satisfactory quality" took decades to develop. For years it was a commercial understanding without any definitive legal basis until it appeared as "merchantable quality" in 1815 in *Gardiner v. Gray*.[45] The implied term was subsequently codified in the Sale of Goods Act 1893.[46] Since the commercial world of cyberspace is not even a decade old, it has obviously not had the opportunity to develop well recognised practices and customs. Also, since the Internet environment is constantly changing, new and novel industry practices continually arise. What is accepted practice today may not be tomorrow. Thus, what the courts will imply into future e-commerce agreements is largely unknown. This creates a rather uncertain environment for vendors.

---

[41] *Deutsche Genossenschaftsbank v. Burnhope* [1996] 1 Lloyd's Rep. 113 at 122.

[42] *Adams v. Richardson & Starling Ltd* [1969] 1 W.L.R. 1645.

[43] *Hutton v. Warren* (1836) 1 M. & W. 466 at 475–476.

[44] The Sale of Goods Act 1979,section states that, unless expressly specified otherwise, customers can imply that the goods they purchase will be of satisfactory quality.

[45] *Gardiner v. Gray* (1815) 4 Camp. 144.

[46] The Sale of Goods Act 1979 replaced the "merchantable quality" found in the Sale of Goods Act 1893 with the term "satisfactory quality."

Even extending traditional implied terms into cyberspace often poses problems, **3.80** particularly for digitised services. For example, does software have to satisfy the implied requirement of satisfactory quality and fitness of purpose for goods? This question is actually one of the few issues the courts have addressed. In *St Albans City and District Council v. International Computers Ltd,*[47] the court indeed held that defective software "would *prima facie* be a breach of the terms as to quality and fitness of purpose."[48] Yet, even this decision leaves questions unanswered. *St Albans* dealt with bespoke software and the damages resulting from its faulty calculations. But what about commercial software that is downloaded as a digitised service? Surely a customer expects that downloaded software will run properly. If the program has minor bugs or is incompatible with the customer's computer, is the customer entitled to a refund because the program failed to meet "satisfactory quality?" Unfortunately, digitised services are insidiously vulnerable to copying and piracy. Would an implied term to refund provide a loophole which dishonest customers could exploit to obtain free services?

Chris Reed has suggested[49] that contracts for the supply of digitised products should as a minimum have implied terms which cover delivery, ownership and use rights and description and quality. However, in the case of digitised products these implied terms will be very different from normal implied terms relating to goods or services. For example, implied terms for the delivery of goods or the performance of services tend to require performance within a reasonable time unless a specific time is agreed. For digitised products this is unlikely to be specific enough. Chris Reed suggests that if a digitised product is transmitted by a supplier via a website download it should try and transmit it within a reasonable number of hours of receiving payment. E-commerce for digitised products will require payment before delivery unless completion of the payment process should trigger the time period. If information is to be collected by providing a customer with a password or creating a customised website with password protected download then it should be made available for inspection within a reasonable time and a reasonable number of hours of payment for these reasons and remain available for collection for a reasonable time. Chris Reed also suggests the addition of the implied terms would also be necessary to deal with communications failures in the file transfer process so that an e-business would provide for re-delivery if delivery fails or that the e-business will make a refund if delivery is impossible.

Similar problems arise in other instances of applying traditional rules to cyberspace. The Sale of Goods Act 1979 further implies, unless otherwise stated, that in a sale by sample, "the bulk will correspond with the sample in quality." Many computer games are promoted online through the use of "shareware" demonstration versions that only allow the user to play a limited game. Could this practice be construed of as a sale by sample? If so, creating a shareware version that consolidated the few, high resolution graphics found in the comprehensive version (to make the game appear more impressive) might form the basis of an action for breach of contract.[50]

In addition to implied terms arising out of industry practice and/or codifying **3.81** legislation, the courts themselves may imply terms from the language of the contract. However, the courts' discretion is severely limited to only what will give business efficacy

---

[47] *St Albans City and District Council v. International Computer Ltd* [1996] 4 All E.R. 481.
[48] *ibid.* at 493.
[49] Paper given to the Third Annual Advanced I.T. Conference on October 16, 1998 available at **http://wsw.scl/org/emag/emagazine/vol19/LSS6–chns–reed–art.htm**.
[50] This practice could also form the basis for an action in misrepresentation, though admittedly, those high resolution graphics do exist in the comprehensive version, just at a different level of frequency.

to the contract and what is the obvious intention of the parties.[51] Thus, as Lord Pearson said in *Trollope and Colls Ltd v. North West Metropolitan Regional Hospital Board*:

> "An unexpressed term can be implied if and only if the court finds that the parties must have intended that term to form part of their contract: it is not enough for the court to find that such a term would have been adopted by the parties as reasonable men if it had been suggested to them: it must have been a term that went without saying, a term *necessary* to give business efficacy to the contract, a term which although tacit, formed part of the contract which the parties made for themselves."[52]

At the moment, not much goes "without saying" in e-commerce. The environment is too new and untested for online merchants to rely on implied contractual terms. In almost all areas, either industry practice has not yet been well developed or accepted, or the applicability of traditional customs and practices is unknown. The courts therefore have very little on which to base decisions except for the express terms found in the standard terms and conditions and perhaps their own common sense. Consequently, wherever any doubt exists, the e-business will wisely state its intentions in express terms.

The E.C. Directive[52a] on certain aspects of the sale of consumer goods and associated guarantees will, when it comes into force imply terms of fitness for purposes and satisfactory quality. The Directive will also provide for a two year period during which the consumer may be entitled to remedies against the seller.

Mandatory terms

3.82　Despite the apparent legal advantage given to e-businesses as the drafters of standard terms and conditions, they certainly do not have complete freedom. Parliament, recognising the dominant bargaining position held by vendors, has imposed mandatory implied terms which may not be excluded or limited in contracts. Many of the terms have arisen through the recent progress in consumer protection, and almost all are felt to be so fundamental that to exclude them would be unfair or unreasonable.

An example of a mandatory term is found in the Unfair Contract Terms Act 1977, which, among other things, prohibits the exclusion or restriction of liability for personal injury or death resulting from negligence.[53]

Contract Formation Terms

3.83　One of the principal areas requiring express terms in an online contract is how the contract itself is formed. In traditional contracts, this topic created less concern, since the "rules" and business practices are better established. However, in online contracts e-businesses will want to expressly delineate the contract formation process to create greater legal certainty and to give themselves as many options and advantages as possible.

The "Contract Formation" clause of the standard terms and conditions can encompass the entire contract formation process, including the following terms. The reasons and rationale behind these terms were discussed in great detail in paragraph 3.28 "Contract Creation".

(1) what constitutes an offer, as opposed to an invitation to treat;

---

[51] *Chitty*, para. 13–004.
[52] *Trollope and Colls Ltd v. North West Metropolitan Regional Hospital Board* [1973] 2 All E.R. 260 at 268.
[52a] 1999/44.
[53] Unfair Contract Terms Act 1977, s.2(1).

(2) whether counteroffers are allowed, prohibition against customer-changed offer terms where there is automated computer acceptance;

(3) if the merchant is making an offer, how long an offer is valid and what constitutes revocation of an offer;

(4) what constitutes acceptance: how, by what method and exactly when an acceptance is effective (postal or receipt rule).

A sample contract creation term is shown in the box below.

> ### Contract Formation
>
> All communications made by the Company thus far are invitations to treat only. Prices and availability of goods are subject to change. You agree not to change these standard terms and conditions from the form presented by the Company. This Agreement represents an offer of contract from you only, and is not binding until acceptance is sent via e-mail by the Company and received by you. The Company reserves the right to refuse your offer for any reason.

Limitation and Exclusion of Liabilities

For online merchants of goods and services, limitation and exclusion of liability clauses are quite similar to the traditional case of a direct mail supplier. Using their standard terms and conditions, e-businesses will try to exclude as much liability for errors and negligence as possible and limit or cap what cannot be excluded.   **3.84**

Liability

In no event will the Company be liable to you for any indirect, incidental or consequential damages arising out of the services or any products provided under this Agreement, even if the Company has been advised of the possibility of such damages. Except for cases of personal injury or death, arising from the Company's negligence the Company's liability to you for actual damages, regardless of the form of action, will be strictly limited to the price of the services or products sold.   **3.85**

English law, heavily regulates the exclusion or limitation of liability in standard form business contracts and consumer contracts. As previously mentioned, a standard form business contract is where one of the parties deals on his own pre-drafted standard terms and conditions. Overlapping in some respects, a consumer contract is defined under the Unfair Contract Terms Act 1977 using three criteria: first, the customer or consumer does not make the contract in the course of a business, and does not hold itself out as doing so; second, the other party, the supplier, makes the contract in the course of a business; and third, the goods being supplied are ordinarily used for private consumption.[54]

One of the uncertainties regarding the definition of a consumer contract is whether a buyer is actually making the contract in the course of business. In *R. & B. Customs Brokers Co. Ltd v. United Dominions Trust Ltd*,[55] the court held that "in the course of business" meant that "the transaction must be an integral part of the business carried on or, if only incidental thereto, be of a type regularly entered into."[56] Thus, a bank ordering flowers

---

[54] Unfair Contract Terms Act 1977, s.12(1).
[55] *R. & B. Customs Brokers Co. Ltd v. United Dominions Trust Ltd* [1988] 1 W.L.R. 321.
[56] *Chitty*, para. 14–052.

online to send to an important customer would probably involve a consumer contract. The definition given in the judgment, however, still offers considerable room for interpretation.

The Unfair Contract Terms Act 1977 regulates exclusion and limitation of liability clauses in most consumer and standard form contracts for goods and services. It does not, however, apply to a few specific types of contract, including ones for insurance, securities, land, and intellectual property rights (creation, transfer or termination). Interestingly, it also does not apply to the international supply of goods defined as[57] where the formation or performance of a sale of goods contract takes place across international borders.[58]

This definition of international supply contracts poses substantial issues for consumers and e-businesses who transact internationally online. If a consumer in the United Kingdom purchases goods or services online from a foreign country, the Unfair Contract Terms Act 1977 will not be applicable. The foreign merchant will be able to ignore the Act's provisions (discussed below) to its great advantage. Similarly, a U.K. vendor can ignore the Act in dealing with foreign customers.

Another potential area of debate is whether international sales of digitised services fall under the definition of "goods" and are thereby excluded from the Act's restrictions. Downloadable software and other digitised services are essentially dematerialised versions of goods, as suggested in paragraph 3.07. This particular interpretation, however, has yet to gain universal acceptance. In any case, international supply contracts will naturally become more popular and important as e-commerce becomes increasingly global and they may require similar "unfair term legislation" in the future.

3.86   The most serious restriction imposed by the Unfair Contract Terms Act 1977 is found in section 2(1). Here, the Act renders any contractual term that excludes or limits liability for personal injury or death due to negligence invalid and unenforceable. Unlike other sections of the Act discussed below, this restriction is applicable to all contracts, including non-standard form contracts. Thus contracts should refrain from making any such disclaimers. The example limitation clause above follows this suggestion.

Besides personal injury or death, all other exclusions or limitations of liabilities in standard form contracts are subject to a test of reasonableness. For example, the popular clauses limiting direct damages to the price of product or service and excluding liability for incidental or consequential damages fall under test this test. Schedule 2 of the Act lists five guidelines for determining reasonableness. Though they are neither exhaustive nor always applicable, they are often used by the courts for evaluating contractual terms:

    (1) the strength of the bargaining positions of the parties relative to each other, taking into account (among other things) alternative means by which the customer's requirement could have been met;

    (2) whether the customer received an inducement to agree to the term, or in accepting it had an opportunity of entering into a similar contract with other persons, but without having to accept a similar term;

    (3) whether the customer knew or ought reasonably to have known of the existence and extent of the term (having regard, among other things, to any custom of the trade and any previous course of dealing between the parties);

    (4) where the term excludes or restricts any relevant liability if some condition is not complied with, whether it was reasonable at the time of the contract to expect that compliance with that condition would be practicable;

---

[57] Unfair Contract Terms Act 1977, Sched. 1.
[58] *ibid.* at s.26.

(5) whether the goods were manufactured, processed or adapted to the special order of the customer.[59]

In addition to these five principles, in House of Lords case of *Smith v. Eric S. Bush*, Lord Griffiths gave a similar set of principles: **3.87**

(a) were the parties of equal bargaining power?

(b) in the case of advice, would it have been reasonably practicable to obtain the advice from an alternative source taking into account considerations of costs and time?

(c) how difficult is the task being undertaken for which liability is being excluded?

(d) what are the practical consequences of the decision on the question of reasonableness?[60]

Both Lord Griffith, referring to (d) practical consequences, and the Unfair Contract Terms Act 1977 in section 11(4) further recommended that the courts consider whether insurance is available to protect the company attempting to limit the liability. As an example, two recent software liability cases hinged significantly on this insurance consideration.

In *St Albans City and District Council v. International Computers Ltd*,[61] a faulty computer **3.88** program designed by ICL for St Albans resulted in a loss of nearly £1 million, but a clause in ICL's standard terms and conditions limited its liability to £100,000. In the originating trial court, Scott Baker J. held that this limitation was unreasonable, considering, among other things, that ICL had the resources to remedy the damage as well as an insurance policy of £50 million. The Court of Appeal affirmed this decision.

Similarly, in *Salvage Association v. Cap Financial Services*,[62] the court held that a clause limiting liability to £25,000 was unreasonable. This decision reasoned that, among other things, a supplier can obtain insurance far more easily and cheaply than the customer. Additionally, the supplier already had insurance covering up to £5 million in damages.[63]

The Unfair Terms in Consumer Contracts Regulations 1994[64] apply to all business contracts with consumers for the sale or supply of goods or services. Unlike the Unfair Contract Terms Act 1977 the Regulations cover all terms in a contract not just those that limit or exclude liability. The Regulations only cover contracts with consumers whereas the 1977 Act covers business to business e-commerce contracts. The Regulations apply to terms which have not been individually negotiated and will therefore apply to e-commerce contracts with consumers which are in the e-commerce businesses standard form, even if a consumer has had the opportunity to negotiate specific terms. The Regulations provide that any unfair term does not bind the consumer. However, issues on the subject matter and price cannot render a term unfair. The Regulations detail an exhaustive list of the sort of terms which may be regarded as unfair. Finally the Regulations require contracts to be in plain intelligible language.

---

[59] *ibid.* at Sched. 2.
[60] *Smith v. Eric S. Bush* [1990] 1 A.C. 831; [1989] 2 All E.R. 514. Also *Harris v. Wyre Forest District, ibid.* (twin appeal cases).
[61] *St Albans City and District Council v. International Computers Ltd* [1995] F.S.R. 686; [1996] 4 All E.R. 481. (CA).
[62] *Salvage Association v. CAP Financial Services* [1995] F.S.R. 654.
[63] *Chitty Supplement* (1997) para. 14–074.
[64] Implement the E.C. Directive 93/13 on Unfair Terms in Consumer Contracts and come into force on July 1, 1995.

Warranties

3.89   Under the Sale of Goods Act 1979,[65] any contract for the sale of goods has an implied warranty of "satisfactory quality", which takes into consideration the description, price, and all other relevant circumstances of the sale.[66] This warranty is strict. There is no defence of having exercised reasonable care in manufacturing, handling and transport of the goods, etc.[67] The goods must also be reasonably fit for the purpose for which they are being bought, though, for unusual instances, English law may require that the buyer inform the seller first.[68]

In contrast to goods, contracts for services have an implied term that the supplier will perform the service with reasonable care and skill.[69] If the supply is for professional services, the level expected is that of a professional person with ordinary skill and expertise. The essential difference between classifying a product as a good or a service hinges on this distinction between satisfactory quality and performance with reasonable care and skill. The law holds goods and services to different standards and, in case of a dispute, one standard may be more easily satisfied than the other.

For the most part in e-commerce, the traditional distinction between goods and services and the warranties those contracts imply will remain exactly the same. Buying a football from the local sporting goods store is no different from buying it from the online version. In order to maintain customer satisfaction and loyalty, most online businesses offer generous return and refund policies, just like their high street counterparts. However, even if an online merchant wanted to exclude the applicable implied warranties, it would not be permitted in the case of consumer contracts. Under section 6(2) of the Unfair Contract Terms Act 1977, the implied warranties of satisfactory quality and fitness of purpose cannot be excluded or limited. The online merchant might succeed in disallowing refunds without cause, but even then would have to contend with the Distance Selling Directive (Chapter 2) which will require a mandatory seven day withdrawal period for the consumer. Thus, most consumers will not see a substantial change in warranty policy as they move from the high street to cyberspace.

3.90   However, one area that continues to pose problems for measurements of quality is digitised services, particularly software. Regardless of whether software is judged to be a good or a service (paragraph 3.08), determining standards for software quality poses a considerable challenge for the courts. Given the complex nature of software programming and execution, all commercial software will almost always have bugs. Do these bugs constitute a breach of satisfactory quality or reasonable care? A similar argument may apply to other digitised services, since they typically depend on a software platform, and bugs in the platform can distort or disrupt the digitised service, whether it is audio, video, text, etc.

Unfortunately, most of the case law deals with bespoke software rather than commercially available, packaged software. However, the bespoke cases do offer a view into the courts' rationale and may be predictive of future decisions on packaged software. In *Saphena Computing Ltd v. Allied Collection Agencies Ltd*,[70] the court recognised the bug and defect removal process as a slow and iterative one, and that:

---

[65] All references to the Sale of Goods Act 1979 assume that it is as amended by the Sale and Supply of Goods Act 1994.
[66] Sale of Goods Act 1979 (as amended), para. 14(2A).
[67] *Chitty*, para. 41–074.
[68] Sale of Goods Act 1979, s.14(3).
[69] Supply of Goods and Services Act 1982, s.13.
[70] *Saphena Computing Ltd v. Allied Collection Agencies Ltd* [1995] F.S.R. 616.

"Just as no software developer can reasonably expect a buyer to tell him what is required without a process of feedback and reassessment, so no buyer should expect a supplier to get his programs right first time."[71]

Thus, software containing bugs were not a breach of satisfactory quality. The supplier **3.91** was merely required to fix those bugs in due course. Similarly, in *Eurodynamic Systems v. General Automation Ltd*,[72] Steyn J. concluded that:

"The expert evidence convincingly showed that it is regarded as acceptable practice to supply computer program (including system software) that contain errors and bugs. The basis of the practice is that, pursuant to his support obligation (free or chargeable as the case may be), the supplier will correct errors and bugs that prevent the product from being properly used. Not every bug or error in a computer program can therefore be categorised as a breach of contract."

These two precedents favouring leniency were then followed by *St Albans v. ICL*, where, as mentioned in paragraph 3.88, the court awarded the plaintiff approximately £1 million in damages stemming from the consequences of a programming error that breached the requirement of satisfactory quality.[73] Thus, on the whole, the courts appear to measure software quality on a case by case basis. As *Eurodynamics* suggests, not every bug is a breach of the implied term to satisfactory quality or reasonable care and skill, but some, more insidious errors can be. In cases where quality is neglected, the damages can be startling.

The above cases involved bespoke software where the parties knew the level of quality expected and the purposes anticipated. Mass-produced application software and other digitised services will be quite different in this respect. With respect to the requirement of fitness for purpose, one might expect a legal distinction between personal use and business use, since errors in business application software can result in far greater damages. One might see digitised service providers in the future restricting programs for personal use only, or charging a premium for business use in order to cover the added liability risk. If a premium is collected, that "business" version will naturally be held to a higher and more stringent standard.

Payment and Delivery Terms

Standard terms and conditions will undoubtedly specify the specific payment and **3.92** delivery terms of the transaction. Online payment methods such as digital cash and the secure transmission of credit card numbers are covered in Chapter 6, "Getting Paid in Cyberspace". However, regarding contractual issues of payment, online vendors and customers should keep two legal principles (and their respective nineteenth century precedents) in mind.

In *Luttges v. Sherwood*,[74] the court held that cash lost in the post consituted non-payment. Thus, the sending of payment is not like the sending of an acceptance; the postal rule does not apply. In order to satisfy the payment terms of the contract, the other party must receive the payment. Applying this rule to cyberspace, digital cash that becomes "lost" *en route* to the online merchant does not constitute payment either. If there is a fault in the line or server connection and subsequently the digital cash disappears, the customer is left with the loss. Due to the rule in *Luttges*, people in

---

[71] *ibid.* at 652.
[72] *Eurodynamic Systems v. General Automation Ltd* (1988) Q.B.D., September 6, unreported.
[73] The damages were reduced by the Court of Appeal.
[74] *Luttges v. Sherwood* (1895) 11 T.L.R. 233.

traditional commerce rarely ever sent cash through the mail; it is too insecure. Besides, an unscrupulous merchant theoretically could even keep the cash and deny ever having received it. In the future, customers in cyberspace may want two systems, anonymous digital cash for small transactions and privacy, and traceable digital cash for larger transactions and accountability.

In *Norman v. Ricketts*,[75] however, the court suggested that if the contractual terms described a method of payment and the sender observes the specified procedures, the sender will not have liability for the lost payment. From the customer standpoint, this case rightfully balances the burden of accountability and record keeping imposed by *Luttges*. However, for the online merchant, the precedent gives a good reason to exercise caution in specifying a payment method. Instead, vendors should probably add a standard term which denies liability and responsibility for lost credit card numbers and digital cash. Let the customer send the payment at his or her own risk.

SUMMARY

3.93 This chapter has addressed the key issues concerning e-businesses contracting online. Why does an online merchant want to select the customer with whom he/she deals? Does e-mail fall under the postal rule or the receipt rule of acceptance? Does an electronic document constitute "writing?" How should an e-business display its standard terms and conditions online? Can a web server constitute a "place of business?" Many of these issues are made academic if online merchants abide by the primary rule:

> Specify everything possible in the standard terms and conditions. English law occasionally restricts the extent of these standard terms but, for the most part, online merchants are free to choose the way by which they contract and do business.

The following is a short list of the key areas which should be explicitly addressed in the terms and conditions of an online contract:

(a) selecting Customers — at whom are the advertisements and contracts directed?

(b) offer/Invitation to Treat — what do the advertisements and order forms constitute?

(c) acceptance Methods and Procedures — what constitutes an acceptance? How and when is a contract formed?

(d) revocations — how can an offer be revoked?

(e) limitations of Liability/Warranty — for exactly what does the online merchant have responsibility?

(f) applicable Law/Jurisdiction — what law and forum govern the interpretation of the contract?[76]

---

[75] *Norman v. Ricketts* (1886) 3 T.L.R. 182.
[76] See Chapter 4.

— 4 —

INTERNATIONAL ISSUES

The global and borderless nature of electronic commerce means that contracting parties **4.01** and customers are just as likely to be from overseas as from the United Kingdom. Consequently, jurisdictional issues are inevitable. This chapter is divided into three sections. The first section considers which jurisdiction will be the forum for any dispute. The second section considers which country's or state's laws will govern the contract the subject of any dispute. The third section briefly considers enforcement of judgments overseas.

JURISDICTION (FORUM)

The issue of forum — which country will hear a dispute, resolve it, and enforce the **4.02** contractual terms — is decided by the laws of jurisdiction. Jurisdictional issues encountered online are not new or novel and are well addressed by legislation and international conventions drafted before the emergence of e-commerce. However, in practice, the borderless nature of e-commerce has raised the importance of jurisdictional issues to a far higher level. Online merchants as well as customers will need to know how to enforce their contracts against foreign parties in the global economy.

Jurisdiction in the U.K. is principally governed by the Brussels Convention on Jurisdiction and the Enforcement of Judgments in Civil and Commercial Matter 1968. This was implemented into U.K. law by the Civil Jurisdiction and Judgments Act 1982. With only a few exceptions,[2] the Convention governs all civil and commercial matters, thereby covering most, if not all, e-commerce transactions.

The Brussels Convention applies to "Contracting States," members of the European Union (E.U.). In addition, European Free Trade Agreement (EFTA) countries are brought under essentially identical rules through the Lugano Convention 1988.[3] In both Conventions, the determination of jurisdiction relies significantly on whether or not a party to

---

[1] *The New Barbarians or How to Survive the Information Age,* a new book by Professor Ian O. Angell, Professor of Information Systems to be published early in 2000.
[2] Exceptions include marriage, wills, bankrupty, social security, customs, taxes, etc. See the 1968 Convention on Jurisdiction and the Enforcement of Judgments in Civil and Commercial Matters, Art. 1.
[3] The Supreme Court Practice 1997, Volume 2, para. 8–037. Thus the countries currently within the Convention are: U.K., Germany, France, Spain, Portugal, Ireland, Greece, Italy, Austria, Luxembourg, Denmark, Holland, Belgium, Finland, Iceland, Sweden, Liechtenstein and Norway.

the contract is domiciled in a Contracting State. If the defendant is domiciled in a Contracting State, the rules of the relevant Convention apply; otherwise English common law will govern the determination of jurisdiction. For convenience, references to the Brussels Convention shall be taken to include the Lugano Convention.

Having been in place for over 30 years, the Brussels Convention will shortly be updated. By way of an E.C. Regulation, the European Union will adopt new rules on jurisdiction and the recognition and enforcement of judgments, based on the existing Brussels Convention. The changes envisaged in a draft Regulation which was published in July 1999[4] include clarification of special jurisdictions, new provisions to cover jurisdiction over all consumer contracts, new provisions relating to individual contracts of employment and a common concept of the domicile of legal persons. Mention of this draft Regulation is made in this chapter on the assumption that provisions similar to it will become a Regulation in due course and will therefore become binding on not only all Member States of the European Union but also the members of the EEA. However, technically it should be noted that the United Kingdom, Denmark and Ireland will not be party to the Regulation unless they "opt in".

Domicile Determination

Persons

4.03   As mentioned above, the key determinant for jurisdiction is domicile. For the Convention to apply, the defendant's domicile must be either in the United Kingdom or another Contracting State. Interestingly, the Brussels Convention leaves the rules regarding domicile to domestic law. Under English law, domicile is defined under sections 41–46 of the Civil Jurisdiction and Judgements Act 1982.

A defendant is domiciled in the United Kingdom if he/she is resident in the United Kingdom and if the nature of that residence indicates a "substantial connection" with the United Kingdom.[5] A substantial connection is automatically presumed, although disputable, if the period of residence is greater than three months.[6] Alternatively, a defendant is domiciled in a Contracting State outside the United Kingdom if he/she would be so viewed under that country's legal system.[7] Under either of these conditions, the Convention rules of jurisdiction will apply.

However, if the defendant does not satisfy either of the above criteria, or if he/she is domiciled in a non-Contracting State, jurisdictional issue questions will be determined by common law. A defendant is domiciled in a non-Contracting State if he/she is resident in that foreign country and his/her residence constitutes a substantial connection.

Corporations and other legal persons

4.04   For corporations, the seat of the corporation is defined as its domicile.[8] Again, if the defendant corporation has its seat in the United Kingdom or another Contracting State, jurisdictional questions will be subject to the Brussels Convention. A corporation has its seat in the United Kingdom if it was incorporated under United Kingdom law or if its

---

[4] Proposal for a Council Regulation COM (1999) 3–8 final.
[5] Civil Jurisdiction and Judgments Act 1982, s.41(2).
[6] *ibid.*, s.41(6).
[7] Convention on Jurisdiction and the Enforcement of Judgments in Civil and Commercial Matters (1968), Art. 52.
[8] Civil Jurisdiction and Judgments Act 1982, s.42(1).

"central management and control" is exercised in the United Kingdom.[9] Similarly, a corporation has its seat in a Contracting State outside the United Kingdom if it was incorporated in that State, or its central management and control is exercised in that foreign State.[10] Furthermore, the foreign Contracting State must recognise that the corporation has its seat there.[11]

Just as in the case of a natural person, if a corporation or other legal person is not recognised as having a seat in the United Kingdom or another Contracting State, jurisdiction will be determined by common law.

Under the draft Regulation on Jurisdiction,[12] the rules might be changed. It is proposed that there should be no reference to the private international law of a Member State to locate the "seat" of a body corporate. Instead, the domicile of companies and other legal persons would be defined by three alternative criteria — the statutory seat, the central administration or the principal place of business.

It should also be noted that Article 15 of the draft Regulation stipulates that where a party is not domiciled in a Member State but has a branch, agency or other establishment in one of the Member States, that party shall, in respect of disputes arising out of that branch, agency or establishment, be deemed to be domiciled in that Member State.

Application of the Brussels Convention

If the Brussels Convention applies, the determination of jurisdiction is greatly simplified. **4.05** Unless the contract has a jurisdiction clause (paragraph 4.14), jurisdiction will usually lie in the courts of the defendant's domicile. A defendant has the right to be sued only in his/her home domicile.

The general rule of the defendant's domicile, however, is subject to a number of exceptions. For example, the general rule does not apply to certain contracts such as insurance,[13–14] land, and intellectual property. In these areas, specific criteria given in the Brussels Convention grant exclusive jurisdiction to a relevant country. For example, for contracts concerning the transfer of intellectual property rights, the courts of the country where those rights are registered or deposited have exclusive jurisdiction.

Expected place of performance

An important exception to the rule of defendant's domicile is that a defendant may be **4.06** sued in "the place of performance of the obligation in question."[15] This exception has great relevance to contracts, since most disputes will involve a defendant who has failed to perform a contractual duty. In the e-commerce transactions, failure to perform will often involve failure to pay for the goods or services rendered. According to *The Eider*:

---

[9] *ibid.*, s.42(2).

[10] However, in case of conflict been a seat in the United Kingdom and one in a foreign Contracting State, the U.K. seat will take precedence. For example, if the defendant is incorporated in the United Kingdom but has its central management and control in France, the English courts will place its seat in the United Kingdom Civil Jurisdiction and Judgments Act 1982, ss.42(6)–(7).

[11] Civil Jurisdiction and Judgments Act 1982, s.42(7).

[12] Proposal for a Council Regulation COM (1999) 348 final.

[13–14] Convention on Jurisdiction and the Enforcement of Judgments in Civil and Commercial Matters (1968) Arts 7–12.

[15] Brussels Convention, Art. 5(1). The reader should note that this place of performance rule is different from the breach of contract rule in common law jurisdiction found in para. 4.12. As discussed in that section, breach of contract can occur in ways other than failure to perform, such as explicit and implicit repudiation.

"The general rule is that where no place of payment is specified, either expressly or by implication, the debtor must seek out his creditor."[16]

This statement implies that when a customer pays an online vendor, the place of performance is at the vendor's location. Thus, if a customer fails to pay, he/she can be sued in the online vendor's jurisdiction.

> A French travel agency orders books online from an English bookseller who promptly delivers them to Lyon. However, the cheque from the travel agency is not honoured and the travel agency refuses to deliver further payment. Under the "place of performance" clause in the Brussels Convention, the travel agency can be sued in the United Kingdom, even though its domicile is France.

However, the converse of the above situation is not true. This may have English customers slightly unprotected. An online vendor who fails to deliver goods or delivers defective goods cannot be sued in the customer's jurisdiction. Under English law, a seller only has a duty to ship the goods, not deliver them, to the buyer. Thus, according to the House of Lords in *Johnson v. Taylor*[17] the substantive part of performance occurs at the seller's location, where it ships the goods, rather than at the buyer's. Consequently, an English customer cannot sue a foreign merchant for breach of contract in an English court because the defendant's domicile and the place of performance is overseas. Notably, however, this rule does not protect English online merchants in the same way, since foreign countries may locate the place of performance elsewhere.

Consumer Contracts

4.07   Another significant exception to the rule of defendant's domicile rule is in consumer contracts. Under Article 14 of the Convention, a consumer may sue the defendant vendor in either the defendant's domicile or the consumer's own domicile. On the other hand, the consumer can only be sued in his/her own domicile. Recognising the limited resources of consumers, this exemption eases the burden on them when responding or initiating legal action.

One should note, however, that the definition of consumer contract under the Convention is slightly different from that found in the Unfair Contract Terms Act 1977 and other areas of English law. While sales of goods to a consumer are included in entirety, contracts for the supply of services are only considered as consumer contracts if two conditions are satisfied. The consumer contract had to be solicited (*i.e.* direct mailing or advertising) by the merchant in the consumer's domicile and the consumer must have completed all contract formation steps there.

This distinction between goods and services, and the advertising requirement in service contracts can cause problems for e-commerce. In the case of warranties (paragraph 3.89), for example, whether digitised services are considered as goods or as services will make a substantial difference. If digitised services are goods (as recommended in paragraph 3.07), consumers will be granted jurisdictional protection when they make

---

[16] *The Eider* [1893] P 119 at 136–137, CA, cited in *Dicey* at p. 336. This is supported by a Scottish case, *William Grant v. Marie Brizard Espana SA* [1998] S.C. 537.
[17] *Johnson v. Taylor* [1920] A.C. 144.

online purchases of software, music, video, etc. However, if digitised services are services, and the consumer was not solicited, no such protection will apply.

The consumer may need to sue the vendor for breach of contract in a foreign court or, worse yet, get hauled into the foreign court.

But even discounting the situation of digitised services, what exactly constitutes a solicitation in the consumer's domicile? Do e-mail and web pages fall under the definition? The implications could be very significant. For example, if services such as banking and web page design were advertised on the web, subsequent contracts may or may not protected by the consumer jurisdiction clauses. The wording regarding solicitations in Article 13(3)(a) is: **4.08**

> "In the State of the consumer's domicile the conclusion of the contract was preceded by a specific invitation addressed to him or by advertising."[18]

E-mail solicitations will probably be considered as specific invitations since they are directed solicitations. However, the status of advertisements on web pages is unclear. Does a "webvertisement" really constitute an advertisement in the consumer's domicile? After all, web pages are never 'directed' at a particular jurisdiction, but instead passively spread all over the globe.[19]

United Kingdom government agencies have taken a subjective approach to this question of "directedness". For example, under the Financial Services Act 1986, all advertising material relating to investment business must be approved by the Financial Services Authority (FSA).[20] However, with respect to a foreign website that advertises investment opportunities, the FSA will consider whether the site is directed at United Kingdom consumers, by examining a list of factors, and then decide on enforcement measures. A similar method might be applied by the courts in determining whether or not a webvertisement for a service transformed the resulting contract into a consumer contract under the Brussels Convention.

Evasion

Since the emphasis of the Brussels Convention is on domicile, contracting parties will probably be unable to avoid their home jurisdictions by merely using an off-shore web or mail server. In many ways reducing uncertainty and potential confusion, the concept of domicile focuses solely on permanent physical locations, such as a person's place of residence or a corporation's seat. Online vendors will not be able to "forum-shop" by placing web servers in countries with more favourable laws. **4.09**

Common Law Jurisdiction

Where the defendant's domicile is not in a Contracting State or, for other reasons, more generally where the Brussels Convention does not apply,[21] English common law **4.10**

---

[18] Convention on Jurisdiction and the Enforcement of Judgments in Civil and Commercial Matters (1968) Art. 13(3)(a).
[19] See Chapter 8 on Webvertising.
[20] See Chapter 2 on Financial Services.
[21] For example, other instances include where the defendant does not satisfy the requirements for being domiciled in a Contracting State, or where the dispute involves non-civil/non-commercial matters.

will settle the issue of jurisdiction. This situation may arise when contracts are formed with parties domiciled outside Contracting States. Under the common law, the principles for claiming jurisdiction are substantially different, providing English courts with a greater opportunity to seize jurisdiction.

Jurisdiction in personam

4.11   The key issue for jurisdiction *in personam* is whether the defendant can be physically served with a writ in England. If the defendant can, then English courts can claim jurisdiction.

Under this doctrine, the courts can exercise jurisdiction over any individual (natural person) present in England, regardless of whether his/her stay is meant to be temporary or permanent.[22] As long as the defendant is served with the writ,[23] the claim of jurisdiction is effective. In addition, according to R.S.C., Ord. 81, rule 9, if an individual conducts business in England, the writ may be served at his English place of business, whether or not the individual himself/herself is in England at the time.[24]

Similar rules apply to partnerships or corporations. A partnership or firm (under a single name) with a place of business in England may be served a writ at that location, whether the partners are in England or not. The rule also applies regardless of the nationality or residence of the partners, thus allowing the courts to exercise jurisdiction over foreigners who do business in England. Companies incorporated in England or registered under the Companies Act 1985 can be served writs at their registered offices. Even a foreign corporation with no officially registered office can be served a writ at its English place of business if that place has been operational for a sufficient period of time and carries on substantial activities.[25] As the court suggested in *South India Shipping Co. Ltd v. Export-Import Bank of Korea*:

> "We have only to see whether the corporation is 'here'; if it is, it can be served. There are authorities as to the circumstances in which a foreign corporation can and cannot be said to be 'here'; the best test is to ascertain whether the business is carried on here and at a defined place."[26]

Jurisdiction *in personam* has ramifications for international online contracts, though its applicability will only lie where one party is from the United Kingdom and the other is from a non-Contracting State. Under the doctrine, a foreign party or consumer can easily use the English courts to sue any online vendor with a place of business in England, provided the forum is relevant to the contract in question (see below). Similarly, a foreign vendor can sue (in the English courts) an English resident or someone who occasionally visits England, provided that the writ is properly and successfully served. These two instances are straightforward, though one should note that, unlike the Brussels Convention, presence, not domicile, determines jurisdiction.

4.12   One uncertainty that arises under jurisdiction *in personam* is whether a writ can be served on a web server. Some have suggested that if a purely foreign company set up a web server physically based in England and directed at English customers, that server might constitute a "place of business". Even though the server is not a traditional form of

---

[22] *Colt Industries Inc. v. Sarlie* [1966] 1 W.L.R. 440, CA, *Dicey* at p. 300.
[23] The procedures and means by which writs may be served can comprise a chapter in itself and will not be discussed here. See Dicey and Morris, *Conflict of Laws*, Chapter 11.
[24] One exception to this rule is that if the person conducts business in his won name, then jurisdiction cannot be exercised via this means. *Dicey*, at p. 301.
[25] *Dicey*, at p. 306.
[26] *South India Shipping Co. Ltd v. Export-Import Bank of Korea* [1985] 2 All E.R. 219.

"place", it is nonetheless where substantial advertising and business transactions occur. In fact, one could even argue that a web server exhibits the "degree of permanence or recognisability" required by *Re Oriel Ltd*[27] If this method of serving writs were possible, English courts would be able to exercise jurisdiction *in personam* over all foreign (non-Contracting State) companies with web servers in England.

The courts would probably be unwise to follow this route. The issue of jurisdiction concerns finding a *forum conveniens*, an applicable forum that will maximise justice for both parties in the dispute. The "web server as place of business" rule would not be in this spirit. Companies place their web servers all over the world, particularly because many Internet/Access Service Providers are located elsewhere. Thus, the physical location of the Web servers of an e-commerce business is often completely irrelevant to the contracts being formed. For example, if an English consumer purchased goods from an English online merchant, why should the courts care that the merchant's website was physically based in the Cayman Islands? The "web server as place of business" rule would create these inconsistencies and, in some cases, might even undermine the ability of the courts to exercise jurisdiction over English companies that cunningly base their web servers elsewhere.

The virtual attributes of the Internet offer no reason for English law to change its traditional and physical definition of a "place of business". Besides, English law does not need to unnecessarily stretch jurisdiction *in personam* to haul foreign corporations into court. It already has a variety of other potent jurisdiction principles as considered below.

Contracts made in England

If a contract is created in England, the English courts can exercise jurisdiction over disputes concerning it. Thus, as already emphasised in paragraph 3.39, the moment of contract creation, whether the courts use the postal rule, the receipt rule or any other rule,[28] becomes extremely important for jurisdiction purposes.   **4.13**

Breach of contract in England

English courts can exercise jurisdiction in cases where the breach of contract occurred in England, regardless of whether or not the contract was originally formed in England. A contracting party can breach the contract in one of three ways: by explicit repudiation, implicit repudiation; or failure to perform. This common law "breach of contract" rule varies in scope from the "place of performance" rule in the Brussels Convention. Breach of contract does not necessarily have to occur at the expected place of performance.   **4.14**

An explicit repudiation occurs when the reneging party expressly informs the other party that it will no longer abide by the contract. The instant at which repudiation occurs is important. According to *Cherry v. Thompson*,[29] for written letters of repudiation, the postal rule is followed. A repudiation by e-mail, however, will probably fall under the receipt rule (see paragraph 3.41). Thus, a defendant who sent an e-mail explicitly breaking a contract to a plaintiff located in England could be sued in an English court, regardless of where the contract would have been performed.

---

[27] *re Oriel Ltd* [1985] 3 All E.R. 216.
[28] It is proposed in the E.C.'s Amended Draft Directive on Electronic Commerce (see Chapter 12) that contracts with consumers shall be formed when the online vendor accepts the notification (be it an offer or an acceptance) of the consumer that he wishes to proceed with the proposed transaction.
[29] *Cherry v. Thompson* (1872) L.R. 7 Q.B. 573 at 579.

Implicit repudiation, on the other hand, involves performing an act that is inconsistent with the contractual performance. For example, if Alice is under contract to sell her car to Bob, selling the car to Cindy would be an implicit repudiation. Where this act of implicit repudiation occurs can form the basis for a jurisdiction claim.

Probably the most common manner of breach, however, is the failure to perform a contractual obligation. If the expected place of performance was in England, the English courts will be able to exercise jurisdiction.[30] This principle is the same as the one found in Article 5(1) of the Brussels Convention, which deals with the "place of performance" (see paragraph 4.05), except here it is applied to defendants from non-Contracting States.

The issues are very similar to the ones described for Article 5(1). Foreign customers who fail to pay English merchants can face litigation in England because payment is performed at the creditor's (merchant's) location. On the other hand, under this rule English customers cannot sue foreign suppliers in an English court. Supplier performance involves only shipping, which occurs at the supplier's location, not complete delivery.

However, English common law does not provide the consumer protection granted in the Brussels Convention. A consumer from a non-Contracting State who fails to pay an English merchant can be sued in England.

Contracts governed by English law

4.15 If the applicable law/choice of law (see paragraph 4.16) of a contract is England and Wales then the English and Welsh courts can seize jurisdiction. However, choice of law does not provide a conclusive determination of jurisdiction. It is a particularly weak factor and, according to Lord Diplock in *Amin Rasheed Shipping Co. v. Kuwait Insurance Co.*, the plaintiff has a burden to show that it could not obtain justice from a more relevant foreign court, or that to do so would require excessive time, resources, or inconvenience.[31] Furthermore, *in Spiliada Maritime Co. v. Cansulex Ltd*, the court held that in determining jurisdiction, choice of law must be considered in light of the context and other facts of the case.[32]

Jurisdiction Clauses

4.16 Relying upon the Brussels Convention or English common law to determine jurisdiction can cause major problems for an e-business. English common law is a confusing legal labyrinth; the principles for determining jurisdiction often conflict and can result in several countries having jurisdiction rights. Thus, as already mentioned, if an American customer purchases goods from an English vendor and then fails to pay, both England and America may have reason to claim jurisdiction. The breach of contract occurred in England and the standard terms and conditions probably stipulated English law. However, since the English vendor probably made the acceptance, the contract was formed in America under the receipt rule, and the American courts could therefore also claim jurisdiction.[33]

For European commerce, the Brussels Convention makes jurisdictional issues more manageable, but situations can still present problems for e-businesses. For example, other

---

[30] Just as in Art. 5(1) of the Brussels Convention, except that this rule now applies to a defendant from a non-Contracting State.

[31] *Dicey*, at p. 332.

[32] *Spiliada Maritime Co. v. Cansulex Ltd* [1987] A.C. 460 at 480.

[33] N.B.: The arguments in this example only consider jurisdictional issues from an English law standpoint; it does not even touch on the American rules, which are different — see para. 4.17.

European laws may provide that suppliers have the duty to deliver the goods, not just ship them (thereby putting the place of performance in the customers' location) Consequently, English online vendors who fail to deliver the ordered materials could be sued in foreign courts.

E-businesses clearly have good reason to specify jurisdiction explicitly in their standard terms and conditions. For example, the following simple clause could be inserted:

Jurisdiction

Each party agrees to submit to the exclusive jurisdiction of the (English) courts as regards any claim or matter arising under this Agreement.

Both English common law and the Brussels Convention attach great weight to express **4.17** jurisdiction clauses and will usually allow the clause to override all other determinations of jurisdiction. Under RSC, Order 11, rule 2a, if a contract has an explicit term granting the English courts jurisdiction, they automatically have the right to examine any aspect of the contract. Similarly, the Brussels Convention states in Article 17:

> "If the parties, one or more of whom is domiciled in a Contracting State, have agreed that a court or the courts of a Contracting State are to have jurisdiction to settle any disputes which have arisen or which may arise in connection with a particular legal relationship, that court or those courts shall have exclusive jurisdiction."[34]

Recognition of jurisdiction clauses under the Brussels Convention, however, is subject to some overriding provisions relating to some consumer contracts. The consumer protection measures given in Articles 13–15, including the consumer's right to sue and to be sued only in his/her domicile, cannot be overridden by contractual terms.

For both commercial contracts and consumer contracts the choice of jurisdiction should be relevant, or at least not blatantly irrelevant. Otherwise, the opposing party could prove that some other forum was more appropriate. For example, if a contract between an English vendor and an American supplier listed Brazil as the jurisdiction, either party would have a strong case for claiming that the *forum conveniens* was either England or America.

Jurisdiction selection in litigation

As previously mentioned, where a contract has no express jurisdiction clause, the plaintiff **4.18** often has an option as to where to initiate litigation.[35] For example, if common law applies, the plaintiff can choose between the location where the contract was formed or breached, or the defendant's place of business. If the Brussels Convention applies and the contract involves a consumer, the consumer can choose whether to sue the defendant vendor in consumer's domicile or the defendant's domicile. These locations, particularly in e-commerce, will not be necessarily the same.

Some changes to the rules relating to consumer contracts have been included in the draft Regulation on jurisdiction. The Brussels Convention affects a large number of e-commerce contracts by including contracts entered into with consumers where the

---

[34] Brussels Convention, Art. 17. Understandably, the Convention requires the selection of jurisdiction to be made in writing. (See para. 3.59 for a further discussion on writing and online contracts).
[35] Indeed, this possibility of plaintiff "forum-shopping" alone represents an important reason why there should always be an express jurisdiction clause!

other party issues a specific invitation or advertisement in the consumer's domicile. The draft Regulation includes all Member States wherever the consumer is actually situated. In effect, most electronic contracts between professional or commercial suppliers of goods and services with consumers are already covered and will remain covered. Thus, the consumer's domicile shall be the country of jurisdiction unless the consumer chooses the supplier's domicile. This will be true regards of any contractual term to the contrary.

A number of e-commerce merchants are concerned that the proposed changes will have the effect of obliging them to trade under local consumer laws in every Member State of the European Union. However, it is submitted that the draft Regulation does not change things radically, because, as is explained in paragraph 4.30, consumers are already entitled to invoke the mandatory rules of the courts of their domicile when conducting a dispute in those courts. Whether this situation, whereby e-commerce merchants which sell goods or services throughout the E.U. must be prepared to enter into the courts of any Member State and be subject to their local mandatory rules, is desirable from the point of view of those who want to encourage the spread of e-commerce, is a debatable matter.

Thus, the laws of jurisdiction permit the consumer plaintiff whether or not agreement has been reached on jurisdiction and the non-consumer plaintiff where there is no jurisdiction agreement to "forum-shop". The plaintiff can balance the advantages and disadvantages of the various forums available and make the most advantageous choice. Some factors include:

- in which jurisdiction is success most probable?

- in what other relevant jurisdictions can a judgment from the chosen forum be enforced?

- does the forum have procedural rules that will help or hinder the action?

- is the chosen jurisdiction relevant? *i.e.* will it accept jurisdiction over the dispute? (see below).

Staying Actions

4.19   However, just because a court can exercise jurisdiction does not necessarily mean that it will. The Supreme Court Act 1981[36] and the Civil Jurisdiction and Judgments Act 1982,[37] provide that, whenever necessary in the interests of justice, English courts have the ability to stay or strike out proceedings. The criteria for the granting of a stay are quite strict, as the House of Lords suggested in *Spiliada Maritime Co. v. Cansulex Ltd*:

> "The basic principle is that a stay will only be granted on the ground of *forum non conveniens* where the court is satisfied that there is some other available forum, having competent jurisdiction, which is the appropriate forum for the trial of the action, *i.e.* in which the case may be tried more suitably for the interests of all the parties and the ends of justice."[38]

Thus, while litigating parties may have some choice over forum, the guiding principles of relevance and appropriateness make the choice far more restricted than it may have initially appeared.

---

[36] Supreme Court Act 1981, s.49(3).
[37] Civil Jurisdiction and Judgments Act 1982, s.49.
[38] *Spiliada Maritime Co. v. Cansulex Ltd* [1987] A.C. 460 at 476.

Foreign jurisdictions

An English e-business will have to compete in a global marketplace knowing that English **4.20** law is not sufficient. Fortunately, for the most part, the actions of other European courts are predictable, since the members of the European Union and the European Free Trade Agreement abide by either the Brussels or Lugano Convention. However, the principles on jurisdiction outside of Europe can be quite different.

In the United States, jurisdiction is often decided based on whether a person makes a "purposeful act toward a forum". For example, in *Minnesota v. Granite Gate Resorts*,[39] the defendant advertised an online gambling service on the Internet, and subsequently formed a mailing list which included Minnesota residents. However, no gambling activities *per se* were considered by the court. The Minnesota Court of Appeals held that:

> "[The defendants] are subject to personal jurisdiction in Minnesota because, through their Internet activities, they purposefully availed themselves of the privilege of doing business in Minnesota to the extent that the maintenance of an action based on consumer protection statutes does not offend traditional notions of fair play and substantial justice."[40]

Similarly, in *United States v. Thomas*,[41] the operators of a pornographic electronic bulletin board[42] in California were convicted of criminal obscenity laws by a Federal court in Tennessee based on Tennessee standards of decency.[43] The Sixth Circuit Court of Appeals held that the material was "sent" to Tennessee and subject to local standards, despite the "sending" being electronic and the bulletin board being essentially accessible world-wide.

In both of these cases, the actions of the defendants were active. In *Granite Gate*, the defendant compiled a mailing list and had even spoken on the phone to the undercover consumer investigator, assuring him that the betting service was legal. In *Thomas*, the defendants charged $55 and required an application requiring age, address, and telephone number. However, U.S. courts may not construe mere passive activity as a "an act purposefully directed toward the forum."[44] In *Blackburn v. Walker Oriental Rug Galleries*,[45] the court held that a website with no purchasing option and only an e-mail response mechanism was 'passive' and thus warranted no claim on jurisdiction.

In related case law on jurisdiction, Dr Lawrence Godfrey, a British lecturer in physics **4.21** and computer science has sued several people and organisations in different jurisdictions in what some believe is a crusade to "force the Internet to comply with national libel laws"[46] Godfrey has sued ISPs, universities and individuals in attempts to force the libel laws of the United Kingdom on other jurisdictions. In 1996, Godfrey sued another British physicist who allegedly posted remarks about him from Geneva, Switzerland. The case settled out of court and therefore provides no precedent in law. However, in 1997, Godfrey sued Cornell University and one of its former graduate students on similar grounds of defamation in the High Court of Justice in London. The High Court issued a

---

[39] *Minnesota v. Granite Gate Resorts,* 568 N.W.2d 715 (Minn. Ct. App. 1997).
[40] *ibid.*
[41] *United States v. Thomas,* 1996 FED App. 0032 P (6th Cir.).
[42] An electronic bulletin board (BBS) is the predecessor to a web site, and was a popular medium among computer enthusiasts in the 1980s. Users do not access it via the Internet, but rather directly call up the computer using their modem.
[43] *United States v. Thomas,* 1996 FED App. 0032 P (6th Cir.), II.C.2.
[44] *Blackburn v. Walker Oriental Rug Galleries Inc.* (E.D. Penn. April 7, 1998).
[45] *ibid.*
[46] Ray C, "The Internet and Jurisdiction: The International Experience"; (1999) 14 *Computer Law Association Bulletin* No. 2.

default judgment against the student (a Canadian studying at Cornell, a New York state university) for £15,000 plus legal costs. In a later settlement Cornell University was dropped from the suit, but in March 1999 it was reported by the BBC that Godfrey was intending to register his judgment against the student in Canada. This case highlights the problems of jurisdiction brought about by the international nature of the Internet. U.S. and United Kingdom notions of free speech and defamation differ and jurisdictional determinations are critical to results. Another example arose in the case of *Pearce v. Ove Arup*,[47] where an English court found that it was entitled to hear a dispute about Dutch copyright law involving a defendant domiciled in England.

Similarly, an affiliate of the Georgia Institute of Technology, based in Lorraine, France, was sued by French linguistic purists for allegedly violating a 1994 law that prohibits advertising in any language other than French. Although French courts decided to dismiss the lawsuit, they did so on purely procedural grounds, leaving open questions of jurisdiction and applicable law.[48]

Although these cases do not deal directly with e-commerce, they indicate the difficulty in applying jurisdictional precedents to Internet law. Full coverage of jurisdictional issues is beyond the scope of this book.

APPLICABLE LAW/CHOICE OF LAW

4.22   Although often confused together, applicable law or choice of law (the law that governs the contract), is not equivalent to jurisdiction (the right to hear a contractual dispute). Jurisdiction deals with issues of forum, whereas applicable law deals with what legal principles that forum applies. The country that claims jurisdiction does not necessarily have to apply its own laws to the case. For example, the High Court in England could resolve a contractual dispute according to French law.

E-commerce does not result in any particularly new or novel issues regarding applicable law. Much of the doctrine has already developed over the past century with the growth of international commerce and shipping. However, in the past, only specialised international importers, exporters, and shippers dealt with these issues on a regular basis. In the global world of e-commerce, applicable law will become a common problem faced by all online merchants.

The Rome Convention

4.23   In England, the issue of applicable law is governed under the Contracts (Applicable Law) Act 1990. The Act implemented the 1980 Rome Convention which harmonised applicable law principles throughout the European Union.[49] The primary interpretative document of the Convention is the Report by Professors Giuliano and Lagarde.

The Rome Convention broadly applies "to contractual obligations in any situation involving a choice between the laws of different countries."[50] Thus, all contracts will fall under its scope, except in a few explicitly stated areas in Article 1(2) such as legal

---

[47] [1997] Ch.293.
[48] Ray C, "The Internet and Jurisdiction: The International Experience"; (1999) 14 *Computer Law Association Bulletin*, No. 2.
[49] N.B.: A few terms of the Rome Convention, notably Art. 7(1) were not implemented by the U.K. Since they are not particle of English law, they will not be discussed here.
[50] 1980 EEC Convention on the Law Applicable to Contractual Obligations ("The Rome Convention"), Art. 1(1).

capacity, land, family matters, trusts and procedural law. The Giuliano-Lagarde Report also interprets the Convention as excluding intellectual property issues,[51] though this exclusion most likely only concerns proprietary rights, not contracts licensing or selling copies of intellectual property (*e.g.* books and software).

Before the passage of the Contracts (Applicable Law) Act 1990, except in specific cases governed by international treaties, common law principles typically governed applicable law disputes in England. However, for all intents and purposes, the Rome Convention now supersedes those principles. Notably, unlike the Brussels Convention and jurisdiction, English courts must apply the Rome Convention in all contractual disputes, irrespective of whether or not the parties are from Contracting States. No connection with a Contracting State is necessary. The Rome Convention universally applies and there are no residual applications for common law.

Despite some suggestions to the contrary,[52] parties most likely cannot "contract out" of the Rome Convention through a contractual clause excluding the 1990 Act. To do so would undermine the whole harmonisation and uniformity purpose that the members of the European Union sought to achieve.

Scope of Applicable Law

The choice or determination of applicable law can be critical in a contractual dispute. By **4.24** defining the rules and principles by which the courts will interpret the contract, applicable law can mean the difference between a breach and no breach, or enforceable and unenforceable. The following list, albeit not exhaustive, shows some of the issues that applicable law governs.

- *Material validity*[53] — the courts will judge the existence or validity of a contract using the law that would govern it if the contract were valid (called "putative proper law" under English common law).[54] Applicable law will govern areas such as mistake, misrepresentation, and contract formation, probably including whether the postal rule or receipt rule is applied under the circumstances. (Paragraphs 3.40 and 3.41)

- *Public policy* — the contract can be held unenforceable because it is manifestly incompatible with public policy (both either to the applicable law or to the forum).

- *Formal validity*[55] — applicable law governs the formal requirements of a contract, such as writing, signature, "every external manifestation required on the part of a person expressing the will to be legally bound."[56] English law has few formal requirements for contracts and, as discussed in paragraph 3.59, is likely to accept the electronic forms of writing and signature anyway. However, other countries may not be as willing to interpret their formal requirements so broadly. One notable exception to this rule is in consumer contracts. Under section 9(5), formal requirements in a consumer contract are governed by the law of the consumer's habitual place of residence, not the applicable law.

---

[51] Giuliano and Lagarde, at p. 10.
[52] Mann (1991) 107 L.Q.R. 353, cited by *Dicey*, at p. 1205.
[53] Rome Convention, Art. 8.
[54] *ibid.*, Art. 8(1). See Current Statutes Annotated [1990] 36–31.
[55] *ibid.*, Art. 9.
[56] Giuliano and Lagardge, at p. 29.

- *Capacity* — The Rome Convention is essentially silent on questions of legal capacity,[57] leaving those determinations to the individual countries. Under English law, the legal capacity of a minor, or any natural person, is governed by applicable law.[58] However, in this particular case, applicable law means "the law objectively ascertained, without taking account of any choice of law in the contract itself."[59] (See paragraph 4.30 on Absence of Choice).

- *Performance*[60] — applicable law determines the expected conditions of performance, such as the diligence required, place, and reasonable time period.

- *Consequence of Breach/Damages*[61] — under the Rome Convention, the remedies and damages available for breach of contract are governed by the applicable law. Although the actual quantification of damages (as a question of fact) remains under the procedural laws of the forum (*lex fori*),[62] limitations on damages and the principles used in measuring damages will be provided by applicable law. These issues were aired in the English case, *Hogg Insurance Brokers v. Guardian Insurance Co. Inc*,[63] in which the judge in the Commercial Court ruled that jurisdiction would extend to all aspects of the contract, including the extent of damages. The court dismissed a claim that punitive damages under Virgin Islands law should apply and found the English court as the forum conveniens. In addition to determining remedies for breach, applicable law will also govern how contractual obligations can be extinguished.[64]

- *Presumptions of Law/Burden of Proof*[65] — to the extent that the principles are substantive and not procedural, the presumptions of law and the burden of proof in a contractual dispute are governed by applicable law. For example, two parties, one from England, the other from Italy, form an online contract for the transport of goods. The goods are damaged in transit. Under English law, the carrier must take "reasonable care" of the goods, whereas under Italian law, the carrier must take "all the necessary measures" to prevent damage.[66] The determination of applicable law may make the difference between whether the carrier is liable for damage or not.

- *Illegality* — if a contract is illegal under the applicable law, the court will not enforce it, regardless of whether it is legal in the court's forum.

4.25   However, despite all these conditions, where applicable law governs the interpretation and enforcement of a contract, the court may refuse to adhere to it under certain

---

[57] Except for the rare and narrow case discussed in Art. 11 of the Rome Convention, which states that "In a contract concluded between persons who are in the same country, a natural person who would have capacity under the law of that country may invoke his incapacity resulting from another law only if the other party to the contract was aware of this incapacity at the time of the conclusion of the contract or was not aware thereof as a result of negligence.".

[58] In this case, applicable means "the law objectively ascertained, without taking account of any choice of law in the contract itself."

[59] *Chitty*, para. 30–091.

[60] Rome Convention, Art. 10(1)(b).

[61] *ibid.*, Art. 10(1)(c).

[62] *Chitty*, para. 30–098.

[63] [1997] 1 Lloyd's Rep. 412.

[64] Rome Convention, Art. 10(1)(d).

[65] *ibid.*, Art. 14(1).

[66] Dicey, at 1209. The Italian law is found in Civil Code, Art. 1681.

conditions. For example, the court may not have the procedural powers to execute the remedy required by applicable law. If the applicable law calls for periodic payments of damages (rather than a lump sum), and an English court has no mechanism for issuing such payments, the court may legally ignore the applicable law's provision under Article 10(1)(c) of the Rome Convention.[67]

Additionally, irrespective of a contract's validity, if the contract is illegal in the country of performance, an English court will not enforce it under the doctrine in *Ralli Bros. v. Compania Naviera Sota y Aznar*.[68] Much debate has arisen over whether the *Ralli* doctrine applies only to situations where the applicable law is English, or to all cases.[69]

As a general principle of the conflict of laws, "a forum will not apply a foreign law which is contrary to the public policy of the forum."[70] An online contract for gambling activities or the distribution of pornography that is illegal under English law will not be enforced by an English court just because the applicable law is of a foreign (and more lenient) country.

Express or Implied Choice

The Rome Convention, following English common law, allows almost complete freedom of choice in selecting applicable law. This freedom applies even in consumer contracts, except for the restrictions discussed at paragraph 4.29. Article 3(1) of the Rome Convention states: **4.26**

> "A contract shall be governed by the law chosen by the parties. The choice must be express or demonstrated with reasonable certainty by the terms of the contract or the circumstances of the case."

Similarly, in *Vita Food Products Inc. v. Unus Shipping Co. Ltd*, Lord Wright (for the Privy Council) held that:

> "Where there is an express statement by the parties of their intention to select the law of the contract, it is difficult to see what qualifications are possible, provided the intention expressed is bona fide and legal, and provided there is no reason for avoiding the choice on the ground of public policy."[71]

As seen in Article 3(1) of the Convention, this choice of law can be made either explicitly or implicitly. Each of these possibilities is discussed in turn.

Express Choice

The specific contractual term or even the standard terms and conditions can expressly select the law which governs the contract. Obviously, express choice is by far the best option for an e-business. The following is an example of an applicable law clause.   **4.27**

Applicable Law
This Agreement shall be governed by, construed, and interpreted in accordance with the laws of England and Wales.

---

[67] Current Statutes Annotated 1990, pp. 36–34.
[68] *Ralli Bros. v. Compania Naviera Sota y Aznar* [1920] 2 K.B. 287.
[69] For further discussion on this debate, see *Chitty on Contracts*, para. 30–108.
[70] *Chitty*, para. 30–109.
[71] *Vita Food Products Inc v. Unus Shipping Co. Ltd* [1939] A.C. 277 at 290, PC.

The chosen law need not have any connection with the contract. As the court held in *Vita Food Products Inc. v. Unus Shipping Co. Ltd*, a contract does not need a connection to England in order for a selection of English law to be valid.[72] Indeed, reasons often exist for selecting a governing law which is not directly or visibly connected to the contract. For example, an underlying intermediary, such as an online auctioneer, may be located elsewhere and select the local laws instead. Alternatively, the auctioneer may choose neutral laws, totally devoid of any connection, on the basis that they are well-constructed for governing auctions. In either case, the purpose of the chosen law is to standardise the contract, so that the other parties know what to expect and the applicable laws do not change from transaction to transaction. However, the chosen laws have no "connection" with the contract *per se*.

However, although the parties have the freedom to choose the applicable law, the Rome Convention imposes a few specific restrictions. These are described in paragraph 4.29. Additionally, in the effort to standardise, choice of law clauses may not select non-national legal systems or "general principles of law". Those choices would probably not constitute an express choice of law under the Rome Convention.

Implied Choice

4.28   As is the case for other contractual terms, where no choice of law is explicitly made, it can be inferred from the circumstances under which the contract was formed. The Rome Convention acknowledges this possibility by accepting implied choices of law where the choice is "demonstrated with reasonable certainty."[73]

However, according to the Giuliano-Lagarde Report, although choice of law may be inferred, a court may only infer it when "the parties have made a real choice of law, although this is not expressly stated in the contract."[74] But in no case does the Rome Convention allow the court to infer a choice of law if the parties had no original intent to choose.[75] This distinction is a fine and tenuous one, and thus the Report suggests a number of situations where the court may infer an intended choice of law. This list is by no means exhaustive, but instead offers examples where an intended choice may be most apparent.

- *Standard Contract* — If the contract is a commonly-used standard form contract where the applicable law is known, the courts may infer the choice of law. A typical example of this type of contract is Lloyd's policy of maritime insurance. In e-commerce, one can imagine that if a particular form became the standard online sale of goods contract in England, the courts may infer that English law was chosen by the parties.[76]

- *Previous Dealing* — If previous contracts or dealings between the parties left no doubt as to the choice of law, the court may infer that choice law into the present contract.

---

[72] *Vita Food Products Inc v. Unus Shipping Co. Ltd* [1939] A.C. 277 at 290, PC.
[73] Rome Convention, Art. 3(1).
[74] Giuliano-Lagarde, at p. 17.
[75] *Dicey*, para. 1224.
[76] One would hope, however, that the contract that becomes the standard on-line contract in the future will already have an express choice of law clause to eliminate this uncertainty!

- *Choice of Forum* — If a contract expressly grants jurisdiction to a specific forum, it implicitly chooses the law of that forum as well. However, choice of forum is only one factor which must be considered in light of other facts in the case.[77]

- *Reference to a Specific Legal System* — If a contract references legal provisions or statutes from a particular country's legal system, the court may hold those laws as the implied choice. For example, mention of the Unfair Contract Terms Act 1977 or the Sale of Goods Act 1979 in a contract might provide grounds for an inference that English law is to apply. Nevertheless, references alone are by no means conclusive. A court must decide if they really imply a particular choice of law.[78]

To infer an intended choice of law, the courts will naturally try to consider as many pre-contractual circumstances as possible. One question, however, is whether the courts can account for conduct after contract formation. In *Whitworth Street Estates (Manchester) Ltd v. James Miller and Partners Ltd*, the House of Lords did not allow post-contractual considerations.[79] However, under the Rome Convention and the interpretation in the Giuliano-Lagarde Report, the position reverses, allowing the court to consider factors after contract formation. English courts will probably consider post-contractual conduct in the future, but only to the extent that it depicts the parties' state of mind prior to contract.   **4.29**

In the absence of an express clause or a definitively implied choice of law, the contract has an 'absence of choice.' In that case, the court will use different principles to determine applicable law, as described below at paragraph 4.27.

Absence of Choice

In the absence of a choice of law, the contract is governed by the law of the country most closely connected to the contract.[80] This rule generally applies, the only notable exception being in consumer contracts where an absence of choice will result in the contract being governed by the laws of the country in which the consumer is habitually resident.[81]   **4.30**

Exactly which country is "most closely connected" is often unclear. Article 4(2) of the Rome Convention therefore provides a presumption:

> "It shall be presumed that the contract is most closely connected with the country where the party who is to effect the performance which is characteristic of the contract has, at the time of conclusion of the contract, his habitual residence or, in the case of a body corporate or unincorporate, its central administration."[82]

Article 4(2) changes the presumption slightly for commercial contracts. In the case of a party effecting characteristic performance during the course of a trade or business, "the country shall be the country in which the principal place of business is situated."[83] Obviously, this latter case is particularly relevant for e-commerce.

---

[77] The situation described here is the exact reverse of that described in the previous section on jurisdiction. There, an express choice of law aided the court in determining jurisdiction, although again, it was only a factor and had to be considered in light of other facts.

[78] For example, the court must determine whether (a) the reference to an English statute implies a choice of English law; or (b) the reference is merely a "shorthand" for a contractual term (*e.g.* the parties seek to include the English standards of satisfactory quality) but the choice of law is a different country altogether (*e.g.* France).

[79] *Whitworth Street Estates (Manchester) Ltd v. James Miller and Partners Ltd* [1970] A.C. 583.

[80] Rome Convention, Art. 4(1).

[81] *ibid.,* Art. 5(3).

[82] *ibid.,* Art. 4(2).

[83] *ibid.*

The above presumption can be overruled if the place of characteristic performance is undetermined or the circumstances suggest that the contract is more closely connected to another country.[84] However, one can imagine that the courts will usually apply this presumption and thus the definition and determination of characteristic performance becomes critical.

Characteristic Performance

4.31 Characteristic performance is defined in the Giuliano-Lagarde Report as:

> "The performance for which payment is due, . . . the delivery of goods . . . which usually constitutes the centre of gravity and the socio-economic function of the contractual transaction."[85]

Consequently, in the online environment, examples of characteristic performance will include the delivery of goods and the supply of services or digitised services. Those goods and services, not the payment exchanged for them, constitute the essence of the contract.

However, the Rome Convention emphasises not the actual place of characteristic performance, but the habitual residence or place of business of the party who performs. Therefore, since the vendor executes the characteristic performance in the typical commercial online contract (non-consumer), the applicable law will be the law of his/her country, not the customer's. The Rome Convention gives the advantage to the vendor.

Since applicable law in the absence of choice will fall to the vendor's place of business, vendors may wonder if the location of the web server could be considered as a place of business. This interpretation would give vendors the flexibility to "forum shop" between their actual physical place of business and the location of the web server. However, as suggested at paragraph 4.09 (*Jurisdiction in personam*), defining a web server as a place of business would be an over extension of the concept and contrary to the spirit of the law. Companies can place their web servers virtually anywhere in the world and the physical location of the web server is often totally irrelevant to how the merchant conducts business. "Place of business" is a holistic determination, not one based on minute objective criteria that may lead to distortion.

In any case, e-commerce vendors are advised to always make a choice of law in their standard terms and conditions. For non-consumer contracts, the rules on applicable law in the absence of choice may be automatically favourable to vendors, but for consumer contracts they are not. Besides, why take chances? Express choice of law solidifies the governing law in nearly all cases, including, surprisingly enough, consumer contracts (subject to the few restrictions set out below at paragraph 4.29.)

Mandatory acts

4.32 Although the Rome Convention allows contracting parties considerable freedom in making their choice of governing law, it does impose a number of restrictions. These restrictions, however, are very limited in scope. They do not prohibit or prevent a choice of governing law under any circumstance; they only ensure that the choice of law does not pre-empt or evade mandatory rules. Although e-businesses establish a great deal of legal certainty by expressly specifying a choice of law, they may therefore still be subject the mandatory laws of other forums.

---

[84] *ibid.,* Art. 4(5).
[85] Giuliano-Lagarde Report, at p. 20.

Domestic evasion of mandatory acts Article 3(3) of the Rome Convention states:

> "The fact that the parties have chosen a foreign law, whether or not accompanied by the choice of a foreign tribunal, shall not, where all the other elements relevant to the situation at the time of the choice are connected with one country only, prejudice the application of rules of law of that country which cannot be derogated from by[*sic*] contract, hereinafter called 'mandatory rules'."[86]

This clause has an extremely narrow application. Its essential purpose is to prevent an otherwise purely domestic contract from evading mandatory rules by specification of a foreign applicable law. Article 3(3) is only applicable if all elements of the contractual situation (not just the contract itself, but the surrounding circumstances) involve only one country. If the circumstances involved other countries, it will not apply. If, however, the clause does apply, the contract will be subject to all the mandatory rules of the forum. For example, two English parties create what is otherwise a purely domestic sales contract, but specify French law as the governing law. The courts will honour the choice of law as French, but will also impose English mandatory rules, such as the Unfair Contract Terms Act 1977.[87]

Superseding mandatory rules Article 7(2) also deals with mandatory acts: **4.33**

> "Nothing in this Convention shall restrict the application of the rules of the law of the forum in a situation where they are mandatory irrespective of the law otherwise applicable to the contract."

Normally, a country's mandatory laws apply only if a contract is governed by those laws. For example, the Unfair Contract Terms Act 1977 is a mandatory law if the applicable law is English, but will not apply if the applicable law is French (except under special provisions).[88] However, section 7(2) recognises the possibility of creating "mandatory rules of a higher order,"[89] rules that would apply to a contract even if it were international in nature and governed by a different law. The Giuliano-Lagarde Report suggests that future rules concerning competition or consumer protection might fall under this category, provided that they are explicitly legislated to be applicable irrespective of a contract's governing law.

Consumer contracts **4.34**

The most substantial application of mandatory acts in the Rome Convention is where it grants consumers protection against choice of law clauses:

> ". . . a choice of law made by the parties shall not have the result of depriving the consumer of the protection afforded to him by the mandatory rules of the law of the country in which he has his habitual residence."[90]

---

[86] Rome Convention, Art. 3(3) from *Current Statutes Annotated* (1990) 36–16.

[87] The Unfair Contract Terms Act 1977 does not apply to international supply contracts. However, in the given case, the contract is of a purely domestic nature and no. goods pass between borders. On a more curious note, the Act will not apply if the example in the text were reversed. If two French parties stipulated English law, normally all the English mandatory rules would apply, since applicable law is English. However, the Unfair Contract Terms Act 1977, it is specifically stipulated that if the choice of law is English but aside from the choice the applicable law would be a foreign country (in the latter example, France), then the Act's provision will not apply. Unfair Contract Terms Act 1977, s.27(1).

[88] For example, where the contract falls under s. 3(3) of the Rome Convention (above).

[89] *Chitty*, para. 30–041.

[90] Rome Convention, Art. 5(2).

However, this consumer protection clause is not automatically applicable. In order to qualify for protection, the contract must satisfy any one of three conditions.

The first condition is that the consumer contract was solicited (*i.e.* by direct mailing or advertising) by the vendor in the consumer's domicile, and the consumer completed all contract formation steps there. This definition of consumer contract is the same as the one found in the Brussels Convention for jurisdiction. (See discussion on issues at paragraph 4.06.) It is also probably the most relevant for online contracts.

The second condition is where the vendor received the consumer's order through an agent in the consumer's country. "Agent" in this context represents anyone acting on behalf of the vendor and not a principal-agent relationship.[91] One potential area of dispute is determining whether an agent is involved, particularly if a website is operated by a third party from the consumer's country. In most cases, as explained earlier, neither the web server nor the third party provider would be considered an "agent" or "place of business". Since the server can be located anywhere and essentially serves as a communications medium, its location is not related to the supplier's business or business practices. However, if the third party operator took active steps, such as order processing, then it might be construed as an agent.

4.35   The third condition, which concerns cross-border excursions for the purchase of goods, is not relevant to e-commerce.

If the contract is a consumer contract, the Rome Convention will not allow the choice of law to deprive the consumer of the mandatory protections offered by his/her place of habitual residence. However, this requirement defines the minimum level of protection. If the choice of law in the contract offers the consumer greater protection, the consumer will receive that higher level instead.

ENFORCEMENT

If one cannot enforce a court judgment, concerns about forum and applicable law become meaningless. Normally, in a domestic case, enforcement flows naturally from jurisdiction. An English court will enforce its own judgment. However, the international nature of many online contracts may require that a judgment obtained in one country be enforced in other countries in which the defendant owns assets.

Enforcement is an extremely broad issue since each foreign country may have its own unique enforcement laws.[92] English judgments can be enforced in many foreign countries through international conventions, particularly the Brussels Convention,[93] but some other countries (notably the United States) have no reciprocal enforcement agreements with England.[94] In the latter case, enforcement will depend on the specific laws of each country, analysis of which is beyond the scope of this book. This section focuses on enforcement within members of the E.U. and EFTA.

Enforcement under the Brussels Convention

4.36   One of the primary purposes of the Brussels Convention was to harmonise the jurisdictional and enforcement laws within members of the European Community. This

---

[91] *Dicey*, at p. 1290.
[92] For a more detailed discussion on enforcement, particularly concerning foreign judgments in the U.K., see *Dicey*, Chap. 14.
[93] 1968 Brussels Convention on Jurisdiction and the Enforcement of Judgements in Civil and Commercial Matters, discussed extensively at para. 4.02 concerning jurisdictional issues.
[94] *Dicey*, at p. 460.

same mission was continued in the Lugano Convention which brought similar harmonisation to members of the EFTA.

In the spirit of harmonisation and legal certainty, the Brussels Convention leaves very little room for interpretation and decision-making in matters of enforcement. In Article 31, it states that:

"A judgment given in a Contracting State and enforceable in that State shall be enforced in another Contracting State when, on the application of any interested party, the order for its enforcement has been issued there."[95]

A person seeking to enforce a judgment need only to make an application to the forum. The enforcing country has very little discretion. Applications can only be denied for a limited number of reasons such as if the judgment is contrary to public policy or if it irreconcilably conflicts with another decision involving the same parties in the enforcing forum. The Convention further prohibits review of the judgment in terms of substance,[96] and binds the enforcing court to the jurisdictional rulings of the original court. In other words, the enforcing court cannot refuse to enforce a ruling because it feels the original court improperly exercised jurisdiction.

As a result of these strict conditions regarding enforcement, there is little difficulty (despite the inconvenience) in enforcing an English judgment in another Contracting State.

Enforcement outside the Brussels Convention

Outside of Europe, the situation regarding enforcement is far less certain. Some **4.37** countries, particularly in the Commonwealth, have reciprocal enforcement agreements given effect under the Administration of Justice Act 1920 or the Foreign Judgments (Reciprocal Enforcement) Act 1933.

However, where a defendant's country has no reciprocal agreement with the United Kingdom, a plaintiff seeking to enforce an English judgment in that foreign country will need to commence a new court action there. This process will be far more complicated; the foreign court may wish to re-assess the merits of the case or re-assess the English court's assumption of jurisdiction before giving effect to the decision.

Enforcement of Arbitration Awards

In the U.K., the Arbitration Act 1996 provides for the enforcement of domestic and **4.38** international arbitration awards. The former are enforceable as if they were judgments of the High Court. The latter are similarly enforceable depending on the country in which an award has been made. New York Convention awards are enforceable if the award was made in a country which was a party to the Convention.[97] The list of such countries is long and includes most developed countries. Provided that such an award is made pursuant to an arbitration agreement in writing, it is enforceable as if it were a judgment or may be relied upon for an order to be sought from the High Court.

---

[95] Brussels Convention, Art. 31.
[96] *ibid.*, Art. 34.
[97] s.100 of the Arbitration Act 1996; New York Convention on Recognition and Enforcement of Foreign Arbitration Awards 1958.

CONCLUSION

4.39   With most consumer e-commerce transactions being for sums of £100 or less, it is unlikely that the application of the complex rules of jurisdiction, governing law and enforcement will be worthwhile considering. However, as the amount of business to business e-commerce increases, it is inevitable that disputes for larger amounts of money will arise where it is necessary to consider which law applies and which forum should hear the dispute. For the e-business, as this chapter shows, the importance of well drafted terms and conditions which contain express choice of law and jurisdiction clause can not be overstated.

— 5 —

INTELLECTUAL PROPERTY RIGHTS

> "The Internet is one Gigantic Copying Machine"[1]

INTRODUCTION — THE RELEVANCE OF INTELLECTUAL PROPERTY RIGHTS

5.01 One area that causes many problems, yet gives rise to the greatest possibilities for e-commerce, is trading in goods and services involving intellectual property rights (IPRs). In the past few years the World Wide Web has become the bazaar of intellectual property. Commerce in ideas, written works, information services and other dematerialised goods is growing at an unprecedented rate. Laws are being tailored to secure intellectual property. However, the laws are hard to enforce; jurisdiction can cause serious difficulties and remedies are difficult to apply.

E-Commerce provides an opportunity for business to communicate with and market products to a worldwide audience. However, the flip side of this universal access is that the user-friendly nature makes it easy for IPRs to be infringed. The Internet does not recognise national boundaries and infringement can take place by someone overseas as easily as from the United Kingdom. For this reason, those involved in e-commerce business, including content providers, website operators, internet service providers (ISPs) and connectivity providers must be aware of the principles of intellectual property and their evolving relationship with digital multimedia environments (the Internet, digital TV, WAP and beyond).

5.02 Each country develops its own intellectual property laws and those rights are only enforceable in that country. Virtually all works on the Internet are protected by copyright but this chapter also considers the other IPRs of trade marks, patents and confidential information.

In making sense of this area two important issues should be highlighted. Firstly, there is considerable research work going on at the international level in specifying what is termed the digital object identifier (DOI). In the United States the Corporation for National Research Initiatives (CNRI) is working closely with Xerox regarding the "digital property rights language". This work is leading toward a standard for "watermarking"

---

[1] David Nimmer, *The Economist*, July 27, 1996.

all electronic documents so that they contain, embedded within them, details concerning their IPR ownership and the uses to which they may be put. These measures will make copyright infringement actions far easier to prove whenever materials containing DOI are in issue. DOI materials will be protected against forgery and tampering by special amendments to copyright laws, which will extend the criminal law into these activities; there was agreement to this effect at the December 1996 meeting of the World Intellectual Property Organisation. Secondly, the debate on "fair use" of copyright materials is currently stalled in Europe although the United States has expended considerable effort in creating a national consensus in favour of fair use amongst educators, libraries and the business community. This European failure to reach agreement makes it likely that U.S. views on what constitutes fair use will prevail. Since the U.S. approach to fair use is rather more liberal than that found in continental Europe this would effectively be a reduction in copyright protection for many media products.

International Law

5.03   Protection of intellectual property rights is territorial. Consequently, if a U.K. copyright or patent owner wishes to enforce its rights abroad, it must rely on the local law of the territory in question and any international treaties to which the country in question has acceded.

The three main international conventions governing copyright are the Berne Convention of 1886, the Universal Copyright Convention of 1952 and the Rome Convention of 1961. The Berne Convention[2] aims to protect "the rights of authors in their literary, scientific and artistic works" and also extends protection to cinematograph films while retaining the rights of the authors of any underlying works. However, it includes protection for items of fact or daily news. As the Berne Convention was established in 1886, it has some difficulty keeping up with advances in technology and affords no protection for computer programs or databases. In fact, due to the rapidly changing environment of trade in intellectual property, the WIPO concluded two new treaties (as a special agreement within the meaning of Article 20 of the Berne Convention) in Geneva in December 1996.[3] The WIPO Copyright Treaty and the WIPO Performances and Phonograms Treaty grant exclusive rights for authors, performers and producers in making available copies of their works to the public "by wire or wireless means" (language intended to cover the Internet). In addition, rights of communication to the public generally exclude the "mere provision of facilities" for enabling communication to the public (in order to exclude the liability of Internet Service Providers). The treaties also cover electronic rights management systems, computer programs and original databases.

5.04   The Universal Copyright Convention[4] sets minimum standards of protection in contracting states for the rights of authors and other owners of rights in literary, scientific and artistic works, including writings, musical, dramatic and cinematographic works, paintings, engravings and sculpture.

---

[2] http://www.wipo.org/eng/general/copyrght/bern.htm.
[3] http://www.wipo.org/eng/diplconf/distrib/press106.htm.
[4] http://www.unesco.org/webworld/com/compendium/4202.html.

The International Convention for the Protection of Performers, Producers of Phonograms and Broadcasting Organisations (the Rome Convention[5]) gives internationally recognised protection to makers of sound recordings, performers and broadcasting organisations. As these three conventions form the backbone of international law covering copyright, members of these conventions must set up minimum standards of protection for copyright. The combination of U.K. law establishing copyright in a particular work and the force of international conventions on copyright is meant to protect U.K.-based intellectual property rights abroad.

In the realm of patents, the Paris Convention[6] on the International Protection of Industrial Property serves as the primary international agreement granting protection to industrial designs and property. As of January 1997, 140 states had signed the Convention which establishes priority for patent applications submitted in one state for 12 months in case an equivalent patent is filed in another signatory state.

Finally, the General Agreement on Tariffs and Trade/Trade Related Aspects of Intellectual Property Rights (GATT/TRIPS) Accord strengthens global trade related intellectual property protection and provides protection for new technology based intellectual property such as software and biotechnology products. The two main principles of protection enshrined in the GATT/TRIPS Accord are national treatment and most favoured nation treatment. The national treatment principle requires signatories to the Accord to provide the same level of protection for foreign intellectual property owners as they do for their own nationals. The most favoured nation principle, similarly requires that nations extend the same advantage, favour or privilege to all nations. In other words, no one nation should have extra privileges or immunities from protection. There are however exceptions that recognise the right to limit protection for nations who do not provide similar national treatment.[7]

5.05

COPYRIGHT

General law

Copyright protects "original" works expressed in various material forms. The expression of an idea is eligible for copyright protection, while the idea itself is not. Designed to improve the efficiency of invention and innovation, the idea/expression dichotomy leaves the protection of ideas to patents. Originally designed to protect works in tangible form, copyright has been recently extended to cover digital works and computer programs as literary works. As the digital revolution continues, new forms of literary works are built and "elegant" and sometimes unintentional means of infringing copyright are discovered.

5.06

Copyright law in the United Kingdom is governed by the Copyright Designs and Patents Act 1988 and allows the author of a work to control the copying or exploitation of the work. Copyright automatically comes into existence when a work is recorded in some way, such as in writing or stored in computer memory. In fact, sometimes the recording of a work has more influence on the rights associated with that work than its creation.

---

[5] **http://www.wipo.org/eng/general/copyright/rome.htm**.
[6] **http://www.wipo.org/eng/general/ipip/paris.htm**.
[7] Williams A. *Multimedia: Contracts, rights and licensing*; (Sweet & Maxwell, London, 1996). at p. 31.

> If I write a speech on paper and deliver it, I have copyright in that work. But, if I deliver a speech without writing it, it is not protected because it has not taken any material form. If someone writes the speech down or records it, I have copyright in the work itself (*i.e.* their recording). This means that they cannot use the work without my permission (although I cannot copy their recording). If, however, the person recording the speech applies sufficient originality to the work, for example a journalist that makes a piece out of an interview, then they retain copyright in the work that they produce. "A sound recording or film cannot exist until it has been created in some medium."[8] There are no rights to works that have not been recorded in some way.

5.07   In the new era of digital interaction, notions of "material form" and "tangibility" fall by the wayside. In fact, notions of material form pull in two separate directions in the information age. In one instance, digitised information rarely takes material form. You can touch the hard drive on which information is stored or the box in which your hard drive sits, but you have no tactile access to the information without some form of processing by the machine itself. On the other hand, as it travels from one location to another during a transfer, digitised information is copied over and over again producing several copies of the original. In this sense, digitised information is both with and without material form. This phenomenon introduces into law several important concepts specific to the copyright of digitised information which will be discussed throughout this chapter.

Internet Routing of Downloaded Information

5.08   As information is passed from a web server to a user over the Internet, the process by which data flows critically effects notions of copyright. For example, when a user downloads an image from a web site, the digital data that makes up the image is broken into packets of bits in order to facilitate efficient flows of information. These packets are fitted with header information that describes where the packet is coming from, where it is going and in what order the packets must be rearranged to reconstitute the original image. After being divided, each individual packet is routed over a series of web servers and routers to the final destination. The path taken by the separate packets is not necessary the same and frequently packets are sent through a variety of paths to the final destination in order to avoid traffic. At the destination, the packets are reassembled into the image that was originally requested. During this process, several "transitory" copies of the image are made at each web server. When the image is then accessed for viewing by the user, yet another transitory copy is made in the Random Access Memory (RAM) of the user's machine. It is the nature and use of these copies that dictates copyright infringement in a networked world. How these copies are used and kept directly impacts the legal status of the actions in question.

Duration of Copyright

5.09   The types of works in which copyright can be found and the period of copyright protection are set out in the following table:

---

[8] Williams A. *Multimedia: Contracts, rights and licensing;* (Sweet & Maxwell, London, 1996, London). at p. 31.

Copyright works	
Type of work	**Period of copyright**
Original literary works	Life of author, plus 70 years from year of author's death
Original dramatic works	Life of author, plus 70 years from year of author's death
Original musical works	Life of author, plus 70 years from year of author's death
Sound recordings, broadcasts and cable programmes	50 years from the end of the year in which the work was first made or broadcast
Computer Generated Works	50 years from the end of the year in which the work was made
Films	70 years from the end of the year in which the last director died
Typographical arrangement of a published edition	25 years from the year of first publication

The convergence of multimedia forms complicates the notion of copyright in many ways. A multimedia work for sale or licence on the Internet may be a combination of sound, film and text. Copyright in individual parts of the product may therefore expire at different times. In addition, copyright protection of different parts of a particular multimedia work may be spread over several individuals or organisations making clearance or licensing more complicated.

Rights of the copyright owner

Copyright owners can prevent the following acts: **5.10**

- copying of the work, including the downloading or printing of material from the Internet;
- issuing copies of the work to the public, including unauthorised dissemination of material on the Internet;
- performing, showing, or playing the work in public;
- broadcasting the work; and
- making an adaptation of the work.

The Copyright Designs and Patents Act 1988 introduced for the first time into English law the concept of moral rights. Four moral rights remain with the author, even if the copyright has been assigned to a new owner: the right to be identified as the author; the right to object to derogatory treatment of the work; the right not to suffer a false attribution of the work; and the right not to have copies of commissioned photographs issued to the public.

In many cases, the author of a copyright work is the person who actually created the work. However, where works are created in the course of an author's employment, subject to any contrary agreement, the employer is the owner of the work. Where an e-commerce business contracts with a third party to create a copyright work it is essential that ownership of such work is assigned to the e-commerce business.

Rights of visitors to a website

5.11   Copyright law also takes into account the interests of users, including vistors to websites, by providing concessions. These concessions are in effect statutory limitations on the exclusive rights of the copyright owner and will provide defences to a charge of copyright infringement. They are as follows:

- *fair use* — fair dealing with a copyright work is permitted for research, private study or for the purpose of review;

- *software* — the Software Directive of 1991 gives the licensee of software a right to make a back-up copy and decompile the software for purposes of interoperability (*i.e.* to ascertain how to operate with other systems, software and networks). It is not an infringement of copyright for a lawful user of a program to copy or adapt it if it is necessary for lawful use and it is an act which is not restricted by the licence.

Protection of material on a website

5.12   An e-business web site will contain a variety of copyright material:

- *written material* — original written material such as advertising narrative and advertisements are protected as literary works;

- *images* — original images such as drawings, charts, maps, plans, diagrams and photographs are protected as artistic works.[9]

- *music and audio-visual material* — music, independent of any accompanying lyrics, is protected as a musical work.[10]

- *databases* — a database is currently protected as a literary work even if computer generated. Qualification for copyright protection in the United Kingdom currently requires only a modest investment of skill and labour in producing the database and that it is original. The Database Directive[11] introduced two levels of protection for databases. If the selection and arrangement of the data involves creativity, the database will attract full copyright protection for the life of the author plus 70 years, as is already the case in the United Kingdom. A database that lacks such creative input (and which may not currently attract copyright protection) will

---

[9] In August 1997 the BBC attempted to shut down numerous sites containing their copyrighted Teletubbies.
[10] In 1997 the management of the pop group Oasis attempted to stop fans from hosting websites which contained music and videos of the group;.
[11] Enacted in all E.U. Member States by January 1, 1998.

acquire the lesser new right of unfair extraction for a period of 15 years. The new right will enable the creator to prevent extraction from or re-utilisation of the whole or a substantial part (either qualitatively or quantitatively) of the database. A website is a collection of pages, each of which may contain several overlapping and adjacent copyright works. A site as a whole may attract copyright protection on the basis that it is, in essence, a database.

- *software* — computer programs are protected by copyright and therefore may not be copied or downloaded without the owner's permission;

- *uniform resource locators* — URLs are the standard addressing system for the Internet. An individual URL is probably not protected by copyright, as it is no different from a telephone number, street address or other type of addressing system[12];

- *web pages* — the design of a web page consists of an arrangement of elements such as text, graphics and audio-visual material. Provided that the arrangement is original and not trivial, the design of the page will be protected by copyright.

When an e-business publishes content on its website, it needs to ensure that either it owns the content that is being used or that it has the right to use someone else's content by obtaining prior permission.

Access to a website

The Internet relies on the principle of implied permission to allow access to material. An **5.13** e-business puts copyright material on its site because it wants it to be browsed and is therefore granting an implied licence to each visitor to the site. Since there is an implied licence the next question is how wide is that licence? This is difficult to determine on a general basis and it will depend on custom, use and the actual circumstances. At the very least there is a licence to permit viewing of a website which entails copying a page/site into the RAM of the computer. It follows that other uses would be an infringement but realistically all that businesses are going to be concerned about is commercial scale infringement, not individual infringement. Valuable material for which a company wants to charge or restrict how it can be used can be made the subject of an express licence. These licences are the ones normally seen on a website where a company or individual stipulates the permitted use(s).

It is vital that visitors to a business website clearly understand what rights are granted **5.14** to use, reproduce and adapt particular material. It is prudent to add a properly drafted licence to each page of a website. It is a simple process to enter into an express licence with every visitor to the website. Having read the terms of the licence, visitors can be required to confirm acceptance of the licence terms by a positive act, *e.g.* by clicking "I accept".[13] An example of a licence and disclaimer is set out below.

---

[12] It is interesting to note here that suits have been brought to prevent registered trade marks from being used in Meta Tags: see Chapter 2.
[13] See Chapter 3, para. 3.71.

The copyright owner [*insert your name*] hereby grants to visitors to this World Wide Web page a licence to make one free copy of the information contained herein for personal use only. All brand names and product names used on these Web Pages are trade marks or trade names of their respective holders. You are granted access to these pages conditional upon your agreement to accept the application of English Law to govern matters between us in relation to this website and you agree to indemnify us and not to hold us liable for the result (foreseeable or unforeseeable) of any actions you may take based on the material contained herein.

Infringement

5.15   Copyright is infringed by doing any of the following acts without the consent of the copyright owner:

- *primary infringement* — copying, issuing copies to the public, broadcasting or mailing adaptations;

- *secondary infringement* — importation, sale or distribution of an infringing article;

- *transient infringement* — making an accidental copy, *e.g.* a temporary copy in RAM;

- *electronic copying* — the conversion of source to object code;

- *remote copying* — transmitting over a telecommunications system.

Either the whole of a copyright work or a substantial part of it must be copied for the copying to amount to infringement. In this sense, "substantial" is both quantitative and qualitative; reproducing the essential features of a work, however small, may constitute infringement. Using five seconds of a piece of well-known pop music would probably be substantial enough to amount to copyright infringement. Plagiarising 10 lines from a lengthy essay, however, may not.

5.16   The legal remedies for copyright infringement on the Internet are the same as for infringement in any other medium. The full range of civil redress is available, including damages, an account of profits and emergency orders. The interactive nature of the Internet on a global scale does, however, cause enforcement problems. Geography is no bar to infringement. Via the Internet, copyright can be infringed from overseas and then disseminated worldwide just as easily as by a user in the United Kingdom. The problems encountered by Nottingham County Council in July 1997 illustrate some of the practical problems faced by copyright owners when faced with a breach of copyright. A report of a 1988 satanic abuse case which was critical of the council was published on the Internet by one of the authors and three journalists. Nottingham County Council obtained injunctions in the High Court prohibiting the authors and journalists from publishing, but a spate of 30 new mirror sites sprang up around the world. The Council was faced with sites infringing copyright in foreign countries; although it threatened to do so, in the end it decided against taking legal action in numerous overseas jurisdictions.

Where to sue and which copyright laws apply therefore become paramount issues. Broadly, copyright laws are limited to national boundaries. There is no such thing as international copyright law, although in many respects these laws are harmonised. The European Union has been harmonising European copyright laws and has adopted

Directives to harmonise, amongst other things, the terms of copyright and protection for databases. As a rule of thumb, the best jurisdiction in which to sue is the jurisdiction of the infringer. If no legal right exists in the infringer's territory, or it is impractical to take action in that territory, there may be scope for suing in another jurisdiction, such as that of the recipients of the infringing work.

Where the infringer is not readily identifiable, is insolvent or too geographically remote, the Internet Service Provider can be an alternative target. As the companies which provide access to the Internet and host websites, Internet service providers can in theory also be liable under English law in certain circumstances for having issued infringing material. Whether an Internet service provider will be liable will often depend on whether it had knowledge of the infringing item.[14]

There are also practical measures which can assist with protecting copyright. It has   **5.17** been said that "the answer to the machine is in the machine". The Copyright Designs and Patents Act 1988, section 296, gives copyright owners rights against those who deal in copy protection circumventing devices where copies of a copyright work are issued to the public in an electronic form which is copy protected. Technical security is available. IBM, for example, developed a system of secure "packaging" for sending digital information over the Internet and a clearing house to track delivery of and payment for the "packages". It is also possible to encrypt (turn into a code) material on the Internet to ensure that a downloaded version will be useless to anyone who does not have the key to decipher it. Furthermore, "sleepers" can be inserted into software to facilitate the proof of infringement. A "sleeper" is something which can be used in legal proceedings to prove infringement. For example, in a piece of software it could be a line of code which does not affect the running of a software program but is clearly incorrect. It is well-nigh impossible to dispute that software has been copied if the defendant's version contains the same sleepers.

Sometimes theft of intellectual property leaves a trail. Thieves are not always technically advanced enough to cover even their most obvious tracks. In the case of **FT.com,** an infringer in Australia was discovered and subsequently convinced to stop stealing material direct from the *Financial Times* website. It seems that this individual had downloaded whole portions of news and data from **FT.com** and subsequently republished the material on his own website hosted in Australia. However, unable to "clean" the material in a sufficient manner, the website operator left most of the HTML code as is on the diverted pages. As a result, the pages requested advertisements from **FT.com** web servers in the United Kingdom. After asking "what business do our advertisements have in Australia?" the FT staff quickly discovered the infringement and successfully convinced the individual to cease and desist.

Hypertext links and "Deep Linking"

Websites are often misconceived as being electronic brochures that are read from   **5.18** beginning to end. Nothing could be further from the truth. In fact, most Internet users are selective in the material they access and may merely access a site to peruse one piece of information before skipping to another site. Hypertext links are the means by which, at the click of a button, visitors can skip from one site to another or from one page to another within the same site.

---

[14] *Godfrey v. Demon* 1999.

The commercial benefits of good "linking" are obvious. Through carefully planned hypertext links Internet surfers can be guided to information about products or services in which they may be interested. Hypertext links to other websites can be used to lure similar target customers. In other words, they can be used as electronic targeted mailshots.

While there are clearly no legal hurdles to establishing intra-site links, the present U.K. law, based on the *Shetland Times* decision of Lord Hamilton in October 1996[15] (so far the only relevant U.K. case), would appear to prohibit in certain circumstances setting up links to another website without obtaining the permission of the owner.

5.19   The *Shetland Times* newspaper obtained a temporary injunction to prohibit its competitor, the *Shetland News,* from linking to its news stories.

Shetland Times owns and publishes a newspaper and also publishes articles on its website. It placed advertising on its home page. *Shetland News* was a competing online newspaper and included in its website headlines from the *Shetland Times,* which were hypertext linked to news stories on the *Shetland Times* website. *Shetland Times* was unhappy that people could obtain access to its news items without having to go through its front page of the *Shetland Times,* thereby bypassing its advertising.

The *Shetland Times* said that its newspaper headlines, which were made available on the company's website, constituted a cable broadcast programme under section 7 of the Copyright Designs and Patents Act 1988 and that *Shetland News'* inclusion of them in its website was an infringement of this Act. *Shetland Times* also claimed that the headlines were literary works and that the copying of them was infringement.

The *Shetland Times'* application was only an interim action and the issues were not fully decided. *Shetland News* claimed that there was no copyright in the headlines and there is case law that words such as "Exxon" are not copyright works; this claim was not accepted. The Scottish court did accept the main argument that the headlines were cable programmes. *Shetland News* said that the Internet did not involve the sending of information and that in any event the service was an interactive one exempted under section 7(2)(a) of the Copyright Designs and Patents Act 1988. Lord Hamilton (the judge in the case) held that the service did involve the sending of information and that there was a case of copyright infringement sufficient for an interim injunction to be granted.

5.20   It is good practice to obtain consent before linking to someone else's site and to set up links in such a way as not to bypass a home page if that home page contains advertising. It seems unlikely that simply providing a hypertext link to someone's web page is of itself a breach of copyright. It is also worth noting that it is possible for a link to be defamatory if the link is to a site with which a company would not want to be associated, *e.g.* if a reputable company site is linked to a pornographic site.

A recent example from the U.S. is the settled case of *Ticketmaster v. Microsoft.* Microsoft's "Seattle Sidewalk" website contained a "deep link" into Ticketmaster's site, bypassing the Ticketmaster homepage and advertising. Ticketmaster, (similar to the *Shetland Times,*) claimed that the opening pages contained certain essential proprietary information and notices, such as the company's logo, copyright notices, disclaimers and advertising. Ticketmaster complaint claimed that Microsoft was depriving it of revenue and infringing proprietary rights and trade marks. The proprietary services and information that Microsoft infringed involved Ticketmaster's live event information and

---

[15] *Shetland Times Limited v. Dr Jonathan Wills* 1997 F.S.R. 604.

services without Ticketmaster's approval.[16] It seems unlikely, however, that web users are willing to follow a hyperlink to a homepage only to have to navigate the site and find the specific document or information they need on their own. This type of narrow and controlled navigation prevents the free workings of the Internet and also prevents efficient navigation.[17] Deep linking can be more easily facilitated if advertising is placed directly on deep pages. Users should not be expected to navigate each and every site they visit on the Web from the home page to the deep page relevant to them.[18]

Framing (Inlining)

Related to hyperlinking and deep linking is the practice of framing. Framing refers to the division of a website into real time "frames" whereby the site owner's proprietary text and material (and potentially banner advertising) is displayed next to linked third party material in the same window. This practice arguably infringes copyright as the website attempts to "pass off" third party material as the proprietary material of the site owner. In the United States case *Washington Post v. Total News Inc.*,[19] the Washington Post and others claimed that *Total News* had designed its website to re-publish news from other sites contributing no original material of their own. *Total News*,[19a] through the use of framing technology, had linked to sites such as the *Washington Post* and framed material from those third party sites alongside banner advertisements which belonged to *Total News*. Those who brought the case alleged copyright and trade mark infringement, false advertising and unfair competition. The case settled out of court and (consistent with the author's views on proper linking) *Total News* was allowed to keep linking to the stories but was prohibited from framing the material next to their own proprietary material, logos and advertisements.[20]

5.21

Caching

Caching refers to the storage of frequently used information in areas more easily accessible to the user. Cached material may be stored on a more powerful computer, a computer closer in proximity to the user or one that receives less traffic. The purpose of caching is to improve the efficiency and accessibility of frequently used information. Local browsers also cache material on the hard disk of the user's computer while ISPs generally cache frequently accessed pages to their local servers. "Proxy" caching refers to any cache created at the server level. Caching involves copying a substantial part, if not all, of the contents of web pages for storage and therefore has potentially significant effects on copyright and trade mark law.

5.22

---

[16] *Electronic Business Law,* Vol. 1, Iss. 4, (May 1999), p. 11.

[17] It seems however that the loss of revenue due to infringement significantly affects corporate decisions about whether or not to allow deep linking. Universal Studios in 1999 asserted what it sees as its legitimate copyright by initiating legal proceedings against a website called Movie-List (http://www.movie-list.com) which aggregates links to movie trailers. Claiming copyright infringement, the major movie studio indicated that linking to their site as a whole was allowed by invitation and authorisation only. Citing *Wired News*, July 27, 1999; **http://www.wired.com/news/news/politics/story/20948.html**.

[18] Another related question concerning deep linking is that of traditional publishing of deep links. In other words, if deep linking is determined to be a violation of copyright, should books such as this one be held liable for publishing the URLs of pages deep within websites. Although this question is similarly unresolved, it seems inefficient to prohibit such publishing.

[19] (No 97 Civ 1190 (PKL) (SDNY 1997).

[19a] See also para. 2.58.

[20] See also Electronic Business Law, vol 1, no. 4, (May 1999), p. 12.

5.23   In most cases, ISPs are the primary target for those whose copyright may have been infringed by the practice of caching. Individual users are too hard to track down and the prosecution of individuals is not an efficient means to blocking alleged infringement. However, the current state of law in this area is quite muddled. At the time this book went to print the two main Directives with relevance to this issue as drafted by the European Union seem to contradict. The draft European Electronic Commerce Directive exempts ISPs from liability for potential copyright infringements due to caching while the European Digital Copyright Directive (as amended) makes them liable for such infringement.[21] ISPs and their counsel are understandably upset by the apparent contradictions in law.[22]

As legal argument hots up in this particular area, the apparent contradiction between the two Directives will surely have to be resolved. Until such a time it may be reasonable to assume that content owners implicitly consent to caching when they make a site available on the Internet. One thing that is clear, however, is that a ban on caching is likely to suffocate Internet traffic and raise access charges.[23]

MP3

5.24   One of the hottest topics of discussion in the field of e-commerce law is the legitimacy and spread of MP3 music files over the Internet. Second only to "sex" as the most widely used term in Internet searches,[24] MP3 files, in the eyes of the music industry, threaten to topple traditional methods of music distribution and unfairly infringe the copyright of music distributors and musicians alike.

MP3 is a file format that stores compressed music files. The major obstacle to the sale of music on the Internet before use of MP3 was file size. MP3 formats, which compress music to a size in which one minute of music roughly equals 1MB of disk space, make the downloading and storing of digital music more feasible.[25] In fact, through the use of "encoders" and "rippers", which facilitate the transfer of music from CD audio format to MP3 and back, users can make MP3 CDs of their favourite music for use in normal CD audio players (or through computer CD-ROM drives). In addition, several firms produce MP3 players which play music directly from the digital MP3 format.[26] This revolution in music compression makes possible the large scale distribution of music over the Internet and therefore has attracted the attention of the music industry and artists interested in protecting their copyrights and royalty payments.

5.25   In the first suit brought by an artist against fan run websites, the Artist Formerly known as Prince is suing a number of sites distributing images, MP3 files and unauthorised biographies over the Internet.[27] Claiming copyright infringement and trade mark violations, the artist is attempting to shut down nine sites involved in the

---

[21] In fact, amendments made by the European Parliament would hold ISPs liable for infringement due to caching, however, the European Commission continues to dispute these amendments and is pushing for exemptions for ISPs on the caching issue. As the current Directive is in a state of debate between the Parliament and the Commission, it is difficult to say what the outcome will be. This legislative negotiation is discussed in further detail in the section covering the Digital Copyright Directive below.

[22] "The current position is ridiculous," . . . "How can you be liable for caching in one Directive but not be liable in another?" As quoted in *E-Commerce Law & Policy,* vol 1, iss 2, (March 1999), p. 1.

[23] *Computing,* April 15, 1999.

[24] *Electronic Business Law,* vol 1 no. 4, (May 1999), p. 5.

[25] **http://www.mp3.com/faq/general.html**.

[26] The Diamond Rio is currently the most popular MP3 player. http://www.diamondmm.com.

[27] *Electronic Business Law,* vol 1, no. 4, (May 1999), p. 5.

distribution of his music, logo and images. MP3 files themselves are perfectly legal. In fact, some music groups have embraced the MP3 movement as the next step in music distribution[28] and several sites legally distribute MP3 music with the authorisation of the copyright holders. However, unauthorised distribution of MP3s infringes the copyrights of the owner and since policing the Internet based unauthorised distribution is nearly impossible, the reaction of the music industry to the MP3 movement is understandable.

In an effort to address the issues of copyright and trade mark infringement brought about by the MP3 movement, several record companies and technology firms have joined forces to promote a unified standard for the secure distribution of music through the Secure Digital Music Initiative (SDMI).[29] On July 13, 1999, the SDMI announced standards for the distribution of secure digital music in a two phase initiative aimed at regaining control over Internet based music distribution channels. The first phase of the initiative would support all formats including MP3, while in the second phase (expected in 2000) music companies would begin inserting digital signatures or "watermarks" into music files to prevent unauthorised copying.[30]

Contributory Infringement

Moves to block the distribution of music through the MP3 format have focused on one of **5.26** the only realistic methods of stopping unauthorised distribution, restraining MP3 search engines. The International Federation of the Phonographic Industry (IFPI) brought a suit in April 1999 against FAST Search & Transfer, a Norwegian partner of Lycos, claiming that their MP3 search engine (licensed to Lycos) contributed to the infringement of music copyrights held by its members. The notion of "contributory infringement" expands the realm of culpability under copyright law to include those who directly contribute to or facilitate infringement although they may not directly copy works themselves.[31]

The legal notion of contributory infringement has significant potential to affect e-commerce in that presumably legitimate businesses that support the online activities of others may be liable for infringements committed by their users. For instance, in the case of the Lycos MP3 search engine, users may simply be looking for legal MP3 files available for personal use. Internet Service Providers and makers of MP3 players may also be implicated by notions of contributory infringement depending on how broadly the legal construct is interpreted.

The U.K. body of law that addresses this type of issue was seen in *CBS v. Amstrad*, in which the British Phonographic Industry took action against Amstrad for selling cassette players capable of recording music. The House of Lords dismissed allegations of copyright infringement, joint infringement and breach of duty of care based on the Copyright Act 1956, (the then relevant Act in law). It is likely that actions against makers of MP3 players would today be considered similarly under the Copyright Designs and Patents Act 1988.[32]

---

[28] The Beastie Boys, a U.S. based rap and funk group, have openly supported the format and its distribution principles.
[29] Set up by the Recording Industry Association of America, SDMI members currently include Sony, Warner Bros, EMI, BMG Entertainment, AT&T Lucent, Microsoft and America Online.
[30] **http://www.cnn.com/TECH/ptech/9907/14/digital.music.html**.
[31] Electronic Business Law, vol 1, no. 4, (May 1999), p. 5.
[32] Morgan G, *IT + Communications Law Journal, no. 5* (February 1999), p. 10.

Digital Copyright Directive

5.27   The E.C. Copyright and Related Rights in the Information Society Directive, originally presented in 1997, is currently in the process of debate between the European Commission and the Parliament. The main issues relating to copyright in the Directive involve the applicability of reproduction and distribution rights in digital environments. Specifically, acts of temporary reproduction, such as caching, which are not economically significant but necessary for the transmission of digital data are expressly exempt from copyright protection giving ISPs some breathing room in their provision of data to the public. In addition, a proposed new right of communication to the public would add to author's rights a "transmission right" for forums like the Internet. Also, protection is explicitly afforded to anti-copying and rights management systems.[33]

After a European Parliament plenary session on February 11, 1999, which formulated a Parliamentary response to the Copyright Directive, the European Commission published an "Amended Proposal"[34] which included ". . . a majority but not all of the changes sought by the European Parliament in its February 1999 Opinion . . ." Significantly, however, the amended proposal maintains exceptions from reproduction rights for "certain technical acts of reproduction" such as caching and rejects Parliamentary suggestions that these technical acts of reproduction should require authorisation from rights holders. If successful, the maintenance of caching exceptions should promote a more efficient flow of information and lessen barriers to e-commerce and the distribution of materials online.

It should be noted, however, that, as of July 28, 1999, the Commission has accepted only 44 of the 56 amendments proposed by the Parliament. Therefore, the Directive remains in a state of legislative negotiation. It may take some time before the Directive is adopted by Member States and begins to impact on e-commerce in Europe.

U.S. Digital Millennium Copyright Act

5.28   On October 28, 1998 President Clinton signed into law the U.S. Digital Millennium Copyright Act (DMCA). Designed to implement the WIPO treaties signed in December 1996 at the Geneva conference, the Act addresses many controversial issues raised by digital copyright such as database protection and the extent of infringement liability in the case of Internet Service Providers. After final debates concerning the Act in the U.S. Congress, certain controversial provisions were excluded. Most notably, provisions to extend copyright protection for databases (including those with material in the public domain) were excluded after opposition from scientists, librarians and the academic community.[35] In addition, many feared the erosion of the fair use doctrine in the Bill. To address these concerns, Congress added explicit language that may provide shelter for fair use of copyrighted material.

[33] *Electronic Business Law,* vol 1, no. 5, (June 1999), p. 10.
[34] **http://www.europa.eu.int/comm/dg15/en/intprop/intprop/copy2.htm**.
[35] Senator Orin Hatch indicated plans to revisit protection for databases in legislation next year.

General Provisions of the DMCA:

- criminalises circumvention of anti-piracy measures in software.

- outlaws code cracking devices used to copy software.

- exemptions to the cracking provisions for encryption research, computer security testing and interoperability of products.

- exemptions from anti-circumvention provisions for non-profit libraries, educational institutions and archives under certain circumstances.

- in general, limits copyright infringement liability for ISPs who simply transmit information and also generally accepts "reasonable" caching as legitimate. (However, does expect ISPs to remove infringing material once made aware of violations)

- requires web broadcasters to pay licence fees to record companies.

- requires the register of Copyrights to submit proposals on how to harmonise the Act with distance learning initiatives while "maintaining an appropriate balance between the rights of copyright owners and the needs of users."

- fair use: Makes explicit that "[n]othing in this section shall affect rights, remedies, limitations, or defences to copyright infringement, including fair use . . ."[36]

The DMCA may have an interesting affect on the propagation of Privacy Enhancing Technologies (discussed in detail in Chapter 7). While the Act addresses personal privacy concerns by allowing the circumvention of "cookies" by online users, this exception is limited to cases in which the user is notified and given capability to circumvent the "cookie". However, this exception does not specifically permit the development or distribution of the means of circumventing identification mechanisms.[37] This may have a significant effect on commercial businesses designed around the goal of providing anonymity to web users.[38] Several online businesses are building technology designed to allow anonymous browsing on the Web while maintaining the legitimacy of their purchases. Strict interpretation of the limits of this exemption may limit the legitimacy of such business and impact the movement towards secure anonymity. **5.29**

The DMCA has significant implications for e-commerce in that it regulates the distribution and dissemination of copyrighted material and products and limits the ability of businesses to provide circumvention tools for copyright or identification mechanisms built into products. Although the Act is U.S. legislation, it effects all business conducted there and any companies targeting sales in America.

---

[36] Cyberspace Law & Policy Institute "The Digital Millennium Copyright Act — Overview" **http://www.gse.ucla.edu/iclp/dmca1.htm**.

[37] Band J, "The Digital Millennium Copyright Act" **http://www.arl.org/info/frn/copy/band.html**.

[38] An example of a business aiming to provide anonymity on the web is Zero Knowledge Systems (whose slogan incidentally is "Nothing Personal"). They are developing a product called Freedom, the Beta version of which was released near the time this edition went to print. **http://www.zks.net**.

TRADE MARKS[39]

Registering trade marks

5.30   In e-commerce one key barrier to entry is to protect the brand. This makes trade marks a valuable right for e-businesses.

A trade mark is any sign capable of distinguishing the goods or services of one origin from those of others. A mark can be protected by registration. In the United Kingdom there are two routes to protection. A national registration can be obtained through the U.K. Patent Office under the Trade Marks Act 1994 or a mark can be registered as a Community trade mark (C.T.M.) under European Community law.[40] The C.T.M. system is administered through the Office for Harmonisation in the Internal Market (OHIM), located in Alicante, Spain. All communications are carried out electronically and it is one of the first truly paperless offices.[41]

5.31   In order to obtain registration the mark must be represented graphically. Sound marks can be represented by musical notation. Shapes and even smells, it has been suggested, can in theory be registered. However, on the Internet it is clearly the traditional word and logo marks that are most readily identified and used. The mark is registered for classes of goods or services that must be specified in detail. It is quite possible for the same trade mark to be registered for quite different goods by different owners. For example, JIF is registered for lemon juice and for floor cleaner.

If a trade mark is to be used on the Internet and the e-business expects to attract customers from a wide geographical area, then ideally the trade mark should be registered in the major countries of the world. This implies the need to amass a large portfolio of registrations, which is an expensive process. For the smaller e-business hoping to develop a reputation in its brand worldwide, a sensible compromise is to register where the business is based, at the U.S. Patent and Trade Mark Office, and at OHIM. The C.T.M. is valid throughout the European Union, thereby obviating the need for separate registrations in different member states. Possession of a registration for a territory allows the owner of the registration to prevent others using the same or a confusingly similar trade mark in relation to the same goods or services.

E-businesses should try and register for trade marks all the elements which give their site distinctiveness.

Infringement on the Internet

5.32   When a trade mark is used on a web page, that page is visible to users all round the world. If goods are offered for sale by reference to a trade mark that is perhaps owned by different parties in different jurisdictions, there is an immediate possibility of a complaint of trade mark infringement. The approach taken by courts is normally to consider the degree to which the website targets a particular country before deciding whether it infringes another's trade mark in that country. If an e-commerce is aware of a conflicting trade mark in a certain jurisdiction the following steps can be taken[42]:

---

[39] Trade marks have already been briefly discussed in Chapter 2 in relation to domain names.
[40] (Council Regulation 40/94 on the Community Trade Mark).
[41] The U.K. Patent Office has an Internet presence at **http://www.patent.gov** and OHIM is at **http://europa.eu.int/agencies/ohim/english/title.htm**. Both sites give useful information about the registration process.
[42] Suggestions from Philip Westmacott of Bristows at Electronic Commerce in Business Conference, October 28, 1999.

- not using the language of that jurisdiction on the website;

- ensure the website makes it clear that individuals in the conflicting jurisdiction territory are not being targeted;

- establish the set up of the website so that orders or even visitors are not accepted from the conflicting jurisdiction;

- insert an acknowledgement of the rights of the third party on the website.

In principle, it is possible to search to ensure that an e-business's trade mark can be used without complaints of infringement being received. This is an expensive process but before launching the use of a new trade mark with an expensive advertising campaign it is clearly necessary to make some effort to evaluate the risk of receiving an infringement complaint.

English courts have held that a website is accessible from every jurisdiction in the world so a German website may constitute passing off in England[43] even if not targeted at the United Kingdom.

Unregistered marks

Unregistered trade marks are not totally without protection. If an e-business has used a **5.33** trade mark in the United Kingdom to build up a body of goodwill, this will be protected against use by competitors, by the tort (or civil wrong) of "passing off". ("Passing off" is the pretence by one person that his/her goods are those of another person.) However, to establish this tort it is necessary to prove the existence of the goodwill and that the use by the adversary has created a misrepresentation that causes damage to the goodwill. Ownership of a registered trade mark makes the complaint much easier to prove, although if the mark used by the adversary is not identical to the registered mark it is still usually necessary to prove the likelihood of confusion.

Use on the Internet

It is legitimate for an e-business to use a third party's trade marks on its web pages **5.34** provided that it is clear that the reference is to the goods or services of that other party. For example, a retail site offering genuine goods from different manufacturers can use the manufacturers' marks to identify the goods just as an ordinary shop keeper does. It is good practice to pick out trade marks in some special manner to show they are not descriptive or generic terms. The likelihood of misunderstanding can also be reduced by including the type of notice that states to whom the various trade marks belong.

When using your own trade marks, it is desirable to emphasise that they are trade marks by the use of a different font or merely upper case characters and the ™ or ® symbols. The ® should only be used where the mark is registered at least in your home country. It is a criminal offence in the United Kingdom to use ® where the mark is unregistered.

Banner Advertising

Web portals such as Excite, Netscape and Yahoo! use keywords to classify websites **5.35** according to their unique classification schemes. As a means of targeting advertising,

---

[43] *Mecklermedia Corporation v. DC Congress GmbH* [1997] F.S.R. 627.

these portal sites sell keywords to advertisers to trigger banner advertisements in their web space. When an Internet user types the keywords and searches for material certain advertisements are triggered. This practice implicates trade marks when trade marked names or words are used by portal sites as keywords and sold to individuals or organisations other than the legitimate owners of the trade mark. Along the lines of this argument, *Playboy* issued proceedings on February 5, 1999 against Netscape and Excite in a California district court seeking an injunction and damages on the grounds that selling registered trade marks as keywords for search engines misappropriates the reputation and goodwill of the trade mark holder. When a user types "Playboy" as a key word in the Excite and Netscape portal sites they trigger banner ads for hardcore pornography, which *Playboy* argued injures its reputation and also misappropriates its goodwill.[44]

A "targeted keyword" can sell for approximately $40 per 1000 displays compared to non-targeted banner advertising which sells for around $25 per 1000 views. "It is estimated that search engines get 20 per cent to 30 per cent of their total revenue from key word advertising sales and that 5 per cent of total advertising sales come from the sale of trade marked keywords."[45] Perhaps in recognition of this loss, Estee Lauder has also filed a similar action recently to stop the sale of its trade mark in the form of keywords to an online beauty products distributor called The Fragrance Counter.[46]

Keywords are not necessarily used to pass off products or organisations as others and the trade mark may be used solely to compare products while maintaining a firm division between the owner of the trade mark and the owner of the banner advertisement. However, U.K. case law suggests in the *One in a Million*[47] case that if there is no need for the trade marked word to be used by the infringer than it should be protected. Therefore, if a similar case was made in the United Kingdom, the defence of the trade mark may succeed based on the *One in a Million* precedent.

Meta Tags

5.36   The term "meta-tag" refers to key word terms imbedded in the HTML source code of web pages to classify them for search engines and portal sites. For example, a web site about e-commerce law may include meta-tags such as "copyright", "law", "legal", "e-commerce", "commerce", "copyright", "contract", and so on, to attract users who type these words into search fields. However, although meta-tags are not readily apparent to the human eye,[48] use of certain words may infringe the copyrights or trade marks of third parties.

In the United States, Playboy Enterprises brought a case against Calvin Designer Label in September 1997, accusing the latter of using "Playboy" and "Playmate", registered trade marks of the plaintiff, as meta-tags. Although the court ruled in favour of *Playboy*, the decision was based on the use of trade marked words as meta-tags and the registration of domain names using those same words. Therefore, the case does not

---

[44] *Electronic Business Law*, vol 1, iss 4, (May 1999), p. 2, citing *Netprofit: Electronic Business Demystified*, March 1999.
[45] Miller, N., "Playboy Challenges Internet Advertising", *IT & Communications Law Journal*, no. 6, (May 1999), p. 23.
[46] *Electronic Business Law*, vol 1, iss 4. (May 1999).
[47] *Marks & Spencers v. One in a Million* is discussed in Chapter 2, para. 2.05 in greater detail.
[48] In fact, you cannot see the meta-tags of web pages while browsing the Internet. However, there is a function on most browsers under the View menu called "Source" or "View Source" which allows a user to see the HTML source code of a particular page. Embedded in the header parts of the source code, the meta-tags for that particular page are visible.

necessarily confirm the use of registered trade marks in meta-tags as infringement of copyright or trade mark.[49]

CONFIDENTIAL INFORMATION

Confidentiality and trade secret law is a widely used form of protection for business **5.37** information and can be used for the protection of certain rights such as copyright in software on the Internet.[50] Confidentiality is often used in preference to other IPRs since, unlike patent and copyright, it offers immediate protection, there is no limit on the period of protection and all types of information can be classified as trade secret.

There are three sources of U.K. confidentiality law:

- *implied or express obligation of confidence* — if there is information which by its nature is confidential (*i.e.* relating to specifics which are given under an obligation of confidence) and that information is used without authority, it may be used as a basis for an action for breach of confidence. Clearly the recipient must be aware either expressly or by implication that the duty of confidence exists;

- *contract law* — under contract law a duty of confidentiality can arise either expressly (*e.g.* in writing) or by implication (*e.g.* by contract);

- *employee confidentiality* — where an individual is an employee and uses information which is confidential and which can be isolated from non-confidential information, an action may also be available for breach of this duty.

Since the Internet is not secure, where possible it should not be used for **5.38** communicating confidential information. If such information is to be sent it should be encrypted. All Internet communications containing confidential information should contain a notice along the following lines, which will assist in showing an obligation of confidence.

> "This message is confidential and intended only for the addressee. No other person is authorised to decrypt this message and unauthorised decryption is prohibited and may be unlawful. Unauthorised decryption will not waive privilege or confidentiality."

For an e-business who contracts with a third party web design company confidential information protection may be relevant in the following ways:

- the developer will keep confidential all materials and ideas it encounters while developing the website;

- the developer may be prevented by a restrictive covenant from working on developing competitor's websites. Such a restriction must be reasonable in term and extent. If the developer is undertaking support and maintenance this may form a basis for a continuing obligation not to complete.

---

[49] *Electronic Business Law*, vol 1, no. 4, (May 1999), p. 2.
[50] *Cantor Fitzgerald International & Another v. Tradition (UK) Limited*, April 15, 1999.

PATENTS

5.39 Patents may at first appear to be the least likely IPR to be relevant to an e-business. However, if an e-business is involved with the technical exploitation of the Internet and tools that allow its power to be harnessed, patent protection may be very valuable in ensuring that the e-commerce business benefits from the inventions that it makes. Technical subjects that have recently attracted much patent interest include methods for securing transmissions and, in particular, payment methods as well as technology for managing the load amongst the connected computers that form the basis of the Internet.

Patents, like trade marks, are granted nationally. A patent is a statutory monopoly over a defined area of technology for a period of time, typically 20 years from the filing date. It is essential to apply for patent protection prior to any disclosure of the idea to be patented. Very few countries (notably the United States)[51] will allow a grace period during which there may be disclosure by the inventor which does not jeopardise the subsequent grant of a patent in that country only. In order to avoid the need to file applications in many countries at once, most countries subscribe to the Paris Convention under which a first home filing starts a priority period of 12 months. Any subsequent application filed in a Convention country within this first year is deemed to enjoy the priority of the filing date of the first application.

In the U.K., patents are governed by the Patents Act 1977.[52] A U.K. patent can also be granted via an application made under the European Patent Convention (EPC).[53] Such applications are filed at the European Patent Office (EPO) in Munich. Surprisingly, no Community patent is available to provide protection for the entire territory of the European Union analogous to the Community trade mark. The 1975 Luxembourg Convention provides a framework for such a patent but it has not yet been ratified by all of the member states and now seems unlikely ever to come into force as drafted.

5.40 A U.K. patent gives the patentee the right to complain of infringement if the patented product is made, disposed of (*i.e.* transferred), used or imported into the United Kingdom. For a patented method, use is infringement. In other countries the infringement rights are similarly defined but always restricted to the territory of the State issuing the patent.

A patent protects an invention. To qualify as an invention an idea must be novel and not obvious. It must also be capable of industrial application. This definition is accepted by all members of the World Trade Organisation which includes almost all industrialised nations. However, as regards computer software, there is a variation in practice across the world as to what is proper subject matter for patent protection. In the United Kingdom a "program for a computer" is expressly declared as not being an invention for the purposes of the Patent Act.

Similarly, under the EPC, a computer program is not regarded as "industrially applicable" although the restriction is interpreted rather more liberally than by the U.K. Patent Office and courts. If there is a "technical effect" the subject matter, although exclusively implemented in software, may be allowed patent protection. The USPTO has even more generous guidelines, published on February 28, 1996 for software related inventions, which focus on the "utility" of the invention. At the EPO, inventions in the

---

[51] The U.S. Patent and Trade Mark Office (USPTO) has a website at **http://www.uspto.gov**. Although the USPTO can grant patents that provide a monopoly only over the territory of the U.S., the size and dominance of that market alone can ensure an adequate reward for a European inventor.
[52] The U.K. Patent Office can be found on the Internet at **http://www.patent.gov.uk**.
[53] The EPO has a web presence at **http://www.austria.eu.net/epo**.

field of text processing and automated language translation are judged to be "linguistic" and not of technical effect. They are, therefore, excluded from patent protection. Nevertheless, corresponding patents are granted in the U.S. and Japan. The U.K. Patents Act 1977 includes a list of excluded subject matter which was drafted to exclude work properly protected by copyright or otherwise not industrially applicable. Computer programs appear in this list as part of a wider exclusion of schemes, rules or methods for performing mental acts, playing a game or doing business. The other exclusions are discoveries, scientific theories or mathematical methods, literary, dramatic, musical and artistic works and the presentation of information.

In the *Fujitsu Application*,[54] decided in the Court of Appeal, software designed to **5.41** display crystal structures on screen was rejected as being a presentation of information, and not because it was implemented in a computer program. Similarly, earlier cases on software to implement a mathematical method for deriving square roots[55] and a data processing system for making a trading market in securities[56] were rejected primarily because they fell within the other exclusions. Encryption methodologies and other inventions which, although implemented in software, have a technical effect and make a technical contribution remain patentable even in the United Kingdom. Accordingly, it is always worth taking professional advice in any given instance.

The U.K. Patent Office published a practice note on May 5, 1999 which states that in the future it will accept applications for computer programs, either themselves or on a carrier (*e.g.* a diskette) provided the program is such that, when run on the computer, it produces a technical effect.

The European Commission is concerned that the difficulties of protecting inventions in this field may undermine the competitiveness of European business. Interested parties were consulted in July 1996 through a questionnaire on industrial property rights in the information society. In a green paper published by the Commission on June 25, 1997 on the Community patent and the patent system in Europe the issue is raised again.

When protecting an invention through a patent, it is necessary to define the monopoly **5.42** sought in the wording of the claim. For much computer software it is frankly impossible to distil any inventive concept into suitable wording for a claim that still satisfies the requirements of novelty and non-obviousness. Such software is still protected by copyright.

Once granted, maintenance of a patent is subject to the payment of annual renewal fees in the United Kingdom and most other countries. In the U.S., maintenance fees are payable at longer intervals. This and the cost of obtaining patent protection as well as the likely commercial benefit of a monopoly are factors that need to be taken into consideration when selecting inventions for patent protection.

The U.S. is the most significant jurisdiction for e-commerce and patents are frequently used to protect software and more recently business methods. The U.S. uses a test of commercial utility rather than technical effect. In the USA Amazon.com has obtained a patent for its one click ordering process. This amongst others have opened the floodgates for e-businesses to obtain patent protection for web site systems and features. As the USA is the epicentre for e-commerce it is worth European e-businesses taking out patents.

---

[54] *The Times*, March 14, 1997.
[55] *Gale's Application* [1991] R.P.C. 305.
[56] *Merrill Lynch's Application* [1989] R.P.C. 561.

CONCLUSION

5.43 As in many areas of law dealing with e-commerce, much of the intellectual property law of the Internet is unsettled and evolving daily. Due to the evolutionary nature of the Internet, it is important to use common sense in the treatment of intellectual property in e-commerce. The *Total News* example is case in point. It seems obvious that framing someone else's proprietary material in your own site without authorisation and running advertisements next to it is a violation of copyright. However, there are still examples of this type of violation on the Internet today.

When displaying the trade mark or intellectual property of others on your website, it is important to be careful to disclaim any unauthorised connection to the material or the mark to avoid passing off your site or material as someone else's. Furthermore, it is considered best practice and good netiquette to ask before linking to the proprietary material of other sites. Although most sites are happy to receive extra traffic, the examples of *Ticketmaster v. Microsoft* and Universal Studios recent unhappiness with links made by Movie-List.com prove that not all sites are happy to receive links. The moral of the story is: "think before you link". In fact, most sites provide guidelines for linking somewhere in their websites. Consulting these notices and e-mailing the owners themselves can clarify the policies of specific sites.

When protecting your own intellectual property on the web, it is important to remain aware of references to your trade marks and material. The case of **FT.com** demonstrates how some infringements get back to the owners of the marks or material. However, in some cases investigative efforts may be necessary in order to police your intellectual property. There now exist several businesses whose sole purpose is to investigate and police intellectual property on the web for clients.[57] This type of intellectual property policing is done in order to limit misappropriation of goodwill and loss of revenue. It is worth e-businesses considering registering their business ideas and methods as a patent in the USA as the Amazon One Click patent shows.

As the information age evolves, new precedents will be set and case law will become deeper on issues of intellectual property. In this uncertain time, it is important not only to use common sense, but to closely follow legal developments.

---

[57] For example, Netnames/IPR at **http://www.netnames.com**.

AN INTRODUCTION TO ELECTRONIC PAYMENT MECHANISMS, ENCRYPTION, DIGITAL SIGNATURES AND ELECTRONIC SURVEILLANCE

> The real price of everything . . . is the toil and trouble of acquiring it[1]

INFRASTRUCTURE AND TECHNOLOGY

E-commerce and electronic communications cannot function without technical **6.01** infrastructures and technologies which are supposed to work within a known legal framework. This chapter looks at the these topics as well as some of the evolving government and international controls and initiatives. Specific legislation is addressed in the last chapter of this book.

GETTING PAID IN CYBERSPACE — INTRODUCTION

> "The cheque is in the mail"[2]

Associated with e-commerce are new ways of getting paid or paying for goods and **6.02** services.[3] These are the logical development of conventional cheques which are a type of bill of exchange. Under the Bills of Exchange Act 1882[4] there is a carefully thought out definition of a bill of exchange as being:

---

[1] Adam Smith.
[2] Anon.
[3] For current methods of payment using credit cards and the regulatory structure of Distance Selling and credit card transactions, see Chapter 2.
[4] Referred to by MacKinnon L.J. in *Bank Polski v. K.J. Mulder & Co.* [1942] 1 K.B. 497 at 500 as "the best drafted Act of Parliament ever passed".

> "An unconditional order in writing, addressed by one person to another, signed by the person giving it, requiring the person to whom it is addressed to pay on demand or at a fixed or determinable future time a sum certain in money to or to the order of a specified person, or to bearer."[5]

A cheque is defined in section 73 of the Bills of Exchange Act 1882 as a bill of exchange, drawn on a banker payable on demand. Combining this definition with section 3 produces the following definition of a cheque:

> "An unconditional order in writing, addressed by one person to a bank, signed by the person giving it, requiring the bank to whom it is addressed to pay on demand a sum certain in money to or to the order of a specified person, or to the bearer."

All of these elements can now be contained in an electronic analogue of the cheque which is confusingly referred to as digital money or digital cash or virtual cash (rather than the more logical term "digital cheque"). Each of the key features of a bill of exchange can be converted into an electronic form through the use of sophisticated cryptography. This allows the creation of digital signatures, authentication of electronic messages and verification of the integrity of electronic messages (confirming that the message has not been tampered with and is received in the same form in which it was sent).

But to enable digital money to replace cheques and bills of exchange the U.K. Government will have to introduce legislation. This it is going to do in the form of the Electronic Communications Bill, a draft version of which was published on July 23, 1999 (see the next chapter).

Wholesale EFT systems — SWIFT

6.03   Over the past twenty-five years the world banking system has developed a number of different networks and services which are used for transfer of funds. Some of these, referred to as wholesale EFT (electronic funds transfer), are closed systems which can only be used between regulated financial institutions.[6] The best know system of this type is SWIFT — the Society for Worldwide Interbank Financial Telecommunications. SWIFT is a co-operative organised under Belgian law, with headquarters in La Hulpe, near Brussels. SWIFT provides communications services to the international banking industry, including payments and administrative messages and, more recently, securities settlements. SWIFT is owned by the member banks — approximately 1,600 — including the central banks of most countries. The U.S. Federal Reserve is not a member, but participates in certain types of payments. Securities brokers and dealers, clearing and depository institutions, exchanges for securities, and travellers cheque issuers also participate in SWIFT.

6.04   However, the profits from taking a cut on the global transfer of funds are vast. Consequently SWIFT has had a turbulent life as its members have sought to gain advantages over each other by producing their own international funds transfer systems. Additionally, SWIFT has always been little more than a secure closed messaging operated under strict rules between banks. Under its rules payment instructions sent by SWIFT are

---

[5] Bills of Exchange Act 1882, s.3.
[6] In the U.K. the main regulatory legislation for financial institutions is contained in the Banking Act 1987 as amended by the Banking Coordination (Second Council Directive) Regulations 1992 (S.I. 1992 No. 3218) which implement, *inter alia*, the Second Banking Directive (89/646).

irrevocable guaranteed unconditional payments. But in electronic terms these are nothing more than messages which are stored and forwarded by one closed e-mail system to another. With the deployment of real-time systems throughout banking and commerce, the SWIFT store-and-forward technology is obsolescent. There are plans to upgrade it but the question of who will pay for such a development in an age of commodity telecommunications and cheap computer power remains unresolved. SWIFT has said that it is going to have to have interactive, query-and-response, as well as store-and-forwarding file transfer, and a new standards paradigm. And, in time, it says it will have to move to an Internet Protocol infrastructure.[7] But the issues of security, of migration to the new systems and how SWIFT intends running incompatible networks together remain unanswered. Since SWIFT pays for its developments out of the profits it earns from its funds transfer activities, and these profits are already under serious attack from rival products, it may be the case that SWIFT does not have a future in the e-commerce marketplace.[8] Instead, its role will be taken over by some form of digital money.

Retail EFT

The real revolution in funds transfer was started by bank-to-customer systems known as retail EFT. To date, these have been corporate cash management systems (allowing businesses to give instructions to their banks either by the use of dedicated terminals or, today, using standard PCs over the Internet), and consumer EFTPOS (Electronic Funds Transfer Point of Sale systems which allow customers to make payments directly from their bank account to merchants: SWITCH being the main U.K. brand in this sphere). National EFTPOS systems have become international through their links to VISA and MasterCard credit cards to become universally accepted payment mechanisms around the world during the 1990s. This has contributed to a change in international business practices driven not from the multinationals doing business with each other but by tourists travelling and spending. The payment mechanisms developed for tourists are now being adapted for e-commerce and may become serious alternatives to conventional bank to bank funds transfer.

6.05

Emerging funds transfer systems such as Mastercard-owned Mondex and Visa Cash use smart cards to store "virtual cash". The idea is that a customer loads up a card from an Automatic Teller Machine (ATM) or a payphone, or a personal computer (if fitted with a smart card reader), and uses it to pay for anything that the customer would use cash for. Mondex was trialled in Swindon and at several U.K. universities. Visa Cash was tested in Leeds. Both have also been on trial elsewhere in the world. The advantage is that transactions go direct from site to site in an instant, rather like handing over cash.

---

[7] Interview with Leonard Schrank, chief executive officer of SWIFT in " Global Custodian" **http://www.assetpub.com/archive/gc/97-04gcwinter/winter97GC036.html**.

[8] SWIFT may well have realised this and is concentrating on the top end of the business to business market rather than small business to small business. It is a 50:50 partner with the TT Club, an insurer that covers the liabilities of shippers and port operators, in Bolero International, an association that's proposing a global electronic network to replace the paper chase of international shipping documentation. It proposes the replacement of documents such as the bill of lading, the physical document carried by the ship's captain which transfers title of goods, by an encrypted communication network to shuffle documents of title around the world., a process that's now hampered by incompatible computer systems and bureaucrats. To make this possible Bolero International has invested in one of the world's largest legal studies into electronic commerce. Thirteen countries, including the United States, have been involved in drafting a patented "Bolero Rulebook." However it will not be an easy task persuading major multinationals to change their business methods so that they match the rules promulgated by Bolero International. See **http://www.bolero.net/**.

But virtual cash is in reality a virtual bearer cheque and the take up of the technology has been slow to date.

It should also be noted that while payment by personal cheque is in decline through the growing use of EPOS, Switch and credit cards in the High Street quite the opposite is happening in the use of cheques between businesses — cheque usage by businesses is growing. This is not because electronic technologies are unable to supplant cheque payments. Rather it is because all bankers are able to charge businesses for every cheque drawn on the businesses' accounts and there is no current consensus regarding the charging regime for electronic payments.

Digital Cash and Microtransactions

6.06   The fact that the cost of a single credit card transaction could be fairly high (up to 7.5 per cent of the value of the transaction for small businesses plus a minimum charge) led to a parallel development of digital cash and what is termed "microtransactions". In the mid-1990s several schemes existed on the Internet which allowed customers to "buy" cash with a once-only credit card deduction, which the customer then used to pay out very small sums online. This was alleged to be an efficient way of paying for subscription sites.

In practice, by the end of the decade, none of the microtransaction systems had found a critical mass of customers or support from any of the major banks. CyberCash[9] merged with First Virtual and effectively went into hibernation. DigiCash,[10] an elegant technology, went bust. They were unable to establish themselves as alternatives to credit cards[11] or one-stop information resources.[12]

Electronic Document Interchange

6.07   All of these systems were only made possible through a standardising and formalisation of the content of funds transfer messages which was part of a larger process — the move towards Electronic Document Interchange (EDI) in all commercial documentation. EDI is the process of replacing the paper medium on which trade data were traditionally communicated by computer-to-computer transfer of structured information. Such trade data may comprise, as on paper, contractual or trade-related information, such as orders, invoices, specifications or parts lists, and increasingly also the EFT information required for the settlement of invoices. Therefore, worldwide message standards have been developed under the auspices of the UN, and constantly expanded. UN/EDIFACT (United Nations/Electronic Data Interchange for Administration, Commerce and Transport) was aimed to enable the worldwide exchange of large volumes of data regardless of the language of origin or the communications and computer systems employed. Its work, which was supported by the American National Standards Institute

---

[9] http://www.cybercash.com.

[10] http://www.digicash.com (Note: Although DigiCash filed for bankruptcy in November 1998 and the offices were closed down its website has not been switched off).

[11] The search for a web currency goes on. For the Internet equivalent of trading stamps see http://www.beenz.com.

[12] Such as the *Financial Times*. Its website sells articles from the *Financial Times* and from thousands of other newspapers and journals at $1.50 each to FT subscribers who maintain a monthly account with it. The single monthly variable debit of a credit card for a large number of microtransactions with a particular information provider during that month appears to be an attractive business model which is supported for all specialist information providers by new technologies such as http://www.pay2see.com.

(ANSI), on technical standardisation and legal standardisation led to the most definitive treatment of the issues for international e-commerce transactions: the United Nations Commission on International Trade Law Model Law on e-commerce (the UNCITRAL Model Law), adopted by UNCITRAL during its 29th Session in December 1996. Since then a number of countries and 40 U.S. states have enacted e-commerce legislation which address the issues of dematerialisation of commercial documents and gives effect to digital signatures which are created using encryption technology. The UNCITRAL Model Law is supported by, what is termed a "living document" called the GUIDEC from the International Chamber of Commerce. GUIDEC[13] (General Usage for International Digitally Ensured Commerce) is a set of international guidelines which aims to draw together the key elements involved in e-commerce, to serve as an indicator of terms and an exposition of the general background to the issue. It also addresses one of the key problems in talking about electronically signed messages, in that they are not signed physically, but require the intervention of an electronic medium. This in turn alters the function of the signer , and introduces problems which a physical signature does not encounter, especially the possibility of use of the medium by a third party.

The OECD, too, has also been active in this field: in March 1997 it adopted Guidelines for Cryptography Policy,[14] setting out principles to guide countries in formulating their own policies and legislation relating to the use of cryptography. The Recommendation is a non-binding agreement that identifies the basic issues that countries should consider in drawing up cryptography policies at the national and international level. The Recommendation culminated one year of intensive talks to draft the Guidelines. More recently, in September 1999, the OECD met to consider consumer issues in e-commerce following a worrying report from Consumers International on goods not being delivered and refunds not being available to e-commerce consumers.[15]

The role of the European Commission

Naturally, the European Commission has also tried to be active in this arena. But its **6.08** work has not been leading edge. In 1994 the Commission published "Europe and the Global Information Society, Recommendations to the European Council (the Bangemann Report) and "Europe's Way to the Information Society: An Action Plan".[16] which gave the development of e-commerce a high priority within the European Union. Following a call for tenders in 1996[17] regarding the security of information services, in October 1997 it published "Towards a European Framework for Digital Signatures and Encryption."[18] In this document the Commission recognised that digital signatures and encryption are essential tools in making "good use of the commercial opportunities

---

[13] **http://www.iccwbo.org/guidec2.htm**.
[14] **http://www.oecd.org/dsti/sti/it/secur/prod/e-crypto.htm**.
[15] **Consumers@shopping** — See **http://193.128.6.150/consumers/**.
[16] COM(94) 347 final.
[17] The Interdisciplinary Centre for Law & Information Technology from the University of Leuven was awarded a contract in mid-1996 by the Commission of the European Communities DG XV to conduct a study on the Legal Aspects of Digital Signatures. A draft report has been issued, which gives an overview of national and E.U. policies, existing and envisaged rules and regulations, as well as practices concerning digital signatures in the Member States and the E.U.'s main trading partners. The Study is not yet available to the general public, but the Executive Summary, Table of Contents, Tables of National Legislation, Tables of Certification Agency (CA) Practices and and further information are available at their website: **http://www.law.kuleuven.ac.be/icri/projects/digisig_eng.htm**.
[18] COM(97) 503.

offered by electronic communication via open networks." With respect to harmonisation, it suggests that "Divergent legal technical approaches would constitute a serious obstacle to the Internal Market and would hinder the development of new economic activities linked to e-commerce. An E.U. policy framework for ensuring security and trust in electronic communication and safeguarding the functioning of the Internal Market is therefore urgently needed." It followed this up in May 1998 with a draft Directive on a Common Framework for Electronic Signatures[19] to "ensure the proper functioning of the Internal Market in the field of electronic signatures by creating a harmonised and appropriate legal framework for the use of electronic signatures within the European Community and establishing a set of criteria which form the basis for legal recognition of electronic signatures." The European Union proposal for a European Parliament and Council Directive on certain legal aspects of e-commerce in the internal market has been published in the Official Journal [1990] O.J. C30/5. The proposal aims at facilitating the use of electronic signatures as well as contributing to their legal recognition. It contains provisions on market access, certification services, electronic certificates, liability issues and international aspects. It does not cover aspects related to the conclusion and validity of contracts or other legal obligations, where there are form requirements prescribed by national or Community law; nor does it affect rules and limits governing the use of documents contained in national or community law.

6.09   However, some European Union states have not felt able to wait for the Commission. Germany,[20] Italy,[21] and Luxembourg[22] have all introduced digital signature laws. The United Kingdom, in contrast, delayed its legislation in this sphere "to ensure that our policy development is compatible with that outlined in the Commission's Communication on Encryption and Electronic Signatures".[23]

At the end of July 1999, the U.K. Government published its Electronic Communications Bill saying that "In the last six months, this Government has been moving vigorously ahead to make Britain the best place in the world to do business electronically." It was strongly criticised and a revised version was published just after the Queen's Speech in

---

[19] COM (1998) 297.

[20] Germany has passed the *Information and Communication Services Act of 1997*. This legislation was enacted on June 13, 1997. Art. 3 of the Act governs digital signatures. It requires the licensing of certification authorities. See **http://www.kuner.com/data/sig/digsig4.htm** for an unofficial translation and commentary by Christopher Kuner.

[21] In Italy the *Italian Digital Signature Legislation* was enacted on March 15, 1997 (Italian Law N. 59, Art. 15, c. 2, March 15, 1997). The Regulations were promulgated on November 10, 1997 (Presidential Decree No. 513). An English language translation of the law (**http://www.aipa.it/english/law[2/law5997.asp**) and regulations (**http://www.aipa.it/english/law[2/pdecree51397.asp**) is available at the website of the Autorita *per* l'Informatica nella Pubblica Amministrazione/Authority for IT in the Public Administration (AIPA). The law gives binding and legal effect to electronic documents, and the regulations enacted November 10, 1997 give the same legal effect to digital signatures attached to such documents as if they were manually signed.

[22] At the end of March 1999, the Luxembourg government introduced the country's draft Bill on electronic commerce to Parliament. Composed of 77 articles, this text adapts national civil, commercial and penal law to the electronic environment by also implementing the E.U. directives 97/66, 97/7 and 93/13 on privacy in telecommunications, distance selling and abusive clauses in consumer contracts. Its declared purpose is to provide Luxembourg with a secure and predictable framework for electronic transactions in accordance with international and European rules by including a set of detailed provisions on proof, electronic contracts, certification authorities, digital certificates and encryption standards. While it allows the use of cryptography, it recognises the same legal validity in both electronic and handwritten signatures, provided their integrity is adequately guaranteed by digital certificates delivered by accredited certification authorities. The bill sets up a voluntary accreditation system with the National Accreditation and Surveillance Authority of the Ministry of Economy being the public body entrusted with this task. The procedures and criteria of accreditation are defined in three Grand Ducal Regulations to be adopted with the law.
The draft Bill can be accessed on the Ministry of Economy web site at **http://www.etat.lu/ECO/**.

[23] **http://www.dti.gov.uk/CII/ana27p.html**.

November 1999. The Bill, a bit of a legislative "dog's breakfast", is intended to receive the Royal Assent in the Spring of this year. We explain its provisions, in outline, in the last chapter of this book. However, before doing so, this it is necessary to say a little about encryption and the science of cryptography.

Encryption's escape

Encryption is the process of disguising a message in such a way as to hide its substance. **6.10** This sounds easy but the problem is that the intended recipient of the message has to turn the message back into a readable text. Cryptography is the science which has developed over the centuries around this problem. Until recently, developments in cryptography were a highly secret topic and ordinary people did not have access to sophisticated technologies. All this changed in August 1977 when the U.S. security services were unable to stop a new type of cryptography called "public key cryptography" being described by Martin Gardner in his column in *Scientific American*.[24] Public Key Cryptography provided a solution to the key distribution problem (see below).

A Cryptographic Primer [25]

Cryptographers start all discussion of cryptography with three characters: Alice, Bob **6.11** and Eve. Alice is the sender of a message, Bob is the receiver and Eve is the eavesdropper. In the basic example, Alice wants to send a message to Bob. She takes the message (which is referred to as the *plaintext*) and *encrypts* it. The encrypted message is called the *cyphertext*. Eve, who intercepts the cyphertext, cannot read it. Bob, however, can *decrypt* the message to convert the cyphertext back to plaintext. He does this using an algorithm.

An algorithm is a mathematical transformation. Alice uses an encryption algorithm to convert the plaintext into cyphertext. Bob uses a decryption algorithm to convert the cyphertext into plaintext. At its simplest level an algorithm might be a rule saying "Shift all characters 5 along in the alphabet". So applying the encryption algorithm to the word "safe" would produce the cyphertext "weji". The decryption algorithm is the rule "Shift all characters 5 back in the alphabet."

Until recently, the security of this type of system depended upon keeping the algorithm secret. But this has never been easy and the secret has always leaked out. And the problem became unmanageable when large numbers of people needed to communicate securely with each other. Each one would need to have their own unique algorithm.

The solution to this problem comes through the use of keys. Again, using the simple example, the encryption algorithm might be put into a general form "Shift all characters X along in the alphabet" where X is the key. Alice now encrypts the message using the algorithm and the key. Eve may know the algorithm but so long as she does not know and cannot guess the key the message is secure. Bob is able to decrypt the message using the key.

---

[24] The U.S. security services said that publication of public key encryption was a potential violation of the U.S. International Traffic in Arms Regulations. For a very readable account of the ongoing battle between civilian cryptographers and U.S. authorities see *Privacy on the Line* by Whitfield Diffie and Susan Landau (MIT Press, 1999).

[25] For further information look at the Counterpane site **http://www.counterpane.com/** which maintains a detailed bibliography. The best textbook on the subject is Bruce Schneier *Applied Cryptography* (2nd ed., John Wiley & Sons, 1996).

The Data Encryption Standard (DES)

6.12   The example above is ridiculously weak encryption and, in practice, designing the algorithm is a major activity. A good real world example is DES, the Data Encryption Standard. In the early 1970s, the U.S. Government sought candidates for its proposed federal encryption standard. IBM submitted a variant of an algorithm called Lucifer. The U.S. National Security Agency evaluated the algorithm and DES, as it was called, was adopted by the U.S. National Institution of Standards and Technology in 1976 and became an international standard.[26] It has been widely analysed by cryptoanalysts around the world. DES is an *iterated block cypher* which means that it encrypts plaintext in block sized chunks — each block being 8 bits in length — and applies its algorithm again and again to the block until it outputs the cyphertext. DES has 16 iterations. As a general rule, more iterations provide greater security. However, DES is constructed in such a way that more than 16 iterations do not increase the security of the cyphertext.

So, if Alice sends a message to Bob using DES, she encrypts the plaintext on her computer. The encryption breaks the message down into 8-bit blocks and using the key applies the DES algorithm to each block 16 times before outputting the cyphertext.

Exchanging Keys and Public Key Encryption

6.13   But there remains the problem of getting the key to Bob. If Alice and Bob have never met and yet want to exchange secure messages, throughout history they have always needed to exchange keys. This problem was solved through the development of public key cryptography which is based upon the inherent mathematical difficult in factoring prime numbers.[27] Public Key encryption is also referred to as RSA encryption (Rivest, Shamir, Adleman — the inventors of public key encryption and the owners of the U.S. patents relating to this development)

In public key encryption there are two different keys one for encryption and the other for decryption. They come in pairs: a specific encryption key comes with a specific decryption key. Everyone has a pair of keys. Alice and Bob each publish their encryption keys which are called their public keys. They keep their decryption keys private. When Alice wants to communicate securely with Bob she encrypts her plaintext using Bob's

---

[26] DES is now getting quite old and in high security banking installations *triple-DES* — a block cypher employing DES three times in a row with three different keys — has arisen as a *de facto* standard. It is being considered for formal adoption by the Banking Security Standards Committee 9ANSI–X9F) of the American National Standards Institute. A competition for a replacement for DES has been underway for several years and in August 1999 the U.S. standards body NIST announced that the finalists in the Advanced Encryption Standard competition were MARS, RC6, Rijndael, Serpent and Twofish. These are three U.S. algorithms, one Belgian, and one which was developed by Dr Ross Anderson of the Cambridge Computer Laboratory in collaboration with colleagues in Israel and Norway.

[27] In greater detail public key cryptography owes its existence to a branch of mathematics known as computational number theory, and involves techniques such as modulo reduction, discrete logarithms, factoring of large prime numbers, and, most importantly, one way functions. A one-way function furnishes security by providing a relatively easy computation in one direction, but an extremely difficult computing problem when trying to reverse the original computation. As an example, the value of Y where:
$A = 2, x = 5, P = 7$, and $Y = A^x \bmod P$, can be computed relatively easily. This is simply the remainder when A^x is divided by P. For this particular example:
$Y = A^x \bmod P = 2^5 \bmod 7 = 32 \bmod 7 = \text{remainder } [32/7] = 4$.
However, given: $A = 2, Y = 4, P = 7$, and $Y = A^x \bmod P$, it is not easy to determine the correct value of x. This is especially true when the values typically range anywhere from 512 bits to 2048 bits.

public key to produce the cyphertext. Bob upon receipt of this is able to decrypt it using his private decryption key.

Public key encryption also provides the solution to digital signatures. If Alice creates a key pair, publishes one key and keeps the other secret, she can "sign" electronic messages. Here the plaintext is encrypted using Alice's private key. Anyone is able to decrypt the cyphertext using Alice's public key. This proves that the person who encrypted the text was Alice since only Alice would know her private key.

In practice, these key pairs tend to be used together. Alice will take a piece of plaintext and encrypt it with her private key. The resulting cyphertext can only be decrypted using her public key. Then she takes the cyphertext and encrypts it again using Bob's public key. The resulting cyphertext can only be read by Bob who, to do so, must go through a two stage process decrypting the text with his private key and then Alice's public key. By this means, the message been securely transmitted from Alice to Bob without either of them having to exchange keys. Additionally, Bob knows that the message is authentic since it had to be decrypted using Alice's public key.

The complexity is not finished. Public key cryptography is not suitable for the **6.14** encrypting of long e-mail messages since the task of encryption and decryption would take too long and long public key encrypted messages could be vulnerable to cryptographic attack.[28] Instead it is always used as a method of communicating a conventional symmetrical key from Alice to Bob — the key that is to be used by both parties when encrypting and decrypting using an algorithm (such as DES) on a particular occasion. Additionally, cryptographic systems use what is termed one way hash functions to generate a kind of fingerprint which proves that messages which "hash" to this value have not been tampered with. The most popular one-way hash function in current use is called MD5.[29]

The complexity is actually handled by e-mail security programs. All Alice has to do is indicate that she wishes to send an encrypted message to Bob and the program does the rest. It generates the secret session key, encrypts the message, finds Bob's public key, encrypts the secret session key, concatenates them together and ships the whole thing off to Bob. On the receiving end, Bob's program automates the decryption process in a similar manner.

The most popular encryption program which in its latest commercial versions does all these things is called PGP which stands for Pretty Good Privacy. It has been through a number of developments but today it uses IDEA[30] for data encryption, RSA[31] for key management and MD5[32] as a one way hash function. PGP also compresses files before encrypting them. It is very secure — so secure that governments resist its use by the general public.

---

[28] But a short message such as a 2048 bit key is totally secure.

[29] Invented by Ron Rivest at MIT in 1991. A hash function is a computation that takes a variable-size input (such as the total number of characters and their value in a document) and returns a fixed-size string called the *hash value*. A one-way function is a function that is significantly easier to perform in the forward direction than in the inverse direction, *e.g.* seconds to compute forward, years to calculate in reverse.

[30] International Data Encryption Algorithm. It was invented in Switzerland in 1991 and has been patented in Europe (patent pending in the USA). It has a 64 bit block and a 128 bit key size. It only uses 8 iterations and on most microprocessors a software implementation of IDEA is far faster than a software implementation of DES. It appears to be extremely secure.

[31] Rivest, Shamir, Adleman — there was been a long running patent dispute regarding PGP's use of the RSA algorithm but this has now been resolved.

[32] See n.16 above. For the full mathematical proof of the strength of MD5 see in Internet RFC (Request for Comment) 1321 which explains MD5 with sample code.

6.15

A worked example of Public Key Encryption using RSA Algorithm (1978)

The mathematics of public key encryption is very difficult to understand. Mr Richard Kemp of Kemp and Co., in his lectures on Encryption and Electronic Signatures, cites the following example from *Tanenbaum on Computer Networks* (Prentice Hall p. 515) which illustrates how this Public Key Encryption works by encrypting and decrypting the word SUZANNE using a public key of 3 and a private key of 7:

PLAINTEXT (P)			CIPHERTEXT (C)		AFTER DECRYPTION		
Symbolic	Numeric	P^3	P^3 (mod 33)	C^7	C^7 (mod 33)	Symbolic
S	19	6859	28	13492928512	19	S
U	21	9261	21	1801088541	21	U
Z	26	17576	20	1280000000	26	Z
A	01	1	1	1	1	A
N	14	2744	5	78125	14	N
N	14	2744	5	78125	14	N
E	05	125	26	8031810176	5	E
-------- Sender's computation --------						
			-------- Receiver's computation --------			
Steps	1	2	3	4	5	6

Encryption using Public Key [C = P3 (mod 33)]
1. Find the mumeric using monoalphabetic substitution of the letter (a = 1 etc)
2. Find the cube of each number in step 1
3. Convert step 2 to ciphertext by dividing each number at 2 by 33 to establish its remainder (modulus) [*Note: use of modulus or remainder, acts as "one way valve" to prevent return to pre-encrypted plain text*]

Decryption using Private Key [P = C7 (mod 33)]
4. Multiply each number at step 3 to the seventh power
5. Divide each number at 4 by 33 to establish its remainder [modulus]
6. Find the letter using monoalphabetic substitution of the numberic

Key Pair
- Public Key = 3 [and 33]
- Private Key = 7 [and 33]
- *Where 3 and 7 are replaced by greater than 500 bit (say 300 digit in base 10) numbers, "cracking" the private key becomes virtually impossible*

*This is what is meant by **"strong encryption"***

Secure Electronic Transactions and the Microsoft Patent

In late 1995, MasterCard and VISA, who had each been working independently on **6.16** secure technologies for use in e-commerce, joined together to develop and promote the Secure Electronic Transaction (SET) protocol as a technical standard for safeguarding payment card purchases made over open networks. SET was published as an open specification for the industry with the statement "this specification is available to be applied to any payment service and may be used by software vendors to develop applications. Advice and assistance in the development of this specification have been provided by GTE, IBM, Microsoft, Netscape, RSA, SAIC, Terisa, and VeriSign."[33] It might therefore be thought that this specification was for public consumption. However, on August 4, 1998, Microsoft was granted U.S. *Patent 5790677: System and method for secure e-commerce transactions.* This appears to be a patent covering the underlying technology set out in the SET protocol in a series of 83 claims. It is difficult to reconcile the invitation given out by MasterCard and Visa in publishing the specification with the patenting of the underlying technology by Microsoft. The latter's conduct would suggest that it was planning to use the technology as part of a Patent Pool agreement with various U.S. partners.

Microsoft's patenting in the U.S. of the underlying cryptographic technology may lead to problems in any commercial developments arising out of the major European Commission funded research project in this area called SEMPER[34] (Secure Electronic Marketplace for Europe). This has been executed by an interdisciplinary consortium, combining experts from social sciences, finance, retail, publishing, IT and telecommunications, with the aim of providing an infrastructure for a secure electronic marketplace in Europe. SEMPER not only supports electronic advertising and sale of goods, but also provides means for a complete electronic market transaction, involving factors like electronic payment, non-repudiation of electronic contracts and exception handling within electronic systems. The fact that the patent has only been granted in the U.S. is unlikely to stop U.S. courts claiming jurisdiction over all transactions on the Internet which pass through servers located on U.S. territory.

SET offers banks the potential for a reduction in fraud owing to the fact that in one **6.17** implementation of the protocol the customer's credit card number does not have to be revealed to the merchant in the transaction but remains at all times within a secure encrypted environment. However, this implementation is not compatible with existing merchant payment systems which require access to the customer's card number. Merchants cannot therefore integrate this way of working into their existing operations. Instead, they have been insisting on an alternative implementation which can reveal the card number to the merchant on a merchant by merchant basis. Unfortunately, this second implementation is considerably more complex and expensive to implement. It also removes one of the main security advantages of SET by permitting merchant personnel to have access to customer credit card numbers.

Additionally, to initiate SET transactions, credit card holders have to obtain digital certificates which are used to sign orders with merchants. The obtaining of a digital certificate remains a non-trivial task. Then, once obtained, the credit card holder has to manage the certificate in accordance with a proper understanding of the risks and liabilities which could arise if his digital certificate is misused or lost or stolen. Very few

---

[33] Full documentation on the SET protocol in both postscript and Word format is available at **http://www.cl.cam.ac.uk/Research/Security/resources/SET/set.html**.
[34] **http://www.semper.org/**.

bankers, let alone cardholders, are aware of the risks which can flow from the misuse of a customer's digital certificate.[35]

Because the additional security benefits which come from use of SET appear to benefit banks more than either the merchants or the customers, there is relatively slow growth in the use of SET in general e-commerce. It is unlikely that this situation will change in the near future. A more likely security route will be the deployment of a biometric system to link a physical person which an electronic record.

Government Regulation of Cryptography

6.18

> (2) The goal of any encryption legislation should be to enhance and promote the global market strength of United States encryption manufacturers, while guaranteeing that national security and public safety obligations of the Government can still be accomplished.
>
> (3) It is essential to the national security interests of the United States that United States encryption products dominate the global market.
>
> (4) Widespread use of unregulated encryption products poses a significant threat to the national security interests of the United States.
>
> **An extract from the proposed U.S. legislation:**
> **HR2616—Encryption for the National Interest Act[36]**

Many governments are concerned about the widespread use of cryptography. They claim that cryptography interferes with law enforcement and intelligence gathering. However, little public evidence in support of their claims has been produced. Privacy advocates[37] suggest that legitimate law enforcement and intelligence gathering are not genuinely inhibited through the availability of strong cryptography to the general public since conventional surveillance using hidden microphones, informers, wiretaps and covert actions can always fulfil the real needs of law enforcement and intelligence gathering.

International Controls

6.19   The basis of international controls over the use of cryptography were formally the subject of CoCom and are now the subject of the Wassenaar Agreement.[38] The Wassenaar Arrangement controls the export of cryptography as a dual-use good, *i.e.*, one that has both military and civilian applications. Software containing cryptography may be subject to controls as a dual-use item although, confusingly, Waasenaar provides an exemption from export controls for mass-market software. The interpretation of Waasenaar is thus open to interpretation.

---

[35] See later in this chapter "Liability Issues concerning Digital Signatures and Cryptography".

[36] Encryption for the National Interest Act, August 2, 1999. For the full text **http://jya.com/crypto.htm**.

[37] See for example Dr Ross Anderson's paper at **http://www.cl.cam.ac.uk/users/rja14/dtiresponse/dtiresponse.html**.

[38] Co-ordinating Committee on Multilateral Export Controls (COCOM), a grouping of Western nations that was abolished in 1994 and replaced by the Wassenaar Arrangement which has been signed up to by Argentina, Australia, Austria, Belgium, Bulgaria, Canada, the Czech Republic, Denmark, Finland, France, Germany, Greece, Hungary, Ireland, Italy, Japan, Luxembourg, the Netherlands, New Zealand, Norway, Poland, Portugal, the Republic of Korea, Romania, the Russian Federation, the Slovak Republic, Spain, Sweden, Switzerland, Turkey, Ukraine, the United Kingdom and the United States..

Internationally, governments currently use two methods to control citizens' use of cryptography. Some, such as Russia, restrict the domestic use of cryptography. In Russia[39] a government authorisation must be obtained in order to use any cryptography for confidentiality purposes (as opposed to authentication purposes). Only if very weak encryption is used will the use of encryption be authorised. The user may also be required to deposit his private key. Additionally, Russia also implements the method used by the U.S. and many other countries — export controls in accordance with the Waasenaar Agreement. In general these require a licence to be obtained from a government agency in order to export cryptographic products and technical data.

In early December 1998 the U.S. announced that it had persuaded the other 32 nations in the Waasenaar Agreement to impose strict new export controls on encryption products under the guise of arms control. Wassenaar countries would restrict exports of general encryption products using more than 56-bit keys and mass-market products with keys more than 64 bits long. But each country was required to draft its own rules to implement the agreement and no further action has been forthcoming.[40]

U.S. Controls on the export of cryptography

The U.S. ban on the export of cryptographic products does not cover everything — there **6.20** are exceptions for weak cryptographic products. As we have seen, the strength of a cryptosystem depends partly on the security of the algorithm and partly on the length of the key. The export ban means that while today U.S. companies can use standard commercial cryptosystems with 128 bit keys within the U.S. (such as the encryption built into the Netscape browser's Secure Sockets Layer (SSL)), if people or companies outside of the U.S. wish to use a U.S. cryptographic product they are only legally allowed to have a version which uses keys of a maximum of 40 bits (*e.g.* the International version of Netscape's SSL). These weaker products can be broken in days.[41]

The present U.S. restrictions on the export of strong encryption are generally considered to be completely unworkable as a means of stopping widespread foreign use of unbreakable cryptography. The controls have not stopped strong U.S. cryptography from getting out of the U.S. since the software has been illegally exported over the

---

[39] Upon the disintegration of the U.S.S.R., the President of Russia issued five degrees of February 22, March 27, April 11, May 12, and July 5, 1992 (Nos. 179, 312, 388, 469, and 507), which, together with the Law on Defense Industry Conversion, laid down certain legal foundations for a national armaments and military technologies control system. These decrees were consolidated in 1994 by the Statute on Controls of Exports from the Russian Federation of Certain Types of Raw and Processed Materials, Equipment, Technology, Scientific and Technical Information Which Can Be Used in the Production of Weapons or Military Equipment as ratified by the President of the Russian Federation under Decree 74 dated February 11, 1994. Included in this statute is a list of commodities, which require an individually approved licence, issued by the Ministry of Foreign Economic Relations for export from Russia. Cryptographic equipment and software (including mass-market) is identified in the list of commodities requiring individually approved export licenses. s.5 of Edict Number 334, of April 3, 1995, issued by the President of Russia prohibits the import of cryptographic products without a license. s.4 of Edict Number 334, of April 3, 1995, issued by the President of Russia prohibits all activities in the development, sale, and use of cryptography without a license issued by the Federal Agency for Government Communications and Information (FAPSI).

[40] Quite a few nations who "gave in" to U.S. pressure to agree to the communiqué were seething in private about it. They subsequently made it very clear in "background briefings" that they had no intention whatsoever of doing anything serious to implement what the U.S. thought that it had got because they viewed Wassenaar as being a method of supporting the U.S. defence industry. And because Wassenaar is only an "arrangement" the agreement carries no real weight in getting anything to happen.

[41] Note that because of the use of session keys every message has to be broken separately and can only be done through use of a substantial amount of computing resources.

Internet.[42] Additionally, the effect of the restrictions has been to drive cryptographic development outside of the U.S. and to provide markets for non-US cryptographic companies who are not bound by such restrictions even though their countries are signatories to the Waasenaar Agreement.[43]

6.21   As this chapter was being finished news came in that the U.S. were going to replace "customer by customer" licensing of cryptographic systems for export with "general" licensing for export to most countries for most end systems applications. This change was welcomed by U.S. industry since it will remove a costly bureaucratic burden and will allow U.S. cryptographic suppliers to compete more easily on cost terms with European and Australian rivals. Full details of these changes are expected in mid-December 1999.

However, the U.S. export restrictions have a secondary purpose. Not only are they intended to stop foreigners using unbreakable cryptography, they are designed to encourage the development of an international key recovery infrastructure. How this infrastructure works in the commercial arena and the legal implications of doing business utilising this infrastructure is a major concern of this book. (see the following sections: "Trusted Third Parties, Certification Authorities and Key Recovery Agents" and "Liability Issues concerning Digital Signatures and Cryptography"). They also form the basis of an international electronic surveillance deployment which is of grave concern to civil rights lawyers (see the section "The Great Eavesdropper goes global").

THE ADMINISTRATIVE INFRASTRUCTURE OF ENCRYPTION

6.22   Public key encryption is an elegant technology which leaves one major problem: how does one correspondent know whether he has the right key for the other correspondent? If two individuals have a secure channel over which they can pass a key — for instance, by sealing a piece of paper or diskette in an envelope and sending it through the mail — they can then communicate in confidence. But if they wish to rely simply on electronic media, they have no such secure channel. No one can trust an e-mail message saying, "Here is my public key," because the very message containing that key may be sent by an eavesdropper. The problem arises whenever two people who do not previously know each other wish to communicate. It comes to the fore most often in e-commerce, where a customer wants to know whether he can trust someone who is claiming to offer goods and is asking for payment.

Trusted Third Parties

6.23   *Trusted Third Parties* ("TTPs") may be the solution that allows an initial contact to be made. If you and your desired correspondent are both known by an intermediary, and you both entrust it with your public keys which it publishes, you can obtain each other's public key from this trusted intermediary and start your communications. For worldwide communication, the TTP will probably be a large organisation with the same public visibility, quality controls, and sense of responsibility as a bank; and in the case of

---

[42] Indeed one enterprising crypto freedom advocate famously produced the best selling PGP T-shirt which had the source code of the strong cryptography software printed on the T-shirt. The T-shirt was advertised as not only being "machine readable" but also "machine washable".

[43] *e.g.* The Swiss government is providing 128-bit encryption plug-ins for browsers for download off of the Internet to secure its Telegiro Internet payment system. Downloads and more information are available at: **http://www.swisspost.ch/E/21.html**.

e-commerce it may very well be a bank.[44] The precise duties of a TTP are the crux of the debate between civil libertarians and law enforcement concerning encryption.

At the moment there are no regulations establishing who or what can be a TTP. The U.K. Government has now committed itself to introduce a voluntary system which will ensure that the TTP can, in fact, be trusted by correspondents. It has done so by establishing a clear policy differentiation between digital signatures and encryption.

Certification Authorities

The first group who will be affected will be TTPs who are in the business of certifying the identity and nature of communicators. It may be the case that a bank may wish to issue digital signatures to its best commercial customers, a digital signature which will indicate not only that it belongs to the high value customer but also that that customer has maintained a £20,000 credit balance in its account over the past year. If a customer wants to do business online with another person the customer sends that person an order signed with his bank-issued digital signature. The person who receives the order looks up the public half to the digital signature on the bank's website and is then in receipt of an instant credit reference as well as reliable proof of the identity of the customer. On the basis of this information the person can instantly decide whether to do business with the customer. The bank which issues the certificate is a special type of Trusted Third Party called a *Certification Authority* or *CA* for short. Under the forthcoming legislation the CA will have to be licensed and will have to show that it is conforming to the procedural and technical standards which such licensing will confer. At a minimum it must be in a position to offer certificates to support electronic signatures reliable enough to be recognised as equivalent to written signatures. But it may well be required to do more to secure consumer and business confidence that its signature mechanism is robust and secure.

6.24

Public Key Infrastructure

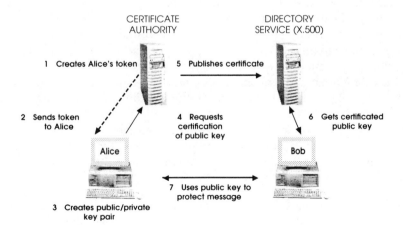

[44] Although this does not have to be the case. Global law firms and major accountancy practices have expressed an interest in getting into the TTP business along with well known systems houses.

Key Recovery Agencies

6.25   There is a special type of TTP known as a *Key Recovery Agent*[45] in the cryptography legislation of some jurisdictions (but not the United Kingdom — see the last chapter of this book). Key Recovery Agents are required to keep, or in the jargon *escrow,* a copy of their customer's private key[46] and are required to hand over a copy of the key within a short time of a request by the authorities. It is an offence, in these jurisdictions, not to hand over the private key needed for decryption of a cryptographic message when the same has been lawfully requested.

It should not, however, be thought that Key Escrow is solely a last ditch attempt by governments trying to regain control over secret communications between its citizens. A reason why Key Escrow schemes are necessary in the commercial world is recovery of information when a private key has been lost, stolen or hidden. If a businessman dies it will be necessary for his executors to be able to decrypt his financial records made using his private key. If a senior employee of a company is fired the company will need to be able to read all correspondence written by the employee while working for the company and encrypted using his private key. Key Escrow systems in cases such as this act as mandatory backup systems ensuring that the private key is always recoverable. It may be thought that e-commerce could be unable to safely function without Key Recovery systems being used.

Biometric Systems

6.26   Key Recovery systems and government requirements for the storage and handing over of decryption keys are likely to become sidelined by a new technology — biometrics.[47] Biometrics are best defined as measurable physiological and/or behavioural characteristics that can be utilised to verify the identity of an individual. They include fingerprints, retinal and iris scanning, hand geometry, voice patterns, facial recognition and other techniques. They are of interest in any area where it is important to verify the true identity of an individual. Initially, these techniques were employed primarily in specialist high security applications. However, we are now seeing their use and proposed use in a much broader range of public facing situations.

Recent work in financial institutions has found wide public acceptance of retinal scanning as an alternative to Personal Identification Numbers in the management of cash dispenser cards. Biometric systems are falling in price and provide a method of uniquely identifying citizens in a manner which, in many cases, cannot be fooled. For example, the pattern in the retina of an eye remains unique and constant from birth until five minutes after death. It cannot be forged but can be captured and compared using a conventional video camera.

If a biometric is used as the private key to secure messages, it will no longer be possible to require a person to hand over his decryption key to the authorities. Instead, any legislation will have to be drafted in terms of a mandatory right to demand decryption by the citizen of his encrypted messages.

---

[45] Unlike every other term of art this one was not shortened to its abbreviation "KRA" when it was mentioned as a U.K. government proposal in a DTI document in 1998. A possible reason for this is that for the DTI to say that "all secret cryptographic keys have to be deposited with the KRAs" could be misunderstood since the Krays or Kray Twins, (Ronnie and Reggie) were a notorious gang of villains who ran major London crime in the early 1960s.

[46] Key escrow or key recovery has been the subject of very heated debate around the world as can be shown by putting either of the two words into any web search engine.

[47] For a very good resource on biometrics see **http://www.biometric.freeserve.co.uk/**.

The Great Eavesdropper goes Global

Lest this complex discussion of encryption prompts the question "why bother — it's too **6.27** complicated" we should indicate that the nature of our telecommunications networks is changing and encryption is becoming essential in competitive international business. The reason for this comes from evidence of the activities of the America's National Security Agency (NSA), the richest security agency in the world. For over forty years the NSA has been eavesdropping on the world's communications networks. In so doing, it has built a spying operation that has reached into the telephone systems of nearly every country.

During 1998/9, members of the European Parliament learned that the NSA in association with the British Government, had created the means to intercept almost every fax, e-mail and telephone call within the European Union. The first report, "An Appraisal of the Technologies of Political Control," confirmed for the first time that the NSA had established a surveillance capacity over the entire European communications network. Of particular interest to Europe was the Report's claim that the NSA was beefing up its *commercial* espionage activities. Its claim is that the NSA has been routinely intercepting sensitive traffic relating to bids, takeovers, mergers, investments and tender offers, all for U.S. economic benefit.

A second report published in June 1999, "Interception Capabilities 2000," set out the technical specifications of a new interception system. This revealed a secret plan amongst the national security agencies to create a "seamless" web of telecommunications surveillance across all national boundaries planned by an organisation called the "International Law Enforcement Telecommunications Seminar". In time, two huge systems — one designed for national security and one for law enforcement — would merge and, in the process, would cripple national control over surveillance activities.

France has been known to use its intelligence services to assist French business interests and there is reason to believe that this practice, by national security agencies, is widespread throughout the world, despite denials. It is clear that, through technology, national borders have disintegrated and that security agencies can intercept any electronic communication worldwide. It is also clear that the distinction between traditional police and security agencies has blurred. The future is, without doubt, a seamless, borderless, surveillance web that touches all facets of our communication. Competitive international business needs to protect itself against such unfair activities through the sensible use of encryption in its sensitive electronic communications.

LIABILITY ISSUES CONCERNING DIGITAL SIGNATURES AND CRYPTOGRAPHY

Doing business using digital signatures requires a different mindset to conventional **6.28** contract management since there are new risks and vulnerabilities. When a digital signature is incorporated in a document it signs every single part of it and links the authority of the signer with every single comma and colon. In practical terms it is far more than signing the end of a document and initialling every page. Yet the digital signature, unlike a physical signature, does not come from a human hand but from an artefact. Unauthorised access to this artefact can lead to the production of signed contractual documents and payment orders which are the same as the genuine articles. The obvious way of controlling such abuse is to make the holder of the digital signature, referred to in the literature as the *keyholder,* liable for all signatures generated by the artefact unless and until the keyholder has revoked the digital signature's authority with the CA.

But it is not easy to establish this new system of working. One business model involves the use of smart cards with the customer's signing and encryption keys recorded in the chip as a replacement for conventional magnetic stripe credit cards. If such a regime were to be grafted onto a U.K. credit card, thereby making the keyholder liable for all transactions made using the card, this would run counter to the current practice whereby a credit card holder is only liable for misuse of his card up to £100. This will not happen. Instead, to deal with the problem, all credit card companies will have to maintain comprehensive, up-to-date lists of stolen or compromised cards. These will have to be far more extensive than today's "stop list" and will require a global infrastructure to enable instant checks to be made every time the credit card is used in a transaction.

6.29   New risks arise through the multiple functions of smart credit cards. If the customer's signing and encryption keys are recorded on the cards when the customer requests a revocation of the card, not only will the credit card company have to invalidate the credit card, it will also have to invalidate the public halves of the personal signing and encryption keys recorded on the cards.

> Paul, a noted investigative journalist, has his home burgled and his smart credit card is stolen along with his PC containing his personal electronic organiser. Paul's digital signature is recorded on the smart card with other secret information recorded on the PC. Paul notifies his credit card company to revoke his credit card and his digital signature. The credit card company fails to do so. A few days later a major foreign newspaper publishes a highly defamatory article allegedly written by Paul. The subject of the article sues the newspaper for libel. The newspaper says it relied upon Paul's digital signature. Paul says he relied upon the credit card company revoking his digital signature. The credit card company tries to rely on limitation of liability clauses in the contract with Paul to absolve it from liability for the defamation arising through its failure to revoke Paul's digital signature.

If a customer is using his smart card not just to buy goods and services using the credit card as a payment mechanism card but also as the repository of his digital signature the credit card company could find itself liable for damages which lie well outside of the scope of e-commerce.

A plethora of problems

6.30   There is also the problem of distinguishing between digital signatures (used for authentication of online messages) and encryption (used for keeping messages secret). They are both generated by the same mathematical functions and based upon the same mathematical principles in computational number theory. The U.K. Government has correctly seen that it should not require the handing over of private keys which are solely used in digital signatures.[48] But there is going to be a major difficulty in explaining to citizens how to manage their signing keys and their encryption keys. Bank staff have been

---

[48] One very significant reason for this is if governments were allowed to have the private keys used in digital signatures of citizens the police and security services could fabricate signed evidence allegedly produced by the citizens.

known to treat a simple check digit system as an encryption system.[49] A citizen could easily need to have several cryptographic keys: a personal signing key (used for all correspondence written by that person in a personal capacity); a commercial signing key (supplied to him as part of his employment which permits him to make binding statements on behalf of his employer which are limited to a pre-defined value of a transaction); a board level commercial signing key (for use in transactions in excess of the pre-defined level made on behalf of company which may inherently incorporate features such as credit reference warranties); a personal encryption key (used when sending private communications in a personal capacity); a corporate encryption key (used when sending private communications in an employed capacity) and a board level corporate encryption key (used when sending private communications in the capacity of being a member of the board). The use of each of the keys and the security needed to be associated with each of them is different. This will lead to disputes and the open question of how the courts would decide the case of an employee using a corporate key for personal purposes. Classical legal analysis suggests that the company would be liable for the employee's actions on the basis of ostensible authority which could only be overcome if the recipient of the signed message knew or ought to have known that the employee was on a frolic of his own. But in real life such cases are likely to get messy as questions regarding whether the company had an adequate system of internal control over the misuse of corporate signing keys and of whether such misuse was condoned at senior levels as a illegitimate boardroom perk but condemned at junior levels, will have to be addressed by the court.

Problems with managing encryption

Companies are also likely to demand, as part of their employment terms, that any **6.31** employee has to escrow with the company any private encryption key he may use in personal correspondence. Were the employer to be unable to demand the private encryption keys of its employees there would be a risk that a disgruntled employee could pass confidential information and trade secrets to rivals secure in the knowledge that cryptography would hide the infamy from the employer. But such a measure would have to be carefully considered. Confusion and litigation could result if this practice were badly implemented and was used as a means of company surveillance over its employees' lifestyles and relationships. Furthermore, corporate ignorance could lead to companies demanding not only the personal private encryption key but the employee's private signing key which would be totally unjustified.

Digital Certificates

"A gentleman's agreement is an agreement which is not an agreement,   **6.32** made between two people neither of whom are gentlemen, whereby each expects the other to be strictly bound without himself being bound at all."[50]

---

[49] In 1979 Dr Lawrence C. Galitz was commissioned by the Committee of London Clearing Banks (CLCB) to develop a "test key" system for the verification of bank messages. This was intended to *verify* messages and warn against simple errors like the substitution of one digit for another, or the transposing of digits. The key he developed was based on "patterns" and "shapes" of 3-digit groups. It was not intended to be used as a authentication system, proving the identity of the sender in a cryptographically secure manner. Most significantly, because the system was intended to be universal, and applicable around the world where varying and very limited technology was then available, it had to be a manual system. Yet despite clear statements to the contrary the "test key" was treated by many bankers at the time as a secure method of message authentication.

[50] Mr Justice Vaisey — an unreported interlocutory observation in *Bloom v. Kinder* [1958] T.R. 91 quoted by Sir Robert Megarry in *A Second Miscellany at Law* (Stephens, 1973).

The digital certificates which are currently in general circulation might be termed "gentleman's digital certificates" (see the above definition). They come with sweeping disclaimers of liability. Both the 40 and 128 bit Netscape SSL encryption that are used for secure web connections rely in part on digital signatures to identify the server and the browser to each other. No one actually guarantees the server's public key. All that the user gets is the practical assurance that if the response back is the same each time he logs on it is unlikely that he is communicating with an impostor rather than the server with whom he wishes to engage in a secure communication. But nobody is accepting liability for the user who is being mislead.

The same situation applies with other current Internet-based certificates including the "authenticode" certificates used to identify the authors of Java-like ActiveX programs. The certificates offer no "bankable" reassurance for Internet users who are understandably reluctant to let code written by strangers gain access to their computer's operating system.[51]

Growing jurisdictional conflict

6.33   The problem is the existing digital signature legislation does not address the liability issue in the same manner from jurisdiction to jurisdiction.[52] If, for example, a comparison is made between two U.S. State digital signature laws, Utah and Washington, important differences can be found. Both states require a CA to suspend a certificate if the CA gets a call from the keyholder saying the private key has been compromised. But to guard against fraud or anti-competitive practices (*e.g.* "Let's hinder our rival in this contract race by faxing its bank and getting its signing key suspended"), the CA can not suspend for long without checking to make sure the suspension request really came from the keyholder. Under Utah law, the check has to be done within two days, but the certificate is automatically suspended whenever the CA gets a request from someone claiming to be the keyholder. Under Washington law, the caller can ask for a four-day suspension, but the CA can only suspend the certificate if the CA is pretty sure the caller really is the keyholder.

Mr Stewart A. Baker of Steptoe & Johnson LLP has considered this point[53] and has commented that while there is the same basic idea in both states ". . . what if you are a CA doing business in both states and you get a suspension request from someone who doesn't sound very much like the keyholder? In Utah, you must suspend; in Washington, you can't. Or suppose the caller asks for three days to come in and verify his identity? In Utah, you can't wait that long; in Washington, you must. CAs simply can't obey the laws of both states."

6.34   This lack of consensus regarding the correct balance of risk between the keyholder and the CA runs though all U.S. states that and can be found in all national systems "How much risk should the keyholder bear and how much should fall on the CA? Different states, and certainly different countries, will arrive at different answers to such questions. But, if CAs must change their practice in each country or each state, there will be very few CAs in ten years, and digital signatures will not live up to their promise."[54] Clearly digital signature legislation requires a great deal more thought than simply trying to

---

[51] See Stewart A. Baker "International Developments Affecting Digital Signatures" October 1997 at **http://www.steptoe.com/WebDoc.nsf/Law + & + The + Net-All/All**.
[52] *ibid.*
[53] *ibid.*
[54] *ibid.*

bring in measures to deal with the de-materialisation of written documents. Somebody has to accept the risk and be adequately compensated for such acceptance. Businesses engaged in e-commerce using digital signatures appear to need similar rights to those given to consumers using credit cards for their payments — a clear limit on their losses when the digital signature is misused.[55] But the speed of modern business may suggest that businesses should also be able to recover unlimited damages for failure of their CA to provide them with round-the-clock services and for failure to supply the business with an instant replacement to a signing key which has been compromised as well as instantaneous revocation of the compromised key.

There is a further problem which has to be resolved before a global system of e-commerce using digital signatures can become a reality. In the White Paper the U.K. Government originally made it clear that it would legislate to ensure that a CA will have to be licensed and will have to show that it is conforming to the procedural and technical standards which such licensing will confer. Although the Government has thought again regarding these procedures (see the final chapter of this book on the new legislation) there remains the question of what "weight" to attach to certificates issued by both licensed and unlicensed CAs. Where does this leave Netscape SSL encryption, "authenticode" certificates and other similar products which are all over the web today? Will every organisation which uses these "gentlemen's digital certificates" have to register? What weight will be given to these certificates? According to Stewart A. Baker: "The German digital signature law implies that no one may issue certificates without meeting strict standards for security; these standards include a requirement that private keys be stored only on a smart card — they cannot be sent over the Internet, and they cannot be stored on a magnetic stripe card or 3.5-inch diskette.[56] In Malaysia, under section 4 of the Malaysian Digital Signatures Act 1997, any organisation issuing digital certificates must register with the Malaysian authorities.[57] Singapore, in their e-commerce law, requires Certification Authorities to be regulated by an appointed Controller of Certification Authorities, who will be responsible for licensing, certifying, monitoring and overseeing certification activities. Licensing will be voluntary, but certificates issued by licensed CAs will be entitled to greater presumptions of validity and limitations on liability. Closed networks may use unlicensed CAs if they choose.[58] None of these regulatory systems are compatible with the system used in the U.S. of voluntary registration by CAs.

CONCLUSION

Recent developments have shown technology and surveillance capabilities to far exceed   **6.35**
the speed at which any reasonable and sensible legal initiatives can proceed. The control over encryption in electronic communications needs to be considered as part of a wider

---

[55] See Chapter 2 for the discussion on the Distance Selling Directive and Consumer Credit legislation.
[56] Cited above. Since Mr Baker published his paper the German position appears to have been modified. See Christopher Kuner of Gleiss Lutz Hootz Hirsch, Frankfurt at
http://www.kuner.com/data/new/gov—digsig—recognition.html.
[57] "s.4(1) No person shall carry on or operate, or hold himself out as carrying on or operating, as a certification authority unless that person holds a valid licence issued under this Act.
s.4(2) A person who contravenes subsection (1) commits an offence and shall, on conviction, be liable to a fine not exceeding five hundred thousand ringgit or to imprisonment for a term not exceeding 10 years or to both, and in the case of a continuing offence shall in addition be liable to a daily fine not exceeding five thousand ringgit for each day the offence continues to be committed. . . ."
[58] s.43 of the Singapore Electronic Transactions Act 1998.

security debate encompassing bugging and secure voice telephony,[59] fairness in the bringing of legal proceedings based on intercepted communications[60] and the need for business to defend itself against illegitimate use of national security facilities to assist local businesses.[61]

All of these topics are well outside the scope of a book on the law of e-commerce. We trust, however, that the footnotes provide the reader with reasonable starting points in considering these issues.

---

[59] See for example Diffie, Whitfield and Landau, Susan Eva, *Privacy on the Line : The Politics of Wiretapping and Encryption* Reprint edition, MIT Press, (March 1999).
[60] See the very useful Human Rights pages of David Swarbrick at
http://www.swarb.co.uk/lisc/Human—Rights—1.html.
[61] See The Annual Report to Congress on Foreign Collection and Industrial Espionage on the U.S. Economic Espionage Act of 1996. **http://www.nacic.gov/fy98.htm**.

— 7 —

EVIDENCE AND SECURITY

INTRODUCTION

It is an unfortunate fact of life that people do not always tell the truth. Sometimes people **7.01** forget, sometimes they lie, or circumstances change which leads one party to remember matters differently. Any modern system of commerce depends partly on trust but mainly on the fact that agreements between the parties are documented. In e-commerce this situation is crucial since the parties to the agreement may never have physically met or spoken to each other by telephone. In most cases, the only evidence of the agreement between the parties will be documents evidencing the transaction. But there may be particular problems because the documents will be computer generated.

TYPES OF EVIDENCE

Computer generated documentary evidence will be of three types. First will be **7.02** calculations or analyses which are generated by the computer itself through the running of software and the receipt of information from other devices such as built-in clocks and remote sensors. This type of evidence is termed "real evidence". Real evidence arises in many circumstances: If a bank computer automatically calculated the bank charges due from a customer based upon its tariff, the transactions on the account and the daily cleared credit balance, this calculation would be a piece of "real evidence". Then there are documents and records produced by the computer which are copies of information supplied to the computer by human beings. This evidence is treated as hearsay material. Cheques drawn and paying-in slips credited to a bank account are hearsay evidence. Finally, there is derived evidence which is information which combines real evidence with the information supplied to the computer by human beings to form a composite record. This too is treated as hearsay evidence in modern evidence statutes.[2] An example of derived evidence is the figure in the daily balance column of a bank statement since

---

[1] A version of a line said by the actor Robin Williams in the Stephen Spielberg movie "Hook".
[2] Although this is not so clear if older statutes are considered. See the section "Hearsay in Northern Ireland" below.

this is derived from "real evidence" (automatically generated bank charges) and individual cheque and paying-in entries.

REAL EVIDENCE

7.03   With rapid improvements in forensic science real evidence is of growing importance in criminal investigation. Fingerprints, DNA samples and bloodstains are all common examples of real evidence which are used to convince a court of the guilt or innocence of a defendant.

Automatic records are fairly recent developments. But the law has not put any barriers into their reception as evidence. Quite early on the recordings from automatic recording devices were accepted as real evidence. In *The Statue of Liberty*[3] the case turned on a record of radar readings showing the location of two ships involved in a collision. The recording was made by a mechanical device without human intervention. Simon P held that such a recording was admissible as real evidence. He cited *R. v. Maqsud Ali*[4] which was authority on the admissibility of tape recordings:

> ". . . if tape recordings are admissible, it seems equally a photograph of radar reception is admissible — as indeed, any other type of photograph. It would be an absurd distinction that a photograph should be admissible if the camera were operated manually by a photographer, but not if it were operated by a trip or clock mechanism. Similarly, if evidence of weather conditions were relevant, the law would affront common sense if they were to say that those could be proved by a person who looked at a barometer from time to time but not by producing a barograph record . . . The law is bound these days to take cognisance of the fact that mechanical means replace human effort."

7.04   In 1981 Professor Smith, in a learned article on computer evidence, developed the ideas put forward in *The Statue of Liberty* and came up with a rule which was later accepted by the courts.

> "Where information is recorded by mechanical means without the intervention of a human mind, the record made by the machine is admissible in evidence, provided of course, it is accepted that the machine is reliable."[5]

"Mechanical" in the above statement means "automatic" and is meant to include electrical, electronic and chemical methods of recording as opposed to just mechanisms made up of machines. In *R. v. Wood* the case, concerning the alleged theft of certain metals, turned upon the computer printouts put forward by a chemist who had performed an analysis of the metal found in the accused possession. The court found that the evidence was admissible as real evidence since the computer was used as a calculator:

> "This computer was rightly described as a tool. It did not contribute it own knowledge. It merely did a sophisticated calculation which could have been done manually by the chemist."

7.05   In *R. v. Spiby* the appellant had been convicted of being knowingly involved in the unlawful importation of cannabis. In support of the allegation of knowledge the prosecution used telephone printouts from the hotel's PBX computer to prove that a particular guest at that hotel had called the appellant at his home. At his appeal against

---

[3] [1968] 1 W.L.R. 739.
[4] [1966] 1 Q.B. 688.
[5] J.C. Smith "The Admissibility of Statements by Computer", (1981) Crim.L.R. 390. This statement was quoted with approval by the Court of Appeal in *R. v. Spiby* (1990) 91 Cr.App.R. 186.

conviction his counsel tried to have the printout ruled inadmissible evidence. The Court of Criminal Appeal held that the printouts were real evidence since the computer had automatically logged the lifting of the phone receiver and the making of the call. It cited and approved Professor Smith's statement (above). The Court of Criminal Appeal also applied the principle that if an instrument was one of a kind which, to common knowledge, is more often than not in working order, then in the absence of evidence to the contrary, the courts will presume that the machine was in working order at the material time. This effectively transfers the burden of proof that the machine was not working properly onto the defendant.

But while the above conclusion may be reasonable for the consideration of individual instances — the reliability of a log of the making of a telephone call or the readings of a speedometer in a motoring offence — they are not an appropriate conclusion where an error in any single instance is replicated and modifies another record: a derived record. Thus, if a telephone system records the number of minutes expended in a telephone call correctly in 99 calls out of 100, the total billing record at the end of a period where 1,000 calls had been made will not be correct since it will contain ten incorrect call records each of which will have affected the total.

In statistical terms[6] it is near certain that the total billing record will contain errors **7.06** when it is made up of 1,000 records. If the total number of calls made is 300 then there is a better than 95 per cent chance that the total billing record contains errors. If the total number of calls made is 70 then on the balance of probabilities it is more likely than not that the total billing record will contain errors.

Number of Records	Likelihood of Errors
1000	99.9956829 per cent
300	95.0959106 per cent
70	50.516134 per cent

To date, the case law on computer evidence has failed to appreciate this important distinction and the consequences which flow from the aggregation of small errors into high probabilities of error. Indeed, the Law Commission accepted a statement by a non-technical legal academic that "most computer error is either immediately detectable or results from errors in the data entered into the machine."[7] — a statement which a

---

[6] The relevent statistical equation to prove this is Bayes' Theorem which has been the basis of statistical analysis for over two hundred years. See: Robertson B and Vignaux GA. *Interpreting Evidence: Evaluating Forensic Evidence in the Courtroom*. (John Wiley & Sons, Chichester, 1995). For the approach of the U.K. Court of Criminal Appeal to statistical evidence and how juries are meant to approch it see *Michael Gordon* [1995] 1 Cr.App.R. 290 and *R. v. Docherty R. v. Adams* 1996, *The Times*, August 16, 1996; *Denis Adams* [1996] 2 Cr. App. R. 467. The Court of Criminal Appeal in these cases appears to have fairly comprehensively rejected the use of probability calculations in English criminal law and dashed the hope expressed by Robertson and Vignaux that logic, probability and inference would provide the language in which lawyers and scientists would communicate with each other. What is not plain is whether the decision in Denis Adams precludes the presenting to a jury of expert evidence explaining the calculations of the statistician as to the effect of his application of Bayes theorem to the evidence. That would seem to be a matter of expert evidence which a jury could consider and accept or reject. Such is the situation in Scots criminal law see: *Welsh v. H.M. Advocate* [1992] S.L.T. 193.
[7] Tapper. "Discovery in Modern Times: A Voyage Around the Common Law World" (1991) 67 Chicago-Kent Law Review 217, 248. Quoted in the Law Commission Consultation Paper "Evidence in Criminal Proceedings" no. 138 1995, para. 13.7.

practitioner who regularly works with computer evidence in criminal cases would find is not supported by the facts.

ADMISSIBILITY AND HEARSAY

> "People were formally frightened out of their wits about admitting evidence lest juries go wrong. In modern times we admit the evidence and discuss its weight."[8]

7.07   When matters are litigated the court has to find that certain facts exist before pronouncing on the rights, duties and liabilities of the parties. Proving the existence of certain facts is done by evidence which is either admitted by the parties as not being disputed or the disputed facts, termed the facts in issue, have to be established by the court. In this determination the court has historically been required to exclude certain evidence under the hearsay rule although the main general rule regarding evidence is that all evidence which is sufficiently relevant to an issue before the court is admissible and all that is irrelevant or insufficiently relevant should be excluded.[9]

The hearsay rule says that: "any assertion other than one made by a person while giving oral evidence in the proceedings is inadmissible as evidence of any fact asserted."[10] Thus, if a witness to a road accident had told a friend that a lady with blue hair was driving the car, under the hearsay rule the friend could not be called to give evidence of that fact because the friend had not witnessed the accident but was only relaying what he had been told. Cross-examination of the friend could not test the underlying reliability of the evidence, it could only test the reliability of the friend's recollection of what he had been told by the witness.

7.08   It will readily be appreciated that this historical rule is extraordinarily inconvenient and is capable of being used to exclude a great deal of good reliable evidence from trials in breach of the main rule that all evidence which is sufficiently relevant to an issue before the court is admissible. In the nineteenth century in England, the business community sought and obtained a statutory exemption to the rule which covered documents created in the course of a trade or business from information supplied by a person who might reasonably be supposed to have personal knowledge of the matters contained therein and where the person in question could not reasonably be expected to have any recollection of the matters contained in the record. Thus, if a clerk working in a business made a note of a sale in a ledger, the ledger could be produced in court as evidence of the sale even if the clerk who had made the entry could no longer recall the matters contained in the ledger. Implicit in this exception to the hearsay rule was a requirement that the exempted evidence was prepared and kept in accordance with the rules laid down by the revenue authorities for the keeping of business records.

The inconvenience of the hearsay rule also led to the creation of a number of common law exemptions which developed in haphazard manner because, when the rule proved highly inconvenient in a particular kind of case, it was relaxed just sufficiently far to meet

---

[8] Coburn C.J. in *R. v. Birmingham Overseers* (1861) 1 B. & S. 763 at 767.

[9] *per* Goddard L.J. in *Hollington v. Hewthorn & Co Ltd.* [1943] 1 K.B. 587.

[10] A formulation of the rule as approved by the House of Lords in *Sharp* [1988] 1 W.L.R. 7 at 11, *per* Lord Havers, with whom Lord Mackay of Clashfern L.C., Lord Keith of Kinkel, Lord Bridge of Harwich and Lord Griffiths concurred. This formulation was also approved in *Kearley* [1992] 2 A.C. 228 at 254H–255A, *per* Lord Ackner, with whom Lord Bridge of Harwich agreed.

that case, and without regard to any question of principle.[11] Considerable work was done in the United States regarding hearsay evidence[12] which was not copied elsewhere.[13]

The position of hearsay evidence in England is today still governed by the majority **7.09** decision of the House of Lords in 1965 in the landmark case, *Myers v. DPP*.[14] The case concerned an alleged conspiracy to deal in stolen motor cars. The defendant would buy a wrecked car and its log book, and then steal an almost identical car. He would then convert the stolen car so that the details matched the log book and proceed to sell it for profit. Evidence produced by the car manufacturers at the time of the production of the cars was critical to the prosecution's case. As the cars moved along the production line, workers recorded details of the serial numbers of the various components fitted to a particular car. These details were recorded on a card by the worker responsible. Eventually, the completed card was photographed and recorded on microfilm. The prosecution sought to put the microfilm records in evidence at the trial under the exception to the hearsay rule in the Evidence Act 1938 which covered business records. The Evidence Act 1938 did not mention microfilm as a type of business record (because the product was not in common use by business in the 1930s). By a majority of three to two the House of Lords held that the evidence was inadmissible as hearsay because any exemption to the hearsay rule had to be construed restrictively. Furthermore, the majority ruled, any further exceptions to the hearsay rule should be introduced by Parliament, not the judiciary.

Lord Reid, giving the majority judgment said: "To admit the evidence is to admit **7.10** hearsay evidence. Further, the records could only go to prove the truth of the assertions contained therein. They did not corroborate any other witness and it was not relevant to show that they had been made unless it was also accepted that the records were true." Lord Pierce (dissenting) said: "In my opinion, where the person who from his own knowledge made business records cannot be found, and where a business produces some proper servant, who can speak with knowledge to the method and system of record-keeping, its records reliably kept in the ordinary way of business, they should be admitted as prima facie evidence".

Over the years the views of Lord Pierce have gained support. They appear to have a great deal in common with the U.S. approach and, although *Myers v. DPP* is still good law in England, it was not followed in Scotland where the Lord Chief Justice in *Lord Advocate's Reference (No. 1 of 1992)*[15] considered the judgment in *Myers* and concluded that

---

[11] See Lord Reid in *Myers* [1965] A.C. 1001 at 1020B–C.

[12] The U.S. addressed the question of hearsay evidence by attempting to codify the evidence law with the publication of the Model Code of Evidence by the American Law Institute in 1942. The Code failed and was not adopted in any jurisdiction in the United States. In 1953, the National Conference of Commissioners on Uniform State Laws promulgated the Uniform Rules of Evidence which was based on the Model Code. The Uniform Rules influenced the development of evidence law in several states. The U.S. Congress then enacted the Federal Rules of Evidence in 1975. The Federal Rules are based on the Model Code and the Uniform Rules and are applicable in the federal courts. More than 30 states have adopted codes of evidence which are modelled on the Federal Rules and a revised version of the Uniform Rules. The Federal Rules of Evidence affirms the rule against hearsay and lists the recognised exceptions by reference to whether the declarant is available as a witness in *Rules 803 804(b)*.

[13] The Federal Rules have been criticised for being too complex. There are 27 specific exceptions and two general exceptions. The Scottish Law Commission were of the view that codification on the American model would not reduce but would in fact increase the complexity of the law. Scottish Law Commission, *Evidence: Report on Corroboration, Hearsay and Related Matters in Civil Proceedings* (Scot. Law Com. No. 100, 1986), para. 3.30 The New South Wales Law Reform Commission also thought that the American approach was conservative and "retain far too much of the technicality and distortion-riddled quality of the present law" New South Wales Law Reform Commission, *Report on the Rule Against Hearsay* (LRC 29, 1978), Appendix B, para. 1.5.

[14] [1965] A.C. 1001.

[15] [1992] S.L.T. 1010.

the judgments of the dissenting minority more accurately reflected Scots Law. Nor was it followed by the Supreme Court of Canada.[16]

7.11   The net result of this situation is that, while the binding authority in English law says that evidence statutes have to be restrictively construed and that it is Parliament alone which can create new categories of admissible hearsay evidence, this is less likely to be the law in other common law jurisdictions. Crown colonies and members of the Commonwealth whose evidence statutes were drafted before computers came into common use are today more likely to be construed in accordance with Lord Pierce's dissenting judgment in *Myers* than in accordance with Lord Reid's majority judgment. Indeed, since the House of Lords is no longer bound by its earlier decisions, it is possible that the majority decision in *Myers* could be overruled today if the right case were appealed before the House of Lords.

Hearsay in England

7.12   In 1993 the Law Commission published a report on the hearsay rule in civil cases[17] in which it made the following points:

(a) Evidence should not be excluded on the ground that it is hearsay. Multiple hearsay as well as simple hearsay should henceforth be admissible.

(b) Existing statutory provisions making hearsay evidence admissible should not be affected by the proposals.

(c) Parties intending to rely on hearsay evidence should be under a duty to give notice of that fact to other parties wherever it is reasonable and practicable in the circumstances to enable those parties to deal with any matters arising from its being hearsay. This duty should be subject to any agreement, or any rules of court, to the contrary. Failure to comply with this duty should not affect the admissibility of the evidence but might attract costs or other sanctions at the court's disposal.

(d) A party should be allowed to call a witness whose evidence has been tendered as hearsay by another party, and to cross-examine him on the statement.

(e) Statutory guidelines should be provided for the courts to assist them to assess the weight they should attach to hearsay evidence.

(f) The requirement that the maker of a statement which is adduced as hearsay should be competent to give direct oral evidence should be retained, and that the date on which the statement was made should be the date on which the statement maker is required to satisfy this condition.

(g) Evidence should continue to be admissible to impeach or support the credibility of a person not called as a witness, and evidence tending to show that such a person made previous or later inconsistent statements should also continue to be admissible.

(h) Previous consistent or inconsistent statements of a person called as a witness should continue to be admissible as evidence of the matters stated.

---

[16] *Ares v. Venner* [1970] S.C.R 608.
[17] Law Commission, *The Hearsay Rule in Civil Proceedings* (Law Com. No. 216, Cm 2321, 1993).

The Government fully accepted these conclusions and, in consequence the Civil Evidence   **7.13**
Act 1995 was enacted in November 1995 to implement the recommendations of the Law
Commission. The relevant provisions in this Act are sections 8, 9 and 12.

Civil Evidence Act 1995

Section 8 (1)
Where a statement contained in a document is admissible as evidence in civil
proceedings, it may be proved—

(a) by the production of the document, or

(b) whether or not that document is still in existence, by the production of a
    copy of that document or of the material part of it,
authenticated in such manner as the court may approve

Section 8(2)
It is immaterial for this purpose how many removes there are between a copy
and an original.

. . .

Section 9(1)
A document which is shown to form part of the records of a business or public
authority may be received in evidence in civil proceedings without further
proof

. . .

Section 12
"document" means anything in which information of any description is
recorded
"copy", in relation to a document, means anything onto which information
recorded in the document has been copied, by whatever means and whether
directly or indirectly.

. . .

However, no statutory guidelines regarding the weight to be attached to hearsay
evidence have yet been produced. This should be of grave concern (see the discussion
below in "The Reliability of Computer Evidence").

Hearsay in Scotland

Scotland addressed the matter of hearsay evidence at little earlier than England: The   **7.14**
Scottish Law Commission published a report on corroboration and hearsay in civil
proceedings in 1986[18] which were substantially implemented by *Civil Evidence (Scotland)
Act 1988*. Under the Act:

(a) The rule against hearsay was abolished and evidence is not to be excluded solely
    on the ground that it was hearsay. Both first-hand and multiple hearsay are
    admissible under the Act.

(b) Assertive conduct as well as oral and documentary hearsay are covered by the Act.

---

[18] Scottish Law Commission, *Evidence: Report on Corroboration, Hearsay and Related Matters in Civil Proceedings*
(Scot. Law Com. No. 100, 1986).

(c) There is no requirement of notification of intention to use hearsay evidence.

(d) The court does not have power to exclude evidence solely on the ground that it is hearsay, nor can a party insists that an available witness whose statement is challenged should attend and give direct oral evidence.

(e) The court has power to allow a witness to be recalled or an additional witness to be called before the commencement of closing submissions when hearsay statements are challenged.

(f) No statutory guidelines are given to the courts to assist them in assessing the weight of the hearsay evidence.

(g) No special provisions are made for computer records.

(h) Statements by witnesses which are consistent (or inconsistent) with their evidence in court are be admissible for the purpose of supporting (or challenging) the witnesses' credibility, and statements proved for such purpose are also be admissible as evidence of any matter contained therein.

During the Parliament debate[19] concerning this legislation the Scottish Office was of the view that to allow the courts to refuse to admit hearsay evidence if the associated notice procedure had not been complied with could have the effect of reintroducing the hearsay rule.[20] If a party was taken by surprise, it could ask that the witness involved be called. If the witness was available but not called, it would be taken account of by the court in assessing the weight of the evidence. But the lack of statutory guidelines on assessing the weight of computer evidence remains a major concern (see the discussion below in "The Reliability of Computer Evidence").

Hearsay in Northern Ireland

7.15   In the first edition of our book we stated that the courts in Northern Ireland still recognised the rule against hearsay and "until the law has been amended, problems can be expected in litigating e-commerce cases." Thankfully this position has been addressed by the Civil Evidence (Northern Ireland) Order 1997[21] which was made on December 17, 1997 and came into effect (apart for section 10[22]) on September 6, 1999. Although this Order makes no mention whatsoever of computers, it is clear that any objection regarding the hearsay nature of evidence is now useless in civil litigation in Northern Ireland.

In 1990 the Law Reform Advisory Committee for Northern Ireland rejected the approach implemented in the Civil Evidence (Scotland) Act 1988 on the grounds that (a) it was a breach of the basic principle that a party is entitled to insist on the production of the best reasonably available evidence against him and (b) it did not safeguard the right of a party to cross-examine the direct source of the hearsay evidence. In its opinion, the Scottish Act did not provide sufficient safeguards.[23] The new Order implements the

---

[19] These matters can now be put before the court in argument since the judgment in *Pepper v. Hart* [1992] 3 W.L.R. 1032 where the House of Lords held that the rules excluding reference to parliamentary materials should be relaxed on certain conditions.

[20] *Hansard* H.C., col. 743–4.

[21] S.I. 1997 No. 2983 (N.I. 21).

[22] A section dealing with Ogden tables in personal injury cases.

[23] *ibid.*, paras 5.39–5.41.

later Report of the Law Reform Advisory Committee for Northern Ireland on Hearsay Evidence in Civil Proceedings (L.R.A.C. No. 3, 1996).

THE RELIABILITY OF COMPUTER EVIDENCE

Computers would be useless if they were not able to record information with a fair degree of reliability.[24] But determining the reliability of a piece of computer evidence is no easy task. The adversarial system of litigation causes problems because it will always be in the interests of one side to suggest that unreliable evidence is reliable and vice versa. Without independent inquisitorial resources to determine reliability the court has a task which it rarely addresses.   **7.16**

As a starting point the court follows a common law presumption:

> In the absence of evidence to the contrary, the courts will presume that mechanical instruments were in order at the material time[25]

In approaching the subject computers have tended to be considered in many cases as little more than a type of filing cabinet. In *R. v. Blackburn*[26] the Court of Criminal Appeal made it clear that they would be extremely reluctant to accept a document produced on a word processor as computer evidence rather than as a written statement from a human author. This would appear to limit the sources of error to be addressed in determining weight solely to inaccurate keying by the human author and would refutably assume the fact that the data had not been corrupted or damaged while being stored on the computer through action by the computer or third parties.

But this assumption needs to be looked as in detail and it is necessary to consider the physical record or artefact which is placed before a court. Documentary evidence in the courtroom consists of printouts which may look like pages from a loose leaf file found in manual systems. But the document may never have existed as a single document, being passed intact from hand to hand. Instead, it may be created "on-the-fly" from an enquiry being made of a database. An error on the part of the computer in conducting the search of the database needed to create the document is unlikely to produce any evidence on the face of the document to indicate that an error has taken place.   **7.17**

It is useful to open this discussion by considering patients records in medical practices since the problems these produce (reliability, discovery, data protection, etc.) are a more acute form of the problems that are encountered with customer records in e-commerce.

---

[24] For more detailed information see Sommer P., *Digital Footprints: Assessing Computer Evidence* [1988] Crim.L.R. (Spec. Ed.), 61 and Sommer, P., "Intrusion Detection Systems as Evidence". **http://www.zurich.ibm.com/dac/Prog—RAID98/Full—Papers/Sommer—text.pdf**
For a slightly lighter but nonetheless realistic indication of some of the problems regarding reliability of computer evidence see **http://csrc.lse.ac.uk/Kelman/Kelman.htm** where Kelman has republished on the web the complete drama *The Case of Grapefruit Sorbet* from his 1981 book *The Computer in Court* (written with Richard Sizer) on admissibility and reliability of computer evidence. Subsequently in a Law Commission Report on Computer Evidence the analysis of the issues set out by these authors was cited with approval. The web extract on the LSE pages contains a new postscript from Kelman bringing the reader up to date with the current situation.
[25] *Phipson,* para. 23-14, approved by the Divisional Court in *Castle v. Cross* [1984] 1 W.L.R. 1372 at 1377B, *per* Stephen Brown L.J.
[26] *The Times,* December 1, 1992.

7.18   In *R. v. Sinha*[27] the defendant, a doctor, was convicted of perverting the course of justice. A patient had consulted him, complaining of palpitations and the defendant had prescribed a course of beta blockers without ascertaining from her medical records that she was an asthmatic. The following day, the patient took one of the beta blockers and later died as a result of an acute asthma attack. The coroner requested that the senior partner at the defendant's practice supplied him with the patient's records. The senior partner could not find the written records, so he sent the computerised version. A later analysis of this computerised version found traces of earlier versions of the patient's records which had been deleted. This led to enquiries and finally the defendant admitted that on three occasions, following the patient's death, he had altered her computerised therapy records which had previously contained four separate references to her asthmatic condition. It was accepted at the trial that it is dangerous to prescribe beta blockers to asthmatics. He was sentenced to six months' imprisonment.[28]

Consider this case in the context of a civil action for medical negligence. The estate of the dead patient brings an action against the medical practice for causing the death of the patient. In the course of the action it would seek discovery of documents which would include the medical records of the practice. Under normal legal discovery practice this would be a printout from the computer system. Such a printout would not have shown the alterations made by the doctor after the death of the patient. Only if the patient's lawyers had promptly insisted on discovery of an "image copy" of the medical practice's computer system and thereafter employed an independent computer expert to review the material would the activities of the errant doctor come to light. Yet to insist upon electronic discovery of documents would be likely to require a special appointment before a Master to argue the relevance of the material with considerable risks of costs being awarded to the other side and any delays in obtaining the order in any event resulting in the loss of all traces of the alterations.[29]

7.19   But the supply of an "image copy" of the database in discovery is unlikely to occur in civil litigation unless the decision in *Derby & Co. Ltd v. Weldon*[30] were reviewed by the court and distinguished. In that case the defendants applied for discovery of a computerised database held by the plaintiff which contained details of transactions which were the subject of the litigation. Vinelott J. held that a computer database which forms part of the business records of a company is, in so far as it contains information capable of being retrieved and converted into readable form, a "document" for the purposes of making discovery. However, the court ruled that party seeking discovery is not entitled to unrestricted access to the database and the court will only permit discovery in the light of expert evidence as to the extent to which the relevant

---

[27] [1995] Crim.L.R. 68.

[28] At the time of completion of this manuscript Dr Harold "Fred" Shipman, 53 of, Hyde, Greater Manchester, was on trial accused of murdering 15 of his women patients. It was part of the Prosecution's case against him that he modified the computerised medical records of a number of these patients after he had killed them to falsely create evidence of medical conditions which were supposed to have been their cause of death.

[29] For a variant on how this situation could occur in practice, where journal records stored on a computer could corroborate witness statements or prove them to be false see the fictional tale "Sam's story" in Chapter 1, where Sam is required to go through the automatic journal entries and compare these with draft witness statements. Users of programs such a Microsoft Outlook may find that, unknown to them, Microsoft Outlook keeps a running journal of work being created or edited on every workstation; recording when documents were produced and when they were modified, when telephone calls were made, etc. Coupled with the caching facilities built into modern web browsers a great deal of corroborating evidence is capable of being found on ordinary business workstations in the course of a forensic examination. There is a good case for requiring this material to be discovered in all civil litigation as a matter of course, particularly since it can be analysed electronically without creating mountains of paper.

[30] [1991] 2 All E.R. 901.

information was available online or from back up systems. The court allowed the defendants to access the database subject to agreement or expert evidence as to what information was or could be made available, to what extent inspect was necessary and whether the provision of print-outs would be sufficient.

Computers used for storing patient records have tended to be small closed networks of standard personal computers running customised software. With the common law assumption that mechanical devices tend to work properly, it is not considered likely that these standard computers used for record taking and the production of prescriptions are not working properly. But the question of weight will turn upon whether the computer records have been altered and whether those alterations could have been made without trace.

In a civil action based on the facts of the *Sinha* case the defendant medical practice **7.20** would have a strong motive to tamper with the evidence prior to discovery. To re-edit a patient's records and remove all traces of the original on the computer system would be relatively easy to do using standard utility software.

But the task of altering records gets a lot harder once the small computer network is part of a large wide area network on which duplicate copies of the data are recorded. The errant doctor has to alter not only the local copy of the record but also the copies which are held and replicated throughout the network. He has to be able to cover his tracks by altering the time and date stamps of his alterations through editing all the log files in a coherent fashion. This may not in fact be possible.

A detailed determination of the reliability of computer evidence beyond the above introduction is outside of the scope of this book. The topic is now being properly addressed in the new science of forensic computing. This fiendishly complicated discipline starts by considering reliability as a combination of two elements:

- the trustworthiness of the *content* of a piece of computer-derived evidence (*content* is what you see with your eyes);

- the trustworthiness of the *process* by which it was produced (*process* is what produced it).

Together, the trustworthiness of *content* and *process* form the actual reliability of the **7.21** evidence. Factors which have to be taken into account in determining this trustworthiness can include the quality of the original source, the quality of the internal computer manipulations, the strength of any control or audit mechanism which might reduce error or provide corroboration, the integrity of the way in which an exhibit — what the court actually considers — has been derived, and integrity of the way in which the exhibit has been handled by or brought into being by investigators. All of these factors will interact with each other. For example, a classic fraud scenario involves a dishonest internal auditor discovering a small fraud by a member of staff involving the putting through of unauthorised transactions for cash and posting the unbalanced transactions to a suspense account which is not monitored on a regular basis. The dishonest auditor adopts this fraud and posts a series of additional transactions for his own benefit, withdrawing the money and creating a false trail to the staff member. He then reports the staff member for prosecution. The staff member's denials regarding the scale of his fraud are rarely believed and the dishonest auditor has an illegal profit which is not subject to further investigation. One role of a forensic computing expert in this situation is to analyse the environment in which the transactions have been created and stop the court or jury from jumping to conclusions by highlighting the fact that the evidence does not reliably point to the staff member as the author of all the unauthorised transactions.

How long must records be kept and what records need to be kept?

7.22   It is well known that under the Companies Act 1985 accounting records have to be kept for six years by a public company and three years by a private company.[31] But other statutes and business risks raise important questions regarding what falls within the scope of the accounting records in e-commerce transactions and whether there are any "long tail" situations which might suggest that it would be prudent for companies to keep their business records for longer than the statutory minimum period.

Historically, accounting records have been considered to be the books of account of the business. In early times these books of account were kept in bound ledgers and clerks would make entries in ink in the bound ledgers whenever transactions took place. This primitive method of record keeping had certain hidden controls:

- it was possible to identify which clerk wrote a record through his handwriting characteristics;

- the accounting entry in a bound ledger in ink meant that any alterations left a visible trace;

- the inclusion of the record within a bound book meant that it was not possible to substitute entries;

- a practice developed whereby a clerk who made an alteration to a record initialled it to signify that the change was authentic.

7.23   As technology permitted new ways of keeping business records other than bound books, legislation was brought in to make this possible. But the hidden controls were not forgotten and modern company law contains important restrictions regarding the keeping of accounting records in Section 722(2) of the Companies Act 1985

Companies Act 1985 — Form of company registers, etc.

722—(1) Any register, index, minute book or accounting records required by the Companies Act to be kept by a company may be kept either by making entries in bound books or by recording the matters in question in any other manner.

722—(2) Where any such register, index, minute book or accounting records is not kept by making entries in a bound book, but by some other means, adequate precautions shall be taken for guarding against fabrication and facilitating its discovery.

722—(3) If default is made in complying with subsection (2), the company and every officer of it who is in default is liable to a fine and, for continued contravention, a daily default fine.

---

[31] s.222 Companies Act 1985.

With e-commerce it is necessary to find analogues for the traditional controls but these **7.24** are not easy to implement or particularly obvious. If an accounting record has been digitally signed (as opposed to being physically signed or initialled) the provisions of section 722(2) appear to indicate that the company needs to be able to associate the digital signature with a particular person. Merely having a smart card and a PIN is unlikely to be sufficient since the signing will have been done by the artefact rather than by a characteristic human hand and that artefact is capable of making unauthorised accounting records when in the wrong hands.

> In 2004 Company X sends an e-mail message to Company Y saying "Your shipment is ready for collection". "What shipment ?" replies Y to discover that Company X says that it received, in 2001, an official e-commerce order for 3 Million gallons of Frozen Orange Juice for delivery in 2004 allegedly digitally signed by "Company Y". Company Y has no knowledge of any such order and has destroyed and replaced the signing key it was using 2001. Company Y finds that its CA does not have a record of Company Y's signing key for the year 2001. It does not know and cannot demonstrate that the order was not a genuine irrevocable order for which it is now liable.

It is quite likely that a company will have to revoke and replace its signing keys and encryption keys several times a year because they have been compromised or staff have left or there have been management changes. To enable the historic accounting records to be verified as genuine a separate archival record will have to be maintained which is able to show which particular cryptographic and signing keys were current at particular times. Companies will turn to their Certification Authority for this information and, if the CA is unable to supply the information, serious consequences will follow.

But it is also true that legal disputes involving documentary evidence can arise long **7.25** after the original events. In *Brian S. Grave v. Leslie & Godwin Financial Services Limited*[32] an insurance broker was held to have been in breach of contract and negligent in not retaining documents that would have identified the reinsurers of the plaintiff's risk. The only document that had been given to the plaintiff was a cover note which did not identify the reinsurers. In that case the reinsurances had been effected nearly thirty years before the plaintiff wished to make a claim under them. The slips could not be found. The court held that there was a duty to take reasonable care of any documents owned by the insured and not to destroy them without first obtaining instructions as to whether to do so or not. The court further held that in the particular circumstances there was a duty not to destroy a slip without the consent of the insured, even if the slip was not the property of the insured.

With improvements in digital storage media it is now possible to keep archival business records in a reproducible form in very little space and at relatively low cost. It would therefore be sensible for a record retention policy to be applied throughout a business as part of the company's risk management strategy. Archival copies of old business records held offsite on inexpensive WORM[33] media for use in limited circumstances would appear to be an appropriate and cost effective means by which a company could continue to have evidence to defend itself when faced with "long tail"

---

[32] *The Times*, May 16, 1995, QBD.
[33] WORM (Write Once Read Many), being storage media on such as CD-ROMs, which used to be referred to as Optical Disks.

claims and liabilities. Such a policy needs to be considered in the light of the provisions of the Data Protection Act 1984 and the Data Protection Act 1998 which requires a business to consider the length of time it holds personal records as well as the amount of personal data it holds on data users.

PRINCIPLES OF GOOD PRACTICE — THE BSI AND DISC CODES

7.26   In 1993 two academics, Mayon-White and Dyer, published a ground-breaking set of principles on good practice for the operation of systems making use of "imaging" technology.[34] They established the Legal Images Initiative (LII) as a consortium of organisations which sought to achieve a position where an imaged document would be treated in law as equivalent to the typed, printed or hand written document. In their report they said that "The primary objective of the LII is to create a framework which, if followed by users of electronic document management systems, will give them confidence in the security of the storage and retrieval processes and in the acceptability of such records in any court of law, should a dispute arise in which the documents stored in this way may be required as evidence."

Mayon-White and Dyer's work became the basis of a British Standard Code of Practice, now published by the British Standards Institute (DISC PD0008).[35] This takes as its starting point their "Five Principles of Good Practice":

1. Recognise all types of information.

2. Understand the legal issues and execute "duty of care" responsibilities.

3. Identify and specify business processes and procedures.

4. Identify enabling technologies to support business processes and procedures.

5. Monitor and audit procedures.

7.27   Each of these principles has been expanded upon. Thus, the first process, recognition of information, is subdivided into classification, storage and evaluation. Classification draws upon the skills of both the librarian or information scientist and those of diligent office administrators. Storage considered the life cycle of the information following its receipt. Evaluation requires the organisation to take appropriate steps to protect its information resource.

This expanding process continues throughout the principles. In relation to the legal issues the code requires the organisation to establish a chain of responsibility and consequently of accountability in relation to information handling within the organisation.

---

[34] Mayon-White W.M. and Dyer B. *The Legal Images Initiative: Towards a voluntary code of practice* ((1993) available from the Image and Document Management Association c/o the Department of Information Systems. The London School of Economics, Houghton Street, London WC2A 2AE).

[35] A second version of this Code, published in April 1999, now covers WORM technology, re-writable media, workflow, boundaries of a system and freezing points in time relating to dynamic information. The first version only covered WORM technology. There is now also a further document PD0009 — *The Compliance Workbook.*

The current position is that there are now two British standards publications[36] and one general publication[37] which can provide courts and lawyers with guidance regarding the management of computer evidence and hence the reliability of such evidence.

But before considering the weight to be attached to evidence it is necessary to consider **7.28** what weight to attach to BS7799 — *The Code of Practice for Information Security Management*. The early work, which led to BS7799, came from the Commercial Computer Security Centre of the U.K. Department of Trade and Industry (CCSC). In the late 1980s the CCSC published two nearly impenetrable documents on computer security.[38] These floated around various worthy bodies[39] in the early 1990s until they were "decrypted" by a number of major commercial users[40] who set about turning the CCSC work into a code which was both meaningful and practical from a user's point of view. Public consultation on these revisions led to the British Standards Institute publishing the code as a guidance document[41] and following a further period of public consultation this code was recast as British Standard BS7799:1995.

BS7799:1995 was submitted for acceptance into the International Standards Organisation (ISO) "Fast Track" procedure in order to become an International Standard, in 1996. ISO were unable to agree on it proceeding by this route and it is still not an International Standard. However the general thrust of BS7799 has been generally accepted. Australia and New Zealand accepted it, changed the U.K. legislative references to corresponding Australian and New Zealand references and re-published it as AS/NZS 4444. The Netherlands fully accepted the approach and went considerably further by establishing a certification scheme in early 1997. This is considered by many within the BSI process to be too radical a step given the developing nature of the work and the likelihood of an elementary low cost certificate giving a false impression of security.

One key weakness of BS7799 is the fact that it is very much a document which focuses **7.29** on information technology quite narrowly. While it contained a great deal of information on technologies such as passwords and access control it is nearly silent on topics such as the Internet. A broader treatment of Information Security is necessary in the form of a standard based upon the revised Code PD0008. Work is slowly proceeding on revision all these documents but it is taking longer than initially estimated.

So far as lawyers are concerned the existence of BS 7799 "A Code of Practice for Information Security Management" along with DISC PC 0008 "A Code of Practice for Legal Admissibility of Information Stored on Electronic Document Management Systems" already presents lawyers with essential material to cross-examine corporate executives who wish to place computer generated evidence before the court. The long term legal consequences of these codes of practice are interesting if an analogy is drawn.

In September 1983 the Accounting Standards Committee the Institute of Chartered **7.30** Accountants of England and Wales commissioned Mr Leonard Hoffman Q.C. and Mary Arden to supply them with a joint opinion of the meaning of "true and fair" with particular reference to the role of Accounting Standards. Leonard Hoffman, who has

---

[36] BS 7768: 1994 *Management of optical disk (WORM) system for the recording of documents that may be required as evidence* and BS7799: 1995 *Code of Practice for Information Security Management*.

[37] Image and Document Management Association (IDMA) *Principles of Good Practice for Information Management*, (London, 1995) available from IDMA, c/o the Department of Information Systems, The London School of Economics, Houghton Street, London WC2A 2AE).

[38] The DTI "Green Books" and the "Users Code of Practice" (1989).

[39] The U.K. ITSEC and the National Computing Centre.

[40] *i.e.* BOC, British Telecom, Marks & Spencer, Midland Bank, Nationwide Building Society, Prudential Assurance Corporation , SEMA, Shell and Unilever.

[41] PD 0003, *A Code of Practice for Information Security Management*.

since become a Law Lord, was at his time at the Bar considered to be one of the best and soundest lawyers around. Mary Arden is now a Chancery High Court Judge and Head of the Law Commission. In their 1983 Opinion the two barristers stated that:

(1) The application of the "true and fair view" involves judgment in questions of degree. There may sometimes be room for differences of opinion over the method to adopt to give a true and fair view. Because questions of degree are involved when a company is deciding on how much information is sufficient to make its financial statements true and fair, it may take account of cost effectiveness amongst other factors.

7.31 (2) It is for the court to decide whether financial statements give a true and fair view in compliance with the Act. But the courts will look for guidance to the ordinary practice of accountants. This is principally because the financial statements will not be true and fair unless the quality and quantity of the information they contain is sufficient to satisfy their readers' reasonable expectations. Those expectations will have been moulded by accountants' practices.

(3) Statements of Standard Accounting Practice have a twofold value to the court. First, they constitute an important statement of professional opinion. Secondly, because accountants are professionally obliged to comply with SSAPs, the readers of financial statements expect those statements to conform with the prescribed standards. Departure from a SSAP without adequate explanation may therefore result in the financial statements not showing a true and fair view.

(4) Consequently, the courts will treat compliance with accepted accounting principles as prima facie evidence that the financial statements are true and fair, and deviations from accepted principles will be prima facie evidence that they are not true and fair. These presumptions will either be strengthened or weakened by the extent to which the SSAP is accepted and applied in practice. A SSAP has no direct legal effect, but it will have an indirect effect on the content the courts give to the "true and fair" concept.

(5) The fact that Accounting Standards can change over time does not alter the effect they have on the true and fair view. The concept of true and fair is dynamic; its content changes but its meaning remains the same.

7.32 In our view it is a short step from the existence of a code of practice to the establishment of a rule of law that information which is handled in accordance with the code of practice should prima facie be considered as evidence in legal proceedings and conversely that information which was not handled in accordance with the code of practice should prima facie not be considered as evidence in legal proceedings. This would mirror the approach the courts take regarding the meaning of "true and fair" in the keeping of business records and the consequences of failing to comply with a Statement of Standard Accounting Practice — failure to comply with an SSAP is prima facie evidence that the business records are not true and fair.

In consequence, a good litigation tactic in e-commerce litigation would be to ask the opponent to specify with full particularity how each and every piece of computer evidence has been handled to be in accordance with BS 7799 and DISC PD0008 (or their successor documents). Failure to respond could reasonably lead to a request to have all the evidence excluded.

But such a draconian request should not be complied with by a court unless and until **7.33** there is near universal acceptance of the Codes of Practice throughout the business community. The current limitations of BS 7799 suggest that it, and PD0008, needs to evolve through a couple more generations before such a position is arrived at.

There is a well known saying in the software industry: "Never buy a commercial software package until it has reached Version 3.0". The rush to release the first version and the pressure of bug fixing on the second version conspire to a situation where programmers only start getting things right in the third release of the software. A similar conservative approach to reliance on codes of practice on information security and legal reliability in the courtroom would appear to be warranted. Both of the academics behind the Best Practice project fully accept and endorse the fact that the their Codes should not be construed as exclusionary rules of law.

— 8 —

DATA PROTECTION

> Businesses are increasingly using the Internet as another medium through which to attract customers. In some cases they trade directly from their websites, although in other cases detailed business transactions are conducted by e-mail, post or telephone. The Data Protection Act applies to personal data obtained and processed over the Internet as it does to information obtained by more conventional sources for automatic processing.[1]

The growth of e-commerce and the "Information Superhighway" gives rise to many **8.01** privacy issues. In every e-commerce transaction a user is forced to trust the security of the World Wide Web. Personal data, such as on individual's name, address and credit card number, may be routed wide via countries with little or no data protection legislation. There is no single authority which controls the web and every message sent can be intercepted at any site it passes and then traced, forged, suppressed or delayed. Every e-mail message contains a header with information about the sender and the recipient (for example name and I.P. address, host name and time of the mailing) and the routing and subject of the message. Increasingly, e-commerce businesses are tailoring their offering to an individual's preferences raising even more privacy and data protection issues.

Virtually every e-commerce transaction will involve the transfer of personal data and will be regulated in Europe by data protection laws. This chapter examines the law on data protection.

The Data Protection Act 1998 (DPA) was enacted on July 16, 1998 and implements the E.U. Data Protection Directive.[2] It came into force in phases starting on March 1, 2000.[3] For the purposes of this chapter it is assumed that the DPA is fully in force notwithstanding transitional provisions.

BACKGROUND AND FRAMEWORK

Fear about the information gathering ability of computers and the power which they **8.02** could have over citizens has been fully appreciated by commentators since the 1960s. Prior to our present legislation there were a series of Parliamentary Bills, Reports and

---

[1] The 14th Annual Report of the Data Protection Registrar published on July 14, 1998.
[2] Directive 95/46 which was adopted in 1995.
[3] This was done by Statutory Instruments available at **http://homeoffice.gov.uk**.

White Papers from 1961 onwards. In the late 1970s the United States, Sweden and West Germany introduced data protection legislation. The Council of the Organisation for Economic Co-operation and Development (OECD) adopted on September 23, 1980 Recommendation with Guidelines on the protection of privacy and transborder flows of personal data (The OECD Guidelines).

The Council of Europe produced its Convention on Data Protection which the United Kingdom signed up to in 1981. This indicated support for the principles but did not commit the United Kingdom to implementing any legislation. That came about once a critical number of countries had also signed up to the legislation. By 1983 major British businesses were asking the Government to bring in data protection legislation. It is unusual for businesses to ask a government to bring in new legislation to regulate them. But industry perceived that the lack of data protection legislation in the United Kingdom was hindering economic activity.

A good example of what was happening arose when a multinational oil company in the early 1980s wanted to centralise its data processing operation for petrol distribution in England. Some of its customers were in Sweden. Most of them were limited companies. But a couple were sole traders — people trading in their own name. The Swedish authorities indicated that they would not permit the multinational oil company to export the personal data concerning these two sole traders because the United Kingdom did not have any data protection legislation.

8.03   Business lobbied Parliament to introduce data protection legislation so that it could fully ratify the Council of Europe Convention. As a consequence the Data Protection Act 1984 was introduced and came into force on October 1, 1985. It was the first piece of legislation in the United Kingdom to address the use of computers. But, being business driven, the approach to data protection in the United Kingdom was to do the very bare minimum to comply with the Convention. This situation needs to be contrasted with other states such as Germany who have developed the concept of data protection to a much greater extent, seeking to elevate the interests and wishes of the individual above those of data users.

The discrepancies between national data protection statutes were identified by the European Commission as constituting an impediment to the attainment of the Single Market. In 1990 the Commission submitted a package of proposals to the Council aimed at promoting the free movement of data within the Community. Included in this was a proposal for a Directive on the topic of data protection.

In addition to the importance of data flows for the attainment of the Single Market, the proposal was also founded in the Treaty of Rome's provisions relating to consumer protection and the promotion of fundamental human rights. In these fields, the Treaty obliges the Community to ensure that harmonisation of national laws occurs at a "high level".

8.04   But there were problems. During the course of its five-year passage through the European legislative process, the Directive was criticised, both by countries such as the United Kingdom which considered that its requirements marked too great an advance over current data protection statutes, and by those such as Germany which were concerned that European legislation might lead to a diminution in the level of protection provided under existing national regimes. A further factor complicating E.U. action is that its legislative competence generally does not extend to matters coming within the fields of criminal law and national security — owing to the concept of subsidiarity.

Additionally, while the Directive was making its slow way through the European legislative process, the Internet appeared. At the start of the process there was no World

Wide Web — but by the time the "Framework Directive" was adopted by the European Union on October 24, 1995, the whole computer and data processing industry had been revolutionised by browser technology and hotlinking. Some lawyers have said that the legislation was unworkable and out of date before it became part of U.K. law.

It is not, however, sensible to look at the U.K. or Europe in isolation. Before we go forward to look at the current British legislation and then to the future of Data Protection we need to return to look again at the history. As technology has developed over the past 40 years, the legal imperatives have changed with them.

THE FOUR AGES OF DATA PROTECTION

The legislative perception of data protection and the nature of the legislation has changed over the past forty years and it is possible to roughly divide the legislation into four ages.[4]   **8.05**

The First Age of Data Protection viewed computers as part of a dismal world where all personal data files were centralised in gigantic national databanks. In the 1960s the Western world had recovered from the Second World War and was bringing in massive social reforms and extensive social welfare legislation. Europe was rapidly creating "cradle to the grave" social security systems which required a sophisticated system of government planning. Government bureaucracies had to constantly collect increasing amounts of information from citizens to fulfil its tasks and to plan for the future. By the late 1960s in Sweden, census and registration records had already been merged, and tax data was stored in centralised tax data banks. Sweden's legislature proposed to merge all these information sources into one national information bank.

The legislation during this First Age concentrated not on the direct protection of individual privacy but on the function of data processing in society. The use of computers itself endangered humane information processing. Data protection was seen as a tool to specifically counter these dangers. Citizens were not given rights to ensure compliance — instead, special institutions were set up to supervise adherence to data protection norms. Citizens could not decide on whether data concerning them should be processed — at best they could merely rectify misleading or inaccurate information about themselves.

These early statutes avoided using well-known words like "privacy", "information", "protection of intimate affairs", and instead regulated "data banks" Complicated registration and licensing procedures were established. It was envisaged that only a few gigantic data banks would be established. Data security could be maintained by simple physical access controls. The legislation sometimes required a specific data protection official for each and every data bank.

However, the nightmare of a Big Brother world of huge centralised databases did not happen. Public concern about huge centralised databases worked against their creation. Also, the computer industry went down a different route with the creation of the minicomputer.[5] These allowed local departmental offices in government to have their own databases. Finally, the sharing of data between databases was found to be a difficult task. It was easy to corrupt accurate databases with bad data arising from incompatible data models or different data-collection procedures.   **8.06**

---

[4] This concept of the four ages of Data Protection was first outlined by Viktor Mayer-Schönberger of Vienna in his essay "Generational Development of Data Protection in Europe".
[5] Computers like the Digital Equipment PDP 8 and the PDP 11.

Later arrivals to the data protection debate (France, Austria, Norway) started to see things differently and produced Second Age legislation. These focused on the individual privacy rights of the citizen. Data protection was seen as the right of individuals to ward off society in personal matters. Their legislation became less linked to a particular stage of the technology. Existing individual rights were reinforced and linked to constitutional provisions. Instead of a licensing regime the legislation merely required registration of users of computers.

Two trends developed during the Second Age. As the number of computer systems increased, continental data protection commissioners not only investigated data protection offences and controlled enforcement but started to act like ombudsmen. Some data protection commissioners were turned into adjudicating bodies on how bureaucracy could legitimately interpret data protection laws.

8.07   But overall there was a growing awareness that citizens could not opt out of the databank society because government required a continuous flow of information from the individuals.

The Third Age of Data Protection developed from a realisation that data privacy decisions were rarely simple binary yes/no issues but required a degree of gradation. The individual should be able to determine how he/she would participate in society. This concept became known as informational self-determination.

The Fourth Age is where we are today. Some countries, forming the view that citizens needed to be protected against readily bargaining away their informational privacy rights, amended their laws to grant absolute protection and created no fault compensation for individuals.[6] But it was also appreciated that some personal data was normally considered more private than the rest and special protection was needed for this material and to protect against its misuse. Finally, it was appreciated that codes of practice for various industry sectors could make data protection legislation relevant and lead to a better protection of citizen's rights. Thus, when the European Commission came to negotiate the creation of the European Data Protection Directive, both sensitive personal data and codes of practice featured strongly in its provisions.

THE DATA PROTECTION ACT 1998 (DPA)

8.08   The DPA replaces the Data Protection Act 1984 in its entirety. It is bigger and more extensive than the 1984 Act it replaces. Whilst the DPA sets out the overall legal framework, much of the detail is contained in secondary legislation. The DPA is divided into six parts and follows closely the structure of the Data Protection Act 1984. The terminology is changed to reflect the increased powers and status of the Data Protection Registrar under the new Act, who is now called the Data Protection Commissioner.

"Processing"

8.09   One major difference in the DPA when compared with the 1984 Act comes through the definition of "processing" which is now very wide. The "processing" of information or data now means "obtaining, recording or holding the information or data or carrying out any operation or set of operations on the information or data, including:

---

[6] *e.g.* recent amendments to German states' data protection laws (*e.g.* s.20 of the Data Protection Act of the German state of Brandenburg and s.7 (new) of the German Federal Data Protection Statute of 1990) introduced no-fault compensation for individual data protection claims thus expanding the Norwegian no-fault compensation model for data protection claims against credit reporting agencies (s.40, Norwegian Data Protection Act).

(a) organisation, adaptation or alteration of the information or data;

(b) retrieval, consultation or use of the information or data;

(c) disclosure of the information or data by transmission, dissemination or otherwise making available; or

(d) alignment, combination, blocking, erasure or destruction of the information or data."

It is a very unusual use of the word "processing" but the significance is really that nothing falls outside of the scope of the DPA.

Manual Records

Manual files are now included within the scope of the legislation provided that they are part of what is termed a "structured filing system" so specific information relating to a particular individual is readily accessible. But the legislation only affects manual files after two transitional periods — the first period up until October 23, 2001 when all manual files are exempted from the provisions of the DPA and the second transitional period up until October 24, 2007 where only some of the data protection principles apply to manual files. Thereafter all the principles will apply. **8.10**

Personal Data and the Data Controller

The DPA regulates the processing of information relating to living individuals. Section 1 of the DPA defines data as: **8.11**

"information which:
(a) is being processed by means of equipment operating automatically in response to instructions given for that purpose;
(b) is recorded with the intention that it should be processed by means of such equipment;
(c) is recorded as part of a relevant filing system or with the intention that it should form part of a relevant filing system; or
(d) does not fall within paragraph (a), (b) or (c) but forms part of an accessible record."

All information carried over the World Wide Web or as e-mail will be data. As long as the data relates to an individual (including a foreign national or resident abroad) who can be identified from the data, the DPA will apply. Accordingly, data about companies will not be caught (save where such data are held by reference to an individual contract at each company). Personal data also includes data which relates to a living individual who can be identified from the data in conjunction with other information. An e-commerce business will hold personal data about its employees.

A data controller under the DPA is a person who alone or jointly determines the purposes for which personal data is processed. There can be more than one data controller. It is the data controller who is primarily responsible for compliance under the DPA.

Data Processor

The data processor is any person (other than an employee of the data controller) who processes data on behalf of the data controller. So for the e-commerce business that outsources functions such as web hosting to third parties the outsourcing company will be a data processor. **8.12**

Notification

8.13   The old system of registration is replaced with a similar system of notification.[7-8] This means that those persons falling within the DPA's ambit are required to notify the Commissioner of their "registrable particulars". The new system is intended to be a simplified less formalistic system and there are some exemptions from the requirement to notify.

A data controller must notify the Commissioner of the registrable particulars and pay the prescribed fee. The registrable particulars are[9] basic items of information about the data controller such as name, address, description of data, purposes for which data is being processed, description of any recipient of the data and those countries outside the European Economic Area to which data may be transferred. In addition, the data controller must give the Commissioner a general description of measures to be taken for the purpose of complying with the seventh data protection principle relating to security.[10]

It is an offence to process data without being included on the Commissioner's register.[11] In May 1996 U.S. Robotics (the U.K.-based company now owned by 3Com) was fined £2,730 for not registering with the data protection registrar when holding customer information on its website.

It is certain that all U.K.-based e-commerce businesses will need to follow the notification procedure and multinational businesses may need to comply with the notification requirements in several countries.

THE EIGHT DATA PROTECTION PRINCIPLES

8.14   There are eight data protection principles with which a data controller must comply. These are contained in Schedule 1 to the DPA. A breach of any of these principles can lead to certain actions being taken by the Commissioner. The Commissioner can also enforce the data protection principles against those who are exempt from registration.

Principle 1 — Data shall be processed fairly and lawfully

The first principle is of particular relevance to e-commerce businesses. Personal data shall not be processed unless one of the six conditions set out in Schedule 2 of the DPA is met.

The first principle also establishes the key principle that personal data shall be processed fairly, regard being made to the method by which the data is obtained including, in particular, whether any person is deceived or misled as to the purposes for which the data is being processed. An e-commerce business should give frank and full information to the data subject about the use and purpose of any personal data including any transfers or disclosures of the information unless it is obvious and also the identity of the data controller. Ideally this should be given ideally on the website before the personal data is obtained. Additionally, a data subject should be provided with any information which is necessary in the circumstances to enable the processing to be fair. In the case of *Innovations (Mail Order) Ltd v. Data Protection Registrar* (September 1993), the Data

---

[7-8] Transitional Provisions mean that existing registrations under the 1984 Act continue to be valid until they expire.
[9] s.16(1) DPA 1998.
[10] s.18(2)(6) DPA 1998.
[11] s.21, DPA 1998.

Protection Tribunal held that data subjects should be informed of any non-obvious purpose for which the data were to be used before the personal data is used.

Where data is not obtained directly from the data subject the data controller must **8.15** ensure so far as practicable that the data subject is provided with the relevant information.

Schedule 2 of the DPA provides that processing may only be carried out where one of the following conditions has been satisfied:

(1) the individual has given his consent to the processing;

(2) the processing is necessary for the performance of a contract with the individual;

(3) the processing is required under a legal obligation;

(4) the processing is necessary to protect the vital interests of the individual;

(5) the processing is necessary to carry out public functions;

(6) the processing is necessary in order to pursue the legitimate interests of the business (unless prejudicial to the interests of the individual).

The conditions most likely to be relevant to an e-commerce business are (1) and (2) above. It may be possible to rely upon the balance of interests test in (6) above but no guidance has been issued yet by the Data Protection Commissioner and its interpretation under English law is uncertain.

An e-commerce business should consider adopting on the website a Privacy Policy which is a convenient way to fulfil the requirements under the Act to disclose certain information. An example of a clause which provides for a Privacy Statement to be used to obtain consent is set out below.

> "Xyz Limited respect the privacy of individuals who visit our website. This Privacy Statement describes the information which we may ask you for and the ways in which we may use the information. This Statement also tells you how you can check that information about you which we keep is accurate and how you can ask us to delete, correct or amend such information from our files. Use of this website from your computer, including submission of a Registration Form or an Order Form, constitutes acceptance by you of this Privacy Statement."

Stricter conditions apply to the processing of sensitive data. This category includes information relating to racial or ethnic origin, political opinions, religious or other beliefs, trade union membership, health, sex life and criminal convictions. Where such data is being processed, not only must the controller meet the requirements of the principles and Schedule 2, but processing is prohibited unless at least one of the conditions in Schedule 3 can be satisfied.

Essentially, the explicit consent of the individual will usually have to be obtained before sensitive data can be processed unless the data controller can show that the processing is necessary based on one of the criteria laid out in Schedule 3 of the Act (which covers matters such as processing necessary for the vital interests of the data subject, data already in the public domain or processing necessary for medical reasons etc.)

There is no definition in the Act of what constitutes explicit consent. The Directive says that it is "any freely given specific and informed indication which signifies agreement." This seems to require some form of active communication from the data subject so that an e-business may not infer consent to process sensitive data from a non-response. Explicit consent involves something which is absolutely clear and which covers the specific details of processing. A blank consent is unlikely to be sufficient.

Consent, either for sensitive data or non-sensitive data is often obtained by "click wrap" consent. This involves having a registration page on the website where the data subject clicks on an "I accept" icon. This ensures that data protection terms are brought to the visitor's attention and requires the visitor to actively communicate consent.

There has been some criticism of the sensitive data requirements in the e-commerce sector as some unlikely activities could fall within the ambit of sensitive data. So an airline which took bookings online and which received requests for special meals such as Kosher, halal or diabetic or wheelchairs could be in possession of sensitive data which relate to religious or health matters.

Principle 2 — Data shall be obtained for specific and lawful purposes

8.16   This principle requires that all purposes for which a data controller holds data be specified in a notice either to the data subject or the Commissioner and that data is not used or processed in any manner incompatible with those purposes.

Principle 3 — Personal data shall be adequate relevant and not excessive

8.17   The third principle requires that personal data shall be adequate, relevant and not excessive in relation to the purpose for which the data is to be processed. Essentially, this means that e-commerce businesses should not obtain excessive and irrelevant data from customers and potential customers. Accordingly, if the e-business is only sending out information by e-mail then postal address details or facsimile numbers may not be relevant. There is a trend among some e-businesses to seek completion of online forms with matters such as salary, age, marital status which are often useful for marketing and statistical purposes but which are irrelevant or excessive for DPA purposes. E-businesses should, when seeking completion of forms, state, often by means of a clearly indicated asterisk, which questions are voluntary and which are necessary to be permitted access to a website.

Principle 4 — Personal data shall be accurate and where necessary kept up to date

8.18   A data controller will not be in breach of this principle if it has held inaccurate data but it has taken reasonable steps to ensure the accuracy of the data or if the data subject has notified the controller of the view that the data is inaccurate and the data indicates this fact. The reasonable steps to be taken to verify data are to be judged in the light of the purposes for which the data was obtained or processed.[12] E-businesses should consider ensuring adequate verification steps are taken when using data which could be inaccurate or out of date.

---

[12] Sched. 1, Pt. 11, para. 7, DPA.

Principle 5 — Personal data shall not be kept for longer than is necessary

Data controllers shall ensure that data is not kept longer than necessary. The data **8.19** controller should give data a set period after which it is reviewed against the purposes given for holding the data. Data storage has become relatively cheap and it is often cheaper for an e-business to retain all personal data than to spend time and money cleansing and deleting data which is out of date. As a result of the fifth principle e-businesses must, however, consider spending the time and money in cleansing their data.

Principle 6 — Personal data shall be processed in accordance with the rights of data subjects

A person contravenes the sixth principle only if:

(1) information is not supplied by a data controller to a data subject where data is being processed by a third party on behalf of data controller;

(2) the data controller does not comply with a notice requiring the controller to cease or not to process data likely to cause damage or distress;

(3) the data controller fails to comply with a notice not to process data for purposes of direct marketing;

(4) the data controller does not comply with a notice not to use data for automatic decision making.

Breach of the principle may lead to the service of an Enforcement Notice from the Data Protection Commissioner.

Principle 7 — Measures to be taken against unauthorised or unlawful processing

This principle requires a data controller to take, amongst other things, reasonable steps to **8.20** ensure the reliability of its staff who have access to personal data. Accordingly, an e-business must provide adequate security guarantees and ensure compliance with these guarantees. The more potentially sensitive the data, the greater the requirement to take security, so, information which is generally available in the public domain will need not as high a standard of security as someone's financial or medical records. Where the processing of personal data is carried out by a data processor on behalf of a data controller the data processor must act under a written contract under which the data processor is to act only on instructions from the data controller and which imposes security obligations on the processor. An e-commerce business which contracts with third parties such as computer bureaux, outsources certain operations to third parties, or engages a company to provide disaster recovery, should ensure that the contracts impose adequate technical and organisational guarantees to comply with the seventh principle and include appropriate warranties and indemnities.

Principle 8 — Personal Data shall not be transferred to a country outside the EEA unless there is adequate protection

8.21   The eighth principle prohibits the transfer of personal data to countries outside the European Economic Area[13] unless there are adequate levels of protection for the rights and freedoms of data subjects in relation to processing personal data. Many countries including the United States do not have equivalent data protection laws and it may be necessary for an e-commerce business to transfer personal data to other countries for processing.

In order to determine whether the level of protection afforded by a country is adequate, the circumstances of the transfer must be assessed. Consideration is given to the nature of the data, the country of origin and final destination, the purposes of processing, the security measures taken in respect of the data and the laws (if any) in force in the country. Adequacy is determined in the light of the "risk" involved in a particular transfer and does not necessarily depend on specific data protection/privacy legislation being in place.

8.22   The eighth principle does not apply in the following situations[14]:

(1) The data subject has given his/her consent to the transfer. For e-businesses, ensuring that a visitor to the web site has been provided either on the web site or by e-mail information about any transfer to an overseas country and obtaining consent by click-wrap or e-mail will be the easiest way of exporting data to countries which do not have "adequate" data protection laws.

(2) Transfer is necessary for performance of the contract between the data subject and a data controller or for taking steps at the request of the data subject with a view to his entering into a contract with the data controller. This is a further exemption upon which e-commerce businesses can rely on.

(3) With respect to a contract between the data controller and a third person entered into at the request of the data subject in his/her interests, and the transfer is necessary for the performance or conclusion of such a contract. This is another exemption upon which an e-business can rely and could cover contacting credit card companies for payment or courier companies for the shipping of goods.

(4) Transfer is necessary for reasons of substantial public interest. This is unlikely to be relied upon by an e-business.

(5) Transfer is necessary with respect to legal proceedings, legal rights or obtaining legal advice. This is unlikely to be relied upon by an e-business.

(6) Transfer is necessary to protect the vital interests of the data subject. This is unlikely to be relied upon by an e-business.

(7) Transfer of personal data on public register. Again this is unlikely to be relied upon by an e-business.

(8) Transfer is made on terms of a kind approved by the Commissioner as ensuring adequate safeguards or the transfer is authorised by the Commissioner as being in manner ensuring adequate safeguards. This exemption is likely to be used by multi-national companies and e-businesses where they are active and need to transfer personal data between operations in the EEA and non "adequate" countries.

---

[13] The 15 E.U. Member States and Norway, Iceland and Liechtenstein.
[14] DPA, Sched. 4.

The Commissioner has stated that she intends to take a pragmatic approach to the issue   **8.23**
of transferring personal data to overseas countries. This involves ensuring a high
standard of adequacy whilst not disrupting unnecessarily international commercial data
flows. Where a country does not have adequate protection, there is likely to be
established model contract clauses[15] which guarantee the protection for personal data.[16]
As data subjects would not be able to assert their rights under a contract between the
controller and the controller/processor in the third country, an additional contract clause
between the data subject and the controller may be necessary. In July 1999 the
Commissioner published a good practice approach to assessing adequacy and considered
the contractual solutions to the restrictions in trans-border data flows.

U.S. SAFE-HARBOUR PROPOSALS

The United States, which prefers to leave regulation to industry, views the European   **8.24**
data protection directive as a classic demonstration of E.U. fondness for bureaucracy and
regulatory overkill. It has threatened to challenge the Directive in the World Trade
Organisation (WTO) if it is ever used against U.S. companies.[17] The U.S. continues to
support self-regulatory industry schemes[18] developed by U.S. business groups to address
privacy issues rather than Federal legislation. At the time of going to press E.U. and U.S.
negotiators have just agreed to recommend a deal on how personal data can be protected
when it is sent from the E.U. to the United States. The agreement is based on "safe
harbour" principles which would allow U.S. industry to conduct business under
European privacy conditions. The parties appear to have agreed on the criteria necessary
for inclusion in the list of companies in the safe harbour scheme and on sanctions to be
applied for violation of E.U. data privacy rules. The arrangements will have to be
approved by the U.s. authorities, E.U. Member States and the European Parliament
before coming into force.

Data Subject Rights

Data subjects have extensive rights under the DPA which an e-business needs to comply   **8.25**
with. A data subject may write to an e-business and ask to be supplied with a
description, purposes and disclosures made of or a copy of any personal data being held.
Within forty days and on receipt of a single fee[19] an e-business must respond to an
individual's request. An e-business must put in place systems to enable it to respond to
such requests.

A data subject has the right to prevent processing for the purposes of direct marketing
and, in certain circumstances, to prevent processing likely to cause him/her damage.[20]

An individual has the right to claim compensation where a data controller contravenes
certain requirements of the DPA. This is a completely new right. It opens up a whole
spectrum of individuals claiming compensation and is one of the most significant new
rights in the DPA.

---

[15] The CitiBank/German Railways agreement of February 1996 which was negotiated with the Berlin Data
Protection Commissioner is being cited as a useful model.
[16] The International Chamber of Commerce has drafted model contract clauses.
[17] See *Financial Times*, "**Regulators@odds**" — October 8, 1998.
[18] *e.g.* Trustee, a non-profit organisation that has established principles of disclosure and informed consent for
on-line services.
[19] Maximum fee to be set by regulations. It was £10 under the Data Protection Act 1984.
[20] See para. 8.13.

In the case of inaccurate data, an individual can apply to the courts for correction, blocking, erasure or destruction.

Data subjects also have the right, subject to exceptions, not to have decisions made about them which are based solely on automated processing. This would cover evaluating candidates for jobs and making decisions about an individual's credit worthiness. The new rules on restricting purely automatic decision-making could impact on an e-business where it is common for decision-making processes to be totally unformatted.

Exemptions From the Act

There are exemptions to certain parts of the DPA. As with the Data Protection Act 1984, there are exemptions for crime, taxation, health and social work, national security and legal professional privilege. There are also some new exemptions which are unlikely to be relevant to e-commerce relating to confidential references, management forecasts and in respect of information by candidates in examination.

Enforcement

8.26   Failure to comply with the DPA may result in criminal penalties for companies and their individual managers. The Commissioner may issue an enforcement notice where a data controller has contravened the data protection principles. She may also issue an "information notice" requiring the controller to provide her with information where she suspects a principle has been breached. Failure to comply with either notice is an offence unless the individual can show that he/she exercised all due diligence.

PRIVACY THREATENING TECHNOLOGIES

Cookies

8.27   A cookie is a computer data storage program which enables a website to record a visitor's activities from his/her computer hard drive, in other words, pieces of information generated by a web server and stored on the visitor's computer. The cookie is then available for subsequent access by the server itself or other servers to read the information stored and thereby analyse and publicise the viewing habits of the visitor to the server which enquires of the information recorded as a cookie. Under the original Netscape standard, cookies existed by default only for the duration of the actual web browsing session and could only be accessed by the web server and the web page that stored the cookie.[21] The original standard, however, and the subsequently revised cookie standards allow web servers to overwrite the defaults. A web server may extend the life-span of a cookie to several years. A web server may also set a cookie so that an almost unlimited number of other servers have access to the cookie information as well. This allows some companies to follow Internet users from website to website to collect information about the personal browsing habits of the visitor for advertising and marketing purposes. The website feeds the Internet user's browser a "cookie" and the

---

[21] Netscape,   Persistent   Client   State   HTTP   Cookies,   Preliminary   Specification (**http://www.netscape.com/newsref/std/cookie spec.html**).

browser being used by the Internet user automatically responds to this by giving out the information requested. This normally happens without Internet users knowing that their computers have been interrogated.

Many cookies are useful and, if asked, most Internet users are happy to accept cookies from any sites, since receiving cookies saves Internet users time and effort. These are the cookies which, for example, keep details of previous visits to the site and thereby save Internet users from having to re-register at websites every time they visit.

8.28

Early versions of the Netscape browser did not contain any facilities to notify Internet users before accepting a cookie. But concerns regarding privacy have led to improvements; the current versions of both Netscape and Microsoft Internet Explorer contain user selectable options which allow users to be notified when a cookie is received. It has been said that merely being notified and allowing the Internet user to reject is not enough and, in consequence, all browsers now contains an option which allows the user to automatically reject all cookies.

The gathering and use of personal data through the use of cookies is certainly an activity which may be within the scope of the DPA if they are used to collect personal data without a user's knowledge or consent. Accordingly cookies which collect anonymous data such as browser name, websites visited, length of visits and items purchased do not raise data protection issues. However, if this anonymous data is combined with personally identifiable information so that together the information identifies living individuals then the Act will apply.[22]

Active Content/Client Based Scripting Technologies

Active content refers to controls or applets which are limited functionality mini-programs that are transferred to a user's computer or active in the web page that a user is browsing. These controls or applets are typically used to add functionality and efficiency to the browsing process. By giving web sites powered by applets access to certain data or functions on a user's computer, active content facilitates efficient exchanges of information between user and host. However, these programs can be used to damage or misuse data on a user's computer. Termed "Hostile applets" by the press and media, these malicious programs may use their wide access to user data to threaten the privacy or security of unsuspecting web surfers. The three main types of active content are Java (a programming language developed by Sun Microsystems), JavaScript (a scripting language developed by Netscape) and Active X (another programming language offered by Microsoft). These languages, when deployed as applets, have the ability to open and close windows, create and delete files, read and write files, create network connections, format the hard drive and reboot the entire system.[23] In essence, these programs are viruses foreign to your computer. Hostile applets have particular implications for privacy in that they can exploit flaws or bugs in a browser's design in order to access personal information such as e-mail addresses and passwords (leaving the user's e-mail wide open

8.29

---

[22] See Mayer-Schönberger, V., *Computer Law and Security Report*, Vol. 14, No. 3, 1998, p.166.

[23] In fact, the level of intrusion allowed depends on which of the three systems of active content you are talking about. JavaScript is the least capable of controlling a user's computer or data while Active X is by far the most capable. Java runs on fundamentally different security models that limit Java code to a virtual machine or 'sandbox' embedded in the browser itself: **http://www.symantec.com/avcenter/security/applets/risk.html**. However, this does not mean that JavaScript is the least dangerous. Depending on the nature of bugs present within the browser, JavaScript applets (which are designed to control you browser) may be able to extract personal information from your browser or POP3 e-mail accounts simply by accessing the preferences available on the browser itself. **http://www.uic.edu/depts/adn/infwww/html/adn20/active.html**.

to inspection), FTP passwords or history bars (revealing detailed accounts of a user's browsing habits). For example, a recent security flaw found in Netscape Navigator 4.0 — 4.04 allows JavaScript programs to read a user's e-mail addresses and passwords found in a browser's preference settings.[24] Microsoft's Internet Explorer is also not immune. A flaw found within Explorer's design allows the right JavaScript to access text added to forwarded e-mails.[25]

It is significant that the technology to capture this kind of information was developed and deployed in the United States which does not have the any equivalent data protection legislation.

PRIVACY ENHANCED TECHNOLOGIES (PETS)

8.30   While Internet users may be willing, in the course of an online session, to give the company a great deal of personal information, the company effectively has a duty to protect them from themselves and their generosity as a result of Principle 3 of the Data Protection Act 1998. There are new technological solutions to this problem which are being given strong support by European Data Protection Commissioners.

8.31   In 1995, the Information and Privacy Commissioner in Ontario Canada and the Registratiekamer in The Netherlands jointly produced a report called "Privacy-Enhancing Technologies: The Path to Anonymity." The authors argued that, at the present time, a person was almost always required to reveal his/her identity when engaging in a wide range of activities.[26] Every time he/she used a credit card, made a telephone call, paid his/her taxes, subscribed to a magazine, or bought something at the grocery store using a credit or debit card, an identifiable record of each transaction was created and recorded in a computer database somewhere. In order to obtain a service or make a purchase (using something other than cash), organisations require that citizens identified themselves:

> "This practice is so widespread that it is simply treated as a given — an individual's identity must be collected and recorded in association with services rendered or purchases made. But must this always be the case? Are there no situations where transactions may be conducted anonymously, yet securely? We believe that there are and will outline a number of methods and technologies by which anonymous yet authentic transactions may be conducted."

The authors then developed their case for privacy-enhanced technologies. Their explanation is somewhat complex and we have instead compared it to a masked ball. At a masked ball the guest arrives at the ball and is identified as someone whom the host has invited to attend. He/she is dressed in a "mask" to hide his/her identity before entering the party. He/she has been authorised to participate in the party but nobody knows who he/she really is.

8.32   PETs perform the same function in an electronic environment. The user arrives at the system and encounters the "Identity Protector" which, once it has established that the user is authorised to proceed, gives the user a mask or "authorised pseudo-identity".[27] This may, in appropriate circumstances, be a different pseudo-identity each time the user connects to the system. Working through the Identity Protector, the user can enter into

---

[24] **http://www.uic/edu/depts/adn/infwww/html/adn20/active.html.**
[25] **http://www.cen.uiuc.edu/~ejk/browser-security.html.**
[26] The Data Protection Registrar gave support for privacy enhanced technologies in the 1997 Annual Report.
[27] This is a good application for a type of public key cryptosystem.

binding transactions. However, the user is in control of information regarding his/her true identity being passed onto the system; any attempts by the system to discover the true identity of the user are caught by the Identity Protector.

Since the European Commission is funding research in this area and the work is fully supported and encouraged by all the European Data Protection Commissioners, it is possible that shortly after the end of this decade privacy law and technology will come together to make it illegal in Europe to use e-commerce systems which do not contain Identity Protectors.

There are serious issues which need to be addressed before such a situation could arise. Identity Protectors must not hinder the investigation of money laundering or serious tax evasion or terrorism or serious crime. PETs are not a fully worked out solution to the privacy problem. But they do provide a useful counter argument to an on-line vendor who claims that it must have personal information in order to authenticate a transaction.

JURISDICTIONAL DATA PROTECTION ISSUES

Many e-commerce businesses will have several severs and databases in different **8.33** countries. This can create difficulties in identifying which data controller is triable for any breach of data protection laws. It has been suggested that laws should be enacted to permit enforcement against internet service providers and internet access providers.[28]

Clause 5 of the DPA applies the requirements of the DPA to both United Kingdom data controllers established in the United Kingdom and also to data controllers established neither in the United Kingdom nor in any other EEA state but who use equipment in the United Kingdom for processing the data otherwise than for the purpose of transit through the United Kingdom Such non United Kingdom controllers who 'uses equipment in the United Kingdom for processing data otherwise than for the purposes of transit must nominate a representative in the United Kingdom to fulfil obligations under the DPA 1998. This specification of transit data through the United Kingdom brings up several interesting questions about the nature of "transit data" and data protection requirements for "transit" situations. For example, if a website in the United States deposited a cookie onto the PC of a user in the United Kingdom and then subsequently reviewed the data collected by that cookie when the user revisited the United States site, the personal data accessed by the site theoretically represents personal data stored in the United Kingdom (*i.e.* on the users PC). It seems ridiculous, but under the auspices of the DPA 1998, the U.S. web site may, in theory, have to nominate the user as representative data controller in order to comply with the 1998 DPA.[29]

The data protection rules which will apply will be those of the place of establishment of the data controller for whose purposes the processing is carried out. It is apparent, particularly for e-commerce businesses, that a data controller may be established in more than on one Member State. Therefore, an e-commerce business which is going to be holding data in a number of jurisdictions may have to comply with the data production laws for each relevant country. In additional e-commerce businesses which transfer data internationally must comply with the transborder data flow restrictions.

---

[28] See France, E. 1997: "Can Data Protection survive?" (1997) *Computers and Law — The Journal of the Society for Computers and the Law*, Vol. 8, Iss. 2.
[29] The idea for this example comes originally from Christopher Millard: "Data Protection and the Internet" *eMagazine*, Feb/Mar 1999, Vol. 9, Iss. 6.
http://www.scl.org/scl/emag/emagazine/vol9/iss6/vol9-iss6-christopher-millard-art.htm.

Telecommunications Directive

8.34　It is unclear whether the E.U. Telecommunications Directive and subsequent U.K. enabling legislation, The Telecommunications (Data Protection & Privacy) (Direct Marketing) Regulations 1998, which came into force May 1, 1999, apply to e-commerce related activities or exclusively to traditional telephony services. Although the Directive specifically states application to "the processing of personal data in connection with the provision of publicly available telecommunications services in public telecommunications networks in the (European Union)",[30] it is unclear whether publicly available telecommunications services include ISPs. However, the U.K. Telecommunications Regulations, which restrict direct marketing over telecommunications networks may apply to e-mail or other broadcast Internet Services. Although the Regulations are intended to apply to conventional voice and fax transmissions,[31] no indication in jurisprudence has been made as to the applicability of these regulations to Internet related activities.

Privacy Policies

A Privacy Policy is an e-business's policy on data collection is a convenient way to fulfil the requirement under the Act to disclose certain information. It is also good marketing for an e-business to tell its potential customers and customers how it protects their personal data and the rights they have in respect of it.

A typical policy might disclose:

- the categories of information which an e-business will collect such as name, e-mail address and contact telephone numbers;
- the purposes for which the e-business collects the information such as billing, delivery, marketing and promotions;
- the way in which the e-business will (and will not) use the information such as to contact customers about products and services, share information with contractors, not sell information to third parties;
- the security measures the e-business will take such as referring to secure socket layer technology;
- information collected automatically such as the visitors internet browser;
- contact details at e-business; and
- the visitors' rights such as for correction and access.

If correctly drafted a Privacy Policy enables compliance with the Data Protection principles while promoting an e-businesses commitment to data protection.

CONCLUSION

8.35　The Commissioner has made it clear that her officers have been reviewing websites and that some of these give her concern. It is clear that the DPA applies to information collected by e-businesses on the Internet as it does to any other method. The

---

[30] Telecommunications Directive, Art. 3(1).
[31] Millard, Christopher in Rowe & Haftke, *A Practitioner's Guide to the Regulation of the Internet* (City & Financial Publishing, 1999/2000).

Commissioner has voiced concerns that the sites she has visited do not contain any notification of the uses and disclosures to be made of personal data as required by the DPA. This may be because in the majority of cases the information is only to be used for obvious purposes such as permitting further direct contract by the e-business concerned (which does not have to be stated). In other situations there could be breaches of the DPA.

Another concern of the Commissioner was that in e-commerce transactions notification to data users are normally only given at the end or at the bottom of an online form. In non-electronic transactions, where disclosures are made on physical paper forms, disclosures are in prominent places such as near the signature on the form. The Commissioner has recognised that e-commerce transactions are different. Where information is imported on to a form of a website, it is immediately capable of being processed as personal data. When warnings are placed at the bottom of a form, it is possible that they may not be seen or read by the user. The Commissioner therefore feels that indication as to the uses and disclosures of data should be given at the beginning of forms so that a user can decide on a fully informed basis whether to enter into the transaction or not. It is likely that the Commissioner's office will be preparing guidance notes on the use of data protection on e-commerce transactions.

European e-businesses must ensure that their websites are data protection compliant. **8.36** The data protection laws are intended to ensure all processing of personal data from the collection, to storage, to manipulation, to disclosure to its destruction is undertaken fairly. A clear statement about the purposes for which personal data is obtained must be given. This may also require adding new terms and conditions to deal with data protection warnings and disclaimers to websites. It is also good practice to have a Privacy Policy on a website setting out an e-business policy on the collection, storage and use of personal data and what visitors can do to correct inaccuracies or to see their records.

The growth of e-commerce does raise a threat to the rights to privacy of individuals. The new DPA, with provision of increased rights to individuals, does help to meet some of these threats. Nevertheless, it is necessary to develop technical means to protect the privacy of e-business users. The use of security encryption methods and the development of the Internet protocol to improve confidentiality by classification of messages and better authentication of procedures is equally important. What is ultimately needed is a global model of data protection. The European model is an important step to protecting data but with the United States government favouring self regulation, an effective regime will only be found when there is a global solution to this transborder problem.

— 9 —
FINANCIAL SERVICES

> "When it is not necessary to change, it is necessary not to change."[1]

INTRODUCTION

Financial services providers have been keen to take up the challenge of using the **9.01** Internet to market, deliver and communicate about their financial services and investment products. The challenger arises from the need to keep sites under constant review for legal and regulatory compliance and to keep up with frequent changes arising from technical and regulatory developments.

This chapter outlines the current regulatory framework in the U.K. governing financial services on the Internet and U.K. and E.U. proposals for change.

THE CURRENT FRAMEWORK

The other chapters in this book explain the general legal issues financial services firms **9.02** need to consider in relation to their websites.

U.K. financial srvices regulators have:

- stated that all existing rules could apply and their jurisdiction extends to all websites which may be accessed in the U.K.;

- avoided creating specific rules for Internet business;

- issued guidance clarifying how the existing regulations apply; and

- developed a realistic enforcement policy.

This approach involves financial services firms adopting a two stage process of considering how the 1986 Act[2] and the relevant regulations apply to a firm's business and then how the regulators will choose to exercise their enforcement powers, based on guidance.

---

[1] Lucius Cary, Viscount Falkland.
[2] The Financial Services Act 1986.

Uncertainty has, to an extent, inhibited innovation by both U.K. and overseas firms. With the risk of private or criminal prosecutions, reliance on indications as to use of enforcement powers is not the ideal way on which to build a new method of doing business. Clarification of how the Internet will be regulated is therefore one of the key elements of the regulatory reforms currently being discussed.

There are two areas to consider. First, advertising including cold calling, and secondly, investment business. They are, of course, interrelated.

ADVERTISING

9.03   The basic restriction on investment advertisements is contained in section 57 of the 1986 Act:

> "No person other than an authorised person shall issue or cause to be issued an investment advertisement in the United Kingdom unless its contents have been approved by an authorised person."

For Internet advertising, you need to ask the same series of questions as for advertising on any other media.

Is it an advertisement?

The term "advertisement" is widely defined to include every form of advertising. An advertisement will amount to an investment advertisement if it contains an invitation or information calculated (*i.e.* likely) to lead directly or indirectly to persons entering into or offering to enter into investment agreements (agreements for the purchase or sale of investments or the provision of investment services).

An advertisement could be:

- a website as a whole, or
- each separate page of a website, being separately identifiable and capable of being accessed without the rest of the site.

Determining this could have significant consequences for website design in order to comply with the requirements for contents of advertisements.

9.04   *Who is issuing the advertisement or causing it to be issued?*

A website owner is likely to be the issuer but there are also third parties, such as ISPs or search engine managers, who may also issue the advertisement or cause it to be issued. For example, search engines may summarise the contents of a website which can constitute an investment advertisement.

However, provided the third party has no knowledge or control over the content of the material put on a site, and no commercial interest in the site, it is unlikely that it would be caught by this provision. There is also a defence for "innocent dissemination" which may apply to those whose ordinary business involves passing on advertisements to the order of another person.

Is it issued in the U.K.?

To be caught by the 1986 Act the investment advertisement must be issued or caused to be issued in the U.K. The 1986 Act treats advertisements outside the United Kingdom as issued in the United Kingdom if they are "directed at" people in the United Kingdom or "made available" to them. The Financial Services Authority ("FSA") has stated:

> "It is the FSA's view that, for the purposes of the Act, an advertisement which can be accessed on a computer screen by a person in the U.K., will have been issued in the U.K."

Even if material is not specifically directed at U.K. investors, it will generally be caught by the availability aspect, as access to website pages is not usually restricted.

Is an exemption or exception relevant?   9.05

There are specific exceptions and exemptions within the 1986 Act and in regulations made under it. Consider:

- whether a particular exemption is applicable. There is an exemption for periodical publications published and circulating principally outside the U.K. — or a sound or television broadcast transmitted principally for reception outside the U.K. The FSA does not consider that Internet material will be a sound or television broadcast although it may amount to a periodical publication depending on the nature of the site. "Newsletter" style sites may fall within this exemption, but the majority of sites will not.

- whether an exemption which provides for promotions to limited categories of persons is applicable. These are likely to be of limited use in relation to Internet materials which are likely to be accessible by the general public rather than by a targeted group. Consideration could be given to implementing access controls to enable an advertisement to fall within an exemption. The regulators suggest password protection systems or screening of applicants.

Are other rules relevant?   9.06

For example:

- in an advertisement for a collective investment scheme, the additional restrictions under section 76 of the 1986 Act need to be considered. Unregulated schemes (*i.e.* ones which are not U.K. authorised or recognised) cannot be promoted to the general public — only to limited categories of persons, either:
  - by anyone under one of the general exemptions mentioned above, or
  - by an authorised person under one of the particular categories for unregulated schemes under the Financial Services (Promotion of Unregulated Schemes) Regulations 1991; and

- general advertising regulations, including the British Codes of Advertising Standard Practice.

If not within an exemption, what should the advertisement contain?   9.07

The general rule is that advertisements should be fair and not misleading.

Regulated firms must apply appropriate expertise and take steps to ensure that the fundamental requirement to provide fair and accurate documents is met. The FSA and the various self regulating organisations have detailed rules for the content, design and format of advertisements which apply to all forms of advertising including those on web pages. How hypertext links are used and the wording and positioning of risk warnings should also be carefully considered. The regulators have each issued guidance on the Internet which comments on the content of advertisments and contains implications for website management and design.

In addition to section 57 concerns, section 47 of the 1986 Act operates independently to prevent any misleading, false or deceptive statements whether or not they are in a regulated advertisement.

9.08 *What about unsolicited calls?*

The 1986 Act prohibits a person seeking to enter into an investment agreement in the course of or in consequence of a personal visit or oral communications without express invitation. Only certain unsolicited calls are permitted. The question is whether Internet materials can be restricted to certain classes of persons.

Although the Internet has not, up to now, been used extensively for voice telephony, the volume of voice calls over the Internet is growing significantly. It is possible that this restriction will become more relevant as a result. It is also possible to make an investment advertisement orally, so the restrictions on advertising outlined above are also relevant.

Certain exemptions from the need for authorisation to carry on investment business in the U.K. can only be available if there is no contravention of advertising or unsolicited calls restrictions.

INVESTMENT BUSINESS

9.09 In addition to considering the advertising restrictions described above, firms should consider investment business issues. There can be investment business concerns even where the site is passive and not interactive with investors.

Section 3 of the 1986 Act provides that:

> "No person shall carry on, or purport to carry on, investment business in the United Kingdom unless he is an authorised person under Chapter III or an exempted person under Chapter IV of this Part of the Act."

The activities which are most likely to be relevant are:

- *dealing in investments* — buying, selling, subscribing for or underwriting investments or offering or agreeing to do so, either as principal or agent.

9.10
- *arranging deals in investments* — "arrangements" are widely defined and the definition has two limbs. The first limb covers arrangements with a view to (*i.e.* with a causal link to) another person dealing in a particular investment, the arrangements bringing about that transaction in that investment. The second limb covers arrangements involving a person who participates in the arrangements dealing in investments generally.

- *investment advice* — this covers advice given to investors or potential investors on the merits of their dealing or exercising rights in relation to a particular investment but not:

  - generic advice, *i.e.* on investments generally or on market trends;
  - neutral information — as this would not be on the merits of the investment concerned. The dividing line is, however, sometimes difficult to draw;

- advice to intermediaries — this would not be advice to persons in their capacity as investors or potential investors.

Who is carrying on the investment business? 9.11

This will usually be the website owner but others may be caught.

An ISP is unlikely to be caught if it merely acts as a conduit in providing technical services and has no involvement in the marketing of the products and services, or share of the profits, of the website owner. Civil and criminal liabilities could arise, for example, for your actions aiding and abetting the criminal activities of a website owner.

Is the business carried on in the United Kingdom

A person carries on investment business "in the United Kingdom" and so needs to be authorised if he/she:

- carries on investment business from a permanent place of business maintained by him in the United Kingdom.

  This provision relies on identifying the person's geographical location which is difficult for Internet activites. If the person has a website or server in the U.K. which is "maintained" and "permanent", this first test may be satisfied. However, traditional interpretations of the terms "maintained" and "permanent" are not particularly helpful. If and when implemented, proposals in the E-Commerce Directive should assist.

or

- engages in investment business in the United Kingdom.

  This test is aimed at overseas persons without a permanent place of business in the United Kingdom but who engage in investment business in the United Kingdom. This could catch overseas persons who use the Internet to do business with U.K. investors.

Does an exemption apply? 9.12

There are no specific exemptions for business carried on via the Internet. There is an exemption for periodical publications circulating principally outside the United Kingdom which is likely to apply to some Internet "newsletter" style publications, but not to all websites.

The question is whether any of the general exemptions can be applied to the Internet activities.

Application of conduct of business rules?

If the activities are carried on by an authorised firm, the conduct of business rules apply as for any other medium. For example,

- *customer agreements:* — The prescribed contents of a customer agreement should be displayed on one website or hypertext-linked sites and should be in the same sequence as the hard copy version.

- *reporting* — Reports and documents may be sent to a customer's e-mail address.

- *record keeping* — Records may be kept in electronic format provided they can be reproduced in hard copy format within one working day.

Some issues remain offline. For example, signatures. In certain circumstances, firms are required to obtain signed documents from their customers, for example, for personal pension applications (although this is likely to change soon).

The position on signatures may change, as the Government is currently considering responses to its draft Electronic Communications Bill which proposes to make all types of electronic signature legally admissible in court and the regulators have indicated that they are reviewing their policy on use of electronic signatures, for example, IMRO has now amended its rules to state that electronic signatures are acceptable in the majority of circumstances where a customer signature is required.

THE FSA'S ENFORCEMENT POLICY

9.13 To an extent, realistic regulation has been achieved by the publication of an enforcement policy which is a statement of what the FSA regards as acceptable.

Investment Advertisements

9.14 Factors indicating an advertisement is outside U.K. regulation include:

Non-U.K. server

Is the site located on a server outside the United Kingdom? The use of a U.K. server is not, however, conclusive evidence that material on that site is aimed at the United Kingdom, and there is a move away from looking at the location of hardware to determine jurisdiction generally.

Availability to U.K. investors

Is the product or service available to U.K. investors? Is it also available through channels other than the Internet?

Positive steps to deter U.K. investors

Are positive steps taken to ensure U.K. investors do not obtain the service? These could include systems and procedures which are in place to ensure that only persons who could lawfully receive it do so.

9.15 *The extent to which any advertisement is directed at persons in the United Kingdom*

Factors which indicate whether or not the advertisement is directed at the U.K. include:

- the existence of disclaimers and warnings;

- hypertext links;

- various other factors relating to the format and content of the site; and

- whether it has been notified to a U.K. search engine or promoted in U.K. media. Website owners may wish to take steps to prevent search engines seeking out and listing their websites without their consent where possible.

Including disclaimers, even where supported by a policy of not dealing with U.K. investors, will not in itself prevent the advertisement from being caught by section 57 of the 1986 Act, although it could reduce the investor protection concerns of the regulators and so the risk of enforcement action.

The extent to which positive steps have been taken to limit access to the site

Access controls will be taken into account in deciding whether or not to take enforcement action. Some access controls which can be circumvented will not, however, be sufficient to remove concerns under the 1986 Act.

Investment Business

Guidance from the regulators confirms that, as for any other medium: **9.16**

- whether a person is carrying on an investment business is a question of fact, which depends on many indicators; and

- the usual exclusions and exemptions apply to the Internet.

The regulators will consider the same factors described above in relation to advertisements in deciding whether to take action in respect of investment business concerns.

PROPOSALS UNDER THE FINANCIAL SERVICES AND MARKETS BILL

Details of the new Financial Services and Markets Bill ("the Bill") which is to cover a **9.17** wide range of financial products, banking, insurance and investments are, at the time of writing, being debated. There is evident interest in developing the new legislation to reflect the need for regulation of financial services on the Internet.

Financial promotion

The financial promotion regime under the Bill is to cover both advertising and cold **9.18** calling. A consultation document setting out the Government's broad approach to regulation of financial promotion was published in March 1999 and a second Consultation Document with a draft Financial Promotion Exemption Order was published in October 1999.

The end result is expected to be that:

- the financial promotion clause will be very wide ranging and note that it is likely to apply to a wider range of products than the current 1986 Act investment advertisement regulations (one of the Governments aims is to address questions posed by the increasing use of the internet).

- the exemptions order will repeat most of the exemptions which already exist to achieve a very similar position to that currently in force.

Issues arising from the proposals to consider include:

Whether the scope of the financial promotion clause causes a problem

The new financial promotion clause states that a person must not "communicate" or cause to be communicated an invitation or inducement to engage in investment activity, unless he is an authorised person or the communication is approved by an authorised person.

9.19   There may be new problems in interpreting:

- what "communication" means and whether or not and when a person will be communicating via the Internet; and

- jurisdictional scope. The Bill is to cover communications which are "capable of having an effect" in the United Kingdom. At the level of statute, still the intention appears to be to exclude communications which cannot have any effect in the United Kingdom, *i.e.* to set the most extreme boundary.

- although further consultation is continuing on this point, the limited exemption originally proposed for hypernet links if they contained nothing more than the name of the website to which it is linked may not be introduced, because of the Government's view that it is not needed.

The Treasury indicates that there will be an exemption for communications which originate outside the United Kingdom and are capable of having an effect in the United Kingdom but which are not directed at the United Kingdom. If this is the case, determining whether a communication is directed at the United Kingdom remains the central issue and the factors which the regulators have already indicated are relevant to this are likely to remain persuasive.

Proposed new exemptions in the Financial Promotions Exemptions Order

The proposed exemptions may include:

- a communication networks exemption providing a limited exemption for networks where certain factors are satisfied; if he carries on the business of transmitting or receiving material provided to him by others; the content of the communication is wholly devised by his customer; and he does not exercise control over the content of the communication prior to its transmission on receipt, *i.e.* he is, in effect a mere "conduit";

- an exemption for solicited "real live" communications (including internet "chat rooms" and oral communications which are not part of a "co-ordinate promotional strategy".

The details of these and other exemptions are not yet finalised and their terms may of course change.

Investment activities

As regards investment business — to be called "investment activities" — the main **9.20** concern is the extension of jurisdictional scope for authorisation.

Although it is apparently intended that the Bill should not significantly change the basic restrictions on carrying on regulated activities in the United Kingdom, it could expand the definition of investment activities to require authorisation of more overseas persons.

E.U. INITIATIVES

In addition to U.K. Government initiatives, there are a number of E.U. provisions and **9.21** new initiatives which contain measures which will affect the use of the Internet and regulation of it. An E.U. Green Paper on e-commerce for financial services is scheduled, under the Action Plan for the Single Market for Financial Services, for issue by mid-2000.

Internet activities need to be reviewed in relation to some existing cross border passport arrangements, including:

Marketing UCITS funds

As mentioning a fund on a website may amount to marketing that fund in other Member States, it is necessary to notify the regulators in those States in accordance with the UCITS Directive (Directive concerning Undertakings for Collective Investment in Transferable Securities) if the fund is a UCITS fund. For example, where the prospectus for a UCITS is displayed on a website and investors can contact the operator or invest online it is likely that notification will be needed.

Passporting investment services

It is likely that the use of the Internet by a firm to promote itself and its investment services to investors in other Member States will require notification to that State's regulators in accordance with the ISD.[3] Lack of notification could result in breach of various local conduct of business rules, *e.g.* the investment advertisement regime described above which relates to authorised persons (which include ISD firms for these purposes).

The Data Protection Directive is also relevant. It aims to balance the free flow of **9.22** personal data around the E.U. whilst protecting the privacy of individuals by harmonising the levels of protection offered by Member States to individuals. It controls the processing of information relating to an individual and imposes greater restrictions on the processing of personal data relating to certain subjects, for example, racial or ethnic origin. There are also restrictions on transfer of data to third countries outside the E.U. where those countries have inadequate protection. This Directive was implemented in the United Kingdom by the Data Protection Act 1998.[4]

---

[3] Investment Services Directive 93/22.
[4] See Chapter 8.

Proposals for new Directives which relate to or have specific provisions for the Internet should also be noted:

Electronic signatures[5]

This Directive will establish a set of criteria which form the basis for legal recognition of electronic signatures. An amended proposal for this Directive was published in April 1999. The Directive will set up common requirements for certification services and bodies to administer those services which will ensure cross-border recognition of signatures and certificates in the E.C. The Directive is also to contain measures to enable recognition of signatures by third countries. When this framework is in place presumably the regulators will accept electronic signatures as being satisfactory.

9.23 ### E-commerce[6]

An amended proposal for the E-commerce Directive was published in September 1999. This is to require Member States to amend any legislation containing requirements, particularly those related to form, which hinder the use of electronic contracts and also clarifies when contracts will be concluded electronically. Clarification would be welcome and should reduce the uncertainty which currently surrounds contracting online.

Distance marketing of consumer financial services

An amended proposal for this Directive was published in July 1999. It is to provide that contractual terms and conditions and a summary of them, including certain prior information, must be communicated in writing or a durable medium *before* the conclusion of the contract. This means that contracts will not be able to be concluded on the Internet until this requirement has been met. In addition, the Directive provides that a general right of withdrawal lasting between 14 and 30 days (dependent on the type of service concerned) must be provided to consumers. Not unusually, such provisions are already in place in the United Kingdom and some harmonisation will be needed as and when the Directive is implemented.

There was a clear move within the E.U. towards home State regulation for electronic commerce activities. However, the terms of the draft Directives are still the subject of much debate. Also, proposed amendments to the Brussels and Rome conventions would, if they proceed, inhibit the E-Commerce Directive from achieving its objective, the promotion of e-commerce.

PRACTICAL IDEAS TO CONSIDER

9.24   Whilst the way forward remains unclear within the United Kingdom and elsewhere, there are a number of practical steps which can be taken to meet regulatory concerns, including considering:

- the content of websites,
- website design,

---

[5] See Chapter 12.
[6] *ibid.*

- use of health warnings,
- restricting access to targeted viewers only,
- introducing terms and conditions specifically for e-commerce activities,
- prescribing the order of access to documents,
- use of hard copy documents in certain circumstances, and
- establishing a formal procedure for review of websites as part of compliance procedures.

Generally, the aim must be to comply with the spirit of the regulation. It is important to demonstrate that all reasonable steps have been taken to meet investor protection concerns. The fundamental purpose is to provide fair and clear information in a timely way to investors and, where contracting is done over the Internet, meeting normal contract law concerns on the best commercial terms basis.

CONCLUSION

U.K. financial services law is currently in the process of major reform and there is no clear position on the approach to regulation of the Internet. There are, however, encouraging signs in recent comments from the Treasury and the FSA.[7] There is also appreciation that there is need for co-operation within the EU and on the wider basis. In the meantime, there are many practical steps which can be taken to ensure that a website's design and contents protect both the interests of the consumer and the financial services provider.

---

[7] H.M. Treasury: "Financial Promotion — Second Consultative Documents: A New Approach for the Information Age", October 1999; speech by Howard Davies, Chairman, Financial Services Authority, September 28, 1999.

— 10 —

WEBVERTISING

> "The advertising and promotional component of the web will far exceed the transactional"[1]

INTRODUCTION

In 1998, it was estimated that businesses spent $1.92 billion[2] worldwide on **10.01** "webvertising" (a 112 per cent increase over 1997). Online advertising soared in the second quarter of 1999 with advertising revenues growing to $934.4 million — more than double that of the same period in 1998.

The opportunities for a business to advertise online fall into five broad categories: advertising in online publications; banner advertising; website advertising incorporating the advertiser's brand name; linking a website with an e-mail address to facilitate the provision of data to the advertiser; and "spamming".

As a general rule, the legal issues that affect advertising in traditional media are of equal application and relevance to webvertising. The problem for electronic commerce businesses is applying national frameworks of laws and regulations to adverts that are disseminated to the world at large. A webvert is potentially subject to the laws of every country in which it is accessed by an Internet user.

The Federal Trade Commission in the United States has been particularly aggressive in enforcing advertising laws against webvertisers. In May 1998, the FTC published a consultation paper regarding the applicability of its consumer protection rules and guides to online advertising and commercial transactions in electronic media.[3] The proposal aims, for example, to clarify that the term "written" in the context of electronic media means information that is capable of being preserved in tangible form and read and that "mail" includes e-mail. The FTC will now be formulating guidelines for businesses on this topic.

---

[1] Chief Executive of TicketMaster, *Wall Street Journal*, April 28, 1997.
[2] Figure provided by the Internet Advertising Bureau. See **www.iab.net/adrevenue/aug99.html**.
[3] "Interpretation of Rules and Guides for Electronic Media", *Federal Register*, Vol. 63, No. 87, 16 CFR Ch. 1. Also see The Rules of the Road at **www.ftc.gov**.

LAWS REGULATING WEBVERTISING

10.02   U.K. webvertisers have to comply with a raft of domestic legislation. This includes the Trade Descriptions Act 1968[4]; the Consumer Protection Act 1987[5]; the Control of Misleading Advertisements Regulations 1988[6]; the Prices Act 1974; the Unsolicited Goods and Services Act 1971; the Trade Marks Act 1994; the Copyright, Designs and Patents Act 1988; the Data Protection Act 1998[7]; the Defamation Acts 1952 and 1996; the Obscene Publications Acts 1959 and 1964,[8] and the Lotteries and Amusements Act 1976.[9]

However, there are also rafts of non-U.K. legislation which may be potentially breached by a webvert as a result of its global "reach". For example, in *United States v. Thomas*,[10] the operators of a pornographic electronic bulletin-board in California were convicted of criminal obscenity laws by a Federal court in Tennessee based on Tennessee standards of decency. The Court held that the material was "sent" to Tennessee and subject to local standards, despite the "sending" being electronic and the bulletin board being essentially accessible worldwide. And in July 1999, the U.K. courts decided that a man responsible for running a pornographic website in the United States was guilty under British law for publishing obscene material.[11]

At present there is no international unanimity on the issue of whether the content of a website is subject only to the law of the country of origin of the advertisement (the place of business of the advertiser, or where its server is based), or subject to every foreign law where the advertisement is capable of being received? The general approach illustrated by existing cases[12] is that the laws of the countries in which there is evidence of "directed" activity will apply.[13]

10.03   Simply placing information on a website should not, of itself, be treated as evidence of directed activity, particularly if there is something about that information which makes it

---

[4] Under the Trade Descriptions Act 1968 any person who, in the course of a trade or business, applies a false trade description to any goods, or supplies or offers to supply any goods to which a false trade description is applied, commits an offence. Offences under this Act are policed exclusively by Trading Standards Officers who are attached to Local Authorities.

[5] The Department of Trade and Industry's *Code of Practice for Traders on Price Indications* gives guidance in respect of the pricing requirements of the Consumer Protection Act and sets out what is good practice to follow in a wide range of different circumstances. If a Trading Standards Officer has reasonable grounds to suspect that a misleading price indication has been given, he has power under the Act to seize and/or detain goods or records which may be required as evidence in any court proceedings.

[6] S.I. 1988 No. 915 which implemented the E.U. Directive 84/450 on Misleading Advertising as amended by Council Directive 97/55 so as to include comparative advertising.

[7] See Chapter 7.

[8] See Chapter 2.

[9] See further section 8.20 (Online promotions).

[10] 1996 FED App. 0032 P (6th Cir.), II.C.2.

[11] *R. v. Graham Wadden*, Lawtel, August 23, 1999. The act of publication took place when the data was transmitted by the defendant to the ISP, and was still taking place when the data was received. Both the sending and receiving therefore took place within the jurisdiction of the court and it was irrelevant that the transmission may have left the jurisdiction in between the sending and receiving.

[12] For example, in 1996 Virgin Atlantic Airways was punished for putting a misleading advertisement on its U.K. server after it was discovered that they were quoting inaccurate fares and listing a fare that was no longer available in relation to flights from the USA. The U.S. Department of Transportation fined the airline $14,000.

[13] For a detailed analysis see Chapter 4 "Jurisdiction". A draft regulation on jurisdiction, recognition and enforcement was adopted by the Commission on June 14, 1999 to replace the Brussels Convention. It will provide that consumers may prosecute a company with which they have had commercial dealings according to the law of the country in which they are domiciled provided they have been solicited in that country (*e.g.* via advertising from a website). There is also a draft proposal for a regulation on applicable law to complement the Rome Convention. Both these measures contradict the draft e-commerce Directive which takes a country of origin approach. The British Government's e-commerce Bill was published as a White paper in July 1999.

clear that it is not targeted at consumers in a particular country. The language of the advertisement may be relevant, but not conclusive. The use of clear disclaimers may help to clarify who is included in the target audience. Disclaimers, such as "This offer is only available for consumers in X country", however, are likely to be construed narrowly and may be void in some countries.[14] One technical method of filtering web users is to use the standard JavaScript function called "get TimezoneOffset" which identifies the time zone in which potential customers are located. For example, a user whose computer responds as being in GMT plus three and a half hours is likely to be in Iran.

Impact of the Single European Market

Businesses using electronic communications for marketing face regulatory differences **10.04** even within the E.U. itself. French laws,[15] for example, require all advertisements to be in the French language. It is also impossible to run a sales promotion campaign that carries a premium, free gift or sweepstakes lawfully across the E.U.[16] In theory, at least, the principles established by the Single European Market, whereby E.U. Member States are meant to recognise, through the principle of mutual recognition, the laws and regulations of the other Member States, should have avoided this problem.[17] However, the right of freedom to provide goods and services is subject to a number of exceptions[18] and the advertising sector has particularly suffered from a lack of compliance with these rules.

In 1992, Yves Rocher,[19] the French cosmetics company, ran a mail order campaign across several countries. The German courts injuncted Yves Rocher on the grounds of unfair competition. The company took the case to the European Court of Justice which ruled that the German prohibition constituted an

"obstacle to trade because it compels a trader either to adopt sales promotions schemes which differ from one Member State to another or to discontinue a scheme which he considers to be particularly effective".

More recently Polygram was prevented from launching CDs in Germany and thereby **10.05** forced to abandon its cross-border campaign. The European Commission sent a reasoned opinion to the German authorities[20] concluding that German legislation imposes a

---

[14] See further Chapter 2, "Disclaimers".

[15] Code de la consommation, Law No. 93–949, July 26, 1993.

[16] See for example the survey published by FEDMA (the Federation of European Direct Marketing) and FAEP (the European Magazine Publishers Federation): "Sales Promotion Rules in the European Union", a country by country survey of sales promotion and advertising rules, self-regulation, privacy policy, codes of conduct and distance selling regulations for companies operation online.

[17] See, for example, *Rewe-Zentral ERG v. Bundesmonopolverwaltung fur Branntwein*, Case 120/78, ECJ, February 20, 1979, ECJ, which concerned a rejection by the German authorities to the plaintiff's application for authorisation to import the alcoholic drink *Cassis de Dijon* from France on the basis that the drink did not contain the minimum alcoholic strength to comply with German rules. The ECJ ruled that there was no valid reason why, provided that they have been lawfully produced and marketed in one of the Member States, products should not be introduced into any other Member State; the sale of such products may not be subject to a legal prohibition on marketing.

[18] Arts 30 and 46 (ex 36 and 56) of the Treaty of Rome where restrictions on foreign nationals can be justified on public policy, public security, public health and other public interest grounds. See, for example, Case C–384/93 *Alpine Investments B.V. v. Minister van Financien* [1995] E.C.R. I–833, 45 where the decision of the Netherlands Government to impose a general measure prohibiting unsolicited calls for the purpose of selling financial services was challenged in the European Court of Justice on the basis that it constituted a restriction on free movement of services within the Community. The Court held that, while the Treaty applied to cold calling and accordingly the measure constituted a restriction, it was justified to protect investor confidence in national financial markets.

[19] See case C–126/91 *Schutzverband gegen Unwesen in de Wirtschafrt e. v. Yves Rocher GmbH* [1993] E.C.R. I–2361.

[20] Under Art. 226 (ex 169) of the E.U. Treaty.

disproportionate restriction on promotional gifts and discounts in breach of Article 49 (ex 59) of the E.U. Treaty on the freedom to provide services, and requested it to withdraw the relevant legislation. As Germany's response was unsatisfactory, on July 2, 1999 the Commission decided to refer this case to the European Court of Justice.[21]

In an attempt to solve these problems, the Single Market Directorate (DGXV) published a Green Paper in 1996.[22] Having invited comments on proposals to improve the ability to disseminate marketing and advertising materials across borders without ensuring compliance with all the laws across the E.U., it issued a follow-up Communication[23] in which it proposed criteria to clarify the laws on the fundamental E.U. principles of country of origin and proportionality.[24] The first report of the Committee of Government Experts, established under the Green Paper, concluded rather disappointingly that "there is no single market in Europe for advertisers" in the area of sales discounts. In 1999 the Expert Group will be focusing on national regulations on premiums, prize competitions, lotteries and sponsorship.[25]

Content Standards

10.06   Whilst it is impractical to obtain legal clearance in every jurisdiction throughout the world, electronic commerce businesses can adhere to some general principles to minimise the risk of infringing against the advertising regulations of other countries. Legal and trade mark clearance should be sought in target countries and in countries in which the electronic commerce business has a presence or assets. Appropriate disclaimers should be used to exclude non-target countries from the invitation. Other practical considerations include: how costly it would be to change a webvertisement if challenged; whether a competitor would be likely to be able to prove actual damage; and whether the authorities in a given country are likely to take a "laissez-faire" approach.

Contractual and Liability Issues

10.07   The risk that an electronic commerce business could incur liability for breach of a foreign advertising regulation makes it even more essential for contracts with advertising agencies to lay down clear lines of responsibility for ensuring legal compliance of advertising material. Third party rights will need to be licensed for both the territories of interest and the medium of the Internet, which is not a use for which consent would necessarily be implied.

The degree of control exercised by an electronic commerce business over material posted on or linked to their website may in itself give rise to liability.[26] Permitting third parties to post material onto its website could leave the website owner responsible for any such material that contains defamatory or otherwise illegal matter. Clear terms and conditions of access and use should be displayed. Open forum discussion areas pose particular risks of libel for the site owner and webvertisers should consider whether, for this reason, discussions via e-mail would be preferable.

---

[21] See **www.europa.eu.int/comm/internal_market/en.services/infring/index.htm** for further information or contact **D3@dg15.cec.be**.

[22] Green Paper on Commercial Communications in the Internal Market, May 1996.

[23] Follow up to the Green Paper on Commercial Communications in the Internal Market, March 4, 1998.

[24] Defined in Art. 5 (ex 3b) of the Treaty which provides that any action by the Community shall not go beyond what is necessary to achieve the objects of this Treaty.

[25] See **www.europa.eu.int/comm/internal_market/index.en.htm** or contact **comcom@dg15.cec.be** for further information.

[26] For further information see Chapters 2 and 3 and section 8.21.

SELF-REGULATION

Throughout the E.U. regimes of self-regulation complement the legal frameworks on **10.08**
matters such as misleading advertising and unfair competition. Although the structures
vary, each country's self-regulatory system is based on the principles enshrined in the
International Chamber of Commerce's Code of Advertising Practice.[27] The Code states
that all advertising should be legal, decent, honest and truthful, and respect the cultural
differences of the given country. Regulatory systems are generally founded on rules of
best practice drawn up, supported and enforced voluntarily by the country's advertising
industry itself.

In 1992 the European Advertising Standards Alliance (EASA) was formed to support
and co-ordinate the roles of the self-regulatory bodies across Europe. Its members now
include 24 bodies from 20 countries, including the whole of the E.U., Switzerland, Turkey
and the Czech, Russian, Slovak and Slovenian Republics. It also has corresponding
members in New Zealand and South Africa. EASA's role in handling cross-border
complaints is now recognised in various E.U. directives and communications. The
decisive factor in identifying a cross-border complaint is that the complaint comes from a
different country from that of the media in which the advertisement appears. The
country of origin of the advertiser or the advertisement is irrelevant.[28] The Alliance has
developed a procedure to enable cross-border complaints concerning webvertisements to
be dealt with on country of origin basis.[29] The British Advertising Standards Authority is
also working with the FTC to enable complaints between Europe and the US to be dealt
with on a similar basis.

The British Codes of Advertising and Sale Promotion

In the United Kingdom the Committee of Advertising Practice (CAP) is the body **10.09**
responsible for devising and enforcing the Codes.[30] The scope of the Codes is broad,
applying to advertisements and promotions in all non-broadcast electronic media,
wording introduced in 1995. The Advertising Standards Authority, the independent body
responsible for investigating complaints of breaches of the Codes, has applied them to
Internet related activities on a number of occasions, usually resulting in the webvertiser
agreeing to amend its website to comply with the ASA's recommendations and to consult
the CAP copy advice team on future site content. The ASA regularly reviews websites for
breaches of the Codes and established a working group to examine how the regulatory
regime should apply to webvertisements. In particular, the ASA is addressing the extent
to which the Codes should apply to a website, distinguishing between what is
"advertising" as opposed to "editorial" or other material which is not intended to be
caught by the rules.

Although the Codes lack the force of law, certain sanctions do apply. An electronic
commerce business may be asked by the ASA to withdraw or amend the advertisement.

---

[27] June 1997 edition available on **www.iccwbo.org/Commissions/Marketing/advercod.htm**.
[28] See **www.easa-alliance.org**. The Alliance publishes reports on cross-border complaints in its newsletter,
Alliance Update and may issue an "Euro Ad Alert" to it members.
[29] See **www.easaalliance.ocq/easaa.html**. This is in line with Commission policy on mutual recognition and
home country control in measures such as the "Television Without Frontiers" Broadcasting Directive under
which a Member State may only impose more restrictive rules on broadcasters under its own jurisdiction.
[30] February 1995 edition. A new version of the Codes is expected to come into force in October 1999. The Codes
can be accessed at **www.asa.org.uk**

The complaint, together with the names of the advertiser and its agency, will be published in the ASA's Monthly Report. If an advertiser fails to comply with an ASA ruling, trade sanctions or a withdrawal of further advertising space may be invoked by CAP members. As an ultimate deterrent, the Director General of Fair Trading under the Control of Misleading Advertisements Regulations 1988 can subject flagrant and persistent abusers of the Codes to legal proceedings. The ASA may also ask the relevant Internet Service Provider to assist it in enforcing any adjudication.

Other Initiatives

10.10   In April 1998, the International Chamber of Commerce (ICC) announced voluntary guidelines on interactive marketing and advertising setting out principles for "responsible commercial communications" via electronic networks.[31-32] The guidelines state that the legality of a webvertisement should be determined by reference to the laws of the country in which it originated. However, the ICC points out that there is no international unanimity as to whether country of origin or country of destination applies, certain countries may, therefore, claim jurisdiction over messages posted online from abroad. The guidelines also fail to address what happens if a webvertiser in one country posts an advertisement on a website where the server is located in a different country. The Direct Marketing Association has also devised a code on marketing on the Internet.[33]

COMPARATIVE ADVERTISING

10.11   Comparative advertising, where an advertisement implicitly or explicitly refers to a competitor or to goods or services offered by a competitor, is another area where webvertisers are at risk because different countries have traditionally applied disparate rules. Whilst the United States and the United Kingdom have tended to encourage comparative advertising on the basis that it is in the interest of consumers to be better informed, most E.U. countries have taken the opposite approach, regarding it as unfair competition. The result has been that a lawful comparative webvertisement in one Member States is likely to breach the rules in another.

With a view to harmonising the laws in the E.U., the Commission adopted a Directive on Comparative Advertising[34] as an amendment to the 1984 Misleading Advertising Directive.[35] The provisions have to be implemented into the national laws of the Member States by April 23, 2000. The Directive states that comparative advertising shall be permitted when the following conditions are met[36]:

- it is not misleading;

- it compares like with like;

- it objectively compares one or more material, relevant, verifiable and representative features of those goods or services;

[31-32] See **www.iccwbo.org**
[33] See **www.dma.co.uk**. Also see Association of British Insurers' Code of Guidance on Telephone sales, Direct Marketing/Direct Mail and the Internet
[34] 97/55 (O.J. L290/18)
[35] 84/450 (1984 O.J. L250/17)
[36] Article 3a.

- it does not create confusion in the market place;

- it does not discredit or denigrate a competitor;

- for products with a designation of origin, it relates in each case to products with the same designation;

- it does not take unfair advantage of the other mark or product; and

- it does not present goods or services as reproductions or imitations of goods or services bearing a protected name or trade mark.

The British Government's Consultation paper[37] proposes to adopt the Directive by means of an amendment to the Control of Misleading Advertising Regulations 1988.[38] The Department of Trade and Industry does not envisage that the Regulations will have much practical impact on U.K. law, although it acknowledges that the permission granted for the use of third party registered trade marks by section 10(6) of the Trade Marks Act 1994 is arguably less restrictive than those provisions contained in the proposal.

PRIVACY ISSUES FOR MARKETING ON THE NET

The ability to collect data through online survey marketing and browser technology has **10.12** obvious advantages for online marketers. At the same time it raises privacy concerns for regulators. Responsible web marketers who wish to stave off greater regulation are now looking to third party organisations to certify their sites as compliant with developing privacy standards. The Council of Better Business Bureau in the United States (the equivalent of the United Kingdom's ASA) has launched its own online privacy initiative that will allow compliant sites to display its seal of approval.

Unlike the United States, however, European laws grant individuals access to and extensive rights over data kept about them. In the United Kingdom, the Data Protection Act 1998 (DPA)[39] places even greater responsibilities on companies that collect and process data for marketing purposes. Companies have to obtain consumers' consent and provide them with certain information before processing their personal data. In practice, express consent is not be required unless the data is "sensitive". However, as well as the name and address of the company collecting and processing the data, companies have to ensure that consumers are aware of the categories of potential recipients of their data, whether provision of the data is obligatory or voluntary, and of the existence of rights of access to and rectification of the data.

Security rules mean that, where data is requested during a visit to a company's **10.13** website, the provider should be informed that its data may not be secure during transmission from one server to the other. A notice in the following form posted on to the web pages where data is requested should suffice:

---

[37] July 27, 1999

[38] The Control of Misleading Advertisements (Comparative Advertisements) (Amendment) Regulations 2000 will amend S.I. 1988 No. 915 giving the Director General of Fair Trading additional powers to take court action in respect of non-compliant comparative advertisements. The amendment will also extend the enforcement responsibilities of the Independent Television Commission, the Welsh Television Authority and the Radio Authority. Financial services advertisements will continue to be excluded. See **www.dti.gov.uk** or e-mail **kevin.davis@cacp.dti.gov.uk** for further information.

[39] For further details see Chapter 7. See also the Telecommunications (Data Protection and Privacy) Regulations 1999 S.I. No. 2093 — which implement the Telecoms Data Protection Directive 97/66 and prohibit the sending of unsolicited faxes to individuals without prior consent and allow individuals to "opt-out" from receiving unsolicited direct marketing telephone calls.

> "Whilst we have taken all reasonable steps to ensure that the information you provide will be kept secure from unauthorised access, the Internet is not a secure environment. We cannot guarantee that the information will be secure during transmission to our web server".

One of the new rights provided to consumers under the DPA is an explicit right to object in writing to data being used for direct marketing purposes. Data subjects have a right to "opt-out" of having their data used in this way and controllers must cease such use within a reasonable period of receiving a request to do so.

The DPA also prevents data being transferred to countries outside the EEA unless those countries have adequate data protection laws in place or the individual has consented.[40] This is extremely relevant for any company wishing to collect U.K. data and transfer it to, for example, the United States whose data protection laws still operate on a self-regulatory basis. Guidance on this[41] has now been issued by the Data Protection Commission.[42] The ICC has also published model contract clauses to ensure the adequate protection of privacy on transborder data flows.[43]

Children Online

10.14   The European Council Recommendation on the Protection of Minors and Human Dignity in Audio-visual and Information Services[44] was the first legal instrument at European level on the content of information services in electronic media. It aimed to provide guidance for national legislation asking broadcasters to develop new digital methods of parental control, and ISPs to develop codes of good conduct and the development of national self-regulation with the objective of enabling minors to make responsible use of online services.[45]

The United States is, however, ahead of the E.U. on the protection of children online. In April 1999 the Federal Trade Commission issued a proposed Rule designed to protect the privacy of children who surf the Internet. This is the first step in the implementation of the Children's On-line Privacy Protection Act 1998. The Rule will require commercial website operators to provide clear notice of their information collection practices and obtain parental consent prior to eliciting personal information from children under the age of 13. It will also allow parents to access and check such information and curtail its use. While website operators are concerned at the logistics of contacting parents and verifying their consent before data is collected, the contrary view is that the burden should be on the party who wants the information. The Rule comes into force on April 21, 2000.

ADVERTISING TO CHILDREN

10.15   Many countries place outright bans or heavy restrictions on advertising to children. However, this is another area where the disparity of laws within the European Union constitutes a barrier to trade.

---

[40] Subject to transitional provisions until October 24, 2001 for processing already underway except for some provisions relating to manual data.
[41] See **www.dataprotection.gov.uk/transbord.htm**
[42] The International Federation of Direct Marketing Associations has adopted its own set of principles governing the protection of personal data in the framework of online service.
[43] See Chapter 7.
[44] COM (97) 570 final, May 28, 1998 adopted under Art. 249 (ex 189) of the E.U. Treaty. This follows the Commission's Green Paper on the subject (COM (96) 483) and its Communication on Illegal and Harmful Content on the Internet (COM (96) 487).
[45] For further information see **www.europa.eu.int/dg10/avpolicy/new_srv/pmhd_en.htm**

After five years of investigation the European Commission has closed its infringement proceedings against Greece. The Toy Industries of Europe ("TIE") had claimed that the country's ban on the advertising of toys on Greek television between 0700 and 2200 hours was a trade protection measure designed to restrict toy imports in violation of Articles 28 (ex 30) (free movement of goods) and 49 (ex 59) (free movement of services) of the Treaty. Toy manufacturers trading internationally have lost 40 per cent of their turnover of advertised brands in Greece since 1994, Greek broadcasters have lost advertising revenue by a similar proportion and children's programming has consequently suffered. Greece claimed that the ban was a measure to protect children and families against disputes thought to arise from purchase requests prompted by TV advertising. The British Advertising Association is leading the U.K. efforts to have the matter reopened with the Commission.

As a result, it is now likely that other complaints lodged by the TIE against Sweden's total ban on television advertising to children, Flander's "Five Minute Rule", and Ireland's ban during pre-school programming will no longer be pursued.

These countries are not alone in proposing statutory restrictions upon television **10.16** advertising aimed at children. Norway disallows advertising to children on television, Spain operates a *de facto* ban on the advertising of "war" toys on T.V. and Denmark is making progress with plans to legislate for a ban on television advertising to children under the age of 12 which is intended to come into effect in 2001. The proposed legislation is intended to ban television advertising of children's products in general and forbid all forms of advertising during children's programmes. Similarly, the German Government has called upon its own German advertising council to bring in tougher regulations on advertising to children especially in relation to television. The German Government has made it clear that if the German Advertising Council does not introduce new regulations which are strong enough, then a statutory ban on the broadcast of advertisements aimed at children will be considered. Also, in Hungary, the advertising industry has recently agreed new guidelines on advertising in schools following recent attempts by the Government to place restrictions upon it.

These bans emphasise the move away from self-regulation to the imposition of statutory regulation and Sweden has made public its wish to push for stricter rules on advertising to children when they assume the presidency of the European Union in 2001.[46]

However, the attempts by Norway and Sweden to block trans-frontier broadcasts **10.17** containing children's advertising have met with disapproval from, respectively, the EFTA Court and the European Court of Justice. In 1997 the European Court of Justice (ECJ) ruled on three joint cases concerning Sweden's ban on advertising aimed at children under 12 and advertising which was deemed to be misleading under Swedish law. The Court decided that Sweden had no right to regulate the content of television advertising aimed at children under 12 which is broadcast from another Member State, and that restrictions on misleading advertising have to meet the overriding requirements of the Treaty in terms of public importance and proportionality. This is a matter for the national courts to decide.[47]

A paper written by the Commission on TV advertising was presented to the Expert Group on Commercial Communications in October 1998.

---

[46] DG XV will be completing its study on the impact of television advertising and teleshopping on minors at the end of 1999. The results may form the basis for an amendment to Art. 16 (Content Rules for TV Advertising to Children) of the Television Without Frontiers Directive during its next review.
[47] Joined Cases C–34/95, C–35/95 and C–36/95, *De Agostini*.

TELEMARKETING ON THE INTERNET

10.18   E-businesses find that the Internet is the perfect tool for sending advertising messages to and soliciting contracts with consumers and businesses by electronic mail. Targets can be reached anywhere in the world for very little cost. While direct mail is tolerated by most national legal systems, provided it does not constitute harassment, spamming[48] raises new issues of cost and inconvenience for the recipient and may provide grounds for legal action to be taken.[49]

The Distance Selling Directive[50] will place some of the existing requirements of the voluntary and trade codes of practice on a statutory footing. It contains similar provisions to the Telecoms Data Protection Directive[51] although it also applies to mail and other forms of communication. The Directive requires Member States to ensure that the express prior consent of consumers is obtained for all uses of faxes or automated calling machines as a means of communications. All other means of distance marketing communications, unsolicited or not, including electronic mail, traditional mailshots and calls, will only be able to be used where there is no clear objection from the consumer. Consumers will have to be given the opportunity to register his/her objection to receiving such communications. Options include either an opt-in or an opt-out system. Whichever form of communication is used, the identity of the supplier and the commercial aim of the communication will have to be stated at the outset.

ADVERTISING REGULATED GOODS AND SERVICES

10.19   Certain types of advertising are particularly problematic in other jurisdictions. E-businesses must therefore be alert to the potential sensitive of the global audience to whom they offer their products. Section 2.42 deals with some of the products which are commonly sold online. With particular reference to webvertising two sectors have received particular attention in recent years, namely tobacco and alcohol advertising.

Tobacco Advertising

10.20   On July 6, 1998 the Tobacco Advertising Directive[52] was adopted. The proposal for a Europe-wide ban, which has been in the pipeline for nine years, will lead to a general European ban on all forms of advertising and sponsorship (excluding television

---

[48] See further section 2.4.

[49] See *Cyber Promotions Inc. v. America Online Inc.* (1996) C.A. No. 96–2486 and 96–5213 which concerned unsolicited e-mails sent to AOL members which AOL intercepted. The Court held that there is no right under the U.S. Constitution to send unsolicited e-mails over the Internet to members of a private company and AOL was therefore entitled to block these transmissions. And in *CompuServe Inc. v. Cyber Promotions Inc.* (1997) Case No. C2–96–1070 the defendant sent unsolicited e-mails to the plaintiff's subscribers and modified their equipment to circumvent the block set up by CompuServe. CompuServe alleged that this constituted the tort of trespass and that Cyber's activities devalued their system and were granted an injunction. Although the position has not yet been tested in the English Courts, in July 1999 in an out of court settlement Virgin Net obtained a £5000 payment and an undertaking against not to spam any of their customers having sued a customer for breach of contract for sending more than 250,000 junk e-mails in an attempt to sell a database of e-mail addresses.

[50] See section 2.2 and the Government's Consultation Paper of June 1998 set out various options for implementing the Directive. The E.U. Commission has also issued an amended proposal on the Distance Selling of Financial Services (See Chapter 2).

[51] See n.38 above.

[52] Directive 98/43 relating to the advertising and sponsorship of tobacco products [1998] O.J. L213/9.

advertising which is already covered by the "Television without Frontiers" Directive[53]). The first implementation date is July 30, 2001, although deferments will be allowed for press and sponsorship, with a further transitional period until 2006 for exceptional global event sponsorship. By October 1, 2006, all the provisions of the Directive are required to be in force in their entirety.

The ban will apply to all forms of commercial communications or sponsorship which have the direct or indirect effect of promoting a tobacco product, including the use of any distinctive features of tobacco products such as trade marks or logos. None of the exemptions will be relevant for webvertisers. Member States may also implement stricter rules at Member State level if this is considered necessary for health protection.

The British Government published its consultation paper to implement the Directive on June 17, 1999.[54] The draft Tobacco (Prohibition of Advertising and Promotion) Regulations 1999 propose a complete and immediate ban on tobacco advertising on billboards, and in British newspapers and magazines by December 10, 1999. Virtually all tobacco sponsorship is to end by July 2003 except for global events with a high dependency on tobacco sponsorship, such as Formula 1, which will be given a further three years but must cut tobacco advertising and sponsorship by at least a fifth in each of those three years. The Federal Association of German Newspaper publishers has complained to the U.K. Government about the proposed Regulations which would prevent German newspapers carrying tobacco advertising being distributed and sold in the United Kingdom despite still being lawful in Germany and have requested an exemption clause.

It remains to be seen whether the Regulations will be completely overturned in due **10.21** course by four major British tobacco companies which in October 1998 launched a legal challenge against the draft U.K. Regulations and to judicially review the Directive on the basis that it is illegal and violates European law against the Directive. In February 1999 a formal reference was made to the European Court of Justice to rule on the validity of the Directive. Germany has also issued proceedings in the European Court of Justice formally challenging the E.U.'s responsibility in this area and it is hoped that the two sets of proceedings will be joined at a hearing in mid 2000. Separate proceedings have also been brought by Davidoff, Salamander (who market Camel shoes), a Greek poster company and an Austrian cinema advert producer. The ECJ's decision is not expected until at least October 2000 so, if it does rule against the Directive, the U.K. implementing regulations would also become invalid.

Alcohol Advertising

This is another area where E.U. rules on television alcohol advertising, contained in the **10.22** Broadcasting Directives,[55] have allowed countries to adopt stricter rules than those laid down in the Directives.[56] This had led to various countries, most notably France since

---

[53] Directive 89/552. The ban was extended to teleshopping programmes by the revised Broadcasting Directive 97/36.
[54] Together with an updated Regulatory Impact Assessment. This followed the Government's White Paper "Smoking Kills" published December 10, 1998. Tobacco advertising in Great Britain is currently regulated by the self regulatory Cigarette Code drawn up by the Departments of Health, the Tobacco Manufacturer's Association and the Imported Tobacco Advisory Council monitored by the Committee for Monitoring Agreements on Tobacco Advertising and Sponsorship, and the Protection of Children (Tobacco) Act 1986.
[55] The *Television Without Frontiers* Directives 89/552 and 97/36.
[56] Under the Directives, alcohol advertising (defined as products containing more that 1.2% of alcohol by volume) cannot be aimed at minors, and cannot give the impression that the consumption of alcohol can lead to enhanced performance or increased success.

1991, banning alcohol advertising altogether. The French "Loi Evin" has been the subject of much controversy, particularly surrounding the France World Cup 1998, due to the large fall in media revenue that it has caused. As a result, the Confederation of Common Market Brewers and the European Confederation of Spirits Producers lodged complaints with the European Commission, which is considering whether to refer the case to the European Court of Justice. In its opinion, these national measures constitute a restriction on trade. Alternatively, it may introduce a separate proposal to harmonise the laws on alcohol advertising.[57]

Online promotions

10.23   Most countries regulate sales promotion schemes, including free prize draws and prize competitions, fairly vigorously.[58] In the United Kingdom, the rules on chance promotions and skill competitions are set out in the Lotteries & Amusements Act 1976. Under the Act, all lotteries[59] which do not constitute gaming are unlawful unless they fall into one of the limited exemptions laid down under the Act, none of which are particularly suitable for advertisers and promoters of commercial products.

In countries where free prize draws are permissible promoters have developed the concept of the "no purchase necessary" route of entry. However, online promotions raise new issues, in particular as to what constitutes a payment to enter a promotion given the online cost to the entrant, particularly if they are required to navigate a site or answer survey questions.

The peculiarities of the Internet must be taken into account in all online promotional rules. For example, to ensure that speed of entry does not give online entrants an unfair advantage over those who use a traditional method of entry; to restrict eligibility to residents of countries where legal clearance has been obtained; to limit liability for system failures; and to include a choice of law and jurisdiction clause in the rules which form the contract between the promoter and the entrants. A number of other special promotional rules will also need to be considered in light of the complexities and technical risks inherent in the online environment.

LINKING AND FRAMING

10.24   More companies are taking advantage of the Internet to increase sales by promoting their own offerings, or for sponsorship or advertising revenue. It is not surprising then, that the question of how to protect the commercial value of websites has become the subject of recent legal claims both in the United States and the United Kingdom. A clear answer is yet to emerge on whether traditional proprietary rights such as copyright and trade mark rights can be used to control information published to the world via the Internet. A frequent argument against such rights being enforceable on the Internet is that it stifles the free flow of information that up to now has been the Internet's unique characteristic. Those who hold this view assert that publication on the World Wide Web implies a licence to use and, perhaps most controversially, a licence to create links to other sites.

---

[57] For further details contact **comcom@dg15.cec.be**.

[58] See further section 2.49 in Chapter 2 (Gaming).

[59] Lotteries are not defined under the 1976 Act but the courts have established the following criteria: a distribution of prizes; by chance; where there is some actual contribution by participants in return for obtaining their chance of winning a prize. *Per* Lord Widgery C.J. in *Readers Digest Association Ltd v. Williams* [1976] 3 All E.R. 737.

Linking is a feature of the Internet that is fundamental to its operation. For many commercial site operators seeking to reach as large an audience as possible, the ability to be found by search engines is all important. Hyperlinks between sites are also commonplace. Hyperlinks are electronic pointers in a web page to other sites (or portions of other sites) on the web. A user may transfer from one site to another by clicking on highlighted text in the original site. Linking has benefits such as increasing the potential audience of a site but can also bring undesired results. The link may be to a specific item on the other site and cause browsers to bypass information or advertising that the site owner would have wished all visitors to the site to see. This could potentially diminish the ability of the site to convey the desired message. It could also affect the potential advertising revenue from the site if it carries third party adverts or affects sponsorship arrangements.

Recent cases in the United States and United Kingdom courts have tested the ability of site operators to object to unauthorised links on the basis that hyperlinks on the web may infringe copyright, trade mark or related business reputation rights. **10.25**

The *Shetland Times* case[60] is the closest there is to a U.K. authority on the subject. This case considered whether the creation of unauthorised links constitutes a breach of copyright. It is a case under Scottish law but the decision of the court was based on copyright legislation common to England, Scotland and Wales. The interim decision of the court found that the linking was a breach of copyright, on the grounds that it constituted an infringement of copyright in a cable programme as defined by the Copyright, Designs and Patents Act 1988. This basis is somewhat artificial because, on a straightforward analysis, linking does not actually involve copying. The case settled before the Court of Appeal. The case does, however, provide an indication of the attitude of the U.K. courts on the question of copyright infringement by hypertext links.

The U.S. courts have also seen claims for breach of copyright, trade mark dilution and unfair competition as a result of unauthorised linking. Again, a case is yet to go to full trial leaving the law in an uncertain state. In the *TicketMaster v. Microsoft* case,[61] TicketMaster asserted that a formal agreement was necessary before another company could offer a link to its site. TicketMaster had sought such an agreement with Microsoft. When no agreement was reached in negotiations, Microsoft decided to create an unauthorised link in any case. TicketMaster claimed that the unauthorised link affected the value of its own sponsorship by companies such as MasterCard and diverted browsers from its pages containing advertising. It also claimed that Microsoft was able to attract advertising to their site because of the link to the TicketMaster content — a Seattle event guide. TicketMaster's Chief Executive put his argument in simple terms:

"The advertising and promotional component of the web will far exceed the transactional — why should they (Microsoft) get the benefit of the advertising when the money is mine?"[62]

Interestingly, the claim did not mention copyright infringement but was based on claims of misrepresentation of a business link between the parties, trade mark dilution and unfair competition. In February 1999, the parties settled the suit but terms of the settlement were not disclosed. Until the issue is finally resolved, "deeplinking" into the website of a third party is to be avoided while linking to a third party's home page may be less risky **10.26**

---

[60] *Shetland Times Limited v. Wills*, (1997) F.S.R. 604, OH.
[61] (1997) U.S. Case No. 97–3055 DDP.
[62] *Wall Street Journal*, April 28, 1997.

Another recent U.S. claim resulted from the use of so-called framing technology which operates so that the title of the page and other windows (often containing advertising) remain static while the user browses linked sites through the frames. The URL of the linked site is often obscured. In the case of *Futuredontics, Inc. v. Applied Anagramatics*,[63] Futuredontics (whose online dental referral pages were referenced by the defendant's link within a frame) claimed breach of copyright and unfair competition when Applied Anagramics linked to and framed the Futuredontics website. Futuredontics argued that such framing creates a derivative work, while Applied Anagramic claimed their link allowed viewers to see material that Futuredontics placed on the web. On July 23, 1998, the U.S. Court of Appeals for the Ninth Ciruit affirmed a 1998 ruling that denied the plantiff's request for a preliminary injunction. The court stated that the plaintiff failed to offer sufficient evidence that the defendant created a derivative work, to show that the framing created irreparable injury or that the balance of hardships tips sharply in its favour.

10.27   So, given the uncertain state of the law, what are the options open to an electronic commerce business which wishes to prevent or stop unauthorised linking or framing? Website operators may prevent hyperlinking in the first place by introducing a registration system with passwords so that only authorised users providing details when accessing via the home page will be given access. However, the technology may be expensive and the effect may be to reduce the potential audience. In the United Kingdom the site operator could threaten a copyright infringement action on the basis of the *Shetland Times* case. Although it is not settled law it may act as a sufficient deterrent. In addition, the Internet Service Provider (ISP) hosting the offending site could be notified. The ISP's contract with the website operator should give it the right to take action — which may include pulling the offending site altogether if it does not co-operate in the event of a legal challenge. Failing that, litigation is the only option but, given the current legal uncertainty, cannot be guaranteed to deliver the desired result. Early indications are, however, that the courts will protect the commercial interests of site operators marking the way for even more Internet promotion, advertising and sponsorship.

---

[63] (1998) 45 U.S.P.Q 2d (BNA) 2005.

— 11 —

TAXATION OF E-COMMERCE

— Graeme Nuttall —

> Walking to a voice that was music, the platinum terminal piping melodically, endlessly, speaking of numbered Swiss accounts, of payment to be made to Zion via a Bahamian orbital bank, or passports and passages and of deep and basic changes to be effected in the memory of Turing[1]

INTRODUCTION

The fact that trading is achieved electronically should, in principle, make no difference to **11.01** how it is taxed and there should be no need for a complete restructuring of existing tax systems. The U.K. tax system and other tax systems worldwide are designed to tax trading whatever its form. The application of existing tax laws to e-commerce is, however, not that straightforward. All the characteristics of e-commerce mean that taxpayers, tax practitioners and tax authorities need to pay special attention to its taxation. This chapter explains how electronic commerce fits into the current U.K. tax system and identifies a number of issues that e-commerce businesses may need to examine further. Inevitably, it deals with many complex areas of tax law only in summary. It concludes by summarising what is happening on a global basis to deal with the various tax issues arising from e-commerce.

Intangibility

Tax law has developed in response to various established methods of conducting **11.02** business. Many tax provisions exist because of the significance physical structures have had and will continue to have in commerce. There is an element of maturity in such tax provisions and in related case law, reflecting, perhaps, that whatever can be done to make a profit from, for example, land and buildings has been tried (and taxed). In contrast, the intangible nature of e-commerce places greater emphasis on, for example, how intellectual property is taxed. There has been concern for some time that the U.K.

---

[1] William Gibson, *Neuromancer.*

tax system could improve the way it deals with intellectual property.[2] In broad terms, different categories of intellectual property have different tax treatments. The treatment of, for example, trade marks is different from that of patents. E-commerce places new focus on the intricacies and inadequacies of intellectual property taxation.

Flexibility

11.03   The flexibility of e-commerce raises many issues. The scope for a business to adapt and evolve rapidly may mean that tax classifications change and with them the tax treatment of the business or aspects of it. What starts off as a trading business could evolve into an investment business. Different tax rules apply to these two activities, particularly regarding the deduction of expenses in computing taxable income. From a value added tax point of view it can be important to establish whether a business is supplying goods or services. E-commerce brings these two categories closer together. The scope for someone to work at home or on the move blurs the distinction between employment and self-employment. The Inland Revenue's preference is for individuals to be employees because tax is then deducted at source by employers under the "Pay As You Earn" system. The scope for businesses to work together more easily, may mean a sole trader's business evolves into a trading partnership, which has tax consequences in addition to other legal consequences.

Many tax rules assume that a trade is of a permanent nature. However, the flexibility of e-commerce means that, in tax terms, there may be a number of trades conducted by one business at one time and, indeed, there could be a succession of different trades. Tax practitioners may struggle to keep up with the tax compliance consequences of a client rapidly starting up and discontinuing a number of trades.

International

11.04   E-commerce, inevitably, involves international considerations. A business based entirely in the United Kingdom with only U.K. employees, equipment, customers, distributors and suppliers, can make the safe assumption that is does not have to consider any overseas tax implications. E-commerce requires a business to understand in more detail when it faces exposure to overseas taxation and the prospect of double taxation. Double tax treaties provide rules to deal with a business trading from an office, factory or other permanent establishment overseas but make no express reference to, for example, web servers.

Anonymity

11.05   The characteristics of the recipient of a payment or of a supply can make a tax difference. The value added tax system, in particular, requires many businesses to identify whether or not a customer is a private customer or a business customer. The scope for anonymity provided by e-commerce makes it harder to distinguish one sort of customer from

---

[2] The Intellectual Property Institute, London, started a review of the taxation of intellectual property in 1995. The U.K. Government's "Innovating for the future" consultation exercise concluded that a rational and less complex system for the taxation of intellectual property is required (Joint D.T.I. and H.M. Treasury consultation document, March 1998).

another. The potential for anonymity also, inevitably, raises concerns with tax authorities that e-commerce will be used for tax evasion or money laundering.[3]

Novelty

The continued novelty of e-commerce for many also adds to the need to pay particular attention to its tax aspects. **11.06**

OVERVIEW

The following paragraphs provide an overview of the taxation of e-commerce and show that, in broad terms, e-commerce is as subject to taxation as other forms of commerce. This can be seen clearly when e-commerce involves buying and selling goods, particularly in a domestic context. **11.07**

> The Smith family have sold toys from their high street shop for many years. Mr and Mrs Smith continue to own and manage the family shop in partnership. In an attempt to compete with the large international and national toy retailers, the shop has recently been redesigned as a "childhood experience". The shop aims to create a nostalgic experience for parents and grandparents whilst retaining a magical atmosphere for children. Demand for toys can arise overnight particularly following the launch of a new film or other merchandising opportunity. Mr and Mrs Smith's son, Douglas Smith, discovered using the Internet that he could locate supplies of the latest toys, often before his family's usual suppliers could obtain such toys. Douglas therefore set up his own business. Using his family's contacts through the local Chamber of Commerce (and a copy of its e-mail address list), Douglas found several busy executives who were prepared to pay a premium price for new products for their children. Douglas conducts his business by e-mail and through a website has built up an impressive customer list. He now employs a friend part time to research the toy market and identify new developments. Douglas works mainly from inside the family shop. He sits in the "New Millennium" section of the shop with his note book.
>
> Mr and Mrs Smith pay U.K. *income tax* on their partnership profits. The partnership is *VAT* registered. *PAYE* is operated on the wages paid to the shop assistants. *Business rates* are paid on the shop.
>
> Douglas pays U.K. *income tax* on his profits. He is *VAT* registered and operates *PAYE* on the salary of his employee. He defers payment of *import duties* (and *VAT*) on toys imported from South East Asia under the duty deferment scheme.

---

[3] See, *e.g.* the Cabinet Office Performance and Innovation Unit Report, September 1999 "e-commerce@its.best.uk" para. 7.26 (available at **http://www.cabinet-office.gov.uk/innovation**) which comments "Where the E.U. does face a problem is in the supply of products digitally to private consumers by suppliers outside the E.U. There is currently no way of tracing that these supplies have taken place, nor are there the mechanisms to collect tax in these circumstances."

11.08   The following paragraphs look at:

- Taxation of trading profits

- VAT

- PAYE and national insurance

- Business rates

- Customs duties

There are various points in relation to the taxation of trading profits and VAT that require more detailed consideration. This is provided in paragraphs 11.41 and 11.80 below. Various tax issues related to starting a new e-commerce business (and expanding it) are covered in paragraphs 11.53.

Taxation of trading profits[4]

11.09   Trade is defined to include "every trade, manufacture, adventure or concern in the nature of trade".[5] Trade is therefore widely defined and it appears that any commercial transaction[6] is taxable as a trade. A Royal Commission in 1955 identified six "badges of trade". Three badges emphasise trading in goods (the subject matter of the realisation, the length of the period of ownership of the property to be dealt in and supplementary work on or in connection with the property realised) but the remaining three badges (the frequency or number of similar transactions by the same person, the circumstances that were responsible for the realisation and motive) are of more general application. This chapter assumes there is a trade, although the versatility of the e-commerce means there may be a number of borderline cases.[7]

Income tax is charged on the profits of:

- any person residing in the United Kingdom from any trade whether carried on *in the United Kingdom or elsewhere*, and

- any person, although *not* resident in the United Kingdom, from any trade exercised *within* the United Kingdom

The profits of a profession or vocation are subject to United Kingdom income tax in similar circumstances.

Tax is charged under Schedule D.[8]

11.10   If a United Kingdom tax resident company carries on a trade it will pay corporation tax on its worldwide trading profits, not income tax. If a non-U.K. tax resident company

---

[4] The legislation relating to income tax, corporation tax and capital gains tax including statutory instruments and supplementary materials such as extra-statutory concessions and statements of practice is published in Butterworths Yellow Tax Handbook Parts I and II. The Inland Revenue website is also an increasingly helpful source of information **www.inlandrevenue.gov.uk**

[5] TA 1988, s.832(1).

[6] Lord Radcliffe in *Edwards v. Bairstow and Harrison*, 36 T.C. 207 at 230 and Lord Reid in *Ransom v. Higgs*, 50 T.C. 1 at 78.

[7] A profit motive is not essential *Torbell Investments Ltd and others v. Williams* [1986] S.T.C. 397 but the impossibility of making profit may prevent there being a trade (*The Religious Tract and Book Society of Scotland v. Forbes* (1896) 3 T.C. 41).

[8] Sched. D to the TA 1988, s.18.

conducts trade within the United Kingdom the profits will be subject to U.K. tax although the tax charged depends on whether or not the trade is conducted through a branch or agency. If it is, corporation tax applies; if not, income tax.

In summary, whatever e-business structure exists, the key issues are:

- is a tax resident involved? and

- in the case of a non-resident, is the trade carried on within the United Kingdom?

These issues are considered below together with what amounts to a branch or agency. There is also a summary of how tax on trading profits is administered. It is clear from the above that if someone is U.K. tax resident it will not, usually, serve any useful purpose to argue that a trade is conducted outside the United Kingdom, in "cyber-space".[9] As a U.K. tax resident, trading profits wherever arising fall to be taxed under Schedule D.[10] In the case of a non-resident, e-commerce does offer scope to avoid a U.K. tax charge on trading profits, even though customers are based in the United Kingdom. Even if a tax charge arises under domestic law, the non-resident may be able to claim the protection of a double tax treaty (see paragraphs 11.73 below).

Tax resident

The following provides an outline of the United Kingdom's approach to determining **11.11** tax residency:

Individuals

There is no statutory definition of a tax resident, although there are some statutory provisions involved in determining whether or not someone is U.K. resident.[11] The Inland Revenue's understanding of relevant law and practice is set out as regards individuals in its booklet IR20. The following are the main rules:

- someone physically present in the United Kingdom for 183 days or more (ignoring days of arrival and departure) in a tax year (April 6 to April 5) is tax resident in that tax year;

- an individual who moves from abroad to live in the United Kingdom permanently or at least remain here for three years or more is accepted as tax resident from the date of arrival;

- an individual who visits the United Kingdom regularly, who after four tax years has visits that average 91 days or more each tax year is tax resident from the fifth tax year;

- an individual coming to the United Kingdom for a purpose (*e.g.* work) that will mean he remains here for at least two years is treated as tax resident from the date of arrival until the date of departure;

---

[9] However, in the case of a non-U.K. *domiciled* tax resident conducting a trade wholly abroad, see para. 11.70 below.
[10] Tax is charged under Case I of Sched. D (Case II for professions or vocations). If a trade is carried on wholly abroad then profits are assessable under Case V not Case I (*Colquhoun v. Brooks* (1889) 2 T.C. 490).
[11] *e.g.* TA 1988, ss.334–336.

- someone leaving the United Kingdom to work full time abroad under one or more contracts of employment can be treated as not resident from the day after departure[12];

- someone leaving the United Kingdom permanently or for at least three years can be treated as not resident from the day after departure[13];

- by concession[14] an individual may be treated as a non-resident for part of a tax year (*i.e.* the period before arrival in the United Kingdom or the period before departure from the United Kingdom).

Improvements in international travel, combined with developments in technology that allow someone to work wherever they are, mean many individuals living in the U.K. spend considerable periods outside the U.K. However, the above rules make it diffficult for someone to cease U.K. tax residency for income tax purposes without taking up permanent residence or full-time work abroad.

11.12 *Corporations*

A company incorporated in the United Kingdom is automatically tax resident in the U.K.[15] A company incorporated outside the United Kingdom is U.K. tax resident if the United Kingdom is the place where "central management and control" actually resides. This latter test of residency arises from case law.[16] Under this test a company is usually accepted as resident where the board of directors meet. This may well be different from the place of business operations and the countries in which directors and shareholders reside. The Inland Revenue, mindful of the scope for board members to act as "little more than cyphers" for a controlling individual, will look to see where and by whom central management and control is actually exercised, rather than necessarily accept a company resides where its board meets.[17] The case law test is not easy to apply to directors located around the world who "meet" by international conference calls or video links. Until law or practice develops, the board of an overseas company that wishes to remain non-U.K. tax resident should meet in person and make decisions at a suitable location outside the United Kingdom. If an overseas incorporated company is treated as resident in the United Kingdom under this case law test but as non-resident under the terms of an appropriate double taxation treaty then it will be treated as non-resident for all U.K. tax purposes.[18]

11.13 *Partnerships*

A trading partnership is resident where the control and management of the trade is located.[19] This is the test and not the resident status of the partners in the partnership.

---

[12] Para. 2.2 of IR 20 sets out the conditions. In particular, visits to the U.K. must average less than 91 days a tax years.

[13] Para. 2.8–2.10 of IR 20 set out the conditions. In particular, return visits must average less than 91 days a tax year.

[14] Extra-statutory concession A11.

[15] FA 1988, s.66.

[16] *De Beers Consolidated Mines Ltd v. Howe*, 5 T.C. 198 at 212.

[17] S.P. 1/90.

[18] FA 1994, s.249.

[19] TA 1988, s.112.

Trustees

A trust can also be used for trading. If all the trustees are non-resident, the trust will be accepted as non-resident. If all are U.K. resident, the trust will be U.K. resident.

Where trustees have mixed residence status the non-resident trustees will be treated as U.K. residents if the settlor was resident, ordinarily resident[20] or domiciled[21] in the United Kingdom at any time when he settled property in the trust.[22] There are separate rules for capital gains tax purposes.

Trade within the United Kingdom

A non-U.K. resident is liable to U.K. tax on profits of a trade exercised *within* the United Kingdom. If all that happens is trade *with* the United Kingdom (*i.e.* with U.K. customers) then this is insufficient to come within the tax charge. If a non-resident wishes to avoid U.K. tax then care must be taken to limit what happens in the United Kingdom, so as to avoid trading within the United Kingdom. Someone visiting customers in the United Kingdom and signing sales contracts in the United Kingdom will be trading within the United Kingdom, even if the goods or services are then provided from outside the United Kingdom. The Internet, of course, makes it easier to distribute information and solicit orders without visiting the United Kingdom. The most important factor, however, is the place where contracts are made.[23] If this is the United Kingdom then there is trading within the United Kingdom.[24] Although, if sales contracts are made outside the United Kingdom, the trade could still be exercised within the United Kingdom if there is sufficient connection in other ways to the United Kingdom.[25] **11.14**

If contracts are made outside the United Kingdom the interesting issue, in the context of e-commerce, is the extent to which equipment sited in the United Kingdom creates an exposure to U.K. tax. The fact that there is equipment in the United Kingdom does not necessarily mean there is trading in the United Kingdom. An overseas company can have a U.K. office (a representative office) without creating a U.K. tax liability.[26] It is the nature of what happens in the United Kingdom that is significant. The Inland Revenue attaches much importance to Lord Atkin's approach in the *Smidth (FL) & Co. v. Greenwood* case and has adopted as the principal criteria for determining whether there is trading in the United Kingdom, the test of "where do the operations take place from which the profits in substance arise?" A non-resident company contracted overseas to provide the services of a property consultant who lived in the United Kingdom. As his activities in the United Kingdom were the essential operations of the company it was subject to U.K. tax.[27] If a non-resident has equipment in the United Kingdom it is necessary to analyse the functions of that equipment and, by analogy with existing case law, determine if those functions amount to trading in the United Kingdom.

The mere buying of goods in the United Kingdom for sale abroad does not amount to trading in the United Kingdom.[28] If equipment in the United Kingdom relays information **11.15**

---

[20] An individual is ordinarily resident in the U.K. if he is "resident here year after year" (Inland Revenue Inspectors' Manual, I.M. 35).
[21] See para. 11.70.
[22] FA 1989, s.110.
[23] See Chapter 3.
[24] *Grainger & Son v. Gough*, 3 T.C. 462.
[25] *Firestone Tyre and Rubber Co. Ltd v. Lewellin*, 37 T.C. 111, 142.
[26] *Smidth (FL) & Co. v. Greenwood*, 8 T.C. 193.
[27] *IRC v. Brackett* [1986] S.T.C. 521.
[28] *Sulley v. A.G.*, 2 T.C. 149.

to customers without any payment for that information then this does not amount to trading in the United Kingdom. The equipment merely provide an electronic "shop window" in the United Kingdom for a non-resident trader and even the relaying of electronic enquiries from potential customers to the non-resident will not amount to trading in the United Kingdom.[29] However, if a server in the United Kingdom provides information to *paying* customers then this could be considered an essential (and taxable) operation in the United Kingdom. When services are provided by non-residents the Inland Revenue tends to give greater weight to the place where the service is provided (rather than the place where the contract is made).[30] In the case of transmission services the service is considered given where the transmission begins.[31] This is based on an old reported case involving the relaying of telegraph messages, although in that case contracts were made in the United Kingdom.[32]

If a non-resident uses an agent in the United Kingdom to accept orders or otherwise habitually make contracts on his behalf, then this also amounts to trading in the United Kingdom by the non-resident.[33] Even if contracts are made abroad, the use of a U.K. agent can bring the trading profits within the scope of U.K. tax.[34] Again, by analogy, if equipment belonging to independent Internet service providers or other third parties is used to make contracts in the United Kingdom, or provides the service which is to yield a profit[35] then there is a risk that such activities come within the scope of U.K. tax, under domestic law.

11.16   In the case of a non-resident company trading in the United Kingdom, the tax charged is corporation tax if the trade is carried on through a "branch or agency".[36] If there is no branch or agency then income tax applies but only at the basic rate. This is because the higher rate of income tax only applies to individuals. This distinction is, of course, easier to make if there is an office, other premises or appointed agent in the United Kingdom. In the case of supplying goods by the Internet, such a presence might exist. If the Internet is used to supply services this is less likely. It is difficult to see how independent Internet service providers, routers and so on, can be categorised as a branch or agent, but the law is unclear. If there is a trade conducted in the United Kingdom by a non-resident company then, possibly, there must be a U.K. branch or agent?[37]

If care is taken over where contracts are made and where profit earning activities take place then non-U.K. tax resident companies and other non-residents can avoid U.K. tax on trading profits. In practice though, there are many who are oblivious to the significance of, in particular, the place of making contracts, and who will as a matter of domestic law be conducting taxable trading in the United Kingdom.

11.17   If the non-resident is based in a country that does not have a double tax treaty with the United Kingdom, then tax liability is determined by the above rules. If there is a tax treaty then protection from U.K. tax may be provided if there is no "permanent establishment" in the U.K. This possibility is considered below in paragraph 11.74 below.

---

[29] See the discussion on identifying profit producing activities in the Inland Revenue International Tax Handbook (ITH at p. 827).
[30] ITH at p. 826.
[31] *ibid.*
[32] *Erichsen v. Last*, 4 T.C. 422.
[33] *ibid.*
[34] *Lovell and Christmas Ltd v. Commissioner of Taxes* [1908] A.C. 46.
[35] *ibid.* at 53.
[36] TA 1988, s.11(1).
[37] See the discussion in Inland Revenue International Tax Handbook (ITH at p. 843 *et seq.*).

If a non-resident conducts trading activities wholly or partly in the United Kingdom, double tax treaties also provide assistance in determining what profit gets taxed in the United Kingdom. Domestic law has no express provisions dealing with this issue. The emphasis in case law on the place of making sales contracts suggests an "all or nothing" approach (so, if there is a U.K. sales contract, all the profit is taxable in the United Kingdom even if all or part of the performance of the contract occurs outside the United Kingdom). The Inland Revenue does, however, accept that an "arm's length" principle applies under domestic law and so a non-resident can argue that economic activity outside the United Kingdom should be excluded from U.K. tax.[38]

Computation of trading profits

A trader must make a tax return in respect of the trade to the Inland Revenue and pay   **11.18**
tax in accordance with the provisions of the Taxes Management Act 1970. Every individual, trustee (and personal representative) is obliged to deliver to the Inland Revenue by January 31 following the end of a tax year a tax return incorporating the taxpayer's self-assessment. Tax is payable on account on January 31 during the tax year and July 31 following the tax year. The balance of tax payable is due on January 31 following the tax year. Self-assessment also now applies to companies.[39] There are procedures for the electronic lodgement of tax returns.[40] Taxpayers' records[41] may, with limited exceptions, be kept as electronic copies of the originals.

An electronic trader has to satisfy the same conditions as any other trader to deduct expenses in computing taxable profits. A deduction is not automatically available because it has been made in computing profits for accounts purposes. The main requirements are that the expenditure is:

(a) wholly and exclusively for the purposes of the trade[42];

(b) revenue expenditure not capital expenditure; and

(c) not expressly disallowed by statute.[43]

Some expenditure is expressly allowed as tax-deductible by statute provided the   **11.19**
conditions set out in the relevant statutory provisions are satisfied. There are several such provisions relevant to technology.[44]

If expenditure is of a capital nature then a deduction may still be available in computing taxable profits but under the capital allowances regime. Capital allowances are available on certain types of capital expenditure for the purposes of a trade. The full amount of a trading expense is deductible in computing profits. Although so-called 100 per cent allowances are available for some capital expenditure,[45] normally only a

---

[38] ITH at p. 857.
[39] FA 1998, s.117.
[40] TMA 1970, Sched. 3A and see S.P. 1/97. The Inland Revenue's Business Support Team can provide additional information.
[41] TMA 1970, s.12B.
[42] TA 1988, s.74(1)(a).
[43] See, in particular, TA 1988, s.74 (general rules as to deductions not allowable), s.577 (business entertaining expenses) and s.827 (VAT penalties, etc.).
[44] See, e.g., TA 1988, s.83 (patent fees, etc. and expenses), s.84 (gifts to educational establishments), s.120 (rent, etc., payable in respect of electric line wayleaves); CAA 1990, s.136 (allowances for expenditures on scientific research not of a capital nature, and on payments to research associations, universities, etc.).
[45] CAA 1990, s.1 (buildings and structures in enterprise zones) and s.137 (allowances for capital expenditure on scientific research).

proportion of the capital cost is allowed. It is therefore generally better for expenditure to be tax-deductible as a trading expense. If the expenditure qualifies neither as a trading expense nor for capital allowances then no deduction in computing trading profits is available.

The above general principles are explained in more detail below (see paragraph 11.42 below) in respect of expenditure on computer software, trade marks, plant and machinery and goodwill.

VAT

11.20   Europe (as defined for value added tax (VAT) purposes) has a common system of VAT[46] with a uniform basis of assessment.[47] Hundreds of millions of consumers throughout the E.U. are familiar with VAT as an extra cost of buying goods and services. In millions of business owners are familiar with VAT as an extra administrative burden.

From a U.K. perspective, VAT is charged on the following:

(a) on the *supply* of goods or services in the United Kingdom;

(b) on the *acquisition* of goods in the United Kingdom from other Member States; and

(c) on the *importation* of goods from places outside the Member States.

These charges, particularly the first, are wide in scope and mean that VAT is as applicable to e-commerce as it is to other forms of commerce. Each of the above VAT charges is explained in more detail in the following sections together with an outline of how VAT is administered by a VAT registered business. All the characteristics of e-commerce, particularly its international dimension, make it likely that some of the more complex aspects of the VAT system will apply to any e-commerce business.

Supplies of goods or services in the U.K.

11.21   VAT is charged on:

(a) a supply;

(b) of goods or services;

(c) which is a taxable supply;

(d) made in the United Kingdom;

(e) by a taxable person;

(f) in the course or furtherance of a business.

Supply

Supply for VAT purposes is a word of the widest import.[48] A supply, for VAT purposes, does however, exclude anything done otherwise than for a consideration. If

---

[46] The legislation relating to VAT, including statutory instruments, E.C. legislation and supplementary materials is published in Butterworth's Orange Tax Handbook.

[47] See, in particular, the Sixth Council Directive, 77/388.

[48] Griffiths, J. in *CEC v. Oliver* [1980] S.T.C. 73 at 74 and see VATA 1994, s.5(2)(a) ("supply" . . . includes all forms of supply).

Internet users are not charged then, as a general rule, there is no supply to them for VAT purposes. The activity is said to be outside the scope of VAT.

Consideration, however, also takes a wide meaning. Consideration can obviously be in the form of money but can be found in something other than money.[49] A barter transaction involves supplies by both parties for consideration. The exchange of information over the Internet could involve supplies for VAT purposes. Case law suggests there must be a direct link between what is provided and the consideration received.[50] The central feature of consideration can be seen as reciprocity.

The wide definition of supply means many users of the Internet may be involved in making supplies for VAT purposes without realising it. There can still be a supply even though no profit is made on a transaction.

Certain events are *treated* as supplies for VAT purposes. This includes the receipt of certain services from abroad. These are the services described in Schedule 5 to the Value Added Tax Act 1994.   **11.22**

Schedule 5 Services, include:

- Transfers and assignments of copyrights, patents, licences, trademarks and similar rights;

- Advertising services[51];

- Services of consultants, engineers, consultancy bureaux, lawyers, accountants and other similar services, data processing and provisions of information (but excluding from this head any services relating to land)[52]; insurance services (including reinsurance, but not including the provision of safe deposit facilities);

- Telecommunications services, that is to say services relating to the transmission, emission or reception of signals, writing, images and sounds or information of any nature by wire, radio, optical or other electromagnetic systems, including the transfer of assignment or the right to use capacity for such transmission, emission or reception (which covers e-mail, Internet access, chatline facilities, teleconferencing and call back services).[53]

If Schedule 5 services are received from abroad by someone in the United Kingdom who uses them for business purposes, then what is known as the "reverse charge" applies. The significance of this and other aspects of Schedule 5 services are explained below. Briefly, the U.K. business customer must account for VAT as if it had made the supply. This mechanism ensures that U.K. suppliers are not unfairly disadvantaged as compared with non-U.K. suppliers. The Government is considering the possible extension of the reverse charge procedure to take account of the growth in services over the Internet.

---

[49] VATA 1994, s.19.

[50] Fox, L.J. in *CEC v. Apple and Pear Development Council* [1985] S.T.C. 383 at 389 and see also the same case at [1988] S.T.C. 221.

[51] This includes advertising space in any electronic location (H.M. Customs & Excise Notice 741 (place of supply of services), para. 11.5).

[52] It does not matter how the supplies of services are delivered which may be by electronic transmission, courier or mail (H.M. Customs & Excise Notice 741 (place of supply of services), para. 11.8).

[53] Someone who simply supplies the content of a transmission (*e.g.* a weather forecasting service) is making a supply of the delivered information and this is not a transmission (*i.e.* it is not a telecommunication service). Someone who supplies a package of Internet services including Internet access and e-mail addresses but where the emphasis is on content rather than communication will not be making a supply of pure telecommunication services and the VAT liability will depend on the nature of the services provided.

11.23   *Goods or services?*

If a supply is made the next step from a VAT point of view is to establish whether it is a supply of goods, or of services, or of neither. The latter category is outside the scope of VAT. There are complex rules to categorise supplies. Goods means tangible, moveable goods. If the whole property in goods is transferred there is a supply of goods.

Other less obvious transactions amount to the supply of goods. The supply of any form of power, heat, or refrigeration is a supply of goods.[54]

It is the definition of services that is particularly wide. Anything which is not a supply of goods but is done for a consideration (including, if so done, the granting assignment or surrender of any right) is a supply of services.

11.24   VAT classification of software provides a useful introduction to the distinction between goods and services.[55] In the case of off-the-shelf software products (so called normalised products) if one price is charged for the package (*e.g.* containing the CD–ROM or floppy disks carrying the software and any brochures) this is treated as a supply of goods. However, H.M. Customs & Excise accept that if separate charges are made for the software and the carrier medium then two supplies are made; one of services and one of goods. If bespoke software is commissioned its supply is generally treated as entirely a supply of services. The carrier medium element is ignored as incidental.

In the case of audio or video recordings, as a general rule, H.M. Customs & Excise consider there to be a supply of goods.

Unless the Internet is used as the medium to buy goods then e-commerce will invariably involve supplies of services.

11.25   H.M. Customs & Excise tried unsuccessfully to argue that the use of a computer ordering system changed the nature of the supply (of sandwiches) from that of goods to one of a supply of services.[56]

The difference from the customer's point of view between receiving a supply of goods and receiving a supply of services is marginal in respect of many Internet supplies and so any difference in VAT treatment can be confusing. VAT legislation describes the transfer and assignment of copyright, patents, licences, trademarks and similar rights as supplies of services. The guidance issued by H.M. Customs & Excise makes it clear that this categorisation does not apply to transfers of normalised products by way of a physical medium. However, increasingly the computer disk, CD–ROM or other such medium is an immaterial part of the transaction. When copyright material is downloaded from a website it is clearly a supply of services and not of goods and yet the VAT treatment can be very different.[57]

11.26   *Taxable supplies*

Supplies of goods and services made for a consideration are categorised for the purposes of charging VAT as either taxable supplies or exempt supplies.

The standard rate of VAT in the United Kingdom is 17.5 per cent. There is currently a reduced rate of 5 per cent for supplies of domestic fuel and power. Some supplies are zero rated.[58]

---

[54] Art. 5, para. 2 of the Sixth Directive states "Electric current, gas, heat, refrigeration and the like shall be considered tangible property". The Internet's use of electric current does not, however, turn supplies over the Internet into supplies of goods.

[55] H.M. Customs & Excise Notice 702/4/94 (importing computer software).

[56] *Emphasis Ltd* [1995] V.A.T.R. 419.

[57] Goods imported from outside the Member States are, in principle, charged to VAT on entry into the E.C. In contrast, services supplied from outside the E.C. to a private customer are not subject to VAT.

[58] VATA 1994, Sched. 8.

All these supplies are generally classified as taxable supplies. However, in the case of zero rated supplies, such as sales of books or children's clothing, the purchaser does not actually pay VAT because it is charged at zero per cent. The significance of this categorisation (and also that of an exempt supply) from the point of view of VAT registered businesses is explained below.

H.M. Customs & Excise state that the storage and dissemination of textual information in non-printed formats (*e.g.* electronically) does not qualify for zero-rating.[59] Goods exported outside the Member States are zero-rated, as are goods exported to a business customer in another Member State.

Certain categories of supply are expressly stated to be exempt from VAT.[60] Purchasers **11.27** of domestic property and certain financial and educational supplies do not, therefore, pay VAT because these supplies are not taxable supplies on which VAT is charged. H.M. Customs & Excise and the British Bankers' Association have agreed that the liability of electronic banking services should be determined according to the status of the individual services. Such services should have the same VAT treatment whether supplied electronically or by conventional means.[61] There are detailed provisions in VAT law dealing with situations when an intermediary (*e.g.* an electrical goods retailer or travel agent) sells insurance with other (taxable) goods and services to avoid exploitation of the VAT exemptions provisions.[62] Electronic data services which provide financial news or share price movements do not, however, make exempt supplies.

A taxable supply will only be charged to VAT if it is made in the United Kingdom, by a taxable person in the course or furtherance of a business. All these conditions must be met, otherwise the taxable supply will be outside the scope of VAT. There is no VAT charged on supplies that are outside the scope.

Made in the United Kingdom 11.28

In the case of goods, if there is no removal of the goods to or from the United Kingdom, then the rule to determine the place of supply is straightforward. A supply of goods is made in the United Kingdom if the goods are situated in the United Kingdom and it is made outside the United Kingdom if the goods are situated outside the U.K. The use of the Internet as a means of buying and selling goods will not, in itself, alter where the goods are located and will not therefore alter the place of supply. It may, however, make it more likely that goods are removed to or from the United Kingdom, with the access it provides to the international marketplace.

Goods removed to the United Kingdom are supplied in the United Kingdom if they are installed or assembled in the United Kingdom. Also, as explained below, there will be supplies made in the United Kingdom if goods are imported from outside the Member States or, in some cases, if the distance selling provisions apply[63] on goods brought into the United Kingdom.

---

[59] H.M. Customs & Excise Notice 701/10/85 (printed and similar matter) and see Forexia (U.K.) Limited LON/1998/879 (the company supplied financial news to customers by e-mail, facsimile and the Internet and failed in its claim that its supplies should be zero-rated).

[60] VATA 1994, Sched. 9.

[61] H.M. Customs & Excise Notice 700/57/99.

[62] In order to treat the supply of arranging insurance as exempt an intermediary is required to disclose *in writing* the premium as well as any fee charged over and above that premium at, or before, the time when the insurance transaction is entered into. In recognition of the problems this causes for telesale and Internet transactions special record keeping requirements have been introduced (S.I. 1995 No. 2518, Regulation 31(1)).

[63] See para. 11.60.

Goods exported are as a general rule considered as supplies made in the United Kingdom (but as mentioned above zero-rating can apply). However if, for example, goods are installed or assembled in the country to which they are removed, then the supply is made outside the United Kingdom and therefore outside the scope of U.K. VAT. If the goods are removed to another Member State and supplied there to someone who is not registered for VAT then the supply may be treated as made by the trader in that other Member State. This is under the local equivalent of the distance selling provisions (see further in paragraph 11.60 below).

11.29   The general rule for services is that they are supplied in the country where the supplier belongs.

A supplier belongs in the United Kingdom if:

(a) he/she has a U.K. business establishment or some other fixed establishment and no such establishment elsewhere;

(b) he/she has such establishments both in the United Kingdom and elsewhere but the U.K. establishment is the one most directly concerned with the supply; or

(c) he/she has no such establishments (in the United Kingdom or elsewhere) but his usual place of residence is in the United Kingdom.

A company or other person carrying on business through a branch or agency in the United Kingdom is treated as having a U.K. business establishment. Any company incorporated in the United Kingdom will have a place of residence in the United Kingdom. These rules raise similar issues to those discussed in the context of non-residents trading in or with the United Kingdom. An establishment has been described as requiring "a sufficient minimum strength in the form of the presence of the human *and* technical resources necessary for supplying specific services".[64] It is therefore possible to argue that equipment on its own does not amount to a business establishment for VAT purposes. E-commerce clearly provides scope through the use of technology either to avoid a U.K. establishment or to ensure that a non-U.K. establishment is most directly concerned with making the supply.

11.30   The general place of supply rule for services is, however, altered for some types of supply. The reverse charge, mentioned above, involves treating certain supplies as made where the recipient belongs.[65] The place of supply of Schedule 5 services (see above) is where the recipient belongs in certain circumstances.[66]

There are various types of services that are treated as supplied where the services are performed. This category includes supplies of services that consist of cultural, artistic, sporting, scientific, educational or entertainment services.[67] Although such services could, on the face of it, be supplied electronically, the relevant statutory instrument makes it clear that such services are supplied where they are "physically carried out".[68]

There is a further special rule for telecommunication services. This term has the same meaning as for reverse charge purposes (see Schedule 5 above). This definition includes basic access to the Internet, e-mail and chatline facilities.[69] If the "effective use and

---

[64] *Berkholz v. Finanzamt Hamburg-Mitte-Alstadt* [1985] 3 C.M.L.R. 667 (a case involving gaming machines on ferries).

[65] VATA 1994, s.8.

[66] S.I. 1992 No. 3121, para. 16 (and see paras 11.83 *et seq.* below).

[67] S.I. 1992 No. 3121, para. 15.

[68] See *British Sky Broadcasting Ltd v. CEC* [1994] V.A.T.T.R. 1.

[69] H.M. Customs & Excise Business Brief 22/97.

enjoyment" of the telecommunication services takes place outside the E.C. then the supply is treated as made outside the United Kingdom. More significantly, for suppliers of telecommunication services that belong outside the E.C., supplies are treated as made in the United Kingdom to the extent that "effective use and enjoyment" of the telecommunication services takes place in the United Kingdom.[70]

Taxable person

11.31

A taxable person is someone who is or is required to be registered for VAT purposes. (This aspect is considered in more detail in paragraph 11.58.)

In the course of furtherance of business

"Business" *includes* any trade, profession or vocation.[71] H.M. Customs & Excise suggest that, in VAT terms, business means any continuing activity which is mainly concerned with making supplies to other persons for a consideration.[72] Such activity must have a degree of frequency and scale and be continued over a period of time. Isolated transactions are not normally business for VAT purposes (in contrast to trading as defined for income tax and corporation tax purposes). If what would otherwise be a supply for VAT purposes (*e.g.* the supply of information over the Internet for payment) does not occur in the course or furtherance of a business, then VAT will not arise. However, what starts as essentially a hobby or recreation may develop into a business for VAT purposes.

Acquisitions of goods from other Member States

VAT is also charged on the acquisition of goods from other Member States.[73] A U.K. **11.32** VAT registered business that receives goods from a business registered for VAT in another Member State will not be charged VAT by the supplier. Instead, it is the U.K. VAT registered business that must account for U.K. VAT. The rate of tax is the one applicable to those goods in the United Kingdom. If the goods are normally zero rated then no VAT will be due.

Someone who is not VAT registered in the United Kingdom who acquires goods from a supplier in another Member State would generally be charged VAT at the rate applicable in the supplier's Member State. But in some cases involving U.K. businesses that are not VAT registered, a liability could arise on the purchaser to register and account for U.K. VAT (see paragraph 11.60 below).

An overseas supplier of goods in the United Kingdom may also have to register for U.K. VAT under the distance selling scheme. This applies if the overseas supplier is responsible for delivery of goods to persons who are not VAT registered. This possibility is also explained in more detail in paragraph 11.60 below.

Importation of goods from outside the Member States[74]

VAT is charged on the importation of goods from outside the E.C. Importation, for **11.33** VAT purposes, has a special meaning, which is the act of bringing goods in from outside the E.C. This is in contrast to the *acquisition* of goods, which refers to bringing goods in from another Member State.

---

[70] See VAT Information Sheet 2/97.
[71] VATA 1994, s.94(1).
[72] H.M. Customs & Excise Notice 700, para. 2.6 and see *CEC v. Lord Fisher* [1981] S.T.C. 238.
[73] VATA 1994, s.2(1)(b).
[74] VATA 1994, s.2(1)(c).

VAT on imports is charged at the same rate as if the goods had been supplied in the United Kingdom, whether or not the person importing the goods is registered for VAT. VAT is charged in addition to any customs duty or other charges due. It is calculated last of all, on a value which includes such charges.

VAT on imports made by a U.K. business is normally either paid outright on importation or later under duty deferment arrangements.[75]

The United Kingdom has a *de minimis* value below which customs duty and VAT do not have to be paid on imports.[76] There are special rules dealing with certain postal imports. A VAT registered business can account for VAT on consignments not exceeding £2,000 in the normal course of events on his VAT return (see below). This does not apply to Datapost packets not exceeding £2,000, on which VAT is due on delivery.[77]

Purchasers of goods over the Internet must therefore be prepared to deal with the payment of VAT (and other duties), even though the goods come from outside the E.C.

Input tax and output tax

11.34   In the United Kingdom, a VAT registered business has to account to H.M. Customs & Excise for the VAT it charges its customers (its output tax). If a customer is VAT registered and the supplies are for use in its business then the VAT it is charged is its input tax. A VAT registered person can, with some exceptions, reclaim input tax to the extent it relates to standard rated and zero rated supplies of that business (and certain other supplies[78]). There is, however, no general ability to recover input tax related to either exempt supplies of that business or non-business activities.

Every VAT registered business has to submit regular VAT returns and account for any excess of output tax over input tax in relation to the return period. In this way, VAT is for most businesses an administrative exercise which involves passing on the cost of VAT to customers.

If input tax exceeds output tax then a repayment of VAT can be claimed by a VAT registered business. This will happen if the business makes only zero rated supplies to customers.

If a business only makes exempt supplies then it cannot register for VAT purposes and so cannot recover any input tax. If a business makes both taxable and exempt supplies it is said to be partially exempt. Such a business is restricted in its ability to recover input tax. This is why the difference between making exempt supplies and zero rated supplies is important from the point of view of a business, although it makes little difference to the consumer.

It is the obligation of the supplier to charge VAT correctly.[79]

11.35   The VAT return has a section for accounting for VAT due on acquisitions. The same amount entered as VAT due on acquisitions can be recovered as input tax, subject to the restrictions on recovering input tax mentioned above.

VAT on imports can be recovered, subject to the normal rules, as input tax of the VAT registered business. It is claimed as input tax on the VAT return for the period in which the importation took place.

---

[75] See further in para. 11.62.
[76] 22 ECU. As at September 1999 the U.K. Government was reviewing the thresholds allowed under E.C legislation. A number of options are under consideration including raising the threshold, eliminating it and maintaining the status quo "e-commerce@its.best.uk", para. 7.42.
[77] S.I. 1995 No. 2518, reg. 122.
[78] VATA 1994, s.26(2).
[79] See further in para. 11.86.

If a business with a turnover that is below the VAT registration threshold (see paragraph 11.58) imports goods for business purposes, it can still opt to defer payment of VAT but it cannot recover VAT as input tax because it is not registered for VAT purposes.

In the case of overseas traders who are not registered for U.K. VAT, there is a system for obtaining refunds. There is one scheme for traders carrying on business in Member States and another for those in business in "third countries".[80]

A VAT registered business must (with limited exceptions) provide a tax invoice to every business customer.[81] Tax invoices provide the main evidence of input tax paid by VAT registered businesses. VAT records may be preserved by electronic means.[82] H.M. Customs & Excise has the power to make regulations to develop electronic VAT return services.[83] E.U. sales lists (required from traders who move goods between E.U. countries) can be sent by electronic data interchange.[84]

Outside the scope transactions

Some transactions are outside the scope of U.K. VAT, including:

- supplies other than for a consideration;
- supplies that are neither supplies of goods nor services;
- taxable supplies that are not made in the United Kingdom;
- taxable supplies that are not made by a taxable person or are not provided in the course or furtherance of a business.

Pay As You Earn

United Kingdom income tax is charged under Schedule E on the emoluments from any office or employment.[85] The Pay As You Earn (PAYE) system imposes a duty on an employer to account to the Inland Revenue once a month[86] for tax that the employer has (or ought to have) deducted from payments to employees.[87] The PAYE system also imposes requirements on an employer in respect of reporting benefits in kind. Although, in theory, the main charge to income tax on employees is the charge under self-assessment, in practice most Schedule E tax is accounted for under the PAYE system. The PAYE system is also used to collect national insurance contributions. The Inland Revenue has power to make regulations to establish systems for the electronic transmission of PAYE information.[88] The following general issues should be noted: **11.36**

Employed or self-employed?

There is often a strong preference on the part of some workers to be classified as self-employed because of the cash flow advantage and the greater scope to claim expenses as tax-deductible, although, in practice, the differences may be less worthwhile than   **11.37**

---

[80] H.M. Customs & Excise Notice 723.
[81] See further in para. 11.85.
[82] See Notice 700, para. 8.1.
[83] Finance Act 1999, ss.132 and 133.
[84] Further information is available from the H.M. Customs & Excise tariff and statistical office help desk on 01702 367248.
[85] TA 1988, s.19.
[86] Quarterly for certain employees.
[87] TA 1988, ss.203 *et seq.*
[88] TA 1988, s.203(10).

imagined. In some cases, it may be advantageous to be an employee.[89] Nevertheless, technology now permits many work arrangements to be structured as instances of self-employment, rather than employment. There is no single test to establish whether or not someone is an employee. The full circumstances are considered. A useful approach is to ask if someone is in business on their own account. Individuals who provide their services through a company may find it easier to establish they are a consultant rather than an employee.[90]

Someone working from home (or where they choose), using their own equipment (PC, printer and so on) is clearly part of the way to establishing self employment.[91]

Who operates PAYE?

11.38   The PAYE system has evolved to try to ensure that, whatever the payment arrangements, someone will operate PAYE on payments to an employee liable to take under Schedule E. An employer with a sufficient taxable presence in the United Kingdom, must operate PAYE. An overseas company with a U.K. branch or agency will satisfy this requirement.[92] If an employee works for someone in the United Kingdom, but the actual employer is outside the scope of the PAYE regulations, the person for whom he works can be made to operate PAYE.[93]

Business rates

11.39   The United Kingdom has a system of business rates (non-domestic rating). In broad terms, occupiers of property used for business purposes pay amounts annually to the relevant local authority based on the rateable value of the property. The amount paid does not increase if the property is used to operate a 24 hour business (*e.g.* worldwide Internet trading).

Customs duties

11.40   Import duties are also (like VAT) E.C. regulated.[94] Duty is paid at the point of entry of goods into the E.C. according to the duties applicable under the H.M. Customs & Excise Integrated Tariff. The World Trade Organisation (WTO) has ruled it will not impose customs duties on electronic transmissions.[95] Customs duties apply to goods. If goods are ordered electronically and delivered physically from outside the E.C. then customs duties will continue to apply at the appropriate rate for the product. However, "goods" supplied electronically from outside the E.C. will be treated as services and therefore be free of import duties. There are currently no plans to introduce additional import duties on electronic transmissions.[96]

---

[89] See, *e.g.*, TA 1988, ss.148 and 188(4) (tax free payments in connection with the termination of an employment).

[90] The Government announced in an Inland Revenue Press Release, dated March 9, 1999, that anti-avoidance legislation will be introduced in 2000 to counteract avoidance in the area of personal service provision through service companies. Detailed information on the "IR35 proposals" is available on the Inland Revenue website.

[91] For more information on the relevant factors see Chapter 14 of *Essential Law for the Tax Adviser* (The Chartered Institute of Taxation).

[92] *Clark v. Oceanic Contractors Inc.* [1983] S.T.C. 35.

[93] TA 1988, s.203C.

[94] Although the customs territory of the E.C. is different in some respects from that of the E.C. for VAT purposes (see H.M. Customs & Excise Notice 703).

[95] The WTO May 1998 "temporary" moratorium on customs duties on electronic transmissions.

[96] This was agreed at the July 1998 E.C. Finance Minister's Meeting. However, further work may be needed to the rules of the WTO (see the U.K. Government's proposals in para. 7.64 of "e-commerce@its.best.uk" and, on customs issues, by the World Customs Organisation.

DIRECT TAXATION IN MORE DETAIL

The following paragraph considers miscellaneous points likely to be relevant to the **11.41**
taxation of the trading profits of e-commerce.

Expenses

Many categories of expenditure related to conducting business electronically will be **11.42**
tax-deductible (*i.e.* they will reduce the amount on which tax is charged) but, as
illustrated in the following cases, care needs to be taken.

Trade marks

Royalties or periodic fees paid for the use of a trade mark in a trade should be tax- **11.43**
deductible against trading profits. This is on the basis that they are revenue expenses
incurred wholly and exclusively for the purposes of the trade.

However, in some cases, a licensee may instead have to claim a deduction against its
total income (a so-called charge on income) rather than just against trading profits. As a
condition for making such a claim, the licensee has to deduct tax from its payments and
account for the tax deducted to the Inland Revenue. Payments subject to this regime are
known as annual payments. Annual payments are explained further in paragraph 11.50.
In broad terms, if the licensor provides services in connection with the trade mark then
the annual payments regime should not apply.

Generally, the Inland Revenue does not expect the cost of creating a trade mark to be
claimed as a tax deduction. The expectation is that a trade mark is an enduring asset and
so expenditure on creating it is capital expenditure. No capital allowances are available
for trade marks.

In contrast, fees paid and expenses incurred registering a trade mark (or renewing a
registration) are tax-deductible. This is because of an express statutory right to a tax
deduction.[97]

If it is clear that a trade mark will have a limited life then there may be scope to claim
the creation costs as revenue expenditure. Revenue treatment may allow a 100 per cent
deduction in the year of expenditure or, perhaps more likely, spread over the anticipated
life of the trade mark.

Computer software

The Inland Revenue has published its views on the U.K. tax treatment of expenditure **11.44**
on computer software.[98] In response to concerns, a provision was introduced into the
Capital Allowances Act 1990 to provide expressly for capital allowances on capital
expenditure on a right to use or otherwise deal with computer software.[99]

In summary, the position is as follows:

- software acquired under licence:
    - regular payments akin to a rental are revenue expenditure and the timing
      of deductions will be governed by accounting practice;

---

[97] TA 1988, s.83.
[98] Tax Bulletin, November 1993.
[99] CAA 1990, s.67A.

— a lump sum payment for software expected to have a useful economic life of less than two years will be accepted as revenue expenditure (possibly also if it will be useful for a longer period but still provides only a sufficiently transitory benefit) and the timing of deductions will be governed by accounting practice;

— a lump sum payment for software as a capital asset of the licensee's trade (*i.e.* it has a sufficiently enduring nature) will qualify for capital allowances.

11.45   • equipment acquired as a package:

— the expenditure between hardware and software should be apportioned;

— capital allowances under the ordinary plant and machinery rules will be due on the expenditure on hardware;

— the treatment of the balance will depend on the above considerations.

• Software owned outright:

— whether the expenditure is capital or revenue depends on the economic function of the software in the trade as it does for licences acquired for lump sums.

Plant and machinery

11.46   There is no statutory definition of plant and machinery. As indicated above, expenditure on computer hardware, telecommunications and other equipment will generally qualify for capital allowances under the plant and machinery rules, although assets incorporated into a building or structure may fail to qualify. Plant is that with which the trade is carried on rather than the setting or premises in which it is carried on. There is a statutory list of assets that are treated as forming part of a building and are therefore excluded from qualifying as plant and machinery. The excluded assets include "mains services and systems of . . . electricity". However, it should be possible to establish that the following are plant:

• electrical systems provided mainly to meet the particular requirements of the trade or provided mainly to serve particular machinery or plant used for the purposes of the trade;

• powered systems of ventilation, air cooling or air purification; and any ceiling or floor comprised in such systems;

• computer and telecommunication systems (including their wiring or other links);

• sprinkler equipment and other equipment for extinguishing or containing fire;

• expenditure on the provision of pipelines or underground ducts or tunnels with a primary purpose of carrying utility conduits.[1]

Goodwill

11.47   In commercial terms, goodwill is the value of a business over and above its net asset value. This is recognised as a capital asset for tax purposes. Expenditure on goodwill on,

---

[1] CAA 1990, Sched. AA1, Tables 1 and 2; *Cole Bros Ltd v. Phillips* [1982] S.T.C. 307 and *Hunt v. Henry Quick Ltd* [1992] S.T.C. 633.

for example, the acquisition of a business as a going concern is therefore capital expenditure. Goodwill is not in itself within the categories of expenditure that qualify for capital allowances.

Traditionally, goodwill has been particularly associated with the location of business premises (*e.g.* public houses, restaurants, retail shops, cinemas, petrol stations). In such cases the value of the property interest will be taken to include goodwill. E-commerce will involve a greater emphasis on "free" goodwill, which is separate from the value of any premises and arises from how the business is carried on, not where it is carried on.

It may be possible to achieve a revenue deduction for expenditure on goodwill if, instead of acquiring goodwill outright, regular payments are made for the use of goodwill for a defined period.[2]

Withholding tax

There are a number of circumstances in the U.K. tax system in which the payer of an **11.48** amount is obliged to deduct or withhold tax from the payment made and account for this to the Inland Revenue.[3] In the context of e-commerce there are two withholding situations in particular that could be relevant if customers are asked to pay recurrent fees. Neither of these concerns apply to one-off fees, so the payment of a once only fee for the use of a software program will not be subject to withholding tax.[4]

The two possibilities in respect of regular fees are as follows:

Royalties where owner abroad

Tax at the basic rate of income tax should be deducted from a payment of royalties to **11.49** use a copyright if the owner of that copyright's usual *place of abode* is not within the United Kingdom.[5] Copyright for this purpose does not include a cinematograph film or video recording or the sound-track of such a film or recording, so far as it is not separately exploited. There is no requirement to withhold tax if the payment is for the use of copyright that has been exported for use outside the United Kingdom. Place of abode is usually taken to be the equivalent of the place of residence for tax purposes.[6] The U.K. Government acknowledges that it is not clear whether a payment to view and download digitised products such as books, photographs, music and software is a payment for the use of a copyright or is a payment for the purchase of goods or services.[7] Unless the website is designed to provide for the operation of the necessary withholding tax mechanism it may be impossible for the user to comply with his statutory obligation and pay a net amount. Statute provides that any agreement to pay gross is void. If a double tax treaty applies this may reduce or remove the obligation to deduct tax.[8]

---

[2] *Ogden v. Medway Cinemas* (1934) 18 T.C. 691.
[3] *e.g.* on the payment of any royalty or other sum paid in respect of the user of a patent (TA 1988, s.348(2)(a) and 349(1)(b)).
[4] Although if a non-U.K. resident sells rights relating to a U.K. patent for a capital payment then a withholding tax obligation may arise under TA 1988, s.524.
[5] TA 1988, s.536.
[6] Inland Revenue Inspector's Manual I.M. 4005.
[7] "e-commerce@its.best.uk", para. 7.29. The U.K. Government's stated aim is to treat electronic and equivalent traditional transactions in the same way for tax purposes.
[8] S.I. 1970 No. 488, reg. 6.

Annual payments

11.50   A withholding tax regime also applies to certain regular payments, known as annual payments, that are charged to tax under Schedule D Case III. Someone contracting over the Internet for merchandising rights, for example, could encounter this requirement.

Payments for the use of registered designs, know how and trade marks could all come within the annual payments regime. If the receipt forms part of the trading profits of the recipient, then the regime will not apply. An important ingredient in identifying an annual payment is that the receipt is pure income profit of the recipient. If the recipient has to do something to earn the payment (for example, providing goods or services), then the annual payment regime should not be relevant.[9] Someone who sold the right to use a secret process in return for a share of profits found themselves within this regime.[10]

If an annual payment is involved, then the following categories of payer may or will be obliged to deduct tax at the basic rate of income tax:

- a payment made by an individual for bona fide commercial reasons in connection with the individual's trade, profession, vocation[11];

- payments made other than by individuals (*e.g.* companies, and trustees).[12]

Digital cash

11.51   The receipts of a trade can take the form of money's worth as well as money.[13] In broad terms, arguments by a trader that non-cash receipts (*e.g.* digital credits) should not be taken into account for tax purposes are unlikely to succeed. The Inland Revenue's approach will be to value such assets. If there is some restriction on the realisation of a non-cash item, then this may reduce its value but it is not an argument that it has no value.[14]

Non-business use

11.52   Non-business use of an asset will either prevent or restrict the ability to claim a tax-deduction or allowance in computing trading profits. This must be borne in mind when claiming deductions for, for example, computer equipment and software. In the case of claiming a trading deduction, if the trader had some purpose in mind other than a trade purpose at the time of buying, for example, a software package, then a trading deduction should not be claimed. Even if there is a subsidiary non-trade purpose, this duality of purpose, prohibits a trading deduction. If, fortuitously, fortunately, accidentally or incidentally there is a non-trade benefit, expenditure may, however, still be deductible.[15] If duality of purpose is a potential problem, then, if possible separate payments should be made in respect of the distinct elements.[16]

Capital allowance claims are not, however, prejudiced by a duality of purpose. Instead, the capital allowance claim is reduced by the appropriate percentage of non-business use.

---

[9] *Campbell v. IRC* (1968) 45 T.C. 427.
[10] *Delage v. Nuggett Polish Co. Ltd* (1905) 92 L.T. 682.
[11] TA 1988, s.347A.
[12] TA 1988, ss.348 and 349.
[13] *Gold Coast Selection Trust Ltd v. Humphrey* (1948) 30 T.C. 209.
[14] *ibid.,* Viscount Simon at 240.
[15] *Mallalieu v. Drummond* [1983] S.T.C. 124 at 129 (and see also [1983] S.T.C. 665).
[16] *Murgatroyd v. Evans-Jackson* (1967) 43 T.C. 581.

STARTING A BUSINESS

The following paragraphs deal with various tax issues that arise on starting a business. **11.53**

Choice of structure

A business can be conducted by a sole trader, a partnership or through a legal entity such **11.54** as a company or trust.

The choice of business structure involves a careful consideration of legal, tax and commercial issues. From a tax point of view the issues to consider are likely to be those that apply to anyone starting a business and, in particular, the tax issues relevant to whether or not to incorporate a business.[17]

The amount of tax payable and when it is paid will vary according to the type of business structure. The main tax point to appreciate is that a company is likely to achieve a tax deferment rather than a tax saving. The main rate of corporation tax is now less than the higher rate of income tax.[18] This tax difference encourages reinvestment of profits by companies. However, at some stage shareholders will want to benefit from their investment in the company. It is then that additional tax will probably be payable. If the shareholders receive income (*e.g.* salaries, dividends) then income tax is likely to be payable. If shares are sold then a capital gains tax liability may arise.[19]

There are a number of detailed tax points that could be relevant. As examples: **11.55**

- the difference in the national insurance contributions payable on the earnings of a sole trader or partner in contrast to those payable by an employer and employee on employment earnings;

- a company may provide a more attractive pension arrangement for its directors, than would be available to a sole trader or partner;

- an unincorporated business may offer more scope to utilise losses that arise in the trade (whether trading or capital losses). (Losses of a company cannot be set off against the income or gains of shareholders);

- there are, in broad terms, more methods of reducing tax on capital gains (*e.g.* on a sale of a business) available to individuals than there are to companies (see further below).

Tax registrations

There are several tax compliance issues that need to be addressed by new businesses. **11.56**

Notice of liability to income tax or corporation tax

If a trader has not received a tax return in respect of a tax year, he must notify his **11.57** Inspector of Taxes by October 5 following the end of the tax year that he is so chargeable.[20] On receiving a tax return the individual is required to make a self

---

[17] Butterworths Business Tax Service, Part II.3 (incorporating a business).
[18] In the 2000/2001 tax year the higher rate of income tax is 40%. In the 2000 financial year the main rate of corporation tax is 30%.
[19] Certain transactions in securities may be subject to income tax and the avoidance provisions in TA 1988, Pt XVII, Ch. 1 apply (cancellation of tax advantages from certain transactions in securities).
[20] TMA 1970, s.7.

assessment. This involves completing the self employment or partnership supplementary pages as appropriate and returning the tax return by no later than January 31 following the end of the tax year. If the tax return is submitted by September 30 following the end of the tax year then the Inland Revenue can be asked to calculate the tax due. Each tax return when received by the Inland Revenue, should be accompanied by a guide which gives instructions on how to complete the tax return and supplementary pages. There are help sheets and leaflets that provide additional information.[21]

There is an equivalent obligation on a company to notify when it is chargeable to corporation tax, although the notification period is 12 months from the end of the company's accounting period.[22] In practice, soon after a company is incorporated, the Inland Revenue will send a letter to the company, asking for basic information on the company, including details of its accounting period.

VAT

11.58   It is vital to consider VAT from the outset. A trader is obliged to register for VAT if his turnover exceeds certain registration limits. Ignorance of the legislation is no excuse for failure to register.[23] A trader will usually become liable to be registered at the end of any month where the value of taxable supplies made in the previous 12 months exceeds the prescribed threshold.[24] If H.M. Customs & Excise can be convinced that turnover in the next 12 months will not exceed a prescribed limit then it should be possible to avoid registration.[25] Alternatively, if turnover in the next 30 days is expected to exceed a prescribed limit, then again registration is compulsory.[26] It should be remembered that turnover includes zero rated, standard rated and other positive rate supplies. H.M. Customs & Excise must be notified within 30 days of any of the compulsory registration events happening. The standard registration form (or forms in the case of group or partnership registrations) must be used.[27]

A business that makes only zero rated supplies (which would normally be a "repayment trader") can apply for exemption from registration. It is still necessary to notify liability to register. Exemption should be claimed in an accompanying letter.

If a business has turnover below the registration threshold it is possible to register voluntarily for VAT purposes. It is also possible to register for VAT as an intending trader, if suitable documentary evidence can be provided to show that taxable supplies will, eventually, be made. There is a VAT leaflet which explains the registration provisions in more detail.[28]

11.59   There are significant penalties for late notification of the liability to register for VAT.

A business faced with compulsory VAT registration may consider arrangements to split the business into two or more separate activities, with a view to each activity falling

---

[21] These are available from the Inland Revenue Order Line, the telephone number for which is 0645–000404 (facsimile number 0849–000604) (open seven days a week between 8 a.m. and 10 p.m.). The help sheets and leaflets include SA/BK3: *Self Assessment. A Guide to keeping records for the Self Employed*; IR220: *More than one Business*; IR222: *How to calculate your taxable profits*; IR227: *Losses* and IR229: *Information from your Accounts*.

[22] TMA 1970, s.10. Self assessment for companies began for accounting periods ending on or after July 1, 1999; see FA 1998, s.117.

[23] *Neal v. CEC* [1988] S.T.C. 131.

[24] From April 1, 2000: £52,000.

[25] From April 1, 2000: £50,000.

[26] From April 1, 2000: £52,000.

[27] These must be ordered from the relevant local VAT Office. In many cases, VAT registration has been delegated to Newry VAT Office. There is an automated VAT registration form ordering system operated by Newry VAT Office (telephone 0345 112114).

[28] Notice 700/1 "Should I be registered for VAT?"

below the VAT registration threshold. This is particularly attractive when the business has relatively small amounts of input tax. However, such arrangements should be approached with caution. H.M. Customs & Excise have powers to counteract the maintenance or creation of any artificial separation of business activities.[29] In determining whether any separation of business activities is artificial, regard is had to the extent to which the different persons carrying on those activities are closely bound to one another by financial, economic and organisational links.[30]

A business that provides only exempt supplies may find it is obliged to register if it receives services from abroad that come within the reverse charge regime. If the value of such supplies exceeds the registration limits then there is a requirement to register and account for VAT on the deemed supplies.

An overseas business may have to register for U.K. VAT under the distance selling **11.60** provisions. Equivalent provisions apply in other Member States. Each Member State has its own distance selling threshold.[31] Once the value of distance sales by a business exceeds this threshold, the business must register in the United Kingdom and account for tax in respect of all further sales made. The threshold is calculated by reference to sales made during a calendar year. Distance selling applies when a business registered for VAT in another Member State supplies goods, and is responsible for their delivery, to any non-VAT registered person in the United Kingdom. In addition to private individuals this will include public bodies, charities and businesses that are not registered for VAT. There is scope to register for VAT even if distance sales are below the threshold. The VAT registration procedure is similar to that described above. A different VAT registration application form is used.[32]

There is another basis on which VAT registration could occur. In broad terms, this applies to businesses not registered for VAT but which acquire goods direct from a VAT registered supplier in another Member State. Such goods are known as acquisitions and the recipient of such goods must register for VAT in the United Kingdom if the total value of the goods exceeds the registration threshold.[33] This limit is based on acquisitions made in a calendar year. Registration is also obligatory if there are reasonable grounds for believing that the value of acquisitions to be made in the next 30 days will exceed this same limit. The registration procedure is similar to those mentioned above. There is a different VAT registration form to complete.[34] There is a VAT Notice which explains the arrangements in more detail.[35]

PAYE

As soon as the business has employees (or payments are planned, if a company, to **11.61** directors) then the business must register for PAYE. The business should contact its local Inland Revenue office to find out which office deals with PAYE for the business. The Inland Revenue will provide the business with a package of documents to enable it to operate PAYE.

---

[29] VATA 1994, Sched. 1, paras 1A and 2.
[30] VATA 1994, Sched. 1, para. 1A(2).
[31] In the U.K. this is set at, €100,000: equivalent to about £60,000.
[32] From April 1, 2000: £52,000.
[33] Form VAT 1A. The H.M. Customs & Excise Notice 700/1A/97: "Should I be registered for VAT? Distance Selling" provides more information.
[34] Form VAT 1B.
[35] H.M. Customs & Excise Notice 700/1B/97: "Should I be registered for VAT? — Acquisitions".

Duty deferment

11.62   A VAT registered business (and certain others) may enter into a duty deferment arrangement with H.M. Customs & Excise. This defers the time of payment of VAT, customs duties and certain other duties due on importation of goods (or the removal of goods from, for example, a customs warehouse). A guarantee from a bank or insurance company is required.[36]

Tax incentives

11.63   The following paragraphs describe tax incentives that may be relevant when establishing a business.

Pre-Trading Expenditure

11.64   If a person incurs expenditure for the purposes of trade within seven years before the trade begins, such pre-trading expenditure can be claimed as a revenue deduction once the trade begins.[37] It is important that the person incurring the pre-trading expenditure is also the person who then starts the trade.[38]

Pre-trading capital expenditure, which qualifies for capital allowances, is dealt with similarly. Such expenditure, incurred for the purposes of a trade by a person about to carry it on, is treated as incurred when the trade commences.[39] If an asset originally acquired for private purposes (*e.g.* a personal computer) is subsequently brought into business use, it is the market value at the time that is eligible for capital allowances.

There is also scope to recover VAT incurred before a business is registered for VAT purposes. VAT incurred for the purpose of the business, on services, in the six months prior to the date of registration, may be recovered together with VAT on goods (*e.g.* stock and office equipment) still retained by the business at the date of registration.[40]

Initial allowances

11.65   The capital allowances regime does provide for 100 per cent initial allowances in some circumstances. These allowances are available to existing businesses, as well as new businesses. Such allowances are, in particular, available for capital expenditure on industrial or commercial buildings (including hotels) in enterprise zones.[41] First year allowances equivalent to 100 per cent of expenditure may also be made available from time to time.[42]

An enhanced allowance in the first year, less than 100 per cent, may also be available from time to time.[43]

---

[36] Further information is available from the Central Deferment Office (telephone 01702 367425).
[37] TA 1988, s.401.
[38] Tax Bulletin (Issue 5), November 1992.
[39] CAA 1990, s.83(2).
[40] See further in H.M. Customs & Excise Notice 700, para. 4.09.
[41] There are Enterprise Zones in Lanarkshire, Dearne Valley, East Midlands, East Durham and Tyne Riverside. An Enterprise Zone designation lasts for 10 years. CAA 1990, s.1(1).
[42] Certain expenditure on plant and machinery for use in Northern Ireland incurred in the period from May 12, 1998 to May 11, 2002 attracts a first year allowance of 100% (FA 1998, s.83).
[43] Certain expenditure incurred from July 2, 1998 to July 1, 2000 qualifies for a 40% first year allowance (FA 1999, s.77).

Trading losses

The amount of a trading loss is calculated according to the same principles, as apply in **11.66** calculating profits. If a loss arises in the first four years of the business the loss may be carried back and set off against income for the three years before that in which the loss arises.[44] This provision only applies to individuals. It is in addition to the normal provision that a trading loss can be set off against general income of the relevant tax year and the preceding year.[45] It is also possible to set a trading loss in a tax year against chargeable capital gains realised in that year.[46]

If relief cannot be given under the above provisions then the loss may be carried forward and set against future profits of the relevant trade.[47] As a general rule, if the trade discontinues then relief for losses is lost.

It is important that the trade is carried on on a commercial basis and with a view to the realisation of profit. If not, the loss will not be accepted as a trading loss for the above purposes.[48] A company can set off trading losses against profits (including capital gains) in the same accounting period and preceding year.[49] It may also carry forward the loss and set it against trading income of the same trade in succeeding accounting periods.[50]

Enterprise investment scheme

The enterprise investment scheme (EIS) comprises various reliefs. EIS reliefs are only **11.67** relevant in the case of a trade carried on by a company which issues new shares for cash. There are various detailed conditions to be met by the company and the subscriber.[51] In outline, the reliefs available, if conditions are satisfied, are as follows:

- 20 per cent income tax relief on the amount invested;

- capital gains tax exemption on a disposal of EIS shares;

- a reinvestment relief for gains on assets where the proceeds of disposal are reinvested in EIS shares; and

- a loss on a disposal of EIS shares may be set against income tax or capital gains tax.

There is an Inland Revenue publication which explains the EIS scheme in more detail.[52] Particular points to note are:

- the business activity of the EIS company must be carried on *wholly or mainly in the United Kingdom* for at least three years after the relevant share issue;

- The EIS company must carry on a qualifying trade. Certain activities are excluded, unless they form an insubstantial part of the trade. From the point of view of e-commerce, receiving royalties or licence fees could prevent the trade from qualifying.[53]

---

[44] TA 1988, s.381.
[45] TA 1988, s.380.
[46] FA 1991, s.72.
[47] TA 1988, s.385.
[48] TA 1988, s.384(1).
[49] TA 1988, s.393A.
[50] TA 1988, s.393.
[51] TA 1988, ss.289 *et seq.* and TCGA 1992, ss.150A *et seq.* Changes are due to be made to make EIS more attractive for shares issued after April 5, 2000.
[52] I.R. 137.
[53] TA 1988, s.297(2)(e).

Interest relief

11.68   Tax relief for certain payments of interest. This include interest on loans to buy shares in certain companies[54] or to buy into a partnership.[55]

Taper relief, employees' share schemes and other reliefs

11.69   Recent changes to the U.K. capital gains tax (CGT) system reduce the effective rate of CGT depending on the length of time and nature of the capital asset owned.[56] For example, a shareholding in a trading company (or the holding company of a trading group) in which the shareholder can excise voting rights of at least 5 per cent (if the shareholder works full time) or 25 per cent (otherwise), is eligible for business assets taper relief on that shareholding. In broad terms, after 10 complete years of ownership the effective rate of capital gains tax for a higher rate taxpayer is reduced from 40 per cent to 10 per cent.[57] This valuable relief may influence how a business is structured.

Many e-business provide share incentives to at least key employees and often to all their employees. There are various types of share and share option schemes available including ones with tax advantages.[58] The U.K. Government has announced proposals for two new share schemes and one of these, in particular, is aimed at providing a tax advantaged share incentive to individuals joining smaller high risk trading companies.[59]

There are other reliefs that may be relevant when structuring an e-business or developing it.[60]

Non-domiciled entrepreneurs

11.70   A *non-U.K. domiciled* individual who is resident in the U.K. benefits from the remittance basis of taxation. In broad terms, capital gains arising on non-U.K. assets are not subject to U.K. tax on capital gains until proceeds are remitted to the United Kingdom.[61] Similarly, income arising from non-U.K. sources is also taxed on a remittance basis.[62] In the case of a U.K. resident individual owning a business overseas, it is, however, difficult to establish such a business as a non-U.K. source of income because the "head and brains" of the organisation will normally be in the United Kingdom.[63]

Domicile for income tax and capital gains tax purposes is a general law concept. Domicile is not the same as nationality or residence. The Inland Revenue's approach is broadly speaking, to ask where someone has their permanent home.[64] Someone born outside the United Kingdom can, live in the United Kingdom for a considerable time without establishing a U.K. domicile. From an inheritance tax point of view, a non-U.K.

---

[54] TA 1988, s.360 (loan to by interest in close company) and TA 1988, s.361 (loan to buy interest in co-operative or employee controlled company).
[55] TA 1988, s.362.
[56] TCGA 1992, s.2A and Sched. A1.
[57] The business assets taper period will be reduced from 10 years to four years for disposals of assets after April 5, 2000 and the scope of the business taper greatly increased by reducing the present 5% and 25% thresholds (Inland Revenue Press Release, March 21, 2000).
[58] Booklets on Inland Revenue approved employee share and share option schemes are available to download from the Inland Revenue website (**www.inlandrevenue.gov.uk/leaflets**).
[59] The Inland Revenue enterprise management incentives draft legislation and commentary, November 1999.
[60] For example, a loss on the disposal of unquoted shares in a trading company or holding company of a trading group can be set off against income if various conditions are met (TA 1988, ss.573 *et seq.*).
[61] TCGA 1992, s.12.
[62] TA 1988, ss.19 and 65.
[63] *Ogilvie v. Kitton*, S.T.C. 338.
[64] I.R. 20, para. 5.

domiciled individual is only subject to inheritance tax on U.K. assets. There is, however, a different test of domicile for inheritance tax purposes.[65]

Non-domicile individuals may prefer to conduct their business through non-U.K. incorporated companies. The shares in such companies will be non-U.K. assets for capital gains tax and inheritance tax purposes. Such a company could be U.K. tax resident under the central management and control test (see above) and pay corporation tax on its worldwide profits. However, if the company is operated so as to be a non-U.K. resident and no part of its business is conducted in the United Kingdom then profits can arise free of U.K. tax (and, possibly, free of any tax if the company operates from a "tax haven").[66]

GOING INTERNATIONAL

Overseas tax issues

The preceding paragraphs explain the scope of U.K. taxation in respect of e-commerce. **11.71** The emphasis has been on e-commerce conducted by U.K. residents and on the tax aspects of conducting that business in the United Kingdom. However, the nature of e-commerce makes it likely that overseas tax will have to be considered. Although U.K. tax residents are, in broad terms, taxable in the United Kingdom in respect of worldwide income and capital gains, this does not mean that overseas tax issues can be ignored.

All the tax compliance issues raised in respect of starting a new business in the United Kingdom could apply equally in respect of a business conducted in another jurisdiction. The other jurisdiction could stake its claim to tax on trading profits within its territory, just as the United Kingdom does in respect of non-resident trading in the United Kingdom. A U.K. based business could have employees in one or more other jurisdictions, which would be subject to the local equivalent of pay as you earn and national insurance contributions. In some territories, tax withholdings are needed on payments to other categories of workers, not just employees. Similarly capital assets held in other jurisdictions could be subject to local taxes on capital gains. There may be local business rates or other property taxes to pay in respect of any interest in land and buildings in other jurisdictions. As explained, in the case of goods sold in other Member States, local VAT may be payable under the distance selling provisions. If there is a place of business overseas that provides goods or services then the local equivalent of VAT clearly needs to be considered.

The United Kingdom's approach to the taxation of e-commerce provides a good guide **11.72** to the overseas tax issues that are likely to arise, but tax legislation does vary significantly from one jurisdiction to another and detailed local advice is likely to be needed.

As explained above, in addition to taxing U.K. residents on worldwide trading and profits, the United Kingdom also taxes non-residents on income arising from trade within the United Kingdom. If a U.K. company, with overseas activities, encounters the same approach to taxation in the country in which it is trading, then clearly there will be double taxation. The overseas jurisdiction will seek tax on the trading profits arising in its jurisdiction and the Inland Revenue will also expect U.K. tax to be paid on those profits. Similarly, a U.K. tax resident employee who works overseas, could face taxation on his salary in both the United Kingdom and an overseas jurisdiction. Double taxation is

---

[65] IHTA 1984, s.267 — "the 17 year rule".
[66] See paras 9.80 *et seq.* regarding the use of offshore companies by U.K. domiciled and resident individuals.

recognised internationally as objectionable and tax systems adopt various approaches to try to avoid or minimise the incidence of double taxation.

In some jurisdictions there are significant exemptions from tax on overseas income. In the United Kingdom two approaches can be identified to deal with double taxation:

(a) double taxation agreements; and

(b) unilateral relief (*i.e.* providing credit for foreign tax paid against the U.K. tax liability or deducting foreign tax in computing business profits).

Both of the above are considered further below and, in particular, the opportunities available under double taxation agreements to avoid or reduce overseas taxation.

In practice, if a U.K. tax resident is conducting business in a country with which the United Kingdom has a double tax treaty then there are significant protections available.

Double taxation agreements

11.73 The Inland Revenue proudly announced in 1996 that the United Kingdom was the first country to enter into double taxation agreements with over 100 countries. The U.K. Government can enter into arrangements with other governments with a view to affording relief from double taxation.[67] The usual approach is for a treaty to follow the latest model treaty devised by the OECD.[68] Relevant provisions in the latest model treaty ("the Model") are considered, as follows[69]:

Permanent establishments and the taxation of business profits

11.74 The concept of a permanent establishment in Article 5 of the Model is vital in determining the right of one government (in tax treaty terms known as a contracting State) to tax the profits of an enterprise of the other contracting State. Under Article 7 of the Model a contracting State cannot tax the profits of an enterprise of the other contracting State unless it carries on its business through a permanent establishment situated therein. A permanent establishment is a fixed place of business through which the business of an enterprise is only or partly carried on. The Model confirms that a permanent establishment includes especially a place of management, a branch, an office, a factory, a workshop and certain places of extraction of natural resources (*e.g.* mines). This gives the impression that some sort of premises are required. However, it is sometimes sufficient for the facility to comprise machinery or equipment (including automated equipment). In the context of e-commerce it is this latter possibility that it is of particular concern (*e.g.* the location of web servers).[70] Various comments in the existing OECD commentary on the Model are also relevant,[71] including:

> ". . . the place of business may be situated in the business facilities of another enterprise. Equipment constituting the place of business [does not have] to be actually fixed to the soil on which it stands. It is

---

[67] TA 1988, s.788.

[68] The Model Double Taxation Convention was first adopted on April 29, 1977 and has since been revised.

[69] Model Tax Convention on Income and Capital' Report of the OECD Committee on Fiscal Affairs, 1992.

[70] The website itself should not be a concern because the software and data comprising a website are not tangible property (*i.e.* they are not a *place* of business) and a website is not a person (*i.e.* it cannot be an agent of an enterprise).

[71] It is intended to revise the existing commentary soon to refer expressly to electronic commerce. The proposed revised commentary is available on the OECD website (www.oecd.org).

enough that the equipment remains on a particular site. If the place of business was not set up merely for a temporary purpose, it can constitute a permanent establishment, even though it existed, in practice, only for a very short period of time because of the special nature of the activity of the enterprise or because, as a consequence of special circumstances . . . it was prematurely liquidated".

"The activity [of the permanent establishment] need not be of a productive character".

"Where tangible property such as facilities, industrial, commercial or scientific . . . equipment . . . or intangible property such as patents, procedures and similar property, are let or leased to third parties through a fixed place of business . . . this activity will, in general, render the place of business a permanent establishment".

". . . a permanent establishment may . . . exist if the business of the enterprise is carried on mainly through automatic equipment, the activities of the personnel being restricted to setting up, operating, controlling and maintaining such equipment".

At one time, the main concern was over gaming and vending machines. In broad **11.75** terms, a permanent establishment may exist if the enterprise which sets up the machines also operates and maintains them for its own account. This remains the case even if the machines are operated and maintained by an agent dependent on the enterprise. The Model does list a number of activities which are treated as exceptions to the general definition of a permanent establishment. The common characteristic of these activities is that they are, in broad terms, preparatory or auxiliary activities. These exclusions allow, for example, a representative office to escape classification as a permanent establishment. This assumes the representative office will restrict its activities to, for example, collecting information and promoting business but not actually conducting it. If e-commerce involves siting equipment in other jurisdictions, for the purpose of routing information only rather than processing it, it should be possible to argue that there is no permanent establishment. This is on the basis that although there is a fixed place of business it is solely for the purpose of carrying on, for the enterprise, an activity of a preparatory or auxiliary nature. Similarly, the acquisition of telecommunications capacity in a country perhaps through leasing telephone lines, should also be considered preparatory or auxiliary. The usual arrangement is that a website of an enterprise is hosted on the server of an ISP. As a general rule this should not create a permanent establishment of the enterprise in the country where the server is located (it has no tangible presence in that country). An enterprise may also create a tax exposure for itself in another country through entering into certain agency arrangements in that country. However, normal contractual arrangements with an ISP should not make the ISP an agent of the enterprise for tax treaty purposes. This is because either ISPs will not generally have authority to conclude contracts in the name of the enterprise or because they will constitute independent agents acting in the ordinary course of their business. There remains, however, general uncertainty as to what amounts to a permanent establishment in the context of e-commerce.

If a permanent establishment is found to exist then under the Model only so much of the profits as is attributable to that permanent establishment can be taxed in the other contracting State. Again, the commentary on the Model provides guidance on how this principle operates.

Independent personal services

A separate provision of the Model is concerned with professional services and other **11.76** activities of an independent character.[72] This excludes industrial and commercial activities

---

[72] *ibid.,* Art. 14.

and also services performed as an employee. Professional services is taken to include independent scientific, literary, artistic, educational or teaching activities as well as the independent activities of lawyers, accountants and so on. Some e-commerce may fall within this provision rather than the definition of business profits. The Model provides a similar protection to that available for business profits. Income derived by a resident of one contracting State in respect of professional services is taxable only in the State of residence, unless he has a fixed based regularly available to him in the other contracting State for the purpose of performing his activities. If he has such a fixed base, the income attributable to that fixed base may be taxed in the other State. It is not clear to what extent (if at all) the definition of a fixed base differs from that of a permanent establishment. The OECD commentary gives two narrow examples of a fixed base (a physician's consulting room and the office of an architect or a lawyer).

Dependent personal services

11.77   The Model provides an important exemption in respect of employment income.[73] An employee who is a resident of one contracting State can avoid taxation in another contracting State if, in outline:

- the employee is present there for no more than 183 days in the relevant tax year;

- the remuneration is paid by or on behalf of an employer who is not a resident of that other State; and

- the remuneration is not borne by a permanent establishment or a fixed base which the employer has in the other State.

Royalties

11.78   Under Article 12 of the Model, royalties are taxed only in the country of residence of the beneficial owner of royalties.[74] However, in practice, many agreements provide for the State in which the royalty arises to charge tax up to a specified level. Under the Model, royalties is defined to include payments of any kind received as consideration for the use of, or the right to use, any copyright of literary, artistic or scientific work. Various examples are given (*e.g.* patents, trade marks and so on). The definition in the Model does not refer specifically to computer software but the commentary does. The commentary on the royalties article contains a discussion on the difficulties of determining where the boundary lies between software payments that are properly to be regarded as royalties and other types of payment (*e.g.* commercial income or a capital gain).[75] The commentary[76] confirms as regards the common situation of making a program copy that:

> "Regardless of whether this right is granted under law or under a license agreement with the copyright holder, copying the program onto the computer's hard drive or random access memory or making an archival copy is an essential step in utilising the program. Therefore, rights in relation to these acts of copying, where they do no more than enable the effective operation of the program by the user, should be disregarded in analysing the character of the transaction for tax purposes. payments in these types of transactions would be dealt with as commercial income [and not as royalties]."

[73] *ibid.*, Art. 15.
[74] *ibid.*, Art. 12.
[75] The relevant OECD Working Party has adopted changes to the commentary dealing with software payments following the OECD Ministerial Conference in October 1998.
[76] *i.e.* as adopted by the OECD Working Party.

Also, payments for "site licences" should in most cases fall to be dealt with as commercial income rather than as payments of royalties.

If royalties are paid in connection with rights effectively connected with a permanent establishment or a fixed base then the relevant provisions (*e.g.* business profit or independent personal services) apply, rather than the royalties article.

Unilateral relief

If a double tax treaty does not apply then unilateral relief is available. Relief from income **11.79** tax and corporation tax shall be given in respect of tax paid overseas by allowing that tax as a credit against income tax or corporation tax.[77] The alternative is to deduct the foreign tax in computing the profits of the business.[78]

VAT IN MORE DETAIL

Points to watch

Many types of business have special VAT rules that apply to them. The following **11.80** paragraphs address some issues that are likely to be relevant to a wide range of e-businesses. In particular, this includes looking in more detail at the differences in VAT liability that arise on supplies of goods and services to customers outside the United Kingdom and some administrative issues. This is a developing area of tax law. The general principles agreed at the OECD Ministerial Conference in October 1998 in respect of consumption taxes (*e.g.* VAT) are:

- cross border trade should result in taxation in the jurisdiction where consumption takes place;

- the supply of digitised products should not be treated as a supply of goods (in the E.C. this means treating them as services);

- countries should consider using some self-assessment mechanism where this would give immediate protection of the revenue base and of the competitiveness of domestic suppliers; and

- appropriate systems should be developed to collect tax on imported physical goods.

Supply of goods to non-U.K. customers

It is assumed that the goods in question would be standard rated if supplied to a **11.81** customer in the United Kingdom. As a general rule, if the goods are supplied to someone in the United Kingdom then it makes no difference if the customer receives the supply for the purpose of a business carried on by him or for private purposes; the supply remains standard rated. If goods are exported to a place outside the E.C. then similarly, it makes no difference to what use the goods are put. The export of goods outside the E.C. to both business and private customers is zero-rated. However, if goods are removed to

---

[77] TA 1988, s.790.
[78] TA 1988, s.811.

another Member State then zero-rating only applies if the goods are acquired in that Member State by a person who is liable for VAT in accordance with the laws of that Member State (the equivalent of the VAT charge on acquisitions described in paragraph 11.32 above). In other cases, either U.K. VAT is charged or, the supplier has to charge local VAT (under the local equivalent of the distance selling provisions described in paragraph 11.60).

Table 1: Supply of goods by a U.K. VAT registered business	
VAT liability	*Place (and circumstances)*
0%	Goods exported outside E.C.
0%	Goods removed to another Member State and acquired by a VAT registered business
Rate applicable in other Member State	Goods removed to another Member State and supplier is registered there under distance selling rules
17.5%	Goods removed to another Member State in other circumstances.

Note: It is assumed that the supply of goods to someone in the U.K. would be standard rated (17.5 per cent).

11.82 If goods are exported outside the E.C. then the U.K. VAT registered business must possess evidence of such export to claim zero-rated treatment. The involvement of the Internet as the means of selling goods for export should not make it any harder to obtain such evidence.[79] In the case of supplies to other Member States, the supply may be zero-rated if:

- the customer's E.C. VAT registration number is included on the tax invoice;
- the goods are sent or transported out of the United Kingdom to another E.C. Member State; and
- commercial documentary evidence is obtained that the goods have been removed from the United Kingdom (there is a time limit for obtaining this).

It is the first of these requirements that may, in particular, cause a practical problem. It is usual to ask the customer for its VAT number. If the number provided is not in the published format for the relevant Member State, it would no doubt be rejected by the trader (or his computer program). Provided all reasonable steps have been taken to ensure the customer is VAT registered and to obtain his VAT number, H.M. Customs & Excise state they will not hold the U.K. supplier liable to account for VAT if it turns out the number is invalid.[80]

Supply of services to non-U.K. customers

11.83 It is assumed that the services supplied would be standard rated if supplied to a customer belonging in the United Kingdom. Again, as a general rule, it makes no

---

[79] H.M. Customs & Excise Notice 703: Exports and removals of goods from the U.K.
[80] *ibid.*

difference if a customer in the United Kingdom uses the services for business purposes or private purposes, the supply remains standard rated.

Schedule 5 services

If services are supplied to a customer belonging outside the United Kingdom it is important to distinguish, in particular, supplies of a description within paragraphs 1 to 8 of Schedule 5 to the Value Added Tax Act 1994 ("Schedule 5 services") from other services.

Examples of Schedule 5 services were given in paragraph 11.22. It is important to realise that the transmission of images and games and so on which are not copyright will probably not come within any of the items in Schedule 5 and so will not be a Schedule 5 service. However, if an Internet package is provided for a single inclusive price (*e.g.* covering access to information pages, on-line shopping, games fora, etc.) then there is a single supply that falls within Schedule 5.[81]

If services are supplied that are not Schedule 5 services, then U.K. VAT at the standard rate applies, regardless of where the customer belongs and whether or not the supply is for business or private purposes.

If Schedule 5 services are supplied to a customer belonging outside the E.C. then the supply is outside the scope but with a right to recovery of input tax. If the services are supplied to a customer belonging in another Member State then the supply is only outside the scope of VAT if made for the purposes of a business carried on by the customer. The local equivalent of the reverse charge should apply. Otherwise, the supply is standard rated.

Table 2: Supply of Schedule 5 services (other than telecommunications services) by a U.K. VAT registered business to a customer belonging in a place outside the U.K.	
VAT liability	*Place (and circumstances)*
OTS	Outside the E.C.
OTS	Another Member State where supply received for customer's business
17.5%	Another Member State in other circumstances
Note: OTS means outside the scope of U.K. VAT. It is assumed that the supply of the services in the U.K. would be standard rated (17.5%).	

There is again a practical issue of identifying whether or not an E.C. customer is in business. VAT registration numbers are the best evidence and should always be requested. If a VAT number is not available then alternative evidence of business status is acceptable. Unfortunately, for an electronic trader, the examples of alternative evidence given by H.M. Customs & Excise[82] are of documents, such as business letterheads which may not be available in an Internet transaction.

---

[81] H.M. Customs & Excise Business Brief 22/97.
[82] H.M. Customs & Excise Notice 741: "VAT: Place of supply of services." See para. 10.06.

Melbourne Agreement

11.84   The Melbourne Agreement[83] permitted the supply of telecommunications capacity by public telecommunications authorities and similar operators to other such authorities to be zero-rated. This aspect of the Melbourne Agreement has, however, been superseded by the new place of supply rules for telecommunications services.[84] United Kingdom providers who fall under the provisions of the Melbourne Agreement do not have to account for the reverse charge on such services.[85]

Tax invoices

11.85   A VAT invoice must contain certain prescribed information. A VAT invoice does not have to be in writing. The requisite particulars can be recorded in a computer and transmitted by electronic means.[86] Various conditions must be met before doing this. H.M. Customs & Excise must be given at least one month's notice in writing of what is planned and a business must comply with any general regulations in existence and such requirements as H.M. Customs & Excise may impose in any particular case.

VAT inclusive or exclusive prices?

11.86   The amount paid for a supply includes VAT. In other words, consideration is a tax inclusive amount.[87] If a price is shown and no reference is made to VAT then the usual implication is that the price is VAT inclusive. This implication may be displaced by the circumstances in which the price is quoted. Care must therefore be taken to ensure that in contract law it is clear whether a price is VAT exclusive or inclusive.

ANTI-AVOIDANCE

Duke of Westminster case

11.87   The United Kingdom currently has no general anti-avoidance provision.[88] A taxpayer is therefore able to organise his affairs, provided it is in a lawful manner, so as to minimise or avoid tax. In the House of Lords in *IRC v. Duke of Westminster*, Lord Tomlin states:

> "Every man is entitled if he can to order his affairs so that the tax attaching under the appropriate Acts is less than it otherwise would be. If he succeeds in ordering them so as to secure this result, then, however unappreciative the Commissioners of Inland Revenue or his fellow taxpayers may be of his ingenuity, he cannot be compelled to pay an increased tax".[89]

There has also been a tradition of interpreting tax legislation in such a way as to place a burden on the tax authorities to show that a taxpayer fell fairly within the scope of the

---

[83] The final acts of the 1988 World Administrative Telegraph and Telephone Conference in Melbourne.
[84] See para. 11.30 above.
[85] VAT Information Sheet 2/97, para. 7.1.
[86] VATA 1994, Sched. 11, para. 3(1).
[87] VATA 1994, s.19.
[88] On October 5, 1998 the Inland Revenue published a consultative document, "A General Anti-Avoidance Rule for Direct Taxes". It examines the advantages a general anti-avoidance rule would have in countering tax avoidance, in relation to the corporate sector, and considers how it might be framed. The document builds on the work of the Tax Law Review Committee report, "Tax avoidance" (November 1997).
[89] 19 T.C. 490 at 520.

charge in question. The development of the *Ramsay* principle provides a general method of counteracting artificial tax planning schemes but this has its limits.[90]

United Kingdom tax legislation does, however, contain a significant number of highly effective provisions to counteract tax avoidance.[91] There are a number of provisions aimed at counteracting tax avoidance through transactions involving shares and other securities. There are also wide ranging anti-avoidance provisions related to the sale by an individual of income derived from his personal activities and in respect of so-called artificial transactions in land. The following paragraphs consider the anti-avoidance provisions that apply and other approaches that can be taken by the Inland Revenue to counteract attempts by a U.K. resident to escape the charges to tax on trading profits explained in paragraph 11.09 above.

U.K. taxation of worldwide trading

A U.K. resident individual is charged to tax on his trading profits wherever the trade is conducted. A U.K. tax resident company will similarly pay tax on its worldwide profits. However, if a non-U.K. resident company conducts a trade, it will only be within the scope of U.K. tax to the extent that trade is conducted within the United Kingdom. There is the considerable potential with e-commerce for a trade to be conducted wholly outside the United Kingdom. A company is a legal entity, separate from its shareholders, directors and employees. Therefore, U.K. tax resident individuals may well be tempted into trying to avoid the *usual* tax charge on trading profits by arranging for a trade to be conducted offshore by a non-U.K. tax resident company. There are a number of tax haven jurisdictions that offer no or low tax regimes and so, in principle, there is a tax planning opportunity. However, in practice, it is difficult to achieve tax savings. **11.88**

> Douglas sells toys (see paragraph 11.07). One of Douglas's customers suggested Douglas sets up a British Virgin Islands incorporated company, with Jersey resident directors. The suggestion is that in this way Douglas does not have to pay any tax on his business profits. There was no suggestion that Douglas should work from Jersey; Douglas would continue to work in the United Kingdom but would use the offshore company's name.
>
> However, another of Douglas's customers, a tax lawyer, warned Douglas that at best he would not save tax and at worse Douglas would commit a criminal offence and incur significant tax penalties and interest.

Offshore companies

In the case of a U.K. resident individual owning an offshore company there are the following obstacles to avoiding U.K. tax: **11.89**

- an overseas incorporated company can still be U.K. tax resident;

- an overseas company may nevertheless have a taxable trade in the United Kingdom;

- in extreme circumstances the arrangement could be ignored as a sham;

---

[90] *Ramsay (W.T.) Ltd v. IRC* [1981] S.T.C. 174; *Furniss v. Dawson* [1984] S.T.C. 153.
[91] TA 1988, ss.703 *et seq.*

- income (and capital gains) arising in the offshore company may be deemed that of a U.K. resident and taxed accordingly.

In the case of a company owning an offshore company or an interest in it there are also the controlled foreign company provisions to consider. Transactions may also be subject to adjustments under transfer pricing provisions.

This chapter assumes that a taxpayer would only consider attempting to reduce his tax liabilities through lawful measures (*i.e.* tax avoidance). If a taxpayer tried to reduce his tax liabilities in a way that is not lawful, this is tax evasion. A tax evader faces criminal prosecution and, in particular, imprisonment. His advisers and associates may also find they have committed criminal offences.[92]

Company residence

11.90   An overseas incorporated company can nevertheless be U.K. tax resident under the central management and control test explained above. It is relatively straightforward to find individuals in tax haven jurisdictions who will act as directors of a company. If such individuals act as mere cyphers for the U.K. resident controlling shareholder then the company will be U.K. tax resident. It will then be subject to tax on its worldwide profits. There are, of course, cases in which the non-U.K. resident directors do genuinely exercise central management and control outside the United Kingdom, e-commerce offers the potential to make this easier to achieve, as more of the trading process is automated. The U.K. resident individual will then more clearly have a relationship with the company as, say, a shareholder, rather than as a shadow director. Nevertheless, in practice, some risk is likely to remain that the activities of a key individual in the United Kingdom could make an offshore company U.K. tax resident.

United Kingdom branch or agency

11.91   Corporation tax is charged on non-resident companies trading through a branch or agency in the United Kingdom. If someone is involved in the United Kingdom in the trading activities of an offshore company, that person may create a taxable branch or agency.[93]

Sham transactions

11.92   It is unlikely that an arrangement will be overturned as a sham transaction but this remains a possibility in extreme circumstances.[94] In which case, the use of the offshore company would be ignored and the trade taxed as if the company did not exist.

Deemed income

11.93   The most formidable obstacle for individuals to overcome is that of section 739 of the Income and Corporation Taxes Act 1988 and related provisions.

Section 739, unusually for a statutory provision introduced in 1936, contains a preamble to explain the aim of the legislation. The preamble reads:

> ". . . this section shall have effect for the purpose of preventing the avoiding by individuals ordinarily resident in the U.K. of liability to income tax by means of transfers of assets by virtue . . . of which . . . income becomes payable to persons resident or domiciled outside the U.K."

---

[92] *R. v. Charlton* [1996] S.T.C. 1418, CA.
[93] *IRC v. Brackett* [1986] S.T.C. 521.
[94] *Snook v. London & West Riding Investments Ltd* [1967] 2 Q.B. 786.

The statutory provisions are drafted in wide terms and have been interpreted widely by the Courts.

Briefly, if by virtue of a transfer of an asset or assets income is payable to a non-U.K. resident then a tax charge will arise on an individual ordinarily resident in the United Kingdom if:

- the individual is the transferor of the asset and has power to enjoy that income (power to enjoy is widely defined);

- the individual is the transferor of the asset and is entitled to receive a capital sum connected with the transfer; or

- the individual is not the transferor of the asset but receives a benefit from the asset.

If the main tax charge under section 739 is not to apply then the transferor must accept **11.94** that neither he (nor any spouse) can have power to enjoy the income of the offshore structure either directly or indirectly. The benefit of the offshore structure must belong to someone else. If this is acceptable then there may be scope to accumulate profits tax free offshore. However, if a U.K. resident wishes to benefit from the profits of the offshore company then a tax charge is very likely to arise under this anti-avoidance provision.

A U.K. tax resident chartered surveyor (Mr B) set up a Jersey trust in 1974 for the benefit of the mother of their two children. The trustees incorporated a Jersey company, (D Ltd), the directors of which were two Canadians and a Jersey advocate. The intention was for the offshore structure to share in the profits of a property development in Jersey. The property development did not, however, go ahead.

Mr B. had retired from private practice but continued to earn fees as a property consultant. Following discussions (outside the United Kingdom) with the directors of D Ltd it was agreed that D Ltd would start a consultancy business. It would employ Mr B to give advice to its clients. When Mr B was asked for business advice he would refer the potential customer to D Ltd. D Ltd would agree to provide the advice and would deal with administrative matters (invoices and payment of expenses).

Mr B received some remuneration from the company. The balance of the fees was retained by D Ltd. These funds accumulated tax free in D Ltd.

D Ltd bought properties from Mr B at what were believed to be market value prices. These purchases were made at a time when there had been a collapse in the U.K. property market and so the properties probably could not be sold on the open market.

The contract of employment between Mr B and D Ltd is the transfer of an asset for the purposes of TA 1988, s.739. Mr B had power to enjoy the income of D Ltd because of the benefits he received from D Ltd: namely the provision of liquidity, payments of salary and also the discharge of Mr B's moral obligations to provide for his children and their mother.

As Mr B was permanently resident in the United Kingdom and his activities constituted the esssential operations of D Ltd's trade, D Ltd was carrying on a trade in the United Kingdom through a U.K. branch or agency. The profits of the offshore structure therefore fell to be taxed in the United Kingdom.

(*IRC v. Brackett* [1986] S.T.C. 521.)

Deemed gains

11.95   If the offshore company realises a chargeable gain, rather than a trading profit, then another anti-avoidance provision may apply. The gains of certain non-resident companies can be apportioned to its shareholders and deemed to be their gains and taxed accordingly.[95]

Controlled foreign companies

11.96   A controlled foreign company (CFC) is one which is not U.K. resident but is controlled by U.K. residents, whether individuals or companies, and which is taxed in its country of residence at a lower level (as defined) than in the United Kingdom. The CFC legislation[96] exists to prevent the accumulation of income in such lower tax jurisdictions. United Kingdom resident companies with an interest in a CFC can be charged to tax on their share of the chargeable profits (less any creditable overseas tax). There are exceptions from the CFC regime. It may be difficult for some e-businesses to come within the exceptions, in particular, for permitted businesses.

Transfer pricing

11.97   Legislation exists to counteract the manipulation of prices by associated businesses.[97] In broad terms, if a U.K. trader sells goods at less than market value or buys goods at more than market value from an associated business, then the prices can be adjusted to market value. The provisions apply to the transfer of rights, interests or licences and the giving of business facilities of whatever kind. The introduction of self-assessment has led to a change in emphasis and restructuring of the legislation. Taxpayers have to use the arm's length principle in making their returns.[98] The complexity of some e-commerce transactions will make it difficult to apply the arm's length principle in practice.

In addition to the above statutory provisions, double taxation agreements contain transfer pricing rules and mutual agreement procedures for resolving disputes between tax authorities.[99]

CONCLUSION

Tax pitfalls

11.98   There are potential tax pitfalls with e-commerce. Traders may not realise the need to register for VAT in other Member States (under the equivalent of the distance selling provisions or otherwise) or an equivalent to VAT in other territories. The Internet does not necessarily offer the best VAT treatment. Information bought in book form is zero rated for VAT purposes, in contrast to receiving an electronic supply of information from a U.K. supplier on which VAT is charged at the standard rate. There are potential practical problems obtaining the necessary information from customers to ensure the correct VAT or other tax treatment. At a governmental level, developing countries

---

[95] TCGA 1992, s.13.
[96] TA 1988, ss.747–756, Scheds 24–26.
[97] TA 1988, s.770A.
[98] FA 1998, ss.108 *et seq*.
[99] The OECD publishes "Transfer Pricing Guidelines for Multinational Enterprises and Tax Administrations."

Diagram: Using the VAT Place of Supply Rules to Provide a VAT Free Service to a U.K. Private Customer

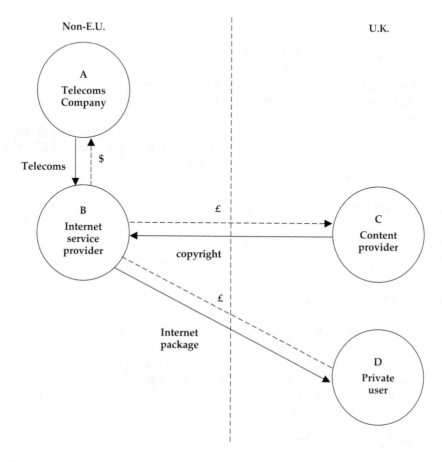

Supply	Comment
A to B	This is outside the scope of U.K. VAT.
C to B	This is a supply of Schedule 5 services and is outside the scope of U.K. VAT. If D bought the copyright material directly from C he would be charged VAT unless he bought, it say, in book form from C.
B to D	This is a supply of Schedule 5 services and is outside the scope of U.K. VAT. The reverse charge does not apply to private customers. If D bought his Internet package from a U.K. service provider he would be charged VAT.

11.99

are concerned at the potential loss of revenue if there is a move from importing goods (on which import duties are raised) to importing intangibles. Governments generally are concerned about the scope for tax evasion.

Tax planning

11.100   E-commerce does provide scope for legitimate tax planning. The Government is aware that betting and gaming duties may be avoided by establishing, for example, "virtual casinos" outside the United Kingdom on the Internet.[1] The place of supply rules for VAT purposes create planning opportunities. It is in the interest of private customers to buy Schedule 5 services (excluding telecommunications services) from suppliers outside the E.C. There remains a competitive advantage purchasing Internet packages from outside the E.C. The rapid growth of e-commerce, makes it easier to receive other services from businesses outside the E.C. Although as at September 1999 it was still thought that the threat to the revenue yield from private customers buying digital items from outside the E.C. was not large.[2]

Tax system refinements

11.101   There are likely to be a number of refinements to the U.K. tax system as e-commerce develops. The changes made to VATA 1994, Schedule 5 from July 1, 1997 in respect of telecommunication services show the commitment of U.K. and European tax authorities to avoid significant tax distortions.

Courts are starting to deal with e-commerce tax issues, the decisions showing the effectiveness or not of current legislation.[3]

The Government is consulting on moving towards a simpler system for intellectual property taxation, essentially following the accounting treatment for relieving intellectual property expenditure and taxing proceeds.[4] There is also consultation on simplifying the taxation of royalty payments. In place of the current variable treatment the aim is to allow as many payments as possible to be made gross and to align withholding tax rules with the terms of double tax treaties.[5]

Taxation policy principles

11.102   The Inland Revenue and H.M. Customs & Excise published a joint paper on U.K. tax policy regarding e-commerce in 1998.[6] This confirmed that the broad policy principles adopted are neutrality, certainty and transparency, effectiveness and efficiency.[7] In broad

---

[1] "e-commerce@its.best.uk", para. 7.49. The U.K. is seeking an international review of the implications of Internet and telephone based betting and gambling. In the Chancellor's November 9, 1999 pre-budget report he announced the strengthening of the ban on advertising by offshore bookmakers on teletext services and other media in the U.K. and announced that further measures may be brought forward in the 2000 budget.

[2] "e-commerce@its.best.uk", para. 7.35.

[3] The VAT Tribunal in the case of *Forexia (U.K.) Limited* LON/1998/879, when refusing to extend zero rating to supplies made by an electronic publisher, commented ". . . with the greatest reluctance, we are forced to the conclusion that [the H.M. Customs & Excise] contention is correct in law . . . and it may be that the European Court of Justice will eventually have to tackle the whole problem of electronic commerce . . ."

[4] Pre-Budget Report H.M. Treasury November 1998 "Steering a stable course for lasting prosperity", para. 3.33.

[5] *ibid.*

[6] Inland Revenue Press Release 128/98 and H.M. Customs & Excise News Release 25/98. See also the Department of Trade and Industry paper "Net benefit — The electronic commerce agenda for the U.K." (issued October 6, 1998).

[7] See further in the OECD Report, dated October 8, 1998, "Electronic commerce: taxation framework conditions".

terms, the Government does not believe any major changes in existing tax law (or new taxes) are necessary to achieve these policy principles. This followed on from a conclusion of the OECD Ministerial Conference in Ottawa in 1998 which has also received support from non-OECD countries. The tax aspects of e-commerce are now actively monitored by the United Kingdom, other Governments and organisations such as the OECD, World Bank, WTO and World Customs Organisation to ensure that existing taxation principles continue to work.

U.K. Government e-commerce tax strategy

The U.K. Government's stated aim is to: **11.103**

> "make the U.K. the best environment in the world for e-commerce"[8]

The Cabinet Office published a strategy paper to achieve this goal in September 1999.[9] This wide ranging paper confirmed the above taxation policy principles and recommended various initiatives relating to the removal of tax barriers to starting up new e-commerce businesses in the United Kingdom, safeguarding the tax base and communicating effectively what the tax rules are for e-business. In summary, the Government has stated that the United Kingdom should continue to aim for:

- international agreement on the direct tax treatment of payments for electronic goods and services (*e.g.* addressing the problems arising from tax rules that require tax to be withheld from royalty payments made to non-residents in respect of patents and copyrights);

- international agreement on the application of the permanent establishment principle to websites;

- a leading role in OECD work to review the application of transfer pricing rules to e-commerce and to develop rules for attributing income to permanent establishments;

- effective mechanisms for VAT collection in respect of consumer purchases of online items from outside the E.C. (*e.g.* some form of automated revenue collection);

- streamlining procedures for the collection of VAT and customs duties on small consignments;

- improved guidance for e-commerce businesses targeted at small and medium sized enterprises explaining their tax obligations and how the tax system will treat cross border transactions (*e.g.* by publishing information on the Department of Trade and Industry's website);

- implementation of the international taxation framework agreed at the 1998 Ministerial Conference; and

- an international examination of the implications of e-commerce betting and gaming.

---

[8] 1998 Competitiveness White Paper.
[9] "e-commerce@its.best.uk".

An updated Inland Revenue and H.M. Customs & Excise joint paper on the tax aspects of e-commerce was published in November 1999 which summarises what is being done to achieve the tax strategy.[10]

Use of new technology

11.104   A particular concern of the U.K. Government is to ensure that efficient use is made of new technology. Since the first edition of this chapter was published in 1998, there has been a notable increase in the information available on tax matters on Government websites. The use of technology goes further than this. The U.K. Government has announced that 25 per cent of transactions with Government should be capable of being done electronically by 2002 and that the Inland Revenue and H.M. Customs & Excise departments will play a large part in this. Arrangements are already in place for the delivery by electronic transmission of tax returns and other information to the Inland Revenue and of import declarations to H.M. Customs & Excise. Most of these arrangements are operated at present by professional advisers. It is hoped soon to introduce systems so that returns and other information can be sent electronically directly by taxpayers, subject to appropriate security measures. The Finance Act 1999 introduced the necessary enabling legislation.[11]

Tax Incentives

11.105   As mentioned above one of the U.K. tax policy principles is neutrality. Nevertheless, the Government may be prepared to create tax advantages for certain aspects of e-commerce to achieve the aim of making the U.K. the best environment in the world for e-commerce. For example, the Budget 2000 introduced an exemption from stamp duty on transfers on or after March 28, 2000 of patents, trade marks, registered designs, copyrights, plant breeders' rights and licences in respect of them. This was done "to boost R&D and foster an environment in which invention and innovation are encouraged".[12]

---

[10] Electronic commerce: the U.K.'s taxation agenda, November 1999.
[11] FA 1999, ss.132 (power to provide for use of electronic communications) and 133 (use of electronic communications under other provisions).
[12] Inland Revenue Press Release, Rev. 5, March 21, 2000.

— 12 —

U.K. AND EUROPEAN LEGISLATIVE INITIATIVES REGULATING ELECTRONIC COMMERCE

"A week is a long time in politics"[1]

INTRODUCTION

This last chapter is an attempt to map out the United Kingdom and European legislative **12.01** landscape at a time when Bills and reports are still being debated and many issues remain in flux. We decided not to include copies of the U.K. Electronic Communications Bill in this book because its inclusion could lead to confusion amongst practitioners as it is amended as it goes through the House. The Bill is available in its up to date form over the web at no charge.[2]

The U.K. draft legislation needs to be considered in the context of both the draft E.U. Electronics Commerce Directive[3] and the E.U. Electronic Signatures Directive[4] each of which are discussed in the context of the relevant parts of the U.K. draft legislation.

The U.K. Government finally published its Electronic Commerce Bill[5] on November 18, 1999 — the culmination of two-and-a-half years of wrangling which had seen the Government change its cryptographic policy from draconian regulator to laissez-faire liberal.[6]

As published the Electronic Commerce Bill is in three parts.

- *Part I, Cryptography Service Providers.* This concerns the arrangements for registering providers of cryptography support services, such as electronic signature services and confidentiality services.

---

[1] Quotation from Prime Minister Harold Wilson.
[2] Available at **http://www.publications.parliament.uk/pa/cm199900/cmbills/004/2000004.htm**.
[3] See **http.://www.ispo.cec.be/ecommerce/legal/documents/legalframew/legalen.pdf**.
[4] See **http://europa.eu.int/comm/dg15/en/media/sign/elecsignen.pdf** for an informal final version of the Directive.
[5] Available at **http://www.publications.parliament.uk/pa/cm199900/cmbills/004/2000004.htm**.
[6] But the regulation of cryptography debate is continuing in the Regulation of Investigatory Powers Bill which seeks to establish a new framework for the police and security forces relating to the interception of electronic communications.

- *Part II, Facilitation of Electronic Commerce, Data Storage, etc.* This makes provisions for the legal recognition of electronic signatures. It will also facilitate the use of electronic communications or electronic storage of information, as an alternative to traditional means of communication or storage.

- *Part III, Miscellaneous and Supplemental.* This part amends section 12 of the Telecommunications Act 1984 and inserts new sections (12A and 12B) into that Act. The proposed new provisions are concerned with the modification of telecommunication licences otherwise than in pursuance of a reference to the Competition Commission. This Part also concerns matters such as general interpretation, the short title, commencement and territorial extent of this Bill.

CRYPTOGRAPHY SERVICE PROVIDERS

12.02   Under Part I of the Bill, the Government will create a licensing scheme for so-called trusted service providers of cryptography products, termed cryptographic service providers. These cryptographic service providers (CSPs) will offer encryption keys used for encrypting e-mail traffic. A cryptographic service provider can also offer value added services such as secure electronic document archiving, proof of e-mail delivery, time-stamping, etc., all of which have non-electronic commerce precedence. The aim is for these cryptographic service providers to work under a voluntary accreditation scheme. Fledgling examples of cryptographic service providers are already operated by the Post Office (called ViaCode[7]) and British Telecom (called Trustwise[8]). The Government, taking the advice of the House of Commons Trade and Industry Committee which studied the matter in detail, accepted the Committee's recommendation to take powers for a statutory accreditation scheme but to hold them in reserve unless and until industry self-regulation is seen to fail. OFTEL will be the initial licensing authority but "the Government does not rule out delegation of some or all of the licensing functions to an industry body in future."[9] Registered providers are expected to have a market advantage over unregistered providers since Clause 1(4)(b) provides for publicity for any withdrawal or modification of approval — hence use of a registered CSP could reasonably be mandated in service contracts in the same way that ISO9000 compliance is often mandated. Clause 6(3) provides that cryptography support srvices are provided in the United Kingdom if they are provided from premises in this country, they are supplied to a person in this country when he/she makes use of those services or they are supplied to a person who makes use of them for the purposes of a business carried on in this country or from premises here.

Cryptographic service providers will adhere to standards, such as security standard BS 7799, and produce certificates against an expected model format. No date has been given for the scheme's inception, although this is expected shortly.

The Bill as published is claimed by the DTI to be compatible with the Cryptography Guidelines, published by the Organisation for Economic Co-operation and Development (OECD) on March 19, 1997[10] and the United Nations Commission on International Trade Law's (UNCITRAL) Model Law on Electronic Commerce.[11]

---

[7] See **http://www.viacode.com/**.
[8] See **http://www.trustwise.com/**.
[9] See   **http://www.parliament.the-stationery-office.co.uk/pa/cm199899/cmselect/cmtrdind/187/18711.htm** note 161.
[10] Available on the OECD website at **www.oecd.org/subject/e-commerce**.
[11] Available on the UN website at **www.un.or.at/uncitral/english/texts/electcom/ml-ec.htm**.

Government control over cryptography

Government policy over encryption is still causing concern since even at this late stage **12.03** there appear to be remains of the proposed draconian policy of a citizen being required to supply the authorities of his/her private key: section 13(2) appears to lay the framework for a requirement on the part of the individual to maintain a copy of the private key. With the possibility that some of these provisions might return in the Regulation of Investigatory Powers Bill it is useful to consider the chronology behind the current U.K. Electronic Communications Bill to understand the main protagonists in the ongoing debate.

Chronology of the U.K. Electronic Communications Bill

Date	Extent
June 10, 1996	DTI paper on "regulatory intent concerning use of encryption on open networks".
March 17, 1997	DTI Consultation "Licensing of Trusted Third Parties for the Provision of Encryption Services"
April 27, 1998	DTI "Secure Electronic Commerce Statement"
October 19, 1998	DTI Consultation paper postponed
November 24, 1998	Queen's Speech announces "Electronic Commerce Bill" this Parliamentary session
December 3, 1998	Trade and Industry Select Committee announces inquiry into e-commerce
January 19, 1999	France abandons key escrow
March 4, 1999	PIU study annonced at No. 10 meeting for industry leaders, key-escrow "not the answer"
March 5, 1999	DTI Consultation "Building Confidence in Electronic Commerce"
March 23, 1999	"Scrambling for Safety III" conference: first public discussion of encryption policy by Home Office
April 1, 1999	26 day response period of DTI Consultation ends: FIPR accumulates submissions on website
May 19, 1999	Trade and Industry Select Committee Report "Building Confidence In Electronic Commerce" The Government's Proposals"
May 26, 1999	Cabinet Office Performance and Innovation Unit Report, "Encryption and Law Enforcement"
June 22, 1999	Home Office Consultation "Interception of Communications in the United Kingdom"

July 8, 1999	Conservatives refuse to allow introduction of Bill under "carry-over" procedure this session
July 23, 1999	Draft "Electronic Communication Bill" published within a consultation paper "Promoting Electronic Commerce" (Cm 4417)
August 1999	U.K. Crypto Listserver debate
September 13, 1999	Publication of the PIU Report "e-commerce@its.best.uk"[13]
September 1999	U.K. Crypto Listserver debate and secret lobbying by Minister to lose Part III of the original Bill
November 3, 1999	Trade and Industry Select Committee Report on the draft Electronic Communications Bill
November 18, 1999	Revised draft Electronic Communications Bill introduced in the House of Commons

12.04   In 1995 the then U.K. government's position was that they had no intention of legislating against data encryption. In 1996, the G7 Summit considered the threat posed by criminal and terrorist use of strong encryption. Following the G7 communiqué, the U.K. Government, in June 1996, announced support for key escrow, in the form of a system of Trusted Third Parties[14] (TTPs). This was ostensibly aimed at protecting the commercial sector, whilst giving the authorities some ability to obtain decryption where deemed necessary. The proposal mixed two separate justifications for trusted third parties, one appealing to private organisations and the other to law enforcement officials. In March 1997 the U.K. Government issued a "Public Consultation Paper on Licensing of Trusted Parties for the Provision of Encryption Services" which was said to be the preclude to legislation and which set out policy proposals for the mandatory licensing and regulation of Trusted Third Parties (TTPs) to provide a range of information security services to their clients. 260 responses, 102 from organisations, and 158 from individuals were received by the Government most of which "expressed their views very strongly."[15]

12.05   The Labour Party while in opposition totally opposed any controls over encryption. However, this position appeared to change following their first year in office. On April 16, 1998 the Department of Trade and Industry (DTI) released a report with a preface by the Prime Minister called "Our Information Age," a general statement about U.K. future plans and current activities regarding uses of Information Technology in education, government and electronic commerce. In support of this report, on April 27, 1998, the DTI Minister for Small Firms, Trade and Industry released her *Statement on the Legal Framework for Secure Electronic Commerce*.[16] This policy statement announced that the DTI had begun the process of drafting legislation to license. Certification Authorities and other trusted Third Parties, and Key Recovery Agents. The statement says "We intend

---

[12] Available from http://www.cabinet-office.gov.uk/innovation/1999/ecommerce.
[13] See **http://www.coi/gov/uk/coi/dept/GTI/coi9303b.ok**.
[14] For a summary of the responses received see **http://www.dti.gov.uk/CII/responses.html**. For a criticism of these U.K. proposals in peer reviewed legal paper see *Cryptography and Liberty "Can the Trusted Third Parties be Trusted? A Critique of the Recent U.K. Proposals"* by Yaman Akdeniz, Oliver Clarke, Alistair Kelman, Andrew Oram at **http://www.ltc.law.warwick.ac.uk/jilt/cryptog/97 2akdz/akdeniz.htm**.
[15] Available at **http://www.dti.gov.uk/CII/ana27p.html**.

that licensed Certification Authorities — conforming to the procedural and technical standards which such licensing will confer — would be in a position to offer certificates to support electronic signatures reliable enough to be recognised as equivalent to written signatures; an essential ingredient of secure electronic commerce." It appeared that the licensing scheme for the use of secure cryptography was not intended to be mandatory but a voluntary system which would be given procedural support in legislation. This statement was followed up on July 1, 1998 by a White Paper containing the British Government's proposals for a new legislative framework for strategic export controls and export licensing, with particular emphasis on the export of military equipment and technology. In section 3.2, "Transfer of technology by intangible means," the paper proposed legislation to provide the Government with the power to control transfers of technology by electronic means. The new laws would provide that "documents transferred abroad containing controlled technology should be subject to export licensing requirements, whether exported physically or in electronic form," and would also govern the posting of information on electronic networks such as the World Wide Web. For the time being, the definition of "controlled technology" was to be limited to that involving weapons of mass destruction and long-range missile systems. But, almost immediately, one leading academic stated that this proposed legislation would "instantly terminate our research in computer security" and was unworkable.[16]

The Government had to think again. It delayed publication of details of its proposals **12.06** but announced in the Queen's Speech in November 1998 that it was introducing an Electronic Communications Bill. A few days later the Trade and Industry Select Committee announced its inquiry into e-commerce in preparation for the legislation. During the subsequent months this Committee took written and oral evidence and produced a Report.[17] Events dragged on — the Electronic Commerce Bill was promised again and again but never appeared.

Finally, on July 23, 1999, the DTI published the government's consultation paper "Promoting Electronic Commerce" (Cm. 4417). The paper was in two parts: Part I: a "consultation document" which was mainly the Government's response to the Trade and Industry Committee's report on the Government's previous consultation document, "Building Confidence in Electronic Commerce"; and Part II: a draft Electronic Communications Bill together with explanatory notes.

This draft Bill was made up of four parts rather than just three in the current Bill — the extra part was an attempt to introduce new criminal offences regarding disclosure of cryptographic keys. If the Government had hoped that publishing this draft Bill in an exceedingly obscure format just before Parliament rose for the Summer Vacation would mean that it would get an easy passage it seriously miscalculated. Throughout August and September a major debate on the implications of the Bill took place in the U.K. Crypto list[18] where top cryptographers and lawyers from all around the world tore into

---

[16] Dr Ross Anderson of the Cambridge Computer Laboratory in a Usenet message "Export Licensing of Intangibles," — August 7, 1998 where he suggests that it would be impossible to implement since "a minimum . . . would have to include . . . numerically controlled machine tools and fibre winding equipment, semiconductor design and test equipment, robots, high performance computers (even top end PCs), optical amplifiers and software radios, aero engine control software, flight management systems, as well as many lasers, gyros, accelerometers and similar components. . . . It will also be illegal to communicate, by demonstration or orally, information relevant to weapons of mass destruction and long range missiles. This is not precisely defined. Will it force the removal of standard textbooks such as Fieser and Fieser's Organic Chemistry (which contains the recipe for mustard gas) and the Feynman Lectures in Physics (which describe how atom bombs work)?"

[17] **http://www.parliament.the-stationery-office.co.uk/pa/cm199899/cmselect/cmtrdind/648/64802.htm**.

[18] **http://www.cs.ucl.ac.uk/staff/I.Brown/archives/ukcrypto/**.

the U.K. proposals. The key civil servant who had been involved in steering the legislation through all its stages tok part in these online debates which were of amazing quality. The Foundation for Information Policy Research[19] produced a formidable analysis and signed up a huge number of M.P.s to oppose the Bill through Stand.[20] They also demonstrated how innocent parties who are in receipt of communications from miscreants could be liable for imprisonment by sending a letter to the Home Secretary with an encrypted confession to a real crime in it. The publicity associated with the story had the required effect — during September a strong rumour circulated that even the Minister for e-business was secretly lobbying to have these provisions dropped from the Electronic Commerce Bill. By the date the House of Commons Select Committee published their Report on the draft Bill the game was up — in private the Government had conceded that it would have to lose these provisions from the Bill if it stood a chance in getting through the House.

12.07 So on November 18, 1999 the Bill finally introduced to the House of Commons shorn of the new police powers. The battle regarding these powers is not over since they are to be addressed in the new Regulation of Investigatory Powers Bill which at the date of completion of this text has not yet been published.

It seems certain that at some stage, despite all the complaints, the Government will again try and introduce controls over cryptography — as may already be there is section 16(3) of the draft Electronic Commerce Bill. The Government's case is that total cryptography freedom is likely to be very damaging in the fight against organised crime and terrorism.[21] There will be laws requiring a suspected person to decrypt his encrypted messages — hopefully after due process and following a full appeals procedure. The person must be suspected of a serious crime — which could include substantial tax evasion. And that person must be given every opportunity (and all reasonable resources) to defend himself/herself against the making of a mandatory decryption order. The devil is going to be in the detail — how is the independent legal profession going to protect citizens from misuse of power by the police, the security services and the Government?

FACILITATION OF ELECTRONIC COMMERCE, DATA STORAGE, ETC.

12.08 Part II of the draft Bill makes provision for the legal recognition of electronic signatures. It will also facilitate the use of electronic communications or electronic storage of information, as an alternative to traditional means of communication or storage (*e.g.* paper). This power is limited by section 8(3) which places a duty on the Minister not to make such an order unless he/she is satisfied that it will be possible to produce a record of anything that is done by virtue of the authorisation. It is also limited by section 8(6) so that a person cannot be required to abandon paper unless he/she has previously chosen to do so.

---

[19] **http://www.fipr.org/**.
[20] **http://www.stand.org.uk/**.
[21] Indeed it is likely that during the course of the passage of the Bill a major International child pornography conspiracy trial called "Wonderland" involving the use by the alleged criminals of unbreakable cryptography to hinder their investigation and discovery will be all over the media see **http://www.nytimes.com/library/tech/98/09/biztech/articles/03porn.html**.

Although the Bill on publication was said to be consistent with the E.U. Electronic Signatures Directive[22] within days of the Bill being published the Minister Patricia Hewitt admitted that the Government would have to amend the Bill to meet the E.C. Directive's provisions, which are intended to harmonise the legal acceptance of certain electronic signatures throughout the European Union by the end of 2000. Political agreement was reached on December 7, 1999 by the Council of Ministers on a common position for the Electronic Signatures Directive. Consequently, it is currently better to look to the Directive for guidance on how this legislation will finally appear rather than the present draft of the Electronic Communications Bill.

The E.U. Electronic Signatures Directive is meant to ensure that Information Society services benefitted from the Internal Market principles of free moverment of services and freedom of establishment and could be provided throughout the European Union if they complied with the law in their home Member State. It establishes "specific harmonised rules only in those areas strictly necessary to ensure that businesses and citizens could supply and receive Information Society services throughout the E.U., irrespective of frontiers."[23] These areas include definition of where operators are established, transparency obligations for operators, transparency requirements for commercial communications, conclusion and validity of electronic contracts, liability of Internet intermediaries, online dispute settlement and the role of national authorities. In other areas the Directive is intended to build on existing E.U. instruments which provide for harmonisation or mutual recognition of national laws.

The E.U. Electronic Signature Directive's main elements are: **12.09**

- *Legal recognition:* the Directive stipulates that an electronic signature cannot be legally discriminated against solely on the grounds that it is in electronic form. If a certificate and the service provider as well as the signature product used meet a set of specific requirements, there will be an automatic assumption that any resulting electronic signatures are as legally valid as a hand-written signature. Moreover, they can be used as evidence in legal proceedings.

- *Free circulation:* all products and services related to electronic signatures can circulate freely and are only subject to the legislation and control by the country of origin. Member States cannot make the provision of services related to electronic signatures subject to mandatory licensing.

- *Liability:* the legislation establishes minimum liability rules for service providers who would, in particular, be liable for the validity of a certificate's content. This approach ensures the free movement of certificates and certification services within the Internal Market, builds consumer trust and stimulates operators to develop secure systems and signatures without restrictive and inflexible regulation.

- *A technology-neutral framework:* given the pace of technological innovation the legislation provides for legal recognition of electronic signatures irrespective of the technology used (*e.g.* digital signatures using asymmetric cryptography or biometrics).

---

[22] See **http://europa.eu.int/comm/dg15/en/media/sign/elecsignen.pdf** for an informal final version of the Directive.

[23] Quotation from the official European Commission Press Release announcing the common position.

- *Scope:* the legislation cover the supply of certificates to the public aimed at identifying the sender of an electronic message. In accordance with the principles of party autonomy and contractual freedom it does, however, permit the operation of schemes governed by private law agreements such as corporate Intranets or banking systems, where a relation of trust already exists and there is no obvious need for regulation.

- *International dimension:* so as to promote a global market in electronic commerce the legislation includes mechanisms for co-operation with third countries on the basis of mutual recognition of certificates and on bilateral and multilateral agreements.

It should be clear that implementing these requirements are likely to require revision of the draft Electronic Commerce Bill as it goes through Parliament. But further amendments are likely to be necessary since the Draft Directive on Electronic Commerce,[24] (see below) is likely to get through all its stages while the Bill is being debated.

MISCELLANEOUS AND SUPPLEMENTARY

12.10 Part III amends the licensing provisions of the Telecommunications Act 1984 to facilitate the modifications of the terms of individual licences without obtaining every licensee's consent (clauses 10 to 14). Clause 10 amends section 12 of the Telecommunications Act 1984 and inserts a new section 12A to permit the Director-General of Telecommunications to modify simultaneously all telecommunications licences of a particular type without obtaining the consent of each individual licensee or making a reference to the Competition Commission. Paragraph 57 of the explanatory note explains that the modification of each and every individual licence is required to comply with the E.C. Telecommunications Services Licensing Directive 97/13 which mandates that telecommunications licensing should not be discriminatory. The new provisions will require the Director-General to refer proposed licence modifications to the Competition Commission only if there are objections from at least a significant minority of licensees and the modification is not deregulatory. Otherwise, the Director may modify the licence term without the licensees' consent upon giving them notice subject only to an appeal to the High Court in England, Wales or Northern Ireland or the Court of Session in Scotland pursuant to clause 21. This Part of the legislation is non-controversial and is expected to go through without serious modification.

THE DRAFT DIRECTIVE ON ELECTRONIC COMMERCE

12.11 Additionally, in November 1998 the European Commission presented the Draft Directive on Electronic Commerce,[25] which aims at removing impediments of form that debar the use of electronic signatures in contracts, *e.g.* the requirement to use paper documents. This original proposal was debated by the European Parliament on May 6, 1999 supported the Commission's initiative and in particular its Single market-based approach.

---

[24] See **http://www.ispo.cec.be/ecommerce/legal/documents/legalframew/legalen.pdf**.
[25] *ibid.*

The Parliament also suggested a number of amendments, largely of a technical nature, generally aiming at clarifying the Commission's original proposal. These were incorporated in an amended proposal for a Directive on September 1, 1999 which was forwarded to the European Parliament and the E.U.'s Council of Ministers for adoption under the co-decision procedure. on December 7, 1999 political agreement was reached by the Council of Ministers on a common position for the propsed Electronic Commerce Directive.

The proposed Directive would define the place of establishment as the place where an operator actually pursues an economic activity through a fixed establishment, irrespective of where websites or servers are situated or where the operator may have a mail box. This definition is in line with the principles established by the E.C. Treaty and the case law of the European Court of Justice. Such a definition would remove current legal uncertainty and ensure that operators could not evade supervision, as they would be subject to supervision in the Member State where they were established. The proposed Directive would prohibit Member States from imposing special authorisation schemes for Information Society services which are not applied to the same services provided by other means. It would also require member States to oblige Information Society service providers to make available to customers and competent authorities in an easily accessible and permanent form basic information concerning their activities (name, address, e-mail address, trade register number, professional authorisation and membership of professional bodies and where applicable, VAT number).

Online contracts

The proposal would oblige Member States to remove any prohibitions or restrictions on **12.12** the use of electronic contracts. In addition, the proposal would ensure legal security by imposing certain information requirements for the conclusion of electronic contracts in particular in order to help consumers to avoid technical errors. These provisions would complement the recently adopted Directive on electronic signatures (see IP/99/915).

Liability of intermediaries

To eliminate existing legal uncertainties and to avoid divergent approaches between **12.13** Member States, the Directive would establish an exemption from liability for intermediaries where they play a passive role as a "mere conduit" of information from third parties and limit service providers' liability for other "intermediary" activities such as the storage of information. The Directive strikes a careful balance between the different interests involved in order to stimulate co-operation between different parties and so reduce the risk of illegal activity online.

Commercial communications

The proposal defines commercial communications (such as advertising and direct **12.14** marketing) and makes them subject to certain transparency requirements to ensure consumer confidence and fair trading. So that consumers may react more readily to harmful intrusion, the proposal would require that commercial communications by e-mail were clearly identifiable. In addition, for regulated professions (such as lawyers or accountants), the proposal lays down the general principle that the online provision of services is permitted and that national rules on advertising shall not prevent professions from operating websites. However, these would have to respect certain rules of professional ethics which should be reflected in codes of conduct to be drawn up by professional associations.

Implementation

12.15 The proposal would seek to strengthen mechanisms to ensure that existing E.U. and national legislation was enforced. This would include encouraging the development of codes of conduct at E.U. level, stimulating administrative co-operation between Member States and facilitating the setting up of effective, alternative cross-border online dispute settlement systems. The proposal would also require Member States to provide for fast, efficient legal redress appropriate to the online environment and to ensure that sanctions for violations of the rules established under the Directive were effective, proportionate and dissuasive.

Mutual recognition/derogations

12.16 The Directive would clarify that the Internal Market principle of mutual recognition of national laws and the principle of control in the country of origin must be applied to Information Society services. This would ensure that such services provided from another Member State were not restricted for reasons falling within the scope of the proposal. The proposed Directive would not interfere with the application of the Brussels Convention on jurisdiction, recognition and enforcement of judgment in civil and commercial matters and the Rome Convention on the law applicable to contractual obligations in consumer contracts or with the freedom of the parties to choose the law applicable to their contract.

On a case-by-case basis, Member States would be allowed under the Directive to impose restrictions on Information Society services supplied from another Member State if necessary to protect the public interest on grounds of protection of minors, the fight against hatred on grounds of race, sex, religion or nationality, including offences to human dignity concerning individual persons, public health or security and consumer protection including the protection of investors. However, such restrictions would have to be proportionate to their stated objective. Moreover, such restrictions could only be imposed (except in cases of urgency and in cases of court actions) after:

- the Member State where the service provider was established had been asked to take adequate measures and failed to do so; and

- the intention to impose restrictions had been notified in advance to the Commission and to the Member State where the service provider was established.

In cases of urgency and in cases of court actions, including preliminary proceedings and criminal investigations, the reasons for the restrictions (and the urgency) would have to be notified in the shortest possible time to the Commission and to the Member State of the service provider. Where the Commission considered proposed or actual restrictions were not justified, Member States would be required to refrain from imposing them or urgently put an end to them.

Once the Common Position is formally adopted without discussion at a forthcoming Council meeting, it will be sent to the European Parliament for its second reading under the co-decision procedure foreseen by Article 251 of the E.C. Treaty.

CONCLUSION

By postponing the promised e-commerce legislation until the new millennium the **12.17** Government lost the opportunity of setting the agenda for the whole of Europe and must now follow what its European masters dictate. The current Electronic Commerce Bill is no big deal. Electronic commerce in the United Kingdom has been developing very rapidly without any legislation explicity addressing the status of electronic signatures nor, with the Government's "flip-flop" over key recovery, is there a pressing need for legislation regarding a voluntary approval system for Cryptographic Service Providers. Yet politically the Government cannot afford to be seen not to be doing something about electronic commerce.

APPENDIX

WHICH WEB TRADERS? — CODE OF PRACTICE FOR WEB TRADERS

A trader displaying the Which? Web Trader logo on their website agrees to follow these guidelines. It does not mean that Which? or any of its associate companies recommends the products you are offering or the customer service you are providing outside the areas covered in the code.[1]

Price

The price of all goods and services you are offering must be clear and easily found. This means you must show the actual price clearly to the consumer. There can be no hidden extras, such as taxes, packaging or delivery. Before signing the contract, you must confirm that actual price the consumer must pay.

If the nature of your business means that you may have to change the price between accepting the order and delivery, you must automatically give the consumer the option to cancel their order and get their money back.

Ways of paying

You must tell the consumer all the different ways of paying and tell them clearly how to pay.

Delivery

You must agree when you will deliver the goods to the consumer. If you cannot deliver within the agreed time you should tell the consumer immediately and, with their agreement, arrange another time for delivery. If you cannot agree another time for delivery, you must offer the consumer a refund.

Security

The site must be secure for sending personal information.

Advertising

All your advertising must meet the conditions of the Advertising Standards Authority code which you can see at **www.asa.org.uk.** If the website contains advertising material from other people or organisations you should clearly identify this material.

---

[1] Source: information taken from **http://www.which.net** Which — Consumers Association reproduced with permission of the Consumers Association.

Promotions

Any promotion you do must meet the conditions of the Sales Promotion Code which you can see at **www.asa.org.uk**.

Consumer law

You must meet your obligations under the consumer protection laws currently in force including:

- the Sale of Goods Act 1979;

- the Supply of Goods and Services Act 1982;

- the Consumer Credit Act 1974;

- the Trade Descriptions Act 1968;

- the Unfair Contract Terms Act 1977 and the 1994 Regulations; and

- the Consumer Protection Act 1987.

Your details

You must provide your full contact details of your website including your phone and fax numbers, an address for correspondence and your e-mail address.

If you trade under the name of a company, you must display its registered name and address, company registration number and VAT number (if you have one) on the website.

Contracts

You must set out the terms and conditions of your contracts clearly and in plain English. They must be easily found on the website. You must say that contracts do not affect the consumers' statutory rights.

Refunds

You must provide the option of a full refund, within a reasonable time, if the goods turn out to be faulty or different from those the consumer ordered. You must give all refunds as soon as possible, and at the latest within 30 days of agreeing to give the refund, taking into account the original method of payment.

Guarantees

You must make it clear if you are providing a gurantee. If you are, you must make clear what is covered, for how long and that the guarantee does not affect the buyers' statutory rights. You must also say if an insurance company is backing the guarantee. If it is, you must give the name and address of the insurer and you must provide the policy.

Receipts, bills and settlement mistakes

You must provide a receipt with the goods. You must correct any mistakes in bills, receipts or payments as soon as possible.

Legal advice and help

Subscribers to Which? Online who have problems after buying online from a trader in the scheme will be entitled to free legal advice and help from Which? Legal Service. You must co-operate with Which? Legal Service to solve the problem.

Handling complaints

You must deal with complaints effectively. Any system for handling complaints must be:

- fair;
- confidential;
- effective;
- easy to use and well-publicised;
- speedy — you should have time limits for taking action and telling customers what you are doing;
- informative — so that you know which services you need to improve;
- simple to understand and use; and
- checked — to make sure that it is working well and getting better.

Solving disputes

You must provide details about any procedure for solving disputes you belong to. You must provide details of any Ombudsman scheme or regulator which you belong to. You must be governed by U.K. law.

Data protection and privacy

You must meet the conditions of the Data Protection Act 1984. You must say if you will send the consumer marketing material, or pass the consumer's details to others. You must give consumers the option to refuse marketing material.

Customer support and service

You must provide a customer service phone number and say when this service is available and state clearly the cost of the calls.

Customer feedback

You must agree to invite Which? Online customers to post comments about their experience of using your service on Which? Online forum discussions. We will invite you to comment on relevant discussions.

SELECTIVE BIBLIOGRAPHY

This is rather an eclectic bibliography which reflects the all encompassing nature of electronic commerce as a discipline and its lack of maturity as a subject. Readers are directed at the books in this list to fire their imagination regarding how the e-commerce world will develop (and the nature of the new risks) rather than to find guidance in drafting agreements for clients.

Author	Title	Publisher and Year	Comments
Baker, Stewart A.	*The Limits of Trust: Cryptography, Governments, and Electronic Commerce*	Kluwer [1998]	Stewart Baker is a Washington based lawyer who has made a special study of cryptographic controls. The Limits of Trust contains several useful features: country-by-country summaries of cryptography and digital signature policies; expert essays from various countries, providing a narrative perspective of the cryptography regime; and an appendix offering translated and untranslated text of many relevant laws
Boyle, James	*Shamans, Software and Spleens*	Harvard [1996]	The role of information technology in the Information Age is dissected — going beyond copyright issues into concerns which question fundamental assumptions regarding ownership of nature
Denning, Dorothy E. (Editor), Denning, Peter J. (Editor)	*Internet Besieged: Countering Cyberspace Scofflaws*	Addison Wesley Publishing Company [1997]	A useful collection of the various kinds of network security risks with accounts of real world security breaches, their effects and suggestions for ways to minimise risks in the future.

Dickie, John	*Internet and Electronic Commerce Law in the European Union*	Hart Publishing [1999]	A small but usefully broad outline and analysis of the emerging European regulatory regime concerning electronic commerce
Diffie, Whitfield and Landau, Susan	*Privacy on the Line*	M.I.T. Press [1998]	A useful analysis of the technology and the U.S. politics associated with wire-tapping in the 1990s
Garfinkel, Simson	*Database Nation — The Death of Privacy in the 21st Century*	O'Reilly [2000]	A fascinating account of how technology is undermining privacy in the USA. A must-read for all privacy lawyers
Gates, Bill with Myhrvold, Nathan and Rinearson, Peter	*The Road Ahead (Revised Edition)*	Penguin USA [1996]	Chapter 8 *Friction Free Capitalism* is a perceptive view of the competitive forces unleashed by Electronic Commerce
Hance, Olivier	*Business and Law on the Internet*	McGraw Hill [1996]	Translated from the French this uneven book has some useful (but dated) pointers to European sources of information but generally it tries to cover too much by attempting to advise on all aspects of U.S. and European Internet law (with 20 standard contracts) in under 400 small pages
Kahn, David	*The Codebreakers (2nd Edition)*	Scribner [1996]	A 1,200 page history of cryptography from ancient times to the 1950s. The second edition does not add much to the first edition (published in 1967) but it remains the definitive text on the history of cryptography.
Lynch, Daniel C. and Lundquist, Leslie	*Digital Money — The New Era of Internet Commerce*	Wiley [1996]	A practical guide to digital money, written from an American point of view. A good starting point and source book

Schneier, Bruce	*Applied Cryptography (2nd Edition)*	Wiley [1995]	An authoritative introduction to the field of cryptography. Readable, instructive, and truly exhaustive.
Schneier, Bruce	*E-Mail Security: How to keep your electronic messages private*	Wiley [1995]	A slightly easier read than *Applied Cryptography* with good coverage of PGP
Singh, Simon	*The Code Book*	Fourth Estate [1999]	The best popular account of the development of cryptography and its likely future
Swire, Peter P. and Litan, Robert E.	*None of Your Business*	Brookings Institute Press [1998]	An book by two of America's leading experts on privacy on the conflict between World Data Flows and the European Directive
Taylor, Paul A.	*Hackers*	Routledge [1999]	A sociological lecturer's look at the perennial battle between the computer underground and the security industry. A very useful book in understanding the risks involved and the motivations of criminals
Westin, Alan F.	*Privacy and Freedom*	Bodley Head [1967]	The modern starting point in any consideration of privacy and freedom — very good for putting later works in context

INDEX

(All references refer to paragraph number)